THE AGE OF ARISTOCRACY

ARISTOCRACY

1688 to 1830

A HISTORY OF ENGLAND
General Editor: Lacey Baldwin Smith

THE MAKING OF ENGLAND: 55 B.C to 1399
C. Warren Hollister
University of California, Santa Barbara

THIS REALM OF ENGLAND: 1399 to 1688
Lacey Baldwin Smith
Northwestern University

THE AGE OF ARISTOCRACY: 1688 to 1830
William B. Willcox
Yale University

Walter L. Arnstein
University of Illinois, Urbana-Champaign

BRITAIN YESTERDAY AND TODAY:
1830 to the Present
Walter L. Arnstein
University of Illinois, Urbana-Champaign

THE AGE OF ARISTOCRACY

1688 to 1830

Fourth Edition

William B. Willcox
Yale University

Walter L. Arnstein
University of Illinois, Urbana-Champaign

D. C. HEATH AND COMPANY

Lexington, Massachusetts   Toronto

FOREWORD

Carl Becker once complained that everybody knows the job of the historian is "to discover and set forth the 'facts' of history." The facts, it is often said, speak for themselves. The businessman talks about hard facts, the statistician refers to cold facts, the lawyer is eloquent about the facts of the case, and the historian, who deals with the incontrovertible facts of life and death, is called a very lucky fellow. Those who speak so confidently about the historian's craft are generally not historians themselves; they are readers of textbooks that more often than not are mere recordings of vital information and listings of dull generalizations. It is not surprising then that historians' reputations have suffered; they have become known as peddlers of facts and chroniclers who say, "This is what happened." The shorter the historical survey, the more textbook writers are likely to assume godlike detachment, spurning the minor tragedies and daily comedies of humanity and immortalizing the rise and fall of civilizations, the clash of economic and social forces, and the deeds of titans. Anglo-Saxon warriors were sick with fear when Viking "swift sea-kings" swept down on England to plunder, rape, and kill, but historians dispassionately note that the Norse invasions were a good thing; they allowed the kingdom of Wessex to unite and "liberate" the island in the name of Saxon and Christian defense against heathen marauders. Nimbly the chronicler moves from the indisputable fact that Henry VIII annulled his marriage with Catherine of Aragon and wedded Anne Boleyn to the confident assertion that this helped produce the Reformation in England. The result is sublime but emasculated history. Her subjects wept when Good Queen Bess died, but historians merely comment that she had lived her allotted three score years and ten. British soldiers rotted by the thousands in the trenches of the First World War, but the terror and agony of that holocaust are lost in the dehumanized statistic that 750,000 British troops died in the four years of war.

In a brief history of even one "tight little island," the chronology of events must of necessity predominate; but if these four volumes are in any way fresh and new, it is because their authors have tried by artistry to step beyond the usual confines of a textbook and to conjure up something of the drama of politics, of the wealth of personalities, and even of the pettiness, as well as the greatness, of human motivation. The price paid will be obvious to anyone seeking total coverage. There is relatively little in these pages on literature, the fine arts, or philosophy, except as they throw light upon the uniqueness of English history. On the other hand, the complexities, the uncertainties, the endless variations, and above all the accidents that bedevil the design of human events—these are the very stuff of which history is made, and these are the "truths" that this series seeks to elucidate and preserve. Moreover, the flavor of each volume varies according to the tastes of its author. Sometimes the emphasis is political, sometimes economic or social; but always the presentation is impressionistic—shading, underscoring, or highlighting to achieve an image that will be more than a bare outline and will recapture something of the smell and temper of the past.

Even though each book was conceived and executed as an entity capable of standing by itself, the four volumes were designed as a unit. They tell the story of how a small and insignificant outpost of the Roman Empire hesitantly, and not always heroically, evolved into the nation that has probably produced and disseminated more ideas and institutions, both good and bad, than any state since Athens. The hope is that these books will appeal both as individual volumes, to those interested in balanced portraits of particular segments of English history, and collectively, to those who seek the majestic sweep of history in the story of a people whose activities have been wonderfully rich, exciting, and varied. In this spirit these volumes were originally written and have now been revised for a third time, not only to keep pace with new scholarship, but equally important to keep them fresh and thought-provoking in a world that is becoming both more nostalgic and more impatient of its past.

Lacey Baldwin Smith
Northwestern University

PREFACE

When I was asked some years ago to become involved in the preparation of first a third and now a fourth edition of *The Age of Aristocracy*, I did not see it as my task to tamper in any significant degree with the widely acknowledged strengths of Professor William B. Willcox's original book: these include his accounts and analyses of warfare, of the fundamentals of politics, and of the attitudes and the way of life of the aristocracy. What I sought to do was to expand somewhat upon those sections of the volume that dealt with economic history, the social history of the lower classes, popular culture, the history of ideas, and Ireland.

In the process I reorganized the original nine chapters into four chronological sections subdivided into a total of thirteen chapters. I am also responsible for all the tables, half the maps, and most of the illustrations, as well as for the revised bibliography. In the present edition, I am responsible for the greater part of Chapters 3, 7, and 9, and for numerous sub-chapters as well as scattered paragraphs and sentences elsewhere: in Chapters 1 and 2, much of the introduction and of the sub-chapters dealing with religion, finance, and Ireland; in Chapter 4, the section on "The Enlightenment"; in Chapters 5 and 6, several paragraphs on finance and domestic policy; in Chapter 8, "Disunion at Home"; in Chapter 10, the paragraphs on humanitarian reform movements; in Chapter 11, "The Impact of War at Home" and paragraphs dealing with Burke and Paine and with Ireland; and in Chapter 13, "The Prince Regent and Regency England" and numerous paragraphs discussing social and economic developments. My intention throughout has been to incorporate the new material with the old without making the seams obvious. Professor Willcox has provided his cordial assistance in and endorsement of that process.

Walter L. Arnstein
University of Illinois, Urbana-Champaign
November 1982

CONTENTS

ILLUSTRATIONS

MAPS

CHARTS AND TABLES

THE AGE OF ARISTOCRACY

1688 to 1830

HAMPTON COURT
(Mary Evans Picture Library)

I THE FRUITS OF REVOLUTION

1688 to 1714

1 THE GLORIOUS REVOLUTION

*T*he seventeenth century in Britain was one of revolution. In 1642 a series of political and religious disputes with socioeconomic implications led to civil war. The partisans of king and Parliament—the Cavaliers and the Roundheads—transferred their debate from the council chamber to the battlefield, and by the time the decade was over King Charles I had been tried and executed by the victors of that struggle. The 1640s secured the authority of Parliament, but the 1650s dramatized the fact that Parliament could not exist without the king. Oliver Cromwell proved to be an able general and a sincere religious reformer, but while he lived there could be no true stability because his rule was based on military power. One political experiment followed another, and it was not until two years after Cromwell's death in 1658 that legitimacy was finally restored—in the person of King Charles II, the son of Charles I.

KING AND PARLIAMENT

The nation required both king and Parliament, and after 1660 it had both. Yet the Restoration did not resolve a number of significant questions: Would the monarch appoint ministers acceptable to Parliament? Would Parliament supply the funds to enable the monarch and his ministers to defend the interests of the kingdom in peace and war? Was the Church of England once again to be the sole legal religious organization, or were Protestant dissenters and Roman Catholics to gain formal toleration? The last question proved particularly troublesome in the later 1670s, when it became clear that Charles II's successor would be his brother James, a Roman Catholic convert, and Lord Shaftesbury and his followers sought to pass an Exclusion Bill denying him the throne. They were known as Whigs, their opponents as Tories. Charles ultimately succeeded in defeating the controversial bill by dispensing with Parliament altogether during the last four years of his reign. His brother succeeded him in 1685, only to provoke within three years another revolution. It was caused in part by the constitutional uncertainties that still enveloped the relationship between king and Parliament. Equally important, however, were foreign policy—the question of whether England was to be an ally, a neutral, or an enemy of France—

and the personalities of two men, King James II and his son-in-law William of Orange.[1]

THE REIGN OF JAMES II

James II came to the throne under auspicious circumstances. A reaction in favor of the crown had followed the Exclusionist Crisis of 1679–1681, and Parliament was as cooperative as the king could possibly have hoped for, granting him the monies he sought and overlooking his Catholicism.

James was a methodical and conscientious monarch, sincere in his religious profession; but he was also an obstinate and unimaginative man— or perhaps he was too imaginative. His dream of returning Britain[2] to Roman Catholicism had died with his great-grandmother, Mary, Queen of Scots, and its ghost had been laid to rest at the time of the Popish Plot of 1678–1679, when Charles II had almost lost his throne. Yet from the moment of his accession, James worked stalwartly and stupidly to realize this dream. What he attempted to do is usually described as reactionary, an attempt to turn back the historical clock. In the European context of the 1680s, however, James might well be described as a modernizer. In the era of Louis XIV, an efficient royal absolutism seemed to be the wave of the future, and a parliament dominated by landed aristocrats, each powerful in his own locality, could (like the French Estates-General) be dismissed as a medieval remnant.

Within just three years James succeeded in alienating almost every powerful group in English society. The king infuriated the Anglican Church not merely by practicing his Catholic faith in public but also by insisting on complete equality for Catholics, in defiance of the law as it then stood. He made his Jesuit chaplain a member of the Privy Council, and he appointed Catholics to command the English navy and the English army in Ireland. James antagonized the universities by insisting that Oxford colleges name Roman Catholics as their heads and by dismissing en masse the fellows of Magdalen College when they refused to do so. He alienated a majority of

---

[1]The "Glorious Revolution" is discussed in detail in a number of recent works, including Stuart E. Prall, *The Bloodless Revolution: England, 1688* (1972), and J. R. Jones, *The Revolution of 1688 in England* (1972). Gerald M. Straka, ed., *The Revolution of 1688 and the Birth of the English Political Nation*, 2nd ed. (1973), provides samples of conflicting historical interpretations. The events of 1688–1689 are set in a broader context by G. N. Clark in *The Later Stuarts, 1660–1714*, 2nd ed. (1956), by David Ogg in *England in the Reigns of James II and William III* (1955), and in the antiquated, biased, but still magnificent Victorian work by Thomas Babington Macaulay, ed. Sir Charles Firth, *A History of England from the Accession of James II*, 6 vols. (1913–1915). Stephen B. Baxter, *William III and the Defense of European Liberty, 1650–1702* (1966), is a highly relevant biography.

[2]*Britain* at this time had no precise political meaning, because until 1707 the island of Great Britain remained divided into two kingdoms with a common sovereign, England (including Wales) and Scotland. But the two were deeply involved with each other, and the inclusive words *Britain* and *British* are a convenience in referring to the island as a whole.

KING JAMES II (1685–
1688) *(National
Maritime Museum,
London)*

country squires by keeping a large standing army and by supplanting numerous county lords-lieutenant and hundreds of justices of the peace with men who lacked wealth and prestige but were regarded as especially loyal to the king. He angered Parliament by failing to summon it after 1685 and by suspending or dispensing with the legal restrictions it had imposed on Roman Catholics and Protestant dissenters. Finally, he revoked the charters of numerous corporate boroughs and of the City of London with the intention of changing the franchise rules so as to "pack" the next Parliament.

Englishmen who were increasingly unhappy about these actions could take comfort in the fact that James II at fifty-five was no longer a young man and that eventually his Protestant daughter Mary would succeed him. In June of 1688, however, James had the audacity to become a father once more, this time of a son by his second wife, the Catholic Mary of Modena. To the dismay of many of James's subjects, the new heir would be brought up as a Catholic and take legal precedence over his Protestant elder sisters, Mary and Anne. While most Protestants denounced the baby as an imposter, many Catholics hailed him as a miracle; and James, never noted for his tact, immediately announced that the pope had agreed to be the boy's godfather. Ten days after the birth, seven English political leaders sent an "invitation" to William of Orange indicating that the kingdom was ready for a change. "The . . . people are so generally dissatisfied with the present conduct," they reported, "in relation to their religion, liberties and properties (all which have been greatly invaded) and they are in such expectation of their prospects being daily worse, that your Highness may be assured there are nineteen parts of twenty of the people throughout the kingdom who are desirous of a change; and who, we believe, would willingly contribute to it, if they had such a protection to countenance their rising, as would secure them from being destroyed. . . ."

THE ROLE OF WILLIAM

In any explanation of the Revolution of 1688–1689, the role of William is as important as that of James. William had been concerned with the Stuart dynasty and the English throne from his earliest years. His mother, after all, had been the sister of Charles II and James II; he was thus in the line of succession to the English throne long before 1677, when he married the most immediate heir, James's daughter Mary. Although the enemies of Charles II and James II had often appealed to William for aid, he had steered a studiously neutral course. He had no desire to usurp or seek to gain by conquest what his wife and he would someday inherit by law. It was only when the church to which his wife was devoted seemed in danger, when her inheritance seemed about to be stolen from her, and when James seemed to be jeopardizing the very survival of the English monarchy, that William agreed to act. If there were to be a rebellion, he was willing to guide it. He would not come as William the Conqueror, but he would come as William the Deliverer.

William served the Dutch Republic as stadholder; in everything but name he was a constitutional monarch. Small in size and population but for two generations the leading commercial nation of northern Europe, the Netherlands had inspired a cultural renaissance, founded colonies in the Americas, in Africa, and the East Indies, and served as the bulwark of a tolerant Protestantism. Ever since 1672 William had sought to make his land the keystone of a military coalition prepared to withstand the expansionist ambitions of the colossus of the age, the France of Louix XIV. It was essential to William's foreign policy to persuade England to cease being the secret ally of France or even a neutral and to join his coalition instead.

William quietly assembled an army of Dutch, English, and German troops as well as French Huguenots (Protestant refugees whose religion had been outlawed by Louis XIV in 1685). He received the secret assent of the Dutch States General for his venture while giving Louis XIV cause to think that the assembled troops would move up the Rhine rather than across the Channel. Early in November 1688, William's flotilla of 250 ships was swept by a "Protestant wind" past the becalmed English fleet, and on November 5 it landed 15,000 men at Torbay in southwestern England.

James's reaction to the prospect of invasion was a sudden reversal of policy. He now promised to maintain the privileges of the Church of England. He replaced the Catholic admiral of the fleet with a Protestant. He restored the fellows of Magdalen College, Oxford, to their former position. He restored the charter of the City of London. Such steps seemed so obviously the result of fear rather than of change of heart that they were cred-

KING WILLIAM III (1689–1702) AND QUEEN MARY II (1689–1694) *(The Granger Collection)*

ited more to William than to James. The former, in a declaration issued prior to sailing, called upon the people of England to aid him in his "Design" so that the nation might be freed from "arbitrary government and slavery" and so that the evils that had beset the English Constitution might be "fully redressed, in a free and legal Parliament. . . ." One by one, the leading men of England deserted James's court and declared their allegiance to William. James's younger daughter Anne did so, so did his leading general, John Churchill, and scores of lesser men in both the army and the county militia.

As William's troops moved toward London, James lost all courage. He decided not to fight at all but to flee to France with his wife and baby son. He disguised himself, hired a fishing boat, and dropped the Great Seal—the symbol of royal power—into the Thames. A group of Kentish fishermen accidentally recognized the king and brought him back to London, where William, unable to think of anything better to do with him, permitted him to escape a second time. By that time William had taken command of the army, which James had at the last moment disbanded. A newly elected Parliament was summoned without royal writ (therefore called the Convention Parliament), and it met in an atmosphere of enormous tension.

WHIGS AND TORIES

The crisis had for the moment brought Whig and Tory together, but they threatened to turn on each other again. Many issues separated them. The Tories were the champions of the crown and of the Church of England, the Whigs the champions of Parliament and of the dissenting Protestants outside the established Anglican Church. Although both Tories and Whigs disliked Roman Catholics, until the Revolution the Tories, professing blind obedience to the Catholic James, muted their hostility to Rome in order to remain obedient. On foreign policy the two parties were as far apart as on domestic. The Whigs, partly because of their ties with the mercantile interests and partly because of their stalwart Protestantism, were belligerent toward France, which was becoming Britain's chief commercial rival and was the major Catholic power of the continent; the Tories, who drew strong support from the rural gentry, had little desire to be drawn into a French war, from which the merchants might profit and for which the gentry would be taxed. These were major issues, and so divisive were they that nothing short of a political miracle could have induced the two parties to collaborate.

James worked that miracle by forcing the Tories to choose between their loyalty to the crown and to Anglicanism, for the two were now in conflict. Most Tories responded, however reluctantly, by discarding their theory that the king could do no wrong and by allying with the Whigs to safeguard the familiar institutions of the country. The alliance was precarious, but the alternative appeared to be civil war. With the lesson of the Cavaliers and Roundheads fresh in memory, the leaders of 1688 were so determined to keep their own revolution from getting out of hand that they were willing to forget past quarrels. Yet they had their awkward moments. In the autumn of 1688 they were saved from bloodshed only by James's decision to flee the kingdom. In the Convention Parliament they argued long and bitterly before agreeing to settle the crown jointly on William and Mary, but, once their decision was reached, the revolution in England was virtually complete. It still had a stormy course to run in Scotland, however, and an even stormier one in Ireland, as will soon be seen; but by the spring of 1689 there was no longer any danger that the attack on James would, like the attack on his father, Charles I, unloose the flood of radicalism.

The Revolution was adroitly managed, but it was orderly for other reasons as well. It commanded a wide degree of popular acceptance and, even more significantly, a high degree of consensus among the oligarchs who dominated the political world of the day. Violently as these men might disagree on specific issues, they agreed on the fundamental point that their own position must be secured against royal encroachment. A few Tories, for whom their old principles were more important than their position as oligarchs, remained loyal to their exiled king; for them, as for Shakespeare,

> The breath of worldly men cannot depose
> The deputy elected by the Lord.

These nostalgic royalists were known as Jacobites, from Jacobus, the Latin form of James, and they and their descendants continued to make intermittent trouble for more than half a century. But they found limited support among their fellow oligarchs, who were satisfied with the Revolution because it confirmed their power.

THE REVOLUTIONARY SETTLEMENT IN ENGLAND

The men who engineered the accession of William and Mary were not abstract political theorists but rather workaday politicians. Although they agreed on branding as unconstitutional certain past actions of King James, they could never have agreed on a definition of how the government should operate in the future; the mere attempt to define would have set them at each other's throats. Instead they concentrated on the needs of the moment: they asserted the rights and privileges of the House of Commons; they settled the crown on William and Mary and then, in default of children, on Mary's younger sister, Anne; they dealt with the status of Protestant dissenters in England, and of the Church and Parliament in Scotland. These were substantial achievements, but they were also incomplete. The position of the House of Commons was only one part of a larger question, the relationship between Westminster and Whitehall or, in other words, between Parliament and the executive; and this relationship remained amorphous for generations to come. The future of the crown was uncertain, statutes to the contrary notwithstanding, until the accession of the house of Hanover in 1714; and so also was the position of English dissenters. Anglo-Scottish relations were in flux until the Act of Union of 1707. All that the Revolution settled, in short, could have been unsettled during the years that followed.

Those years were filled with problems.[3] The brief alliance of Whigs and Tories was dissolved by success, and the old factionalism revived. The fiscal system of Charles II and James II proved hopelessly inadequate, and new ways of financing the state had to be found. Behind all the developments of the period, furthermore, molding them in greater or lesser degree and rendering their outcome unpredictable, was a great foreign war that lasted, with one brief intermission, from 1689 to 1713. In the heat generated by armies fighting abroad and parties fighting at home, the revolutionary settlement remained fluid; and it did not cohere into a stable system of government until the war ended and the Stuarts gave place to the Hanoverians. By then the original architects of the Revolution would not have recognized their handiwork.

Those Whigs and Tories were no more democrats than Charles I had been. They would have shared his view that the common people have no claim to a part in government but only the right to have a government that safeguards their lives and goods. The oligarchs were ready enough to speak in the name of the people and did so in the Bill of Rights of 1689, which holds that all freeborn English have "their undoubted rights and liberties" and proceeds to list some of them: the right to petition; the right to jury trial; freedom from "excessive bail," "excessive fines," and "cruel and unusual punishments." But direct participation in government was not a right; it was the privilege of property owners. If the state itself existed for the

---

[3]Most of these problems are discussed, in clear and concise topical essays, in Geoffrey Holmes, ed., *Britain After the Glorious Revolution* (1969).

preservation of property, as John Locke argued, the conclusion was obvious that only men of substance should have a voice in determining, primarily through the legislature, the actions of the state.

But the constitutional role of the legislature was still undefined. The Revolution established the principle of parliamentary sovereignty: in a basic disagreement between the monarch and the two houses, the monarch must either yield or lose the throne. The means of implementing the principle, however, had not yet been found; the modern concept of responsible government, in which the executive branch is responsible to Parliament for the day-to-day workings of administration, still lay in the future.

The revolutionary settlement, for all its safeguards against misuse of the king's executive authority, created no mechanism by which that authority could be effectively subordinated to the authority of Parliament. The ministers of the crown, although they normally sat in the House of Lords or the House of Commons, were not servants of Parliament but of the king. A major part of their service to him, it is true, consisted in marshaling enough votes in the two houses—the first hereditary, the second elected—to ensure passage of legislation that was acceptable to him; their position therefore depended in great measure on their parliamentary influence, and when they lost influence they usually lost office. But the king alone determined their tenure. He could, if he chose, keep for a time the most unpopular ministers to carry out the most unpopular policy; Parliament could eventually force him to change his ways but had no means of securing from him the men and measures of its choice. It might bankrupt a government by withholding funds, overturn a minister by the cumbersome process of impeachment, and in a great crisis even destroy a king. What it could *not* do was control the executive sufficiently to dictate a continuing line of policy. The two houses were able, given time, to eliminate obstacles to their will; they were unable to implement their will through the day-to-day operation of the ministry. Although by now their power was enormous, it was still, as it had been throughout the century, in essence negative.

The final sanction behind that power was revolution, a sanction on which no constitutional government can rest. The right of revolution is the right to violate constitutional procedure and to substitute force for law. The conservative revolutionaries of 1689 had the conservative's dislike of force but had no substitute for it as their final argument. They were in much the same dilemma that had confronted their remote forebears in 1215: the barons who had extracted the Magna Carta from King John had feared, with good reason, that he would break the promises contained in it and had tried to meet the difficulty by inserting a clause to legalize rebellion against him if he did so; but their attempt to enforce the law by lawlessness had come to nothing. The makers of the Glorious Revolution, moved by the same fear, inserted a similar provision in the Bill of Rights: the oath of allegiance no longer precluded resistance to the crown, and all Protestant subjects were permitted to bear arms. The implication was clear: sovereigns who owed their throne to one revolution might lose it by another. This was perhaps a salutary warning, but until the right to revolution was forgotten—as it would not be for years to come—government could not find its constitutional feet.

The Tories had foreseen the instability that would come from altering the succession. Their insistence on the strict law of heredity had made them, at the time of the Popish Plot, vehement opponents of the Whig plan to exclude James from inheriting the throne; and their position had been rooted in more than traditionalism. To change the descent of the crown was almost as dangerous in the seventeenth century as it had been in the fifteenth, when the deposition of the Plantagenets in the person of Richard II had led to almost a hundred years of instability. The sovereign was still in fact the chief executive, and an executive without a clear title invited conspiracies in the name of a pretender. The Tories had not used this prosaic argument before James's accession but had talked of divine right and of the sin of resisting God's anointed. When the new king's conduct had forced them to realize that such talk created enormous difficulties, they had joined in ousting him, but they had done so with great hesitation. They now made heroic efforts to invest William and Mary with some shreds of James's legitimate sovereignty. The Tory logic was ridiculous or pathetic, depending on the point of view; but the purpose behind it was practical: to stabilize the settlement by capping it with a legally valid crown.

The Whigs cared little about such legalism. After 1689 the labels of Whig and Tory, in the words of a modern historian, "distinguished those who welcomed the Revolution as a notable constitutional advance from those who grudgingly accepted it as a sinful and infinitely regrettable necessity."[4] The advance that the Whigs welcomed was primarily in ways of controlling the sovereign, and to gain control they were more than willing to sacrifice the law of heredity. Although they had to admit that the royal prerogative was necessary, they intended to keep it subordinate to the will of the oligarchy as expressed through Parliament, that citadel of oligarchic power. Precious little divinity, in consequence, hedged their king.

The Whig position was writ large in the statues of William's reign. The Bill of Rights guaranteed the House of Commons control of its own procedure and ended the royal claim to suspend or dispense at will with acts of Parliament. Judges gained at long last security of tenure, subject only to removal by Parliament, and so acquired that independence of the crown for which they had been struggling since the days of James I. The first in a series of Mutiny Acts, in 1689, established parliamentary control over the army by legalizing martial law—the basis of all military discipline—for only a stipulated period; the acts have been renewed continuously from that day to this, usually for a year at a time, and have achieved two purposes at

---

[4]J. P. Kenyon, *The Stuarts: A Study in English Kingship* (1959), p. 189. This short, well-written, and vivid account is focused, as the title indicates, on the personalities of the sovereigns. J. P. Kenyon is also the author of *Revolution Principles: The Politics of Party, 1689–1720* (1977).

once—to subject the army to periodic parliamentary examination and to ensure that Parliament was in session at least once a year. Last, but far from least, the course of the Revolution underlined the Whig principle, largely derived from Locke, that the state rests on a contract between government and governed. In the Bill of Rights the people of England, represented by the Lords and Commons in Parliament, "claim, demand, and insist upon" specific liberties and *then* declare that William and Mary are joint sovereigns. The point is unmistakable: sovereignty is not an indefeasible right but is rather the result of a bargain in which the subjects offer their allegiance on condition that the crown maintain their liberties. If the condition is violated, the contract is void.

The enthronement of William and Mary was the beginning, not the end, of the problem of the succession. Mary died without children in 1694; William remained king for his lifetime. At his death, according to the Bill of Rights, the throne would pass to his sister-in-law, James's younger daughter Anne, and then to her offspring by her husband, a dull Danish prince. Anne had thirteen pregnancies in thirteen years, but no child lived to grow up. The last died in 1700, and with him died the hope of carrying on even the semilegitimate line of James's children by his first wife. That line would end at Anne's death, and the question of who would succeed her had to be settled all over again.

There were two possibilities. One was to bring back James or his son by his second marriage, both of whom were Roman Catholics. The other was to turn to the nearest Protestant branch of the Stuarts, which was a remote one; it was represented by James I's granddaughter Sophia, the widowed electress of Hanover, and her son the elector George.[5] Bringing in the Hanoverians, petty German princes with their wholly German outlook, would not only extinguish the glamor of royalty but also embroil Great Britain in the politics of central Europe. Restoring the Catholic Stuarts would be even worse: their faith and their heritage almost committed them to undoing the Revolution. Even the Tories could not stomach that prospect. In 1701, the year after the death of Anne's last child and the year before King William died, a Parliament dominated by Tories passed the Act of Settlement, which stipulated that after Anne's tenure of the throne it should pass to the Hanoverian line. Thus the Tories, for the moment, con-

---

[5]The family tree below shows how the problem arose. Sovereigns are in Roman capitals, and the claimants after 1700 in italics.

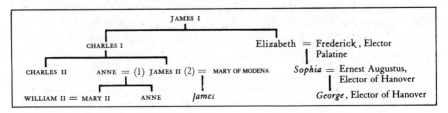

fessed that their doctrine of legitimacy was untenable; for they passed into law their opponents' doctrine that the crown was at the disposition of Parliament. But only for the moment. The Tories' creed of legitimacy died hard, and within a decade some of them were intriguing to bring the son of James II back to his father's throne.

If Whigs and Tories could be brought together in a crisis by their hatred of Roman Catholicism, they were poles apart in their attitude toward the Protestant dissenters. The Tories, traditional champions of the Anglican Church, were enemies of dissent who wished to maintain the restrictive policy that the Clarendon Code had imposed a generation earlier. The Whigs had long ago realized that the code had failed in its purpose of making life so unpleasant for its victims that they would return to the fold of the established church. Instead, legal harassment had merely kept the Presbyterians, Congregationalists, Baptists, and other sects a discontented minority. But that minority had proved so loyal to the parliamentary cause, despite all the blandishments of Charles II and James II, that the Whigs considered dissenters to be humble champions of Whiggism who deserved their reward. By 1689 even the Tories were ready to make some grudging concessions to them. The question was how far to go, and here the two parties were at loggerheads.

The result was a compromise that satisfied no one. The Toleration Act of 1689 was as important for what it did not do as for what it did. It did not cover Jews, Roman Catholics, or a small body of Protestants who denied the doctrine of the Trinity (the later Unitarians); it did not apply to Ireland; it did not give English dissenters political rights, for they remained excluded from local and national government. It did relieve all English Protestants, including Quakers, from the restraints on their civil liberty and freedom of worship that the Clarendon Code had imposed, and made them for the first time full-scale participants in all aspects of the national life except those that the oligarchs reserved for themselves: politics and officeholding. There the entrée was still the fantastic one set up in the Test Act of 1673—taking communion in the established Church of England. A particular form of the eucharist remained the hallmark of the ruling class.

Whatever its limitations, the Toleration Act had significant implications for about half a million of the five-and-a-half million people who lived in England and Wales. The act made it possible for dissenters to worship in public meetinghouses rather than in private homes; more than 2,500 such houses were licensed during the twenty years after 1689, and in London they soon outnumbered Anglican parish churches by a ratio of two to one. Whereas the act did not go far enough for the dissenters and their Whig champions (who had to be at least nominal Anglicans to hold office), it went much too far for most Tories. The latter were particularly disturbed by the manner in which some dissenters wormed their way into office by the practice known as occasional conformity, or taking Anglican communion once a year to satisfy the letter of the law. Tories were concerned also with the way in which the expiration of the Printing Press Licensing Act in 1695 had liberated heretical and anticlerical pamphleteers from government censorship. (Critics of the government were also freed from press censorship, but they still had to abide by a strict libel law.) Tories were troubled most of all by the manner in which the legal authority of the Church of England had been undermined first by James II and now by William III and his Parliament. In the past, church courts had dealt vigorously with cases ranging from blasphemy and failure to attend church to marriage, adultery, and illegitimate births. Now church courts found it difficult to exert such legal discipline. The spiritual revival of the 1690s took the form not of a legally strengthened state church but of voluntary organizations. The Society for the Promotion of Christian Knowledge and the Society for the Propagation of the Gospel set up charity schools and parish libraries and sent missionaries to the American colonies, while members of the Society for the Reformation of Manners used the civil law courts to initiate prosecutions for immorality against their neighbors. The proper role of the Church of England remained very much in dispute after 1689, because on the issue of dissent, more than on most other issues, the Tories were reactionary, trying to undo the measure of toleration that had been granted. The religious struggle, like the uncertainty over the succession, helped to keep the whole settlement in suspense until the day of Queen Anne's death.

THE REVOLUTION IN FOREIGN POLICY

Behind these domestic conflicts, and often overshadowing them, was another and far greater conflict. The upheaval that ousted King James was a revolution not only in internal affairs but also in foreign policy, for it launched the English into European involvements they had never known before. Since the 1660s, when Louis XIV had begun to reach for the hegemony of Western Europe, the English government had done nothing to stop him. Twice it had helped him by fighting the Dutch Republic, the power that barred his way to the lower Rhine; the rest of the time Whitehall had preserved a largely benevolent neutrality. As long as Britain's chief executive was Charles II or James II, both of them Louis's first cousins, thoroughgoing war against France was out of the question. Neutrality ended, however, when William became king.

By the 1680s the Dutch Republic was squarely in the path of French aggression; and its stadholder was forging a European coalition against Louis. William was a mediocre soldier but a skilled diplomat, and it was largely in the cause of his diplomacy that he made his bid for the British throne. When he succeeded, he brought his subjects into their first continental coalition with the Grand Alliance of 1689—Sweden, Spain, Savoy, the Holy Roman Empire, Bavaria, Saxony, the Palatinate, the Dutch Republic. Britain was unknowingly beginning that series of struggles against France that is often called the second Hundred Years' War. It was a duel of giants that occupied almost half of the next 125 years and profoundly affected the history of the world.

The British oligarchs did not go to war merely because they took William for king; they had reasons of their own. Merchants had long been alarmed by the rise of French commerce and naval power; diplomats had realized that Louis, if he secured for France the "natural" frontiers of the Pyrenees, Alps, and Rhine, would upset the balance of power in Europe; politicians had feared his intrigues in Whitehall and Parliament; Protestants had come to see in him a new Philip of Spain, scheming to bring the British Isles back into the arms of Rome. The causes of war antedated the Revolution, and the coming of William made war inevitable.

Tories and Whigs were agreed on opening the struggle but not on how far to carry it. France was too strong to be brought down quickly, and the Tories had no taste for long years of fighting. Their party did not have its center of gravity in the mercantile interests, which were largely Whig, but in the landed gentry; and the gentry neither knew nor cared much about distant dangers in Europe. Their background and tradition made them isolationists, and, even when they themselves were sitting on the benches of Parliament and confronting the affairs of the great world, they tended to restrict their vision to the rural limits of squire, vicar, and justice of the peace. They disliked the French more as foreigners than as a threat to the balance of power; they detested papists but did not see in Louis the malevolent champion of Rome. In consequence, willing as they were to embark on war, they had no compelling incentive to wage it through thick and thin.

They had one compelling reason not to—the taxes that a long war entailed. The system of taxation rested, as it had for centuries, predominantly on land, the easiest form of property to discover and assess; and by 1689 the land tax stood at 20 percent of assessed value. The landowners, who were the backbone of the Tory party, paid what many of them considered, with some reason, a disproportionate share of the nation's bills. As the campaigns in Europe dragged on from year to year and the cost mounted, so did the discontent in Tory circles. Long before the first phase of the conflict ended in 1713, the Tories had become the party of peace.

Yet the struggle, much as the Tories grumbled, brought to them and the rest of the oligarchy enormous benefits. The Revolution was secured at home, primarily by the defeat of James II's attempt to regain his throne from Ireland. Scotland and England, not daring to fly at each other's throats in wartime, came together instead as a single state. The strain that military operations put on the treasury produced a new financial structure. Britain learned to employ its naval strength and dazzled Europe with its victories on land. War is always to some degree revolutionary, because it accelerates the rate of change; and these wars were no exception. The kingdoms of England and Scotland entered them in 1689 as two parochial states that had been concerned for centuries with their own affairs. The kingdom of Great Britain emerged in 1713 with new interests in North and South

America and in the Mediterranean, with a new status as one of the great powers of Europe, and with the revolutionary settlement deeply rooted at last against the wind of reaction.

The first phase of the conflict, from 1689 to 1697, was known as the War of the League of Augsburg or simply as King William's War; its chief strategic importance for Britain was naval. The nature of the Grand Alliance created a problem that was to recur over and over again in the future—how to hold the alliance together. The states that composed it, because they surrounded France on all sides, were exposed to attack and destruction piecemeal; the French were at the center of a circle and could strike at the circumference wherever they pleased. The allied war effort depended on effective communications between Spain, northern Italy, central Europe, the Dutch Republic, Scandinavia, and the British Isles. The distances involved were enormous, but the British had an advantage, if they could develop it, to compensate for the French advantage of position. Moving supplies and armies was slower and more cumbersome by land than by sea, and naval control of the waters around Europe would give the allies the upper hand. A successful war of coalition, in short, depended on the successful exertion of sea power.

As an instrument of sea power the Royal Navy of 1689 seemed to be a weak reed. It had not seen action since the third Dutch war, fifteen years before, and its performance then had been lamentable. Now it was outnumbered by the French and had no apparent advantages; tactics were crude, gunnery inaccurate, and strategic ideas embryonic. But in some ways the navy was more effective than in the days of its past glory under Elizabeth and the Roundheads. The warship had become differentiated from the commercial carrier; no longer could merchant ships be pressed into service in the line of battle, as they had been against the Armada. A naval career had become differentiated from a military; gone were the amphibious heroes of Cromwell's time, like Blake and Monck and Rupert, who had transformed themselves from generals into admirals. The "senior service" was emerging as a specialized profession: a start had been made on a marine corps, on training youngsters systematically for a career at sea, and on maintaining reserve officers in peacetime. The challenges that remained were to build and man more ships and learn how to use them.

King William's War opened with a crisis in which sea power was of paramount importance. In March 1689 King James landed in Ireland, which he intended to use as a base for reconquering the British throne. Two years earlier he had appointed a faithful Roman Catholic, the earl of Tyrconnel, as his Irish lord-lieutenant, and the latter had placed all the major political, judicial, and military offices in Roman Catholic hands. In 1689 the Irish took advantage of James's presence to induce him to summon a Parliament that immediately set to work for Irish independence by condemning to death some two thousand leaders of the Protestant Ascendancy in Ireland and confiscating their estates. Most of the Protestant leaders fled to the northern province of Ulster, where they proclaimed William and

Mary king and queen and organized an army of their own with which they successfully defended Londonderry and Enniskallen against James's besieging army. Since the French were superior at sea, it seemed only a matter of time, however, before the entire island fell under James's control. William could not come to the rescue unless the navy could clear a way for him, and this the navy had no idea how to do. Fortunately for him, however, the French admirals were as inept as their British counterparts.

The result was what looks by hindsight like a comedy of errors, although it was in fact more a comedy of ignorance. In the summer of 1690 the French concentrated against the Anglo-Dutch fleet in the English Channel, defeated it, and, instead of gathering the fruits of victory by blockading Ireland, then did nothing at all. Meanwhile, King William sailed (with a convoy of only six warships) and landed at Carrickfergus in Ulster, where he began the march south toward Dublin, James's capital. William's army (made up of English, Dutch, Danish, and French-Huguenot troops) met James's (French and Irish) at the Battle of the River Boyne. Although William's deputy commander was killed and although an Irish cannonball grazed the king's shoulder, his frontal assault succeeded. James, with his troops in retreat, sought refuge on a French warship and fled back to France. The remnants of his army held out until October 1691, still with little support from the sea, and then in the Treaty of Limerick surrendered on reasonable terms. The French had lost the best chance in their history of turning Ireland into a satellite. When they tried again a century later, the British had learned how to handle a navy.

THE REVOLUTIONARY SETTLEMENT IN IRELAND

The effect of James's failure was to save the Revolution at the cost of the Irish.[6] If he had been victorious or even maintained his hold on part of the island, he might have regained his hold on part of England; for the Dutchman and his wife were newly on their thrones, and many would have been glad to see them toppled off again. But such thoughts were suppressed as soon as James scuttled back under Louis's wing and became the pensioner of France. The exiled king never again landed in the British Isles, and the Jacobites who waited for him there grew more and more discouraged. They had to nourish their faith on a secret ritual; when one of them toasted "the king," for example, with his wineglass held over a goblet of water, he meant that he was toasting the king-over-the-water. Such antics revealed a loyalty that was overlaid, as well it might be, with circumspection. From the Battle of the Boyne to the end of the wars, the Jacobite cause, whether in Ireland or Scotland or England, was the cause of France as well as of James, and was therefore tinged with treason.

---

[6]In *Ireland in the Empire, 1688–1770* (1973), Francis G. James provides a clear and systematic account of the long-range impact on Ireland of the Revolution of 1689.

Scottish and English Jacobites paid chiefly in heartache for their failure, but Ireland paid a heavier price. Three times in a century the Irish had turned on their masters and had always met defeat. They had rebelled against Elizabeth and had been chastised by her and James I; they had rebelled against the Long Parliament and had been chastised by Cromwell; now they had rebelled against King William, and the vengeance exacted was more civilized but more effective than that of the Puritans. The Treaty of Limerick was repudiated, the penal laws against Roman Catholics were strengthened, and Catholic landholders were slowly strangled by legal restrictions on their property. They were neither to buy land nor to inherit it from Protestants. When a Catholic landowner died, the law compelled him to divide his lands equally among all his surviving sons. Catholic tenant farmers were for the most part deprived of the protection of custom and were transformed ir o "tenants at will" whose rents could be raised and who could be turned out at their landlord's whim. Catholics were barred from certain trades and professions and from both the Irish Parliament and local government office. They could neither vote nor sit on juries; nor could they serve as teachers, constables, sailors, or soldiers. As a consequence 14,000 soldiers chose to serve with King Louis XIV of France. Even some of the Protestants of Ulster, who had held a beachhead for William, were decreed second-class subjects. Most of them were Presbyterians, and an act passed in 1704 excluded them also from the right to hold public office in Ireland. The Dublin Parliament was limited, from that point on, to the small minority who belonged to the Irish branch of the Church of England.

This Anglo-Irish clique, determined to keep its monopoly of power, was responsible for some of the most savage legislation of the period. The Westminster Parliament also contributed its share, particularly in economic restrictions. Though it encouraged the Irish linen industry, it forbade the Irish to export woolen goods either to foreign countries or to the colonies. Indeed Ireland itself was still treated like a colony. Throughout the eighteenth century it was to remain predominantly a land of Gaelic-speaking peasants engaged in subsistence farming, although there were pockets of industry, commerce, and cultural life, such as Dublin, the second largest city in the British Isles. Nor were all the penal laws and economic restrictions consistently enforced: in spite of numerous hardships, some 1,000 Roman Catholic priests and 4,000 monks and nuns carried on their work. The penal laws themselves were doubtless the products of fear on the part of the English and of the Anglo-Irish Ascendancy, but it remains fair to conclude, as Edmund Burke did later in the century, that in British history they constituted an "unparalleled code of repression" motivated by "national hatred and scorn towards a conquered people." During no other era was the majority of the Irish population so obviously in subjection as during the first three-quarters of the eighteenth century. The few who could escape did so, thereby inaugurating the first of those waves of emigration that continued for the next two centuries and disseminated far and wide the Irish hatred of Britain.

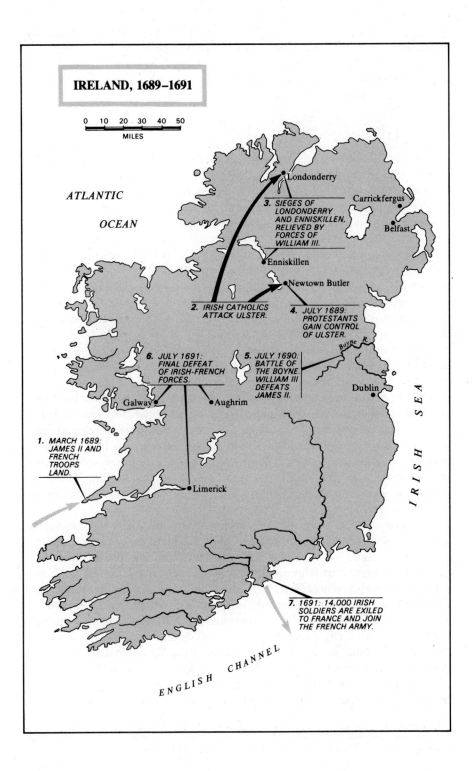

IRELAND, 1689–1691

0 10 20 30 40 50
MILES

ATLANTIC

OCEAN

Londonderry

Carrickfergus

*3. SIEGES OF
LONDONDERRY
AND ENNISKILLEN,
RELIEVED BY
FORCES OF
WILLIAM III.*

Belfast

Enniskillen

Newtown Butler

*2. IRISH CATHOLICS
ATTACK ULSTER.*

*4. JULY 1689:
PROTESTANTS
GAIN CONTROL
OF ULSTER.*

Boyne R.

*6. JULY 1691:
FINAL DEFEAT
OF IRISH-FRENCH
FORCES.*

*5. JULY 1690:
BATTLE OF
THE BOYNE.
WILLIAM III
DEFEATS
JAMES II.*

Dublin

Galway

Aughrim

*1. MARCH 1689:
JAMES II AND
FRENCH
TROOPS
LAND.*

Limerick

IRISH SEA

*7. 1691: 14,000 IRISH
SOLDIERS ARE EXILED
TO FRANCE AND JOIN
THE FRENCH ARMY.*

ENGLISH CHANNEL

THE REVOLUTIONARY SETTLEMENT IN IRELAND 19

In Scotland, unlike Ireland, William and Mary gained power not by military conquest but on the basis of an affirmative vote by the independent Scottish Parliament. However, the nature of the long-term relationship of the still separate kingdoms of England and Scotland remained in William III's day very much an open question.

FINANCIAL INNOVATIONS

The revolutionary settlement had yet another facet: the reordering of public finance.[7] By 1689 the archaic fiscal system that the Stuarts had inherited from the Tudors, although improved at the Restoration, was still a long way from the system of a modern state. Money was in ample supply, but much of it lay idle; the wealthy were accustomed to keeping coins and gold bars locked up in safes or buried in their gardens. Until such treasure could be readily channeled into investment, whether in private enterprise or government securities, commercial growth was restricted and the waging of a prolonged war was impossible. Mechanisms for tapping the nation's wealth were needed, and these were found. Although complex and undramatic, they were as much responsible as the navy for Britain's emergence as a great power.

One mechanism was the public debt. By the early 1690s the government, it was clear, could not continue to finance the war by increasing taxation or by short-term loans. The solution that was found was to create a system of permanent borrowing—to issue annuities, not repayable but bearing interest for specified terms of years; investors could thus buy from the state a guaranteed income. By 1696 the system was fully developed, and what had once been a short-term loan to the government had become a government security. So began the national debt. It did not solve at one stroke the financial problems of the state: a debt rarely does. But it did permit the government to utilize private capital more freely than before, and in this case to turn it into war making.

Almost from the start, the evolution of the public debt was intimately associated with the rise of the Bank of England. Here many factors were at work, of which two were especially significant. One was the government's need for an agency to administer the complicated machinery of the debt; the other was the rising demand for a reliable form of paper currency. Private banking, largely in the hands of London goldsmiths, had grown by leaps and bounds since the Restoration and had already developed the two techniques that chiefly concern the average citizen of today—the personal check and the bank note (or, as it is known in the United States, "the bill") that constitutes paper currency. The check is in essence an order to the banker to pay from money deposited, the note a promise by him to pay from his own resources. By the 1690s bank notes were becoming a kind of

---

[7]The most authoritative modern account is P. G. M. Dickson, *The Financial Revolution in England: A Study in the Development of Public Credit, 1688–1756* (1967).

informal currency; but their value depended on the financial reputation of the particular bank that issued them and might vary enormously from firm to firm and year to year. What was needed was a bank of issue that was as far above suspicion as Caesar's wife.

In 1694 a group of Whig financiers made a bargain with the government. They lent it £1,200,000 at a lower interest rate than that on the debt and in return were chartered as a bank with certain unique privileges, which grew as the years passed. Soon the new corporation, the Bank of England, had the entire management of the debt and a monopoly of joint-stock banking, and it was the most sizable institution permitted to issue bank notes. Its volume of business was so large, and its connection with the government so close, that it commanded the confidence of the business community. In the course of the eighteenth century its notes became what they have remained to this day: the dominant paper currency of Great Britain. From the beginning the Bank has thus held a unique position in that it is both a private corporation and an arm of the state.

Many Tories vehemently fought the Bank on the ground that it was a Whig device for tying the financial world to the leading strings of the Whig party. If that party was synonymous with the cause of the Revolution, the point was well taken. Political changes tend to be lasting when money is invested in them; Henry VIII, for example, perpetuated the breach with Rome by transferring the monastic lands to new owners, who thereafter saw in Rome a threat to their pocketbooks as well as their souls. An analogous process was going on in the 1690s: the Revolution was becoming a gigantic vested interest; the more money poured into government securities and the more powerful the Bank of England grew, the more the new financial structure of the nation was fused with its political structure. A Jacobite restoration would threaten not only those who governed under William and later under Anne but also those who invested in government, and security-holders were far more numerous and formidable than officeholders. By the 1710s there were some 40,000 such security-holders; they included a few aristocrats and country gentlemen, some foreigners, a significant minority of women (unmarried heiresses and widows), and a majority of London-based merchants and financiers.

The Bank also strengthened the sinews of sea power, by which the Revolution was secured. The climax of the naval war came in 1692, when Louis attempted an invasion only to have his fleet destroyed under the eyes of his army. After that, his resources were more and more drained away from the navy by the needs of the land war, while the British pushed a shipbuilding program that soon gave them predominance at sea. But ships were so expensive that only the creation of the Bank permitted the Royal Navy to function. Half of the initial loan of 1694, with which the Whig Bankers bought their charter, went at once to the treasurer of the Navy: and throughout the war, and the one that followed it, squadrons plowed through distant seas because suitable arrangements had been made in the London money market. Almost a third of the cost of King William's War was met by borrowed money, while the remainder was met by excise taxes, customs duties, and the land tax. The ancient distinction between ordinary and extraordinary taxation was brought to a close. After voting King William his "civil list," a fixed income for nonmilitary government expenses, Parliament became accustomed to meeting annually in order to levy taxes and authorize their expenditure. A series of short-run expedients was being transformed into a financial system.

The thirteen years of William's reign were thus a period of far-reaching change: the constitution was altered; dissent was recognized; Ireland was pacified effectively, if brutally; Scotland started on the autonomous road that led to union five years after William died; and the two kingdoms fought their first great European war and achieved the financial means for waging it. In 1697, peace returned to Europe as eight years of war ended with the Treaty of Ryswick. The tide of Louis's aggression began to ebb; he was forced to restore most of his recent conquests and to permit the Dutch to garrison defensive fortresses in the Spanish Netherlands, which separated the Dutch Republic from France. In the peace treaty Louis also recognized William as king and Anne as William's successor.

For these solid achievements the Dutch king might have expected some thanks from his subjects, but he got none. Even the Whigs had never been enthusiastic about him, and he lacked both the virtues and vices by which his uncle, Charles II, had endeared himself to much of the public. William was a cold, withdrawn man, and such heart as he had remained in the Dutch Republic. He had Charles's political acumen without his laziness, and a deeper insight into European diplomacy than any sovereign since Elizabeth; but these qualities did not appeal to the oligarchs, who were far more interested in managing their king than in learning from him. While the war lasted they were forced to cooperate with him after a fashion, but the moment peace was signed they made his life miserable. Parliament took the bit in its teeth, forced the sale of Irish lands that the king had given his favorites, cut his standing army drastically, and packed home his beloved Dutch guards. After a decade on the throne he was on such bad terms with the men who had called him to it that he talked of quitting the country.

But he could not do so, for the same reason that he had been unable to resist the call in 1688. The storm clouds of a new and greater crisis were boiling up over Europe, and he dared not lose such control as he had over British policy. In the four years of peace after 1697, his gift for diplomacy was stretched to the limit, first in his efforts to ward off the coming storm and then in preparations for it. Parliament was asleep, and he could only hope that it would wake in time to meet the danger. The "Glorious Revolution" was now history, but the Revolution settlement remained in great risk of being unsettled.

2 THE REIGN OF QUEEN ANNE

*P*rolonged and expensive as William's wars had been, they proved to be a dress rehearsal for the conflict to come. During the last months of the king's life, England became involved in a worldwide war that lasted for eleven years and overshadowed the highly significant constitutional developments that took place during Queen Anne's reign (1702–1714).[1]

THE WAR OF THE SPANISH SUCCESSION

The question that confronted Europe at the opening of the eighteenth century was what to do with a state that was too weak to determine its own future. The state, or rather collection of states, was the empire of the Spanish Habsburgs. With Spain as its focus, the empire included the Spanish Netherlands, possessions in Italy, and most of Central and South America. The crown of these vast dominions was on the head of a weak and sickly king, Charles II, who had no direct heirs. What would happen when he died?

The answer would affect the whole power structure of the continent. By 1700 there were two principal contenders for the inheritance, both claiming it by right of descent: Archduke Charles of Habsburg, a younger son of the Austrian branch of the family headed by the Holy Roman Em-

---

[1]The early eighteenth century is discussed in many of the works cited in Chapter 1 as well as in G. M. Trevelyan's classic, *England Under Queen Anne*, 3 vols. (1930–1934). Sir Winston S. Churchill wrote in appreciative detail about his distant ancestor in *Marlborough, His Life and Times*, 6 vols. (1933–1939). Briefer accounts are provided in C. T. Atkinson, *Marlborough and the Rise of the British Army* (1921), and, with numerous illustrations, in Correlli Barnett, *Marlborough* (1974). Institutional changes are taken up in J. H. Plumb, *The Origins of Political Stability in England, 1675–1725* (1967), and parliamentary activities in Geoffrey Holmes, *British Politics in the Age of Anne* (1968). Edward Gregg's *Queen Anne* (1979) is excellent in setting the monarch in her historical context, although he tends to exaggerate her personal importance. David Green has provided reliable biographies both of *Queen Anne* (1971) and of *Sarah, Duchess of Marlborough* (1967).

peror; and Philip of Bourbon, the grandson of Louis XIV.[2] Neither could succeed to the entire Spanish empire without threatening the balance of power, in one case by reestablishing the old Habsburg predominance of the early sixteenth century, in the other by creating an even more menacing Bourbon predominance. The only way to maintain the balance was to split the prize and give part to each claimant. Even Louis XIV was attracted by this idea as the alternative to a European war, and he and King William agreed to a partition treaty. But the Austrian Habsburgs refused to cooperate, and the king of Spain was not so weak or so lacking in Spanish patriotism that he was willing to see the empire partitioned. He willed it in its entirety to Philip with the proviso that, if the Bourbon refused, all the empire should go to Archduke Charles. Then, in 1700, the king died.

Louis was faced with a difficult choice. He might respect the partition treaty, which could well mean fighting Austria for his grandson's share, or accept for him the entire empire and fight all who objected. He chose the second alternative and thereby ensured a war against Austria. Britain was far from ready to fight, but during 1701 Louis acted as if he were trying to force its hand: he moved his troops into the Spanish Netherlands, announced that France would henceforth have special trading privileges with Spanish America, and in September, when James II died, formally recognized his cousin's son as James III, king of England, Scotland, and Ireland. Almost simultaneously Louis banned British imports into France and urged his grandson, Philip, to do the same in Spain. These actions gave Britain major war aims—to preserve the Dutch Republic from French dominance, to redress the balance of power, to safeguard the Protestant succession in England against a Stuart pretender who was the protégé of France, and to protect British trade in Europe and overseas. When King William returned from the continent after organizing another coalition, he found that Parliament at last was solidly behind him. The War of the Spanish Succession had begun.

---

[2]The family tree below shows how the claims arose. Claimants after 1700 are in italics.

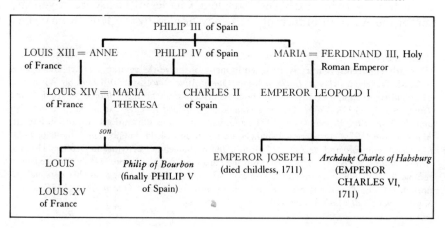

William did not live to manage it. He had never been robust, and this latest crisis drained his stamina. In February 1702, he fell from his horse and broke his collarbone; two weeks later he was dead. But, fortunately for both his countries, he left behind a war leader much more talented than he was—John Churchill, then earl and soon duke of Marlborough, the most brilliant soldier-diplomat of modern British history.

Marlborough, like William, had a cool intelligence and almost infinite patience; unlike William, he was endowed with tact, good looks, and the charm to melt a basilisk. Under this winning surface he was greedy and unscrupulous, like most of the men about him. In a peaceful era he might have left no more of a mark than they did; but in wartime his genius, aided by the luck that brought him to power, carried his name across Europe. He had begun as a trusted servant of James II (who had taken his sister for a mistress), had deserted him at the critical moment of the Revolution and been rewarded with an earldom by the new sovereigns, and had then begun to intrigue with James again. William never liked or, for good reason, trusted the earl but was compelled as time passed to bring him into prominence. Although the king did not know what talent lay hidden in his slippery servant, he did know that Marlborough's wife Sarah was the close friend and confidante of Princess Anne and that the earl and countess would play crucial parts in the new reign.

So they did. Anne was born to be dominated by someone, and Sarah was born to dominate. Anne's life had been dogged by embarrassment and misfortune. Her mother, a commoner whose marriage to the future James II had first been kept secret, had died early. Her father had long been estranged by differences of religion and politics. Her husband, Prince George of Denmark, was a stupid man who drank too much and who failed to provide the emotional support she craved. (According to tradition the prince never learned more than a single English sentence: "Is it possible?"—admittedly a phrase suitable for a great variety of occasions.) All her children had died in childbirth or in childhood, and by the time Anne ascended the throne she appeared prematurely old; she was sickly, corpulent, dull-witted, narrowly pious, and suspicious of all except her few friends. But friends she had to have, and those she trusted she trusted completely—for the time being. Her strong sense of duty prevailed over her ill health sufficiently to permit her to confer with ministers, preside at cabinet meetings, and make known her often strongly-held opinions. Yet she decided most issues less on their merits than on the personalities of their advocates.

"Her friendships," Sarah was to write, "were flames of extravagant passion, ending in indifference or aversion." Anne's whole-souled admiration for Sarah, though spiced with a touch of fear, lasted for years and extended to Sarah's husband. The queen was scarcely on the throne before Marlborough became the power behind it; he was made commander in chief, a duke, and a Knight of the Garter. His duchess bullied Anne in his interest and provided the strange liaison that tied the direction of the war to the source of executive power in St. James's Palace.

QUEEN ANNE (1702–1714)   The last of the Stuarts was a doggedly dutiful monarch. *(National Portrait Gallery, London)*

For a liaison with Parliament, Marlborough trusted primarily to the manipulations of a moderate Tory, Lord Godolphin, whose chief responsibility was to hold together a working majority that would support the war. Success in this task depended in great measure on military success, which depended in turn on how well the allies could coordinate their efforts. They were again scattered across the map of Europe: Britain, the Dutch Republic, Austria, some of the German states, and before long Savoy and Portugal. The second coalition had the same weakness that King William's had had—dispersion—while France had new advantages. Its armies already occupied Spain and the Spanish Netherlands and commanded the lower Rhine, and France had the alliance of Bavaria in southern Germany, a wedge thrust between Anglo-Dutch and Austrian power. France consequently began the war in a vastly stronger position than in 1689.

Politics and geography created three main theaters of operations, to which a fourth was soon added. The three were the Low Countries, the Danube valley, and northern Italy; the fourth was Spain. Each of the continental allies had its own particular interests. The Austrians were intent on defending themselves on the Danube while they acquired the Spanish possessions in Italy, and they wanted to see Archduke Charles made king of

THE DUCHESS OF
MARLBOROUGH The
brilliant wife of Britain's
premier general was, for
a time, the queen's best
friend. *(National Portrait
Gallery, London)*

Spain only if they did not have to do the fighting there. Neither the British
nor the Dutch, at the start, dreamed of doing it for them. The Dutch were
focused on the Low Countries and, like the French in the First World War,
opposed any distant operations that weakened the defense of their own soil.
Only the British, secured at home by sea power, were in a position to see
the struggle as a whole and the need to coordinate its many parts. But they
were not inclined to do so, and Marlborough's chief task was to imbue
them with his own broad vision.

Many of them were impervious to his vision, but no one was impervious to his charm. Lord Chesterfield, who knew him well, has left a sketch
of him that deserves quoting. "He was eminently illiterate, wrote bad English and spelled it worse. . . . His figure was beautiful, but his manner was
irresistible by either man or woman. It was by this engaging, graceful manner that he was enabled, during all his war to connect the various and jar-
ring powers of the grand alliance and to carry them on to the main object
of the war, notwithstanding their private and separate views, jealousies, and
wrong-headednesses. Whatever court he went to (and he was often obliged
to go himself to some testy and refractory ones), he as constantly prevailed
and brought them into his measures."

During the first two years of the struggle Marlborough did not notably prevail with either Parliament or Britain's allies. Although he showed his skill by parrying the French threat to the Netherlands, the threat to Austria steadily increased; by the spring of 1704 the French and Bavarians were poised for a blow at Vienna that might well knock the Habsburgs out of the war. Neither the Tories nor the Dutch could see the danger. Marlborough did, and he rose to it. In the deepest secrecy, taking only the queen and Godolphin into his confidence, he kidnapped the British, Dutch, and German army in the Low Countries for a lightning march to the Danube. There at Blenheim, in August, he won the first great victory that had come to a British general in Europe since the Middle Ages. King Louis's army was shattered, his marshal a captive in Marlborough's coach; and Versailles had its first word of the disaster in letters from prisoners of war. France, although still far from having been defeated, after Blenheim was forced progressively onto the defensive. The gilded panoply of the French regime, which had fascinated and terrified Europe for half a century, was shown at last to be vulnerable.

Meanwhile, the workings of British sea power had begun to be felt in the Mediterranean. In the autumn of 1703 the Royal Navy helped to induce the duke of Savoy, Louis's ally in northwestern Italy, to change sides and

THE BATTLE OF BLENHEIM (1704)   A German village was the site of Marlborough's greatest victory. *(Reproduced by permission of the British Library)*

bring into the coalition an army of 16,000 men. Almost simultaneously Portugal likewise deserted France for Britain, thereby changing the whole face of the war. The allies now had a base for the conquest of Spain and began to take seriously the idea of installing the archduke in Madrid. This was a war aim to arouse the enthusiasm of the powerful merchants, Dutch and British, who were eager to enlarge their trade; Spain and its overseas empire under Habsburg rule would be their happy hunting ground.

But Philip V, backed by French land power, was reigning in Madrid. To oust him would require attack from the sea and therefore command of the sea. For that purpose the Portuguese harbor of Lisbon was inadequate, because a fleet based there could not control the Mediterranean coast of Spain or contain the French fleet based at Toulon. What was needed was a base inside the straits, a good harbor immune to land attack and therefore on an island. The obvious place was Port Mahon on Minorca, in the Balearic Islands. Here the British established themselves in 1708 and remained for seventy-five years.

Meanwhile they had picked up another prize. In 1704 a British admiral, frustrated by a cruise in which he had accomplished nothing, had attacked and captured the Rock of Gibraltar. It was not a base like Port Mahon because its harbor was too small, but it was invaluable as an observation point for shadowing any hostile fleet that entered or left the Mediterranean. Gibraltar and Minorca together proved in the long run to be the keys to naval operations off southern Europe: large ships based on Port Mahon could blockade enemy squadrons in the harbors of the mainland; if a squadron ran the blockade and made for the open Atlantic, frigates based on Gibraltar could follow it and call up a battle fleet from Minorca or Britain. This was the strategy of the future, but it took many years to develop. Britain, retaining its two conquests at the end of the war, had no inkling that they would eventually be worth far more than all Marlborough's victories.

Those victories continued after Blenheim, for the duke never lost a major battle. But those he won were never conclusive, and their principal effect was to breed violent controversy at home about the conduct of the war. As one campaign dragged on to the next, the Tories became more and more restive, the Whigs more and more ambitious. Marlborough's strategy now had for its political aim the expulsion of King Philip from Spain, and for its military aim the invasion of France by way of the Spanish Netherlands and Flanders. The Tories believed (and they proved to be right) that these aims were unattainable and urged instead what they called a "blue-water" policy, concentrating on the war at sea while supporting Britain's continental allies by subsidies, which were less expensive than the interminable land war. The eyes of the Whigs were fixed on the Spanish prize, and Marlborough's victories made them overconfident. They dreamed of France conquered by invasion from the Low Countries, of Louis brought to his knees and his grandson exiled from Madrid, and of Spain and Spanish America opened to British trade. Year after year, however, Louis refused to kneel,

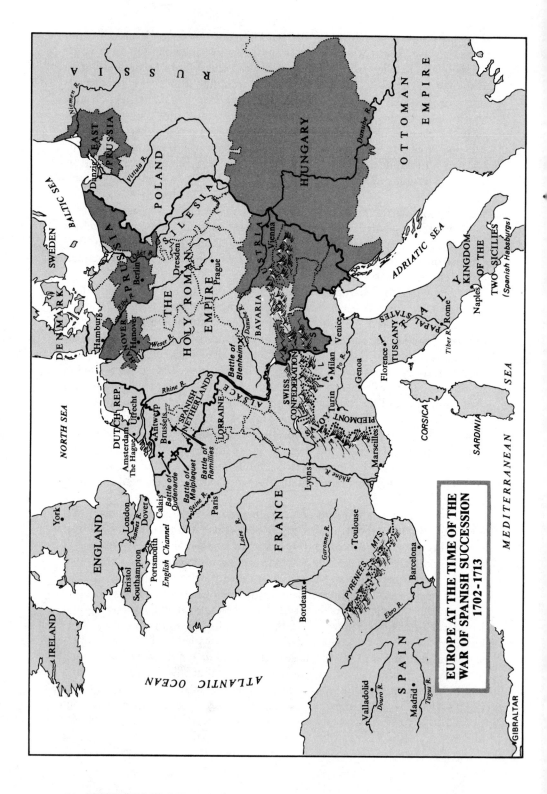

EUROPE AT THE TIME OF THE
WAR OF SPANISH SUCCESSION
1702–1713

and the Spaniards held to their Bourbon king. "The Whig formula of 'no peace without Spain' would mean 'no peace till Doomsday.' "[3]

In order to carry on the war, Marlborough and Godolphin turned more and more during those years from the Tories to the Whigs, and by 1708 the Whigs dominated the queen's ministry. The duchess of Marlborough persuaded a doubtful Queen Anne to go along with this process for a time, but by 1710 a royal and popular reaction in favor of the Tories was well under way. By then the years of war had altered both the constitution and the institutions of England and Scotland in fundamental ways.

ENGLAND AND SCOTLAND

The years of the War of the Spanish Succession were the years during which the troubled relationship between the separate kingdoms of England and Scotland was resolved by the Act of Union of 1707. Since 1603 the two kingdoms had known the same monarch, but in a century as unstable as the seventeenth a union of crowns had led neither to a union of cultures nor to a sense of security. It remained readily conceivable that eventually the two kingdoms might once more go their separate and perhaps hostile ways. Not that the situation in Scotland was identical to that in Ireland. The Glorious Revolution and the wars that followed it, like the era of revolution and wars between 1640 and 1660, had indeed dramatically different effects in those two lands. To Ireland both upheavals brought disaster; to Scotland they were, in the long run, a blessing. The reason is largely that the Scots, in dealing with the English, had three great advantages over the Irish: a political system that gave them considerable autonomy, a church that was dourly Protestant, and a fighting force that commanded respect. Seventeenth-century Scotland was not strong enough to avoid defeat and partial domination by England but was too strong to be exploited as Ireland had been.

The Restoration in 1660 had been little more popular with the Scots than the "sword government" of Cromwell's Ironsides. Presbyterians had been furious to see the Church of England reestablished, and merchants had been enraged to see their trade with England and its colonies curtailed. The first of these grievances the Scots dealt with in 1689, when their own Convention Parliament independently offered the throne to William and Mary on condition that the Presbyterian Church be recognized as the national church of Scotland. The condition was promptly met, and the northern kingdom finally shook off the rule of the hated Anglican bishops, against which it had been struggling for a hundred years.

The Highlanders remained a problem. In the wild hills and glens of the north, a region without roads or commerce or church, the king's writ

---

[3]G. M. Trevelyan, *England Under the Stuarts* (1949), p. 413. Although this book, first published in 1904, is now out of date, its insight and vividness still make it a classic example of history writing as a fine art.

scarcely ran. There the clans, who cared almost as little for the government in Edinburgh as for that in London, were a tumultuous law unto themselves, speaking a Gaelic tongue unrelated to English, and swayed by loyalties that had little to do with the religion or politics of the Lowlands. Jacobitism was strong among the Highlanders. King James was nominal head of Clan Stuart, and the clansmen were romantics at heart. In 1689 some of them rose and were suppressed by force, the first bloodshed in the hopeless saga of the north that went on for the next half-century. In 1692 the Macdonalds of Glencoe, who had been slow to make their peace with King William, were butchered by soldiers drawn from a rival clan. This massacre, for which William had not been directly responsible but which he condoned, increased his unpopularity in the north. Every Scot who resented the heavy hand of Whitehall was a potential Jacobite.

These troubles coincided with a weakening of the king's political control over Scotland. Before the Revolution the Scottish Parliament had been largely under the thumb of the executive; privy councillors responsible to the monarch had picked a committee of members of Parliament that arranged most of its business. After the Revolution this committee disappeared, and Parliament changed its character: no longer a tool of royal authority, it began to speak for the nation to a distant sovereign. That sovereign now had to work with two legislatures, English and Scottish, each jealous of its own prerogatives, and, if friction arose between them, the crown would be in an impossible position.

Friction did arise, largely from economic causes. The Scots were turning to trade and commercial ventures overseas with the avidity that they had once shown for the theological niceties of John Calvin. English financial and mercantile interests, entrenched in the Westminster Parliament and determined to keep the resources of the empire for themselves, feared Scottish competition even more than Irish. In the 1690s a Company of Scotland was formed to trade with the Indies, with Africa, and with Spanish America. The directors attempted, indeed, to establish a colony at the Isthmus of Panama, which one promoter looked on as "the door of the seas, and the key to the universe." After London financiers had discouraged English investment in the company, the Scots took it over as a national enterprise, undeterred by William's failure to support them. William's ambassador then found himself in the extraordinary position of trying to explain to the Spanish court that, although a group of William's subjects had invaded Spanish territory, Spain should bear William no ill will since those subjects were defying their king. The Company of Scotland collapsed less because of Spanish resistance than because of the inexperience of the company's directors: they sent too few supplies; they did not know how to cope with the tropical diseases that felled the colonists; they underestimated the difficulty of building a road across the isthmus. The Scots preferred to blame the debacle on England, however, and behaved "like raging madmen."

Early in Anne's reign, the Scottish Parliament took the opportunity to assert national autonomy in political terms. The climax came with the passage of the Scottish Act of Security of 1704, which provided that the dynastic union of the two countries, unless it were amended in a way to satisfy the Scots, should end at Anne's death. The Scottish crown would then go to a Protestant Stuart, but not necessarily to the same one who wore the crown of England. When the queen refused to sign the act, the Edinburgh Parliament, for the first time in its history, put pressure on her by refusing supplies. She signed, the act became law, and the crisis was at a boil. The English government did not dare coerce the Scots in the middle of a great war for fear of driving them into the enemy's hands. Waiting for time to heal the quarrel was even more dangerous, however, for at any moment Anne's death might open the northern kingdom to the French.

Breaking the ties between the two countries was unthinkable, and their existing constitutional relationship was unworkable. The only other possibility was a closer union. Members of a committee drawn from the English and Scottish Parliaments overcame their suspicions of one another sufficiently to begin negotiations that in due course achieved a compromise, the Act of Union of 1707.[4] By the decision of their respective Parliaments, the two nations were amalgamated in the Kingdom of Great Britain, the union denoted by a new flag. Scotland retained its own courts and legal system, and of course its own church. It received forty-five seats in the House of Commons of the new combined Parliament, and sixteen seats in the House of Lords for representatives elected by the Scottish peers. The Scots were henceforth to meet at Westminster rather than at Edinburgh, but if Scotland became the junior partner in the union such status represented harsh reality. Scotland, with a third of the island's area, had less than a sixth of its population and, according to a contemporary estimate, only a thirty-ninth of its wealth. Union gave the Scots a most important economic concession, however: free trade with England and within the empire. The island of Great Britain thereby became the largest free-trade area in Europe. At last the Scots could export their cattle, their linens, and their raw wool duty-free. The union was an act of necessity on both sides, not of choice, and it remained extremely unpopular for years to come. But it was the response to centripetal forces that had been at work for two centuries.

When Henry VII's daughter Margaret Tudor had gone as a bride to Edinburgh, her father had said that in this marriage alliance between the two kingdoms the greater would draw the less. Time proved him right. The first pull came at the beginning of Elizabeth's reign, when the Scots threw off Catholicism, broke away from France, and called on England for aid; the next came when the house of Stuart moved its capital from Edinburgh to London; the third came during the Puritan Revolution, which brought

---

[4] The most detailed modern account, P. W. J. Riley's *The Union of England and Scotland: A Study in Anglo-Scottish Politics of the Eighteenth Century* (1979), stresses the short-term political ambitions of the leading negotiators. T. C. Smout provides a balanced brief introduction to the background of union in his contribution to Geoffrey Holmes, ed., *Britain After the Glorious Revolution, 1689–1714* (1969).

the two countries into more intimate contact than ever before—sometimes in collaboration, sometimes in war—and culminated in a brief political union that was forced on the Scots by the Cromwellian Protectorate. The Glorious Revolution was achieved by both nations together, and after it the idea of a voluntary and lasting union was periodically broached. But what brought the idea to fruition was the outburst of economic and military activity that swept the whole island at the turn of the century. England and Scotland had parallel aims, in war and trade as much as in their search for dynastic security, and their need of each other undercut their jealousies. They could no longer afford individual governments, little as they cared to admit it, and by fusing their sovereignties they gained strength for the future.

ADMINISTRATION AND POLITICS IN WARTIME

It is customary to look on the Glorious Revolution as weakening the executive and strengthening the legislative and judicial branches of the British government. The appraisal is accurate in that, from 1689 on, not a year went by without a meeting of Parliament and, by the practice of William and the dictate of the Act of Settlement, judges were now appointed for life and in no sense subject to dismissal at the monarch's pleasure. These limitations on the crown gave rise to the eighteenth-century theory of the English Constitution, that Britain possessed a "mixed government," a happy balance of executive, legislative, and judicial power. The Constitution was thought to be balanced in yet another way: the forms of government first defined by the ancient Greeks—the monarchical, the aristocratic, and the popular—were exemplified respectively by the sovereign, the House of Lords, and the House of Commons.

In the age of William and Anne, the monarch was still regarded as personally in charge of the executive branch of government. William was quite literally the commander in chief of the kingdom's armies; Anne presided over all the formal meetings of her leading ministers, called "cabinet councils," which took place almost every Sunday and lasted for several hours. Her officers of state were generally members of one of the houses of Parliament, but Anne considered them her ministers. As she once explained: "All I desire is my liberty in encouraging and employing all those that concur faithfully in my service, whether they are called Whigs or Tories, not to be tied to one or the other. . . . "

A period of war might necessitate yearly meetings of Parliament to vote taxes and authorize army discipline, but, in the eighteenth century as in the twentieth, war was likely to strengthen the executive branch of government. At the very least it vastly increased the number of persons employed by the crown. The royal court was no longer expanding, but various departments of state were growing rapidly, especially the Admiralty, the War Office, and the Treasury. During the war years the British navy doubled in size, until it maintained more than 300 ships and some 50,000 sailors and was the largest in Europe; it employed more people than any other industry in the country. The army grew even more quickly, and, though far from the largest in Europe, it employed 70,000 men by 1711. Both services, furthermore, required a far more complex bureaucratic structure.

The biggest nonmilitary branch of the national government was the Treasury, whose growth too was the result of war and of the increased taxation and government borrowing that war necessitated. The Customs, the Excise, the Mint, and the Tax Office were all brought under the jurisdiction of the Treasury, and new tax collectors were employed as new taxes were imposed—taxes on land, on salt, on servants, on paper, on glass, and even on hackney cabs. The employees of the enlarged Treasury were scarcely noted for honesty or efficiency: patronage rather than merit was the criterion by which most of them were chosen. But the increasing number of career government servants operated with sufficient ability to enable the necessary funds to be raised and the expenses of war to be paid.

Although the growing executive branch of the government was a potential force for political stability, parliamentary strife was not—and never in English history had party rivalry been so lively as in the reign of Queen Anne. The Triennial Act of 1694 guaranteed a general election every three years, although not all seats were contested each time. The total English electorate grew to over 250,000, one adult male in four or five; electioneering was rowdy, and bribery was prevalent. Party rivalry between Whigs and Tories involved not only a struggle for office, but also genuine differences of both principle and emphasis. By the middle years of Anne's reign, the Whigs had become the war party, the party of parliamentary management and government finance, and the party of the aristocratic magnates, cosmopolitan in outlook and sympathetic to religious dissenters and London merchants. The Tories were predominantly the country squires, fearful of the influence of the burgeoning bureaucracy, eager to reduce taxes and electoral corruption, suspicious of foreigners abroad and of religious dissenters at home. By 1710 they had also become the peace party. Strife between the parties, although it was sometimes confused by factional division and moderated by those members of Parliament who consistently supported the queen's ministers, was the order of the day. Yet neither its legitimacy nor its utility was truly accepted, and the winners were still tempted to impeach or to exile the losers. Political opposition to the ministers of the queen could not easily be distinguished from potential treason, and, as the final years of Queen Anne's reign demonstrated, a change of party dominance might alter the succession to the throne.

THE END OF THE STUART ERA (1710–1714)

Every year seemed to bring another victory by Marlborough's forces over the French: there were the Battle of Ramillies (1706), the Battle of Oudenarde (1708), the Battle of Malplaquet (1709). Yet somehow peace seemed further away than ever, because thus far the anti-French alliance had failed to budge the grandson of Louis XIV off the Spanish throne. On all other points in dispute, the French seemed eager to make peace, but the Whigs refused to negotiate. Tory landowners wondered whether a conspiracy was at work on the part of the new "moneyed interest" to impoverish both them and the Anglican clergy, a quarter of whose income went in taxes to help pay the costs of war. Queen Anne became increasingly disenchanted with the bullying of the duchess of Marlborough and transferred her affections to Abigail Masham, a relative of the moderate Tory leader Robert Harley. She distrusted advisers who appeared to mock at princes and churchmen alike.

The rising tide of discontent came to a head with the impeachment and trial of Dr. Henry Sacheverell. A handsome young High Church clergyman, he utilized Guy Fawkes Day, 1709, to preach in London an explosive sermon against religious dissenters, occasional conformists, unlicensed schools, "moderate" bishops, and all who questioned the pre-1689 doctrines of loyalty and obedience to monarch and church. The Whig government decided to prosecute Sacheverell for the sermon and thereby brand all such Tory ideas as Jacobitical and treasonous. The House of Commons duly impeached the preacher for "high crimes and misdemeanors," but the tactic backfired. In the House of Lords, Sacheverell's advocates shrewdly defended him as the victim of misrepresentation by enemies of the Church of England. One hundred thousand copies of his sermon were sold, and pro-Sacheverell mobs swept through London, wrecked dissenter meetinghouses, and even attacked the Bank of England. Although the House of Lords, by a vote of 69–52, declared him guilty, Sacheverell escaped with a minimal sentence: a three-year suspension from public preaching. He became the hero of the hour as church bells were rung, toasts were drunk, and celebrations were held in his honor.

In the summer of 1710 the queen dismissed Godolphin as her chief minister and replaced him with Harley. In the parliamentary elections that followed in November, the Tories also triumphed. They were committed to making peace, and for domestic reasons they had to make it fast. At the queen's death, which might come at any moment, they dreamed of a Stuart restoration. The Tories had never liked the prospect of a Hanoverian king, even though they themselves had passed the Act of Settlement; and in the years since 1701 they had been increasingly intrigued by a Stuart youngster, growing up in France, whom the Jacobites called James III and others called the Pretender. If he could be persuaded to change his religion he might make a Tory king—*provided* that the war was over by the time the question arose. Even the most fevered Tory fancy could not picture the British public's accepting in wartime a king who was a pensioner of France.

Two factors helped the government in its hurried efforts to make peace and force the treaty through Parliament. One was that Archduke Charles succeeded to the Habsburg dominions in 1711 as the emperor Charles VI; his accession vitiated the Whig argument for conquering Spain, because success there would unite the Austrian and Spanish empires under a single crown and thereby upset the balance of power. The other factor was that the queen gave her ministers the support they needed to force the treaty through the House of Lords. The upper house, unlike the lower, was still dominated by Whigs because it was immune to the electorate, and without royal intervention the Lords could not be coerced. But Anne could pack the house and did so at the end of 1711 by creating twelve new Tory peers. Her action was more momentous than she or her ministers realized. Two other and greater crises of the future, in 1832 and 1911, were resolved by the government's threatening to take the same course, and the fact that Anne had taken it sufficed to bring the Lords to heel.

The final Anglo-French peace was signed at Utrecht in 1713, after Britain had shocked its allies by deserting them in the field. Other treaties were concluded in the following year, and the whole complex, which goes by the name of the Utrecht settlement, was a landmark in European history. An examination of its terms will show why it was also a landmark in British history. France accepted the Hanoverian succession and banished the Pretender; in return the allies recognized Philip V as king of Spain and of the Spanish overseas empire on condition that he should never inherit the French crown. The Habsburgs received the former Spanish possessions in Italy and the Spanish Netherlands, which until the 1790s remained Austrian; and the border between them and France was garrisoned by Dutch troops to protect the road to Amsterdam. Spain ceded to Britain Gibraltar and Minorca, and by an agreement known as the *asiento* accorded to British merchants a monopoly of importing slaves into Spanish America and limited trading rights there.[5] In North America France ceded to Britain Hudson's Bay, Nova Scotia, and Newfoundland. These were the dry details.

The settlement respected the principle of the balance of power by giving something to every strong belligerent. The Dutch gained security for their frontiers. The Austrian Habsburgs gained the whole of the European Spanish empire, except Spain itself, and so increased their weight in the scales of power to balance the Bourbon accretion. France gained a dynastic, and therefore a political and economic, link with Spain and South America but lost part of the inheritance for which Louis had originally gone to war. Only Britain, among the major contestants, seemed to make minor gains: a rock by the Straits of Gibraltar, a Mediterranean island, and some North American wilderness. But appearances were deceptive.

The settlement furthered the long-standing British interest in keeping a strong power out of the Low Countries, for the Austrian Netherlands were henceforth protected by the Dutch and governed by the distant Habsburgs. British merchants gained concessions that started them on their century-long struggle for the trade of Latin America. The Royal Navy, faced with the possibility that the Franco-Spanish fleets might unite against it in overwhelming strength, received in Gibraltar and Minorca the bases it needed for keeping Bourbon forces in the Atlantic separated from those in the Med-

---

[5]See Chapter 5.

iterranean. Britain came out of the struggle, in short, with little to show on the surface for eleven years of fighting but with solid foundations for its power.

The end of the war was the beginning of a final, bitter domestic crisis. Its crux was the succession, but it also involved the status of landowners, taxation, and religion. In 1711 the Tory Parliament passed a law making only substantial landowners eligible for election to the House of Commons. Wealth in the form of bank deposits or stock holdings did not count. Two years later Parliament substantially reduced the burden of the tax on land. On the subject of religious dissent, the Tories were as intolerant as ever. In 1711 they banned the practice of occasional conformity to evade the Test Act and three years later gave the Church of England a monopoly of secondary education; dissenters now could neither hold office nor keep their children from Anglican indoctrination. As even their precarious position of 1689 was being undermined, they looked for deliverance to the Whigs and Hanover. The Tories, in turn, could rely on a large segment of the country squires and the Anglican clergy, whose attitude toward dissent would have won the approval of Archbishop Laud.

Persecuting a minority might win votes for the Tories but did not touch their basic dilemma over the crown. Time was running out; Anne clearly could not live for many more months, and some preparation had to be made for the succession. But for whose? If Hanover was unpopular with the Tory government, the Tories were even more unpopular with Hanover. The elector George became sole heir to the throne when his mother Sophia died early in 1714, and George believed that the great Tory achievement, the Treaty of Utrecht, had flagrantly betrayed the interests of the German states in general and Hanover in particular. Unless the angry elector could be shorn of power before he set foot in England, the Tory ministers would be finished, politically if not physically. Yet their only alternative to the Hanoverian was the Pretender, who far from giving them help dashed their hopes, in the spring of 1714, by announcing that he would not abandon his Catholic faith for the sake of a throne.

As spring wore on toward summer, the unity of the Tory ministry began to disintegrate in a quarrel between its two leading members. Robert Harley, earl of Oxford, was an enigmatic and skillful politician who wanted to wait on events in the hope of profiting from whatever came. Henry St. John, viscount Bolingbroke, sought to gather into his hands the full power of the state, by putting his agents into every position of influence. How he intended to use the power is not clear to this day, because he did not quite have the chance to demonstrate: Lord Oxford stood in his way. The two men, who by now detested each other on a number of grounds, fought for the upper hand. On July 27 Bolingbroke won; Oxford was dismissed. But the victor had only three days in which to try to exploit his victory. By July 30, when the queen was obviously dying, few men were willing to risk their necks for whatever Bolingbroke's schemes might be. The moderates gained control, and a stream of orders went out to prepare the way for the coming of the Hanoverian. On the morning of August 1 the last of the Stuarts died. Edema and a bad heart in a woman prematurely old ended Bolingbroke's career and destroyed his party, and he of all men had reason to remember his *Macbeth:*

> She should have died hereafter;
> There would have been a time for such a word.

The years 1713–1714 were a watershed in British history. They marked the end of a quarter-century of wars, from which Britain emerged as the first sea power of Europe and during which the changes set in motion in 1688 were completed and secured. If defeat of the Royal Navy had ever opened the way to invasion and a Stuart restoration, if Scotland had broken the dynastic union and resumed its independence, if the Bank of England had failed, if the Pretender had turned Protestant and Anne had lived a few months longer—these are the *if's* of history, which produce no answer. All that can be said is that the revolutionary settlement was never really safe until George I was proclaimed king, and never in serious jeopardy thereafter. The settlement, like the persons who made it, was a combination of political wisdom and expediency, principles and grasping self-interest, and was built in the dust of battling parties in Westminster and battling armies in Europe. It was revealed, when the dust finally cleared, as the structure of Britain's Augustan Age.

TEA PARTY AT LORD HARRINGTON'S HOUSE, 1730, BY CHARLES PHILIPS
(Yale Center for British Art, Paul Mellon Collection)

II *T*HE WHIG OLIGARCHY

1714 to 1763

3 THE STRUCTURE OF SOCIETY

*A*society, past or present, can be described only in generalizations, which by their nature are unsatisfactory. Observers of a society today can at least live in it, but historians cannot; they have to view it through the eyes of men and women long dead, who saw only what they were able to see from their particular positions and with their particular preconceptions. The "facts" that they provide, and on which any general description of a period must in great part depend, are consequently unreliable.[1]

This is no modern discovery. It was clear to a sophisticated observer in the reign of George II and underlay his skeptical view of the data that make history. "Do we ever hear the most recent fact related exactly in the same way," the earl of Chesterfield asked, "by the several people who were at the same time eyewitnesses of it? No. One mistakes, another misrepresents, and others warp it a little to their own turn of mind or private views. A man who has been concerned in a transaction will not write it fairly; and a man who has not, cannot."

In this passage, nevertheless, the earl was urging upon his son the value of studying history. That study was becoming, as never before, the recognized prerequisite for understanding the present, which is the reason that the eighteenth century saw the beginning of history-writing in the modern sense. Chesterfield, although in accord with this trend of the times, also had a healthy strain of what he called "historical incredulity." He urged his son not to accept at face value historians' generalizations about causes and motives, but to try to pry into them for himself and to remember the complexities and inconsistencies of human nature with which history deals—the fluctuations of passion and will, the accidents of bodily health, the admixture of petty and evil in the best of men, of greatness in the worst. "As for the reflections of historians, with which they think it necessary to interlard their histories or at least to conclude their chapters . . . do not adopt them

---

[1]Chapters 2, 3, and 5 of W. A. Speck, *Stability and Strife: England, 1714–1760* (1977), incorporate recent scholarly research on many of the topics taken up in this chapter. Three somewhat older books retain great value: Charles Wilson, *England's Apprenticeship, 1603–1763* (1965), T. S. Ashton, *An Economic History of England: the Eighteenth Century* (1955), and Dorothy Marshall, *English People in the Eighteenth Century* (1956). M. Dorothy George, *London Life in the Eighteenth Century* (1925), and George Rudé, *Hanoverian London, 1714–1808* (1971), are reliable guides to life in the kingdom's capital and sole metropolis.

implicitly upon the credit of the author, but analyze them yourself and judge whether they are true or not."

His words are a sound caution in approaching his world. We know a great deal about the oligarchs among whom he moved, from their politics and architecture to their farming and views of life, but no one knows enough to generalize confidently about them. It is even more hazardous to generalize about the lives of the vast majority of English men and women who were not members of the oligarchy.

THE ENGLAND OF GREGORY KING

The eighteenth century was not so absorbed with statistics as the nineteenth and twentieth centuries, but it was more so than the sixteenth or early seventeenth. The kingdom was making increasing use of large-scale government borrowing and of nationally organized tax collections. Some of the merchants at Edward Lloyd's coffeehouse in London were developing the principles and practices of insurance—for ships, fire protection, and human lives. Isaac Newton, the greatest scientist of the day, was appointed in 1699 to the Treasury office of master of the Mint, and its standards of accuracy proceeded to improve. Surviving business and household accounts remind us with what conscientiousness many men and women recorded every shilling and penny they spent.

There was no national census in Britain until 1801, however, so demographers seeking to calculate the population of the preindustrial world and its growth or decline have been compelled to make do with a great deal of circumstantial evidence drawn from parish registers and tax records. They have also utilized the estimates made by contemporaries, and by general consent the most reliable guide to the approximate population and social structure of early-eighteenth-century England was provided in 1696 by Gregory King, the secretary to the commissioners of the Public Accounts. He justified his "Natural and Political Observations and Conclusions upon the State and Condition of England" on the basis that, in the midst of a long and expensive war, knowledge of "the true state and Condition" of its people and their wealth "must be of the Highest Concern. . . ." Since it is generally agreed that the population grew slowly during the first half of the eighteenth century, King's figures provide an approximate guide for that entire period.

Gregory King's assumptions are as revealing as his conclusions. He assumed, for one thing, that the fundamental unit of society was not the individual but the family. Furthermore, he took for granted what social historians have recently confirmed—that the nuclear family (made up of father, mother, and children) was the fundamental social unit in the British Isles and northern Europe long before the Industrial Revolution. In the higher social strata, the family would clearly include a number of unmarried live-in household servants. Modern scholars conclude, indeed, that King underestimated both the size of the average household and the annual

Number of families	Rank, degrees, titles and qualifications	Heads per family	Number of persons	Yearly income per family £
160	Temporal lords	40	6,400	2,800
26	Spiritual lords	20	520	1,300
800	Baronets	16	12,800	880
600	Knights	13	7,800	650
3,000	Esquires	10	30,000	450
12,000	Gentlemen	8	96,000	280
5,000	Persons in greater offices	8	40,000	240
5,000	Persons in lesser offices	6	30,000	120
2,000	Merchants and traders by sea	8	16,000	400
8,000	Merchants and traders by land	6	48,000	200
10,000	Persons in the law	7	70,000	140
2,000	Eminent clergymen	6	12,000	60
8,000	Lesser clergymen	5	40,000	45
40,000	Freeholders of the better sort	7	280,000	84
140,000	Freeholders of the lesser sort	5	700,000	50
150,000	Farmers	5	750,000	44
16,000	Persons in sciences and liberal arts	5	80,000	60
40,000	Shopkeepers and tradesmen	4½	180,000	45
60,000	Artisans and handicrafts	4	240,000	40
5,000	Naval officers	4	20,000	80
4,000	Military officers	4	16,000	60
50,000	Common seamen	3	150,000	20
364,000	Laboring people and out-servants	3½	1,275,000	15
400,000	Cottagers and paupers	3¼	1,300,000	6½
35,000	Common soldiers	2	70,000	14
—	Vagrants	—	30,000	—
1,360,586			5,500,520	—

income of the top families in the land. Families of merchants, tradesmen, and artisans were also likely to include live-in servants and apprentices. A widowed parent, a spinster aunt, or a bachelor uncle might be found at all social levels. But the nuclear family was the norm. If King's estimates are correct, it is equally clear that early eighteenth-century England was a highly inegalitarian society. About one-fourth of the total national income went to 3.5 percent of all families, while three-fifths of the population shared a sixth of that income. King's own comments took such a state of affairs for granted. Indeed he praised the families of nobles, merchants, professionals, shopkeepers, and artisans for "increasing the wealth of the kingdom," while he criticized the vagrants, the paupers, and even the common laborers, cottagers, seamen, and soldiers for decreasing its wealth. His criterion was whether income exceeded or fell short of expenditure. Those whose income surpassed expenditure were praised for investing in the commerce and industry of the kingdom. Those in the lower half of society were

A VILLAGE PILLORY In the countryside, as in London, the pillory was used both to punish criminals and to entertain the public. *(The Bettman Archive)*

thought all too liable to resort to the charity of others or to the parish overseer of the poor.

The society that Gregory King analyzed was evidently one that recognized a great many gradations of social status, of status that in practice could roughly be equated with annual income. Yet King ranks government officials above merchants, and clergymen above freeholders, even though merchants and freeholders were materially better off. The society King describes was in no sense a castebound world; some individuals found it possible both legally and practically to climb the social ladder or to topple from it. Nor is it appropriate to describe the society as one based on class. There was, of course, a small group of legally defined aristocrats at the top of the social ladder, whom one was well advised to address as "Your Lordship," or "Your Worship," or as "Sir," and whose life-style will be discussed in greater detail in Chapter 4. But which of the groups that King classified ought to be defined as "middle-class" and which as "lower-class" is in some cases far from apparent: such phrases are either too simple to represent human reality or too fuzzy around the edges. What is clear is that relatively few members of eighteenth-century English society were "class-conscious" in the manner that some of their nineteenth- and twentieth-century descendants came to be. Loyalty was less likely to be to a class than to a particular community. The people that a landed aristocrat or country squire concerned himself with in the course of a day or a year were in no sense limited to his own rank in society. They included the immediate members of his family, a bevy of household and estate servants, his tenant farmers, and, only slightly further removed, the village parson, the local tradesmen, and the neighborhood artisans. It is true that they deferred to him, and as justice of the peace he possessed the legal authority to supervise their behavior; but in times of distress they would expect his assistance. Many of them might owe their position or that of their children to his patronage, and they might extend comparable patronage at a lower level to servants, day laborers, and apprentices. When the landed squire entered Parliament, he readily pictured himself as responsible for and representative of his particular portion of the country. Members of different social ranks thus tended to be tied to one another by complex relationships of patronage and dependence.

In Chapter 13 of the novel *Joseph Andrews* (1742), Henry Fielding compares the pattern of patronage and dependence to "a kind of ladder."

> Early in the morning arises the postillion, or some other boy, which no great families, no more than great ships, are without, and falls to brushing the clothes and cleaning the shoes of John the footman; who being dressed himself, applies his hands to the same labours for Mr. Second-hand, the squire's gentleman; the gentleman in the like manner, a little later in the day, attends the squire; the squire is no sooner equipped than he attends the levee of my lord; which is no sooner over, than my lord himself is seen at the levee of the favourite, who, after the hour of homage is at an end, appears himself to pay homage to the levee of his sovereign. Nor is there, perhaps, in this whole ladder of dependence, any one step at a greater distance from the other than the first from the second, so that to a philosopher the question might only seem whether you would choose to be a great man at six in the morning or at two in the afternoon. And yet there are scarce two of these who do not think the least familiarity with the persons below them a condescension, and, if they were to go one step farther, a degradation.

THE FARMERS

Early-eighteenth-century England was preindustrial, but in no sense was it a wholly self-sufficient agricultural society. Many more people were involved with farming than with any other economic activity, but there was a sizable population of artisans, merchants, and other town and city folk who bought their food in the shop or the marketplace rather than growing it themselves. Even family farmers specialized in particular crops from which they derived their cash income.

Independently owned family farms were to be found, but large estates were more common. These estates were units of ownership rather than of production, for most of the land that constituted them was rented out, on long lease or short, to tenants who, with members of their family and hired hands, did the actual cultivating of the soil. By the end of the century some three-quarters of the agricultural land was worked by such tenant farmers; many of them had once been small freeholders, who had sold out to the great landowners in return for capital to invest in cattle, seed, fertilizer, and plows.

BULL ON THE RUN   An
exciting episode depicted
by painter John Nixon
(c. 1790). *(Rose-Hulman
Institute of Technology)*

The life of the farmer in the first half of the eighteenth century remained very much dependent on the success or failure of each year's harvest. Haymaking and harvesting would not only absorb all available local
labor but also attract thousands of young workers from Ireland and Wales,
who then went home for the winter. A run of bad harvests in the early decades of the century gave way to a series of plentiful ones in the 1730s and
1740s. Farm production did not merely keep up with a slowly rising population but surpassed it, so that food prices fell and Britain became an ex-
porter of wheat to continental Europe. Although a blessing for Londoners,
the decline in food prices caused many tenants to fall behind in their rents.
Landlords, compelled to concede rent reductions, were given new incentive
to search for changes in technique that might increase agricultural
efficiency.

One potentially revolutionary discovery in agriculture was that land
need not lie fallow in order to regain its fertility. This simple fact undermined the system of cultivation that in the more fertile areas of England
had prevailed from time immemorial: the arable land of a manor was divided into two or three great fields, each subdivided into the lord's and tenants' strips; in the two-field system one of the two fields lay fallow each
year, in the three-field system one of the three. In any given year, therefore,
at least a third of the fertile land of the country was bearing nothing but
weeds. There was consequently not enough fodder grown to keep all the
cattle through the winter, and many had to be slaughtered every fall. These
limitations on the supply of grain and meat seemed to be imposed by the
nature of the soil: century after century no one thought to question whether
they might be imposed by human ignorance.

The increase in scientific activity that began with the Restoration was
essentially a process of questioning, and one of the earliest inquiries of the
Royal Society was into methods of farming. At the same time pioneers were
bringing in the idea, long a commonplace in Flanders, that judicious rota-

THE PROCESS OF ENCLOSURE Surveyors use "cross head" poles and knotted strings to measure and reallot the fields of a Bedfordshire village. *(Courtesy of the Bedfordshire County Council)*

tion of crops would keep a field producing every year. Wheat one summer, turnips the next, then oats or barley, then clover, then wheat again—this was the cycle that slowly revolutionized British agriculture. The primary reason was that the new crops, turnips or clover, did two things at once: they replenished the soil with nitrogen and provided winter fodder for cattle. Bigger and better-fed herds gave the farmer more meat to sell and more manure for fertilizing, which made for more and better crops and hence still larger herds. Simultaneously came the first experiments with the scientific breeding of sheep and cattle for meat. Progress was extremely slow, but by 1750 modern farming was coming to birth.

The rotation of crops and the new emphasis on stock breeding forced a change in the face of the countryside. Now that the old system, two or three open fields divided into strips, was no longer necessary, landholders gradually came to realize how wasteful it was. The only way to rotate crops efficiently was to consolidate scattered strips into a single holding; the only way to improve farm stock was to prevent the animals' wandering together over the fallow ground as they had always done, a practice that ensured "the haphazard union of nobody's son with everybody's daughter," and to segregate them for breeding purposes. Improving crops and meat, in other words, required enclosed land. The requirement was met by the enclosure movement, which was essentially the conversion of strips and pasture rights in the open field, under communal supervision, into individual fields and pastures, walled or fenced, in which each owner or tenant could do as he pleased. The great age of enclosure in the English midlands by act of parliament was just beginning, but perhaps a third of all land had already been enclosed when the century began.

In a society so deeply rooted in the land these changes were momentous. The predominance of the landed interest, unchallenged until after the Napoleonic Wars, did not rest solely on turnips and clover, mutton and beef; for wealth was accruing from many other sources. But the wealth that was most accessible to the landowner was that which lay in his fields. The more profit his farmers made, the fatter his rent rolls grew. As harvests and herds improved from year to year, so did the income of the progressive squire with his few acres and the great magnate with estates all over England.

In accordance with seventeenth-century legislation, grain growers were largely protected from foreign competition and were even granted a bounty for any grain they exported. Much grain was exported during the middle years of the eighteenth century; later in the century a growing population would catch up with the available domestic food supply. Upper-class menus could be very elaborate, but for most farm and town laborers bread (made of wheat or rye), cheese, and beer (made of barley and hops) served as food staples. By the middle years of the century imported tea and sugar had become part of that diet as well. Those who could afford it ate beef several times a week, while the rest made do with mutton or bacon, and, in coastal areas, fish. In Scotland and northern England oat porridge and oat bread were customary, whereas in Lancashire, as in Ireland, potatoes were increasingly becoming a standard food. Cabbage and other leafy vegetables were available but often spurned.

Many other economic activities depended on agriculture. Even a small farming village would have its blacksmith, its shoemaker, its tailor, its glazier, and its thatcher. Wheat made its way from the farms to millers, bak-

COTTAGE INDUSTRY
William Hincks provides an idealized eighteenth-century view of the way in which yarn was spun, reeled, and boiled. (The Bridgeman Art Library Ltd.)

ers, distillers, and starchmakers. Cattle provided hides for tanners and ultimately for dealers in leather goods. The fat derived from cattle and sheep
was utilized by soap-boilers and candlemakers, and the wool shorn from
the same sheep was fundamental to the textile industry.

MERCHANTS AND ARTISANS

Although eighteenth-century industry was thus largely carried on by a variety of individual rural craftsmen, in London and in several other regions
there had developed relatively large-scale, specialized forms of manufacture.
Textiles were the most significant of these, and, in the eighteenth century as
in the fourteenth, woolen cloth was England's most important nonagricul-
tural product. It has been estimated that as late as 1740 woolen cloth constituted one-third of all English manufactured goods. No wonder that Parliament had long been eager to make sure that domestic raw wool was
reserved for English producers, not smuggled abroad, and that Parliament
protected these same textile manufacturers from foreign competition. Wool
was manufactured in a variety of grades and forms, and, although total
production is estimated as having risen by 50 percent between 1700 and
1760, the industry underwent no technological revolution during this period. In Devon the industry was indeed declining at the same time that it
was reaching its heyday in Norfolk; in Norwich and vicinity 12,000 hand
looms kept some 72,000 weavers busy. The industry was growing most rapidly in Yorkshire, where labor was cheaper and the merchant-capitalist organizers more enterprising. Like most other industries, woolen cloth manufacture was concentrated not in factories but in small workshops. Much
of the work took place in the very cottages in which the workers lived, and
the major task of the merchant-clothier was to superintend the multifaceted
process whereby the wool was spun in one place, woven in a second, fulled
(or thickened) in a third, dyed in a fourth, and sold in yet another.

Other textiles were produced as well. The Lombe silk factory that operated in Derby during the 1720s foreshadowed the pattern of manufacture
of the early nineteenth century. The complex machinery, which had been
copied from an Italian model and which supposedly involved "97,746
wheels, movements, and parts," was powered by a waterwheel and employed more than 300 women and children working day and night on successive twelve-hour shifts. Silk proved in the event to be a declining industry; linen manufacture, on the other hand, was growing in northern Ireland
and Scotland, and in Lancashire a group of English entrepreneurs took advantage of an act that kept out Indian cloth to begin a domestic cotton industry that became before long an economic giant.

There was no obvious revolution before 1760 in metal manufacture
any more than in textiles. But forges, anvils, smithies, and glassworks utilized an increasing amount of coal: the amount mined more than doubled
during the first sixty years of the century. Perhaps half the iron output of
the English Midlands was transformed into nails by some 10,000 nailmak-

COALBROOKDALE IN SHROPSHIRE   In this village Abraham Darby founded his pioneer iron works in 1709. Here pig iron was first smelted successfully with coke instead of wood. *(Reproduced by courtesy of the Trustees of the British Museum)*

ers. Techniques were continually improving. A workshop industry like watchmaking involved considerable division of labor, as some workers made dials, others cases, and yet others wheels and springs. By mid-century some 120,000 clocks and watches were produced each year in London; of these 70,000 were exported abroad. In specific skills, Dutch, French, and German artisans were on a par with the English, or superior, but by 1757 one Englishman could boast that "few countries are equal, perhaps none excel, the English in the number of contrivances or their Machines to abridge labour." Although in many regions the pace of change was slow, observers discerned bustle and vitality. Daniel Defoe adopts a "Chamber of Commerce" tone when, in his *Tour of the Whole Island of Great Britain* (1724–1726), he tells of "the New Buildings erected, the Old Buildings taken down; New Discoveries in Metals, Mine, Minerals; new Undertakings in Trade; Inventions, Engines, Manufactures, in a Nation pushing and improving as we are: These Things open new Scenes every Day, and make England especially show a new and differing Face in many Places, on every Occasion of surveying it."

THE INHABITANTS OF LONDON

In preindustrial as in postindustrial Britain, London constituted a unique phenomenon. In 1700, when Bristol and Norwich could claim perhaps 30,000 people each and Edinburgh was just a little more populous than

A LONDON SQUARE IN THE 1730s   An open-air market may be seen on the right. The statue shows King Charles II triumphing over Oliver Cromwell. *(Reproduced by courtesy of the Trustees of the British Museum)*

that, the number of inhabitants in London surpassed 600,000. It was the largest city in all Europe. Less than one-third of its people now lived within the old city walls. The metropolis that one Englishman in nine called home had not merely spread westward along the Thames and linked up with Westminster, where Parliament met and judges sat, but also swallowed up a score of small villages to the east and the north. Until 1747 the London Bridge of nursery rhyme fame sufficed as the sole land link with Southwark and the suburbs to the south, but two more bridges were added at mid-century. For the enthusiastic Defoe, London was made

> *glorious* by the Splendor of its Shores, gilded with noble Palaces, strong Fortifications, large Hospitals and publick Buildings; with the greatest Bridge, and the greatest City in the World, made famous by the Opulence of its Merchants, the Encrease and Extensiveness of its Commerce; by its invincible Navies and by the innumerable Fleets of Ships sailing upon it, to and from all Parts of the World.

Other eighteenth-century observers were troubled by the implications of that growth. The novelist Tobias Smollett saw mid-century London as "an over-grown monster; which, like a despotical head, will in time leave the body and extremities without nourishment and support." Visitors were likely to comment more prosaically on "the smoke, which being mixed with a constant fog, covers London." Coal had replaced wood as the prime fuel for cooking and for heating homes and workshops; and in consequence one pessimist feared that "the inhabitants must at last bid adieu to all hopes of ever seeing the sun."

Although the city was the site of large breweries and shipyards as well as of numerous small workshops, it was primarily devoted to commerce rather than industry. It served, first of all, as the kingdom's largest port, where as many as 1,400 sailing vessels might at any given time compete for the opportunity to load or unload their wares. Secondly, it was a community of markets and exchanges, such as Billingsgate for fish, Covent Garden for fruits and vegetables, and Smithfield for meat. "Every county," wrote Defoe, "furnishes something for the supply of London." There was cider from Devon, cheese from Cheshire, cattle from the Scottish Highlands, and from East Anglia drovers urged on thousands of geese and turkeys that waddled to the capital on their own feet if not their own volition. For well-to-do country gentlemen who built town houses around elegant new squares—each with its private park in the center—London was not merely the political and legal capital of the realm but its social center and the site of "balls and assemblies," of theaters, and of pleasure gardens such as Vauxhall and Ranelagh. Having paid their shilling admission, visitors could wander along Vauxhall's winding wooded paths, illuminated at night by hundreds of decorated oil lamps: they could listen either to nightingales or to outdoor singers and fiddlers, and stop at pavilions to dance or to purchase wine, cider or beer, and slices of beef and ham—so thin, according to

VAUXHALL GARDENS   One of London's chief pleasure gardens at mid-century. *(The Victoria and Albert Museum, London)*

a contemporary critic, that you could read a newspaper through them. The comment is a reminder that London's first daily newspaper began publication in 1702: by 1760 there were four. Young men often escorted young women down garden paths that turned so confusingly that, according to one observer, "the most experienced mothers have often lost themselves in looking for their daughters." The gardens at Ranelagh, reputedly more sedate, centered on a huge rotunda, inside which visitors could promenade and listen to music. The rotunda balcony was divided into fifty-two open alcoves where groups of seven or eight could eat, observe, listen, and wait for the outdoor fireworks that climaxed the evening.

Only a fourth of the people who lived in eighteenth-century London had been born there. The city attracted tens of thousands of the destitute from the countryside, along with immigrants from Ireland, Scotland, and the continent. There they produced the variety celebrated by Ned Ward, the early-eighteenth-century rhymster.

> Young Drunkards reeling, Bayliffs dogging,
> Old Strumpets plying, Mumpers progging [beggars scrounging],
> Fat Dray-men squabling, Chair-men ambling,
> Oyster-Whores fighting, School-Boys scrambling,
> Street-Porters running, Rascals batt'ling,
> Pick-pockets crowding, Coaches rattling,
> News bawling, Ballad-wenches singing,
> Guns roaring, and the Church-Bells ringing.

London was a dangerous and often brutal metropolis in which the favorite public amusements included cockfights, bullbaiting, and wrestling matches between half-nude women. Some people found diversion in the Tower of London, where the crown jewels, medieval weapons and suits of armor, and the royal menagerie were on display, while others peered reverently at the lavish tombs in Westminster Abbey. Still others sought out curio collections, of which the most elaborate and well-organized, Sir Hans Sloane's, was bought for the nation in the 1750s with funds raised by a government-sponsored lottery and transformed into the British Museum. Londoners could also visit wax museums, peep shows featuring mechanical figures operated by clockwork, and freak shows advertising giants and dwarfs, three-breasted women and two-headed men, and what a later generation came to call Siamese twins.[2] On Sundays sightseers paid their pennies for the right to gape at the lunatics behind the bars of Bethlehem Hospital, whose name was contracted into "Bedlam." Others stared at—or even stoned—convicted criminals bound to the pillory or watched the floggings at Bridewell (the "House of Correction") and the hangings at Tyburn. Henry Fielding, the novelist and magistrate, was moved to complain that "we sacrifice the lives of men not for the reformation but for the diversion

---

[2]In *The Shows of London* (1978), Richard D. Altick writes informatively about numerous half-forgotten chapters in the history of popular culture.

of the populace." Whatever the punishment, crime continued to flourish, and in 1718 London's city marshal lamented that it was "the general complaint of the taverns, the coffee-houses, the shop-keepers, and others, that their customers are afraid when it is dark to come to their houses and shops for fear that their hats and wigs should be snitched from their heads or their swords taken from their sides, or that they may be blinded, knocked down, cut or stabbed."

London was a magnet for all elements of society, including the poor. To them it offered variety, excitement, and the chance to make a dishonest penny, but neither security nor comfort. During the first half of the eighteenth century the urban death rate was significantly higher than the rural, and, according to one estimate, of every four children born in London during those decades only one survived to the age of five. The mass of the urban poor lived on the edge of subsistence in conditions that would have made a modern slum seem like paradise. Home meant one room per family—often a room in a garret or a cellar—and as many as eight adults and children in the family bed. The houses lacked both piped-in water and plumbing, and the sewers were the gutters outside the door. Overcrowding eliminated privacy and almost assured sexual promiscuity.

Those who could afford to do so escaped in the evening to the tavern and alehouse. Never did so large a number of English men and women find

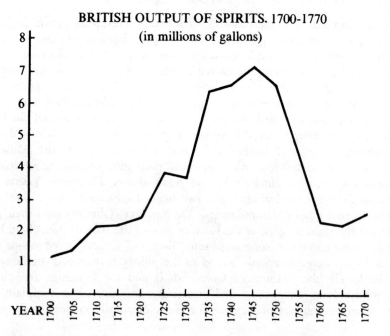

BRITISH OUTPUT OF SPIRITS. 1700-1770
(in millions of gallons)

Adapted from T. S. Ashton, *An Economic History of England: The Eighteenth Century* (1955), p. 243.

it so easy to drown their sorrows as during the 1720s, 1730s, and 1740s—the so-called "gin age." That potent beverage had become easy to distill from domestic grain, and thousands of gin-shops opened in London during the early years of the century. Although farmers, distillers, and retailers all profited, the disastrous consequences had become apparent by 1736, when the preamble to an act of Parliament observed that "the drinking of spirituous liquors or strong waters is become very common, especially among the people of lower and inferior rank, the constant and excessive use whereof tends greatly to the destruction of their healths, rendering them unfit for useful labours and business, debauching their morals, and inciting them to perpetuate all manner of vices. . . . " It required several additional acts of Parliament, a widespread change of attitude, and a rise in grain prices before high license fees and strict enforcement of the law brought the "gin mania" to an end in the early 1750s.

Taverns served not only as social centers but also as unofficial employment agencies and as places where workers were paid. London wages tended to be high when work was available, but preindustrial London, like most of the third world in our time, was plagued with chronic "underemployment." In trades that had one or more slack seasons a year, laborers would all too often find themselves imprisoned for debt or seeking relief from the parish overseers of the poor.

THE POOR LAW

The Elizabethan Poor Law of 1601 had placed on the parish, the smallest unit of civil as well as ecclesiastical government, the responsibility of choosing each year two overseers of the poor to levy a tax called the "poor rate" on local property holders, to be used for relief of those too young, too old, or too sick to help themselves. The overseers also sought to find employment for the able-bodied but jobless of the parish. Although the Elizabethan Poor Law was amended in detail from time to time, it provided the basic framework of social welfare in England for well over 200 years. What the law did not do was to set up a national or even a county administrative system to supervise the work of the overseers: they were unpaid nonprofessionals whose efficiency and sympathy for their charges varied greatly from parish to parish.

Studies of surviving parish records suggest that, although many overseers felt a greater sense of responsibility to the parish rate payers than to the "undeserving poor," paupers and aging widows were not left to starve. They received a small weekly allowance and at times bedding, cooking utensils, and shoes; when they were ill, the parish paid the local doctor to prescribe quinine for fevers and "Godfrey's cordial" or "Daffy's elixir" for other ailments; when they died the parish paid for the funeral and the burial. Orphan children were supported until they were old enough to be apprenticed. Unmarried pregnant women might be bribed to move to the next

GIN LANE, BY WILLIAM HOGARTH *(Reproduced by courtesy of the Trustees of the British Museum)* A caption at the bottom of the print reads:

Gin, cursed Fiend with Fury fraught,
    Makes human Race a prey;
It enters by a deadly Draught,
    And steals our Life away.

Virtue and Truth, driv'n to Despair,
    It's Rage compells to fly,
But cherishes, with hellish Care,
    Theft, murder, perjury.

Damn'd Cup! That on the vitals preys,
    That liquid fire contains
Which Madness to the Heart conveys,
    And rolls it thro' the veins.

BEER STREET, BY WILLIAM HOGARTH *(Reproduced by courtesy of the Trustees of the British Museum)* A caption at the bottom of the print reads:

Beer, happy produce of our Isle
    Can sinewy Strength impart,
And wearied with fatigue and Toil
    Can cheer each manly Heart.

Labour and Art upheld by Thee
    Successfully advance,
We quaff Thy balmy Juice with Glee
    And water leave to France.

Genius of Health, thy Grateful Taste
    Rivals the Cup of Jove,
And warms each English generous Breast
    With Liberty and Love.

parish so that their offspring would not become a parish liability, but, when that ploy failed, the parish would pay for the midwife and search for the father. Although less than 10 percent of the people of the average parish were looked upon as incorrigibly poor, as many as 50 percent might seek parish aid at least once in their lifetime because of a personal or a national crisis.

The Elizabethan Poor Law required the overseers to set the able-bodied to work, but this task proved difficult. Some parishes did buy supplies of wool to set women to spin or used jobless men to repair roads and wells, but the cost of supervision generally exceeded the monetary gain. During the early eighteenth century, parishes received permission to solve the problem by joining together to set up workhouses in which the poor were to be brought together, given food and shelter of a sort, and put to work. Enthusiasts hoped that these workhouses would give pauper children enough elementary training so that they, "instead of being bred up in irreligion and vice to an idle vagabond life, will have the fear of God before their eyes, get habits of virtue, be inured to labour, and thus become useful to their country." The reality was often quite different. The rules of one London workhouse insisted that inmates attend church on Sunday or forfeit supper; those who missed church twice were to be confined inside the workhouse for six months. There were separate dormitories for men and women and boys and girls—with three children or two adults per bed—and inmates had to be in bed by nine in the summer and by eight in the winter. Such a regime deterred all but the truly needy from seeking parish aid. Many a workhouse became a dumping ground where the aged as well as the young, the ill as well as the healthy, were jammed together in filthy buildings that bred disease and despair.

The people of eighteenth-century Britain lived in a paradoxical society in which elegance in architecture, furniture, and sometimes in manners went hand-in-hand with widespread callousness and cruelty, a clamorous and abusive press, and intermittent riots. Election-time tumults in numerous communities in 1715 led to the passage of the Riot Act later that year. The act permitted local magistrates to "read the Riot Act" to an assembly of twelve or more. Those who failed to disperse within the hour could be found guilty and hanged. The rapidity with which capital offenses were added to the statute book in the early eighteenth century testifies to the sense of concern of such magistrates, who lacked any police force more formidable than the parish constable. In a typical year (1740), seventeen men and one woman were hanged in England: the great majority of those convicted, even for capital offenses, were ultimately spared the hangman's noose. Both rich and poor appealed to the common law, and, when dissatisfied, Britons of the day appeared ever ready to fight for their rights as they saw them. When a new turnpike road or an enclosure of common land undermined ancient custom, or when a bad harvest created a bread shortage, or when a change of fashion led to a depression in a particular trade, laborers and their wives as often as not resorted to violence.[3] At least once a decade, a particular cause would rouse "the London mob" to a flurry of destruction, and even the king's ministers were likely to have their windows smashed and to go about armed against assault. Yet the first half of the century witnessed neither a political overturn, nor an explosion in population, nor a revolution in industry. The mood of the age was more favorable to individual achievement and self-assertion in war, trade, and politics than to ready popular subordination to some national master plan.

---

[3]E. P. Thompson, in "The Moral Economy of the English Crowd in the Eighteenth Century," *Past & Present* 50 (February 1971), and his associates in D. Hay et al., *Albion's Fatal Tree: Crime and Society in Eighteenth-Century England* (1975), look upon the criminal law as predominantly an instrument of class oppression, while John Brewer and John Styles, eds., *An Ungovernable People: The English and Their Law in the Seventeenth and Eighteenth Centuries* (1980), emphasize that eighteenth-century society involved more than two classes and that the rich, the poor, and those in between all appealed to the law, a law that gave legitimacy to the authority of the upper ranks and at the same time limited that authority.

4 THE STRUCTURE OF THE OLIGARCHY

*L*ife in eighteenth-century London was often turbulent, but the kingdom's underlying social structure remained remarkably stable. Society was organized in a hierarchical manner, with a small group of families at the top furnishing political, economic, and cultural leadership. Their activities and aspirations were abundantly recorded in the letters, diaries, pictures, furniture, and buildings of the age. This chapter will begin with their political structure and will touch on their architecture, their problems in providing for their families, their education, their view of the world, and their taste in literature. It will turn at the end to Lord Chesterfield as the exemplar of a social code by which many of them lived. Generalizations will appear in abundance but will be no more than tentative conclusions. As Chesterfield advised his son, "Analyze them yourself and judge whether they are true or not."

THE DEFEAT OF TORYISM

The political structure of the oligarchy changed after 1714, for the Hanoverian accession marked the end of parties in the old sense. They had scarcely been parties in the modern sense, because, except for a few years during the reign of Queen Anne, they largely lacked national organization, cohesion, or discipline: they had rather been expressions of contrasting points of view. Out of the great cleavage that had produced the civil war of 1642 had come the Whigs and Tories of the Restoration—one the intellectual heirs of the Roundheads, the other of the Cavaliers; and from the 1670s until the death of Anne the party struggles had had in them an undercurrent of violence. Great issues had been at stake in domestic and foreign policy, and they had all been tied to the disposition of the crown. Now that the issues were settled, much of the venom went out of the political world.

So did the old Tory party. The Glorious Revolution had shaken its twin pillars of principle, the Anglican Church as the sole church of the nation and the royal prerogative as divinely ordained. Toleration of Protestants outside the church had been legalized, and God's laws of hereditary monarchy had been subordinated to man's law made in Parliament. The Tories had continued till 1714 to fight bitterly *against* these changes, without knowing what they were fighting *for*. The idea of a narrow church that persecuted Catholic and Protestant outsiders with equal fervor had become as unrealistic as the idea of restoring divine-right monarchy in the person of a Roman Catholic Stuart. In the frenzied pursuit of these will-o'-the-wisps the Tories had gone to their destruction.

After 1714 their twin principles and their party were dead and buried. The Whigs extended the practice of toleration in a typically pragmatic fashion. Parliament repealed the legislation of Anne's reign against dissenters and annually indemnified those of them who took local office illegally. Yet the Test Act and the Clarendon Code, as modified in 1689, remained on the statute book. Politically ambitious dissenters moved into the Anglican fold. The rest were still underprivileged and had no voice in national or even local politics, except in communities where they were numerous. But they were no longer a minority persecuted to the point where they excited controversy. Their acute grievances were over, and their religious zeal was flagging. They gradually settled down, alongside the Anglicans, to what Edward Gibbon in later years called "the fat slumbers of the church."

If dissent was not a major political issue after 1714, neither was monarchy. George I was enough to dissipate the last wisps of Tory romanticism, and his court was as dull as he was. In his early years he had divorced and imprisoned his charming young wife for a love affair and had probably had her lover murdered; but by the time he came to England, in his mid-fifties, he had lost even the glamor of scandal without acquiring that of royalty. He had nothing regal about him. He never learned English and scandalized his courtiers when, on his arrival, he could not even distinguish the different ranks of the peerage.[1] Except when it seemed politically necessary, he shunned the pomp that his office demanded. Although he impressed his German associates as a reasonable, kind-hearted man, highly knowledgeable about European diplomacy, he failed to win the affection of his new subjects. Lord Chesterfield found the king gross even in his pleasures. "No woman came amiss to him," he reported, "if they were very willing and very fat. . . . The standards of his Majesty's taste made all those ladies who aspired to his favor, and who were near the suitable size, strain and swell themselves like the frogs in the fable to rival the bulk and dignity of the ox. Some succeeded, and others burst."

The Tories could not worship a crown that rested on such a head, but George would not have welcomed them even if they had. He recognized that he owed his throne to the Whigs and accordingly gave them the plums of office: to be Tory was to be in permanent and hopeless opposition. A few of the erstwhile Tories turned Jacobite, scheming for the day that never arrived when a Stuart would again be king. Many more came to terms with

---

[1]J. H. Plumb provides caustic pen portraits of George I and his immediate successors in *The First Four Georges* (1956). Ragnhild Hatton's assessment in *George I: Elector and King* (1978) is far more favorable. John M. Beattie presents a detailed account of the royal household in *The English Court in the Reign of George I* (1967).

GEORGE I ENTERS LONDON   A splendid procession, on September 20, 1714, escorts the new king to St. James's Palace. *(BBC Hulton Picture Library)*

the new regime, called themselves Whigs, and joined the scramble for office. The rest became disgruntled onlookers, longing for they knew not what.

The demotion of Toryism to apparently permanent minority status meant that Britain, for close to a century after 1714, did not have two parties in any meaningful sense.[2] Everyone who aspired to office was by definition Whig, and the political conflicts of the period were among cliques within this universal party. As the balance of power shifted between the cliques, ministries came and went. There was always an opposition, and its leaders thundered against corruption in government, but they were usually trying to increase their nuisance value in order to force their way into office and were quick to change their tune when they got there. Although politics remained tumultuous, it was a different kind of tumult from that under the later Stuarts: a struggle for place rather than for principle. Only the Jacobites, with their antiquated principle, could on occasion revive the old threat of civil war. The rest of the time the politics of Whiggism produced only factional skirmishing.

---

[2]The title of one of the major works on the politics of the period seems to belie this generalization, but the author in fact supports it: Keith G. Feiling, *The Second Tory Party, 1714–1832* (1938).

THE CABINET AND PARLIAMENT

Great causes and principles are not prerequisite for great developments, which often come in undramatic periods. So it was with the first half-century of the Hanoverians, when the very dullness of the new monarchy contributed to the rise of cabinet government. George I and his son, who succeeded him in 1727 as George II, had some prestige because they were kings, and more because advancement depended on their favor, but they had neither the brains nor the will for leadership. Consequently a subtle shift of executive power set in, from the sovereign to his ministers. They became less agents of his policy and more makers of policy themselves; under the king's surveillance, sometimes sharp and sometimes perfunctory, they steered through Parliament measures that were essentially their own. The eighteenth century was evolving the mechanism, which the seventeenth had lacked, for amalgamating executive and legislative authority in the king's cabinet.

The beginnings of this process went back to the Restoration and can best be sketched here. The cabinet originated as an inner, secret committee of the Privy Council. Secrecy was vital, because Parliament could not call cabinet members to account unless it knew what they had done. As long as they were protected from prying eyes at Westminster, and as long as the king was able to direct them, they were servants of his will. Charles II, when told that

> He never said a foolish thing
> And never did a wise one,

answered that "my words are my own, my acts are my ministers.' " But the reply was deftly misleading. He acted for himself, and so did his immediate successors. Just as he forced the earl of Danby to be his reluctant tool in negotiating with Louis XIV, so William III forced his cabinet to authorize unnamed persons to treat with Louis for unnamed ends. Ministers of the Stuarts had no doubt about who determined policy.

William began his reign by drawing cabinet members from both parties, but in his last years he preferred to draw them from whichever party had a parliamentary majority. The reason was merely that government could function more effectively, and with less legislative interference, if it had a solid base of support than if it depended on segments of both parties. At the end of the reign, however, when Parliament was at its most obstreperous, it interfered with a vengeance: it attacked the whole cabinet system as a device for vitiating parliamentary supremacy. The Act of Settlement of 1701 barred the cabinet from offering secret advice to the sovereign and provided that after Anne's death cabinet members should also be barred from the House of Commons. These two provisions would have made the new experiment unworkable. Prohibiting ministers from advising the crown privately would have ended their usefulness to it. Excluding them from the

Commons would have destroyed the essential characteristic of the cabinet: that it is an executive selected from and based in Parliament. Both provisions, by good luck, were soon repealed, and the cabinet continued its unplanned growth.

The Hanoverian accession began a new phase of growth. The principle that cabinet members—who included both peers and commoners—should be drawn from the majority party lost its meaning as soon as everyone became a Whig, and the rise of factions within the all-encompassing party left the king leeway in choosing his ministers. He had to be sure that they commanded the support of a sufficient number of factions in the Commons to carry on his government, but this proved to be a problem that he could leave largely to the men of his choice. The conduct of administration became a matter of manipulation, bargaining, and influence, which the Whig politicians soon developed into a fine art. Understanding how they did so— in other words, how the Hanoverian political system worked—demands some understanding of the structure of the House of Commons.

The knights of the shire, the two members representing each county, were elected at large by those who held freehold property worth forty shillings a year. Powerful local families, as time went on, learned to control most of the elections by adjusting differences and balancing interests so as to present only two candidates, whom the voters were expected to return and usually did. These county members had to hold land worth £600 a year and therefore belonged to the well-to-do gentry; but they composed only a quarter of the House. The majority was made up of borough representatives.

A parliamentary borough was any town to which the sovereign had accorded one or more representatives. But "town" was often a euphemism, for boroughs ranged from great cities to decaying hamlets. The way in which they had been apportioned at the beginning of Parliament in the Middle Ages had reflected, in a rough and ready fashion, the distribution of urban wealth and population at that time, but the vast changes since had brought no commensurate change in apportionment. An eighteenth-century borough might be a heap of stones in a pasture or engulfed by the sea; it continued to send its member or members to Westminster, whereas many new and bustling towns sent none. The system was logically absurd and politically indispensable.

Although the qualification for voting in the boroughs varied as widely as their size, in almost all of them the electorate was small. Only three had more than 4,000 voters, most had less than 500, and several had thirteen or fourteen. The possibilities of influencing an election in such tiny constituencies were increased by the fact that a candidate did not need to be a resident. If a candidate had landed property worth £300 a year he might stand for any borough, and he did not have to look far to find one where the voters would return whoever offered them the most. Offers varied from bribes and favors to individuals, through paying for public improvements in the town, to supporting its interests in Whitehall and Westminster.

If the candidate did not personally have the wealth or influence to meet the terms demanded, he needed only to discover a patron who had, or better yet a patron who controlled a "pocket" borough. In these the voters were so well in hand that they returned whoever was offered them; at each election the patron reached into his pocket, in effect, and pulled out the member or members for that borough. In such cases no candidate needed to lift a finger. "Your seat in the new parliament is at last absolutely secured," Lord Chesterfield wrote his son in 1754, "and that without opposition or the least necessity of your personal trouble or appearance." A patron had been found, and "he brings you in with himself at his surest borough." The wheedling and bargaining that preceded such an agreement were often difficult, but the election itself was a mere formality.

As the century wore on, patronage became a highly developed system. A Whig aristocrat, usually a peer and sitting in the House of Lords, would work through agents and friends to gain and keep control of a group of boroughs. Some needed constant attention and constant guarding against predatory rivals, but with enough persistence and money every large landholder could build up what the period called his "interest," a group of members of the lower house who owed him their places and voted substantially as he told them to. The larger his "interest," the greater his political weight, and out of the great "interests" ministries were built. Four or five territorial magnates, pooling their resources in the cabinet, could command a substantial bloc of votes in the Commons, and many of the remaining votes they needed would come to them because they were in office. The king, one of the greatest landholders in the country, had a borough "interest" of his own to put at his ministers' disposal: as his agents they also had a variety of other ways in which to influence votes in the Commons.

The key to this influence was the Septennial Act of 1716, which extended the life of any Parliament to a maximum of seven years. Not until after the American Revolution was a Parliament dissolved before the end of its legal term, and the reason is apparent. From the viewpoint of members of the Commons and their patrons, elections were expensive and time-consuming and so to be avoided. Whereas 156 English and Welsh seats were contested in the election of 1722, only 66 were fought in 1757. From the perspective of the cabinet, a long parliamentary session provided the opportunity to explore the weaknesses and needs of members, to determine those who could be counted on and those who could be bought with promises and favors, and so to create a phalanx of government supporters.

Some votes went almost automatically to any administration in power. Many army and navy officers sat in the House of Commons, and so did placemen, who would now be called civil servants. These groups were rarely in opposition—officers because they had their eye on promotion, placemen because they were themselves a part of government. Other members responded to more indirect influence: one might have a clerical brother who hungered for a bishopric, another a father anxious to be raised from

CANVASSING FOR VOTES   A painting by William Hogarth. *(Courtesy of the Trustees of Sir John Soane's Museum)*

the Irish to the British peerage; a third might want a local henchman made postmaster or customs collector; and a fourth might have such heavy debts that only a colonial governorship could keep him out of jail. The king was still the source of promotion, honors, offices, and cash: his ministers could barter his favors for political support.

But their "interests" combined with his influence could never secure a working majority. For that the government always had to have substantial assistance from the independent members, those who were beholden to no one in office and voted as they pleased. They are sometimes called the Country party, as distinct from the ministerial or Court party, but the phrase is misleading, because they were even less a party in any meaningful sense than the pre-Hanoverian Whigs and Tories had been. The independents, although they included the troublemakers who hoped to harass the ministry into silencing them with an office, were for the most part men who were uninterested in office, who in earlier days might have been Tory, and who were concerned primarily with the needs of their own localities and secondarily with such national questions as they could grasp. They were the solid substratum of the House of Commons—merchants and financiers with a sharp eye on the government's commercial policy, country gentlemen intent on keeping down the land tax and keeping up the prosperity of agriculture. They were largely immune to political manipulation but alert to their own special interests, which no cabinet could neglect for long and stay in office.[3]

Thus a ministerial majority, like an electoral majority in a borough, was the result of careful bargaining and arrangement. To call this way of doing things corrupt is to impose today's moral judgment on the past. Politicians of that day, even when out of office and inveighing against ministerial corruption (by which they usually meant that others were getting the plums they wanted for themselves), would never have called the system itself corrupt. They knew no other. They and their ancestors in the feudal hierarchy had always scrambled for favors from the king, and only their scramble had made government possible; they had given services in return for rewards. This two-way process still operated, with the difference that a small group of the oligarchs, ministers of an acquiescent king, now dispensed the rewards. At a time when parties were in abeyance and the cabinet was delicately balanced between crown and Parliament, rewards were the means of securing votes, and votes were the means of getting the king's business done. What the ministers called influence, not corruption, was only a part of the governmental process, but in the circumstances it was an essential part.

The formal, organized opposition that the modern British political system requires was unthinkable under the Hanoverians. In a world where all the ambitious were Whigs and where the symbol of Whiggism triumphant was the new dynasty, loyalty to it—if not enthusiasm for it—was incumbent on all. Ministers were still the servants whom the king chose to carry out his policy. They were fair game in debate, but only on their specific measures; to attack them on principle, because they were ministers, would have been tantamount to attacking the throne. Although when they fell from power they might criticize the succeeding administration, they rarely if ever attempted to undermine it. What is formally known today as "Her Majesty's loyal opposition" can be both loyal and in opposition because majesty no longer plays a personal role in government. The Hanoverians did play such a role and hence could not have such an opposition.

Once every generation, however, opposition was able to assume a kind of dynastic loyalty. The reason was an odd family characteristic of the Hanoverians: each sovereign in turn became, sooner or later, bitterly estranged from his heir, the Prince of Wales. George I and his son George were at loggerheads as long as the father lived; George II and his wife quarreled furiously with their firstborn, Prince Frederick, whom the Queen once described as "the greatest ass and the greatest liar and the greatest *canaille* [scoundrel] and the greatest beast in the whole world." George II outlived his son (a great good fortune for the kingdom) only to find himself at odds

---

[3]For a fuller analysis of the composition of Parliament, see Dorothy Marshall, *Eighteenth Century England, 1714–1783* (1962) or chap. 1 of W. A. Speck, *Stability and Strife: England, 1714–1760* (1977). The most detailed account of the subject remains E. and A. Porritt, *The Unreformed House of Commons*, 2 vols. (1903).

with his grandson, the future George III; a generation later George III in turn was made miserable by his eldest, the prince who eventually became George IV. This repetitive antagonism of father and son had a political significance. Malcontents could rally around the heir to the throne, as long as he opposed his father, and attack the royal ministry in the name of royalty-soon-to-be. The king was the setting sun; those who championed the prince were likely, when the sun set, to be the ministers of the new reign. Meanwhile they could be both loyal and in opposition.

Another trait of the first two Georges had major political repercussions. Both men were more devoted to the electorate of Hanover than to the kingdom of Great Britain. George I accepted the throne from a sense of duty to his house, not from love of the island. "His views and affections were singly confined to the narrow compass of his Electorate," said Lord Chesterfield. "England was too big for him." George II spoke English, unlike his father, but with a marked German acent; in his heart he was equally German and longed to escape the cares of British kingship. "I am sick to death of all this foolish stuff," he once burst out, "and wish with all my heart that the devil may take all your bishops, and the devil take your ministers and the devil take the parliament, and the devil take the whole island—provided I can get out of it and go to Hanover."

Both kings spent part of each year in their electorate, were intent on safeguarding its interests, and expected their British ministers to provide the means for doing so. This expectation posed a new kind of problem. For the first time since the Middle Ages, except for the brief Dutch connection brought by William III, Britain had a territorial stake in Europe. The location of Hanover made it far more vulnerable and difficult to defend than the Dutch Republic. It lay across the lower Elbe and Weser, the two great waterways from central Europe to the North Sea; on the east was the rising power of Prussia, on the west the Dutch and Austrian Netherlands and France. Hanover was directly or indirectly involved in every struggle for power in that part of the continent. Whenever a crisis arose, the great question was how far Britain would be involved in consequence.

That question, arising over and over again, emphasized the equivocal position of the king's ministers. They were responsible to him and also to Parliament and were therefore in a dilemma whenever Hanoverian and British interests conflicted. Sacrificing the first to the second would never be forgiven at court; sacrificing the second to the first would never be forgiven at Westminster, where the independent country gentry cared little or nothing about the electorate and were quickly aroused by the argument that the Hanoverian tail was wagging the British dog. For half a century the problem of how to coordinate tail and dog plagued successive administrations. It was never settled because it was the expression of a more fundamental problem—how ministers could both serve a king who was pulling in one direction and keep control of a legislature that was pulling in the other. That problem was insoluble until the king ceased to pull and became a constitutional figurehead.

So much for the political structure of the regime. It was a confused and rambling structure that would have been the despair of a modern political scientist, by whose standards the government that operated within it would seem unbelievably inefficient. But modern standards of efficiency, like modern views of corruption, are irrelevant in understanding the past, which has to be taken on its own terms. People of the time might realize dimly that there were constitutional problems and even absurdities in their political system, yet for half a century they accepted that system because by their standards it provided effective government.

THE RULING CLASS

Britain was ruled by amateurs. A professional politician or administrator, in the sense of a specialist who devotes his or her whole life to that career, would have struck an eighteenth-century Whig as an aberration of the human species. Gentlemen had careers and might even spend a great deal of time at them, but they were not prepared for them by formal education. If they went into either of the armed services, they did not attend college—let alone a military or naval academy—but were trained in the regiment or at sea: one admiral remarked that for forty years his ship "has been the only university he has been permitted to study at." If they elected a political career, they were likely to start with an education of sorts at Oxford or Cambridge, and perhaps an exposure to the law at one of the Inns of Court; but then, when they secured local office or a seat in Parliament or membership in the cabinet, they learned their job as they went along, trusting to their wits and, with luck, to an experienced secretary.

This is not to say that gentlemen were uneducated. Almost all of them were versed in the classics and had some command of French, while many were well grounded in history and informed by foreign travel and wide reading. What they lacked was a training in principles, in the theory of what they were doing: they were improvisers rather than specialists and would have scorned to be anything else. Their self-assurance, even when they were ignorant, was that of men who know that they are to the manor born; their amateur status was synonymous with their being gentlemen.

Their rule was as expensive as it was successful. They were profligate in wasting time and money; they often made decisions on inadequate information and unexamined premises; they ignored much that cried out to be done. Yet they also achieved surprising results in the hundred-odd years that their regime lasted. They conquered an empire overseas, fought France to a standstill and eventually to defeat in Europe, presided at home over an economic revolution in agriculture and industry, and brought the art of living among the favored few to a high peak. They had faults aplenty, but they also had an energy that made even their system work.

Early Georgian society, for all its self-assurance, was less sophisticated than it became later in the century. The court did much to set its tone, and the sovereign to set the tone of the court. Anne had been no patron of the

GEORGE FREDERICK
HANDEL (1685–1759)
A naturalized English-
man, musician-com-
poser Handel provided
a background of elegance
and entertainment for
courtiers and ordinary
citizens alike. *(National
Portrait Gallery,
London)*

arts, and by comparison with her the first two Hanoverians were boors—as
witness the bluff comment of George II, in his Germanic English, "Damn
the Bainters, and the Boets Too!" Only for music did the first two Georges
make an exception: both became loyal patrons of George Frederick Handel
(1685–1759), German by birth, Italian by musical training, and English by
residence and naturalization. Handel's *Royal Water Music* was dedicated to
George I, and many of Handel's thirty-six Italian operas were performed
before him. In his later career the composer specialized in oratorios, un-
staged operas performed in concert halls to English texts, the best-remembered of which, *The Messiah*, was first performed in Dublin in 1742. He
helped implant choral singing in the English musical tradition, and he dominated the London musical scene until his death in 1759.

Many of the great magnates provided patronage to painters and poets,
musicians and architects, but their taste was far from impeccable: they often
mistook ostentation for elegance. An example in point is Blenheim Palace,

completed at the beginning of the period. When Parliament voted the duke of Marlborough a great country house, a fashionable architect, Sir John Vanbrugh, was commissioned to design it. The duke himself had much to do with the plans, and after his death his termagant duchess brought the work to completion. It bears the impress of Marlborough's personality. "As the Pharaohs built their Pyramids, so he sought a physical monument which would certainly stand, if only as a ruin, for thousands of years. About his achievements he preserved a complete silence, offering neither explanations nor excuses for any of his deeds. His answer was to be this great house."[4]

Although the "house"—three acres of it—answers no questions explicitly, it does tell something about what the duke and his age considered to be monumental. The palace is not only huge but as ponderous as the Great Pyramid. Its heaviness is accentuated by the fact that it broods over one of the most serene and spacious parks in England. The mass of the building is enough in itself to explain the epitaph on Vanbrugh, its architect: "lie heavy on him, Earth, for he laid many a heavy load on thee." But massiveness is not the only characteristic: another is multiplicity. Despite the symmetrical plan, the sense of unity is lost in a maze of pavilions, wings, colonnades, and indentations; the eye is kept busy in racing from window to cornice to statuary to pilaster without ever coming to rest. The interior is of a piece with the facade: monumental staircases, vast rooms hung with tapestry or gleaming with marble (some of it real, some painted on the walls), and never a quiet moment. This is the architecture of show. It is a collection of impressive parts jostling each other for preeminence, like politicians jostling for office. The restless energy within the structure itself results in an imposing chaos.

The same restlessness ran through much of society, although it did not always appear on the surface. Many members of the eighteenth-century nobility and gentry added to their country houses or built new ones, securing, if they were fortunate, the services of Lancelot "Capability" Brown (1716–1783), the prime landscape architect of the age. Brown would dam rivers to create artificial lakes, shear away old hillsides and build new ones, cut away underbrush and plant new groves of trees—all in order to provide a series of varied but serene parkland views to be admired from the manor house and from the winding gravel walks that surrounded it. The inhabitants of such country houses seemed to have an almost inexhaustible appetite for social life. They loved to eat, to dance, and to attend what they called an assembly—defined in 1751 as "a stated and general meeting of the polite persons of both sexes, for the sake of conversation, gallantry, news and play." The invention of carriages with springs made it possible for country squires and their wives to travel to London in relative comfort and also to take the waters at Bath or at one of the other fashionable spas. The great

---

[4]Churchill, *Marlborough, His Life and Times*, vol. 6 (1933–1939), p. 319. For an illustration of Blenheim and a fuller discussion of its architecture, see Chapter 10.

BURLEY-ON-THE-HILL, RUTLAND   An eighteenth-century country house, designed in the baroque style, with formal gardens and landscaped grounds. *(Aerofilms Limited)*

lords usually had permanent town houses in London, but aristocrats and gentry alike retained their roots in the country.[5]

The eighteenth century was their heyday. They had freed themselves from the attempts of the Stuart monarchy to control local as well as national government and had taken both into their hands. It is well to remember that the central government, except in the person of excise collectors and wartime impressment gangs, was far removed from the day-to-day concerns of most Britons. More important to them were the local officials, particularly the unsalaried justices of the peace. These Tudor workhorses continued to serve as both judges and administrators. They met four times yearly, in appropriately named quarter sessions, to try a great variety of offenses ranging from physical assault to short-weighting by shopkeepers. They also administered the county bridges, jails, and houses of correction and licensed alehouse proprietors and innkeepers. Occasionally they still set

---

[5]Mark Girouard is concerned with both the architectural setting and the inhabitants' social customs in *Life in the English Country House* (1978).

maximum wage rates and bread prices, and in a period of distress they requisitioned grain. Finally, they were influential in nominating parochial officials: the churchwardens, the overseers of the poor, the surveyors of highways, and the petty constables. The justices had the power to indict such officers for failing to carry out their duties, and they served as a court of appeal against the decisions of parish poor-rate assessors. The local oligarchs were free from administrative supervision from above and largely free from popular control from below. In the eighteenth century the parish vestry, in theory the assembly of all householders, was democratic in form but seldom in substance. In this situation aristocrats and squires might have been expected to settle into placid enjoyment of their power. But political power was a function of their status as gentry, and status depended on money: rulers who went bankrupt would cease to rule. They had to maintain their incomes, and this need kept their world in flux.

They themselves were not farmers, or they would never have had the leisure to govern. Their estates were tilled either by hired hands, whom a steward normally supervised, or by tenants—farmers in the English sense. The nobleman or squire lived on the labor of others, which enabled him to be a local official or member of Parliament and still have time left over for the vigorous life of a country gentleman. But the economic foundation of that life could not be taken for granted. If his estate was entailed, he had only a life interest in it and had to keep it intact, to go at his death to his eldest son. If it was not entailed, dividing it between several sons would fatally lower their positions in the world. How then, could he keep it together and also provide for his children? Not by sitting still, but only by exploring every possible way to increase the family fortunes.

One way was matrimonial. If a father could find rich wives for his boys and rich husbands for his girls, his troubles would be over. Even if he could do nothing more than find an heiress for his eldest son, the estate might then be stretched to take care of the other children. The conscientious father would rarely try to make a marriage alliance with a monster or a moron, no matter how well endowed with earthly goods. The mid-eighteenth-century aristocratic family in England was likely to show both greater affection and a greater sense of equality between husband and wife, more direct involvement in the bringing up of children, and a wider degree of detachment from the everpresent household servants than had comparable families during the Tudor and Stuart eras.[6] Admittedly, the father seeking

---

[6]Marriageable daughters were less likely to encounter imbecilic suitors such as the one Ann Page describes in Shakespeare's *The Merry Wives of Windsor:*

> He is my father's choice.
> O, what a world of vile ill-favored faults
> Looks handsome in three hundred pounds a year!

The entire subject is explored in Lawrence Stone, *The Family, Sex, and Marriage in England, 1500–1800* (1977), and in Randolph Trumbach, *The Rise of the Egalitarian Family: Aristocratic Kinship and Domestic Relations in Eighteenth-Century England* (1978).

spouses for his children remained as concerned with social status and financial stability as with love. Achieving his goal required luck in finding wealth, diplomatic and business acumen in bargaining with the other parent, and shrewd lawyers in drawing up the contract. Such contracts, though they could not ensure happy marriages, often ensured the survival of families.

The largest market for rich husbands and wives was among those who had more money than lineage. The *nouveaux riches* of the day, who had made their fortunes in banking, commerce, or the wool trade, or abroad in the service of the East India Company or one of its lesser competitors, were eager to rise above their origins into the ruling class. The way to do so was first to settle on the land, then to contract judicious marriages. No one could begin the climb toward gentility until he severed all active connection with trade and bought a country estate; then he could inaugurate the long series of moves by which his son might gain admission to county society. The boy would go to an acceptable school such as Eton, then to Oxford or Cambridge, then perhaps to Europe for a year or two of polishing on what was called the Grand Tour. On his return he would be eligible, if his father had enough wealth, to marry even the daughter of an impecunious earl: such a marriage would in all likelihood make him socially acceptable by right of his wife. Their son, two generations removed from money grubbing, would in any case be a gentleman above reproach.

In this and similar ways the oligarchy was constantly getting new blood. "Trade in England," said Daniel Defoe, ". . . has peopled this nation with gentlemen. . . . The tradesmen's children, or at least their grandchildren, come to be as good gentlemen, statesmen, parliament-men, privy councilors, judges, bishops, and noblemen as those of the highest birth and the most ancient families." One of these newly arrived noblemen, catapulted into the peerage by his father's wealth, summed up the process more succinctly: "I am William Lord Craven. My father was Lord Mayor of London, and my grandfather was Lord knows who."

If what is now termed upward mobility characterized the ruling class, so did downward mobility. Not all the younger sons of squires or even peers could find heiresses to ease their way; families were large and opportunities limited. The careful father would use all his connections, relatives and influential friends, to find openings for his boys in the world in which they were reared; but he could not always do it. Take the case of an imaginary country squire, Sir Roger Broadacres, Bart., who is the father of six sons. The estate is entailed on young Roger, the eldest, who will inherit it along with the baronetcy. No problem there. Secundus, his younger brother, is marked out for the army; and Lady Broadacres's cousin at the War Office will watch out for his advancement. Tertius, a studious boy, will obviously go into the Church, for his uncle is a bishop. Quartus is attracted by the sea and has for godfather a captain in the Royal Navy. But connections cannot be overused, and the prospects for Quintus and Sextus are slim. So Sir Roger puts one to work with the family solicitor, to be trained for the law, and the other with the wool merchants who have long marketed the produce of the family's sheep. Two out of the six brothers, in other words, leave the world of the gentry.

A man in Sir Roger's position had to do more than provide for his children by arranging marriages and pulling strings: he also had to look sharply to his income. The status, perhaps the survival, of his family depended on how well he used his land, and in the course of the eighteenth century many of his ilk became leaders as well as beneficiaries of agricultural improvement. Charles Townshend, a secretary of state in the 1720s, retired from politics in order to pioneer the utilization of root crops and to win historical renown as "Turnips Townshend." Such men had an economic incentive, of course, but it was not their only one. Like Antaeus, they drew their strength from the earth, and familiarity with it was in their blood. The discovery that it had greater potential than they had dreamed of was a challenge to their adventurousness, and they responded by innovating with the same energy that they brought to politics and empire building.

BRITAIN AND THE "ENLIGHTENMENT"

The mental world of educated Europeans in the eighteenth century is usually summed up as the "Enlightenment."[7] That term may be defined as the era when "philosophes," the contemporary term for inquirers into the ways of man and nature, examined almost every facet of the world as they saw it in order to discover relatively simple, yet fundamental, "natural laws" comparable to those mathematical equations by which Isaac Newton had explained the workings of the cosmos. The human mind was regarded as a torch that could cast a beam into a deep and complex cavern and in course of time reveal every crevice. In the words of the age's most famous poet, Alexander Pope (1688–1744),

> Nature and Nature's laws lay hid in night
> God said Let Newton be! and all was light

Newton, building on the work of earlier scientists, had found the formulae that described the revolution of the earth and planets about the sun, and his findings had superseded complex ancient and medieval theories. Just so did other men seek to become the Newtons of the moral or economic world, to dispense with ancient superstitions, substitute the natural for the fanciful, and supplant outmoded dogma with the power of human reason.

---

[7]The eighteenth-century world of ideas is the subject of Peter Gay, *The Enlightenment: An Interpretation*, 2 vols. (1967–1970). That Victorian classic, Leslie Stephen, *History of English Thought in the Eighteenth Century*, 2 vols. (1876), concentrates on the British scene, as does R. W. Harris, *Reason and Nature in Eighteenth Century Thought* (1968). Jane Rendall examines *The Origins of the Scottish Enlightenment, 1707–1776* (1978). A. S. Turberville, in *English Men and Manners in the Eighteenth Century*, 2nd ed. (1929), provides brief sketches of numerous authors and artists as well as of politicians and military men.

Newton's compatriot John Locke had taken several giant steps in that very direction. In his *Two Treatises on Government* he had sought to justify human government on the basis of reason rather than dogma. Men were to obey government not because of habit or religious sanction but self-interest, for only by creating a government could they protect their lives, their liberty, and their property. The governments they set up had to justify themselves in turn on the basis of reason, for it was presumed that a contract existed between the governed and the governors for the benefit of the former. When governments, such as that of James II, did not abide by this contract, they could and should be supplanted by others that did. In his *Essay Concerning Human Understanding,* Locke had outlined similar axioms in the area of human psychology. Man was not born, he wrote, with a host of innate ideas; his mind at birth was rather a blank slate to be filled by experience—by sense impressions and his reflections upon them. The implications of Locke's psychology seemed optimistic: if one could improve the environment in which human beings were educated, one could make the next generation better than the one that had gone before. One could emphasize the potentialities of human beings rather than their limitations, their possible achievements in this world rather than the "original sin" that, according to traditional Christianity, deferred ultimate happiness to the world to come.

To the leading exponents of the eighteenth-century Enlightenment throughout Europe—to Voltaire, Diderot, and Condorcet—Newton and Locke served as "founding fathers" of reform. In England itself they became the bastions of the status quo. As the Whig party had been transformed within half a century from a quasirevolutionary opposition group to a pillar of respectability, so the ideas of Newton and Locke lost many of their radical implications and became the conventional wisdom of the day. The English, unlike the French, could claim to have limited arbitrary royal power, to have established an independent judiciary, and to have begun to tolerate a diversity of religions; these achievements bred complacency. Thus the Royal Society, which had been in the forefront of scientific experimentation in the later seventeenth century, became less innovative in the eighteenth. The universities of Oxford and Cambridge, although they provided a setting in which young gentlemen might socialize for several years and dip into books at their leisure, paid little attention to scholarship and virtually ceased to impose examinations on their students. As the historian Edward Gibbon recalled in his *Autobiography,* the Oxford dons of the 1750s "supinely enjoyed the gifts of the founder [but] from the toil of reading, or thinking, or writing, they had absolved their conscience."

It was Scotland rather than England and the universities of Edinburgh and Glasgow rather than Oxford or Cambridge that participated more energetically in the European Enlightenment. In the aftermath of the Act of Union, numerous Scots—such as the novelist Tobias Smollett, the surgeon John Hunter, and the diarist and biographer James Boswell—found fame and sometimes fortune in London. Edinburgh, though it ceased to be a national capital, remained the cultural center for most of the Scottish upper class, who found London too distant and too expensive a mecca. They took advantage of the wide degree of Scottish literacy and of a new, less dogmatic temperament on the part of the leaders of the Presbyterian Church, to transform their former capital into "the Athens of the North." While the University of Glasgow shone in mathematics and philosophy, Edinburgh developed the best medical school in the English-speaking world. Adam Smith, professor of moral philosophy at Glasgow, laid the foundations for the modern study of economics as a separate social science, and Adam Ferguson of Edinburgh became "the father of modern sociology." Joseph Black, who taught at both Glasgow and Edinburgh, laid many of the foundations of modern chemistry and was the first person to isolate carbon dioxide in the laboratory. Perhaps the most original of all eighteenth-century Scottish thinkers was David Hume, who followed up Locke's theories of human knowledge in so rigorous a fashion as to cast doubt not merely on the fallacies and superstitions of past ages but also on the assumptions and methods of reasoning of his fellow philosophers. Hume's skepticism seemed to undermine the very basis of the prevailing belief in a benevolent deity that ruled the world by means of natural laws, and cost him appointments to the chair of philosophy at both Edinburgh and Glas-

WILLIAM HOGARTH (1697–1764), A SELF-PORTRAIT Hogarth's paintings and engravings were barbed criticisms of the foibles of all classes of English society in the first half of the eighteenth century. (The Tate Gallery, London)

gow. Hume thereupon applied his rigorous rationalism to the writing of a history of England.

The world view of the educated in England and Scotland remained formally a Christian one, and they thought it proper for most people—especially the poor—to attend church regularly. Yet for many of them, the God that had been an overwhelming personal reality to both Puritans and Cavaliers was fading into the abstraction of deism, "more a polite bow to the unknown than an act of faith." Any individual experience of Him—or It—was branded as "enthusiasm" and dismissed as bad form. Although the leaders of the Church of England were more than deists, they too came to put less emphasis on burning conviction or biblical prophecies and miracles than on uprightness, benevolence, and sober good sense. Passionate denunciations of the devil gave way to moral homilies. One of the most influential preachers of such moralism was neither a writer nor a churchman but the painter and engraver William Hogarth, many of whose pictures, such as *Gin Lane* and *Beer Street*, were intended not merely as deft pictorial satire but as graphic moral tales.

AUGUSTAN CALM

If the general acknowledgment that the universe operated according to discoverable natural laws could inspire some eighteenth-century thinkers to search for similar laws in the social sciences, it persuaded others that life on earth was already natural and reasonable if one would but ask the right questions. As Alexander Pope wrote in his "Essay on Man":

> All nature is but Art unknown to thee;
> All Chance, Direction, which thou canst not see;
> All Discord, Harmony not understood;
> All partial Evil, universal Good:
> And, spite of Pride, in erring Reason's spite,
> One truth is clear, WHATEVER IS, IS RIGHT.

Such an attitude could indeed lead to an inner tranquillity that expressed itself outwardly in good manners and good form. To be civilized meant to be free of the passions, religious as much as political, that had convulsed the past; and good form was the mark of freedom. A gentleman's or gentlewoman's goal, it seemed, was no longer to be saved but to keep calm.

> Void of strong desire and fear,
>   Life's wide ocean trust no more;
> Strive thy little bark to steer
>   With the tide, but near the shore.
>
> Thus prepared, thy shorten'd sail
>   Shall, whene'er the winds increase,
> Seizing each propitious gale,
>   Waft thee to the port of Peace.

This almost complacent serenity appears over and over again in the literature of the period. The savage satire and political pamphleteering of Queen Anne's reign gave way to a quieter mood in which even satire lost its barb. It is true that the embittered Irishman, Jonathan Swift, published *Gulliver's Travels* in 1726, but this attack on the human race was as exceptional as it was masterly. A much more typical satire, mixed with light nonsense, was *The Beggars' Opera* by John Gay, which appeared in the following year and took the country by storm. This featherweight comedy (for it is not an opera) is peopled with highwaymen, jailers, pickpockets, and their womenfolk, all talking and behaving like—and busily poking fun at—the gentry. A father, for instance, asks his newly wed daughter,

> "Had not you the common views of a gentlewoman in your marriage, Polly?"
>
> "I don't know what you mean, sir."
>
> "Of a jointure,[8] and of being a widow."
>
> "But I love him, sir: how then could I have thoughts of parting with him?"
>
> "Parting with him? why that is the whole scheme and intention of all marriage articles. The comfortable state of widowhood is the only hope that keeps up a wife's spirits."

This is not great comedy; John Gay's fondest admirers would scarcely rank him with the Elizabethans. But in one respect he has an advantage over them for readers of today: he is completely intelligible. Little more than a century had passed since Shakespeare's death, and in that time the English language had changed its nature. It had lost its wealth of metaphor and simile, its elaborate sentence structure, and at that price had gained in lucidity.[9] Georgian England conversed and wrote in a prose that had already taken on its modern form.

The age was essentially prosaic. Although it had its famous poets, notably Alexander Pope, even he substitutes flawless technique, wit, and occasionally wisdom, all smoothly packed into heroic couplets, for the soaring music of such earlier lyrics as

> Beauty is but a flower
> Which wrinkles will devour:
> Brightness falls from the air;

---

[8]A settlement that the wife received on marriage and retained in her widowhood.

[9]For comparison with the prose of *The Beggars' Opera* take this passage from *Much Ado About Nothing,* written at the close of the sixteenth century:

> "I can tell you strange news that you yet dreamt not of."
>
> "Are they good?"
>
> "As the event stamps them: but they have a good cover; they show well outward. The prince and Count Claudio, walking in a thick-pleached alley in my orchard, were thus much overheard by a man of mine: the prince discovered to Claudio that he loved my niece your daughter, and meant to acknowledge it this night in a dance; and, if he found her accordant, he meant to take the present time by the top and instantly break with you of it."

Queens have died young and fair;
Dust hath dimmed Helen's eye;
I am sick, I must die—
Lord, have mercy on us![10]

Much of what the Georgians called poetry was in fact pretentious prose, dressed up in rhyme and regular meter and adorned with archaisms and the flowery clichés of which Pope complained:

And ten low words oft creep in one dull line,
While they ring round the same unvaried chimes
With sure returns of still-expected rhymes.
Where'er you find "the cooling western breeze,"
In the next line it "whispers through the trees";
If crystal streams "with pleasing murmurs creep,"
The reader's threatened (not in vain) with "sleep."

Georgian prose was also marred by clichés, particularly classical tags and allusions. All gentlemen shared a knowledge of the Roman classics (not many were so fluent in Greek) and often poured out their knowledge in a flood of Latinity that drowned the meaning of the English. They give the impression that they were dressing up their prose with Latin just as poets dressed up their verse with flowers of speech. Lord Chesterfield, who was as fond as anyone of invoking the Romans, recognized at least that they did not belong in business correspondence. "Carefully avoid all Greek or Latin quotations," he cautioned his son, "and bring no precedents from 'the virtuous Spartans,' 'the polite Athenians,' and 'the brave Romans.' Leave all that to futile pedants. . . . There is an elegant simplicity and dignity of style absolutely necessary for good letters of business; attend to that carefully."

Chesterfield, like many of his contemporaries, was obsessed with style. He insisted on it in writing, and he insisted on it in living. His *Letters to His Son* are a rambling, discursive exposition of what he conceived to be a gentleman's proper style of life.[11] In them he revealed a great deal about the values and concerns of his world, and a survey of that world may well end with a glance at what he had to say. The letters preach an egoism as cold as Machiavelli's; repetitive and often trivial, they never probe the depths of experience. For Chesterfield has a narrow vision: he sees only the surface, the outward form, the style. But he sees with the eyes of a hawk, and he is completely honest.

---

[10]Thomas Nashe, 1593. To call the age of Pope prosaic would shock his admirers, who argue that he stands comparison with any of the great poets in the language. The issue boils down to the question of what poetry is, and each reader must perhaps answer this individually.

[11]They are published in condensation in the Everyman series, and Oliver H. G. Leigh edited them in full and sumptuous form for the Navarre Society, 2 vols. (1926). The period was one of assiduous letter writing, much of it designed for publication. The most prolific and famous of all correspondents was Horace Walpole (1717–1797), for whose epistolary output see Wilmarth S. Lewis et al., eds., *The Yale Edition of Horace Walpole's Correspondence*, 48 vols. (1937–1983).

THE WORLD OF LORD CHESTERFIELD

Philip Stanhope, fourth earl of Chesterfield (1694–1773), belonged to one of the political dynasties of the period. He was a diplomat, a cabinet member, a friend and patron of French and British writers, and a voluminous author himself. His life bore out his conviction that "any man of common understanding may, by proper culture, care, attention, and labor, make himself whatever he pleases, except a good poet." His primary concern, however, was not with politics or diplomacy or literature but with being a gentleman. Here by his own rigorous standards he succeeded. But his success did not extend to his illegitimate son Philip, to whom his letters were written: the boy had in him a touch of boorishness, which his father tried for more than a decade to eliminate by sage admonitions. What mattered to Chesterfield was that he failed; what mattered to posterity was that he expressed, in failing, his concept of what a gentleman should be.

The essence of the concept was to be pleasing. "You had better talk trifles elegantly to the most trifling woman than coarse, inelegant sense to the most solid man; you had better return a dropped fan genteelly than give a thousand pounds awkwardly; and you had better refuse a favor gracefully than to grant it clumsily. Manner is all, in everything; it is by manner only that you can please, and consequently rise." The central rule of life, there-

LORD CHESTERFIELD (1694–1773) His letters to his son provide a guide to "the age of aristocracy." (*National Portrait Gallery, London*)

fore, was never to impose yourself on those around you or try to make them admire you, but always to cater to their tastes and interests in order to buttress their self-esteem. "Those whom you can make like themselves better will, I promise you, like you very well."

This creed is obviously based on pure, if sophisticated, egoism. The *Letters,* said Samuel Johnson, "teach the morals of a whore, and the manners of a dancing master." But there is something else as well: a love of form for its own sake. Chesterfield had an almost physical aversion to those who lacked the graces of good breeding and admitted frankly that he cared more for the clothing of ideas than for their intrinsic worth. Awkwardness was for him the sign of worthlessness. He was honest enough to suspect that he might be wrong, but he resented the suspicion and did all he could to keep from putting it to the test. "If a speaker should ungracefully mutter or stammer out to me the sense of an angel, deformed by barbarisms and solecisms or larded with vulgarisms, he should never speak to me a second time if I could help it."[12]

This worship of form was amoral, because it permitted any kind of dissimulation that was gracefully garbed. Religious belief, for example, was important for the simple reason that society did not trust freethinkers; therefore a wise atheist would pretend to a belief that he did not hold. Chesterfield deemed women a much more important case in point, for they also required a gentleman to pretend. Although they were only grownup children, they played a crucial part in the school of good manners; "the concurrence of the two sexes is as necessary to the perfection of our being as to the formation of it." A man must flatter and humor women and, because they always suspect that they are being dallied with and crave to be taken seriously, must give them the impression that he is opening his inmost secrets to them. "Weak men really do, but wise ones only seem to do it."

He believed females to be only a little more gullible than males. Chesterfield, although he lived in an age of rationalism, had no illusions about the role that reason plays in governing human conduct. "Those who suppose that men in general act rationally, because they are called rational creatures, know very little of the world, and if they act themselves upon that supposition will nine times in ten find themselves grossly mistaken." Everyone is a blend of reason and passion and appetite; no two blends are identical, and each contains weaknesses that are waiting to be manipulated. All that is required of the manipulator is to address himself to the whole man, heart as well as head, and he will find the weak spots soon enough.

---

[12]Such fastidiousness was far from universal; otherwise Samuel Johnson, whose manners were notorious, would never have exercised the dominion that he did over the literary world. A tribute to Johnson by a friend provides the common-sense rebuttal of Chesterfield's position: "To reject wisdom because the person of him who communicates it is uncouth and his manners are inelegant—what is it but to throw away a pineapple, and assign for a reason the roughness of its coat?"

This was Chesterfield's recipe for success in the drawing room and also in the House of Commons. He had been a member of the lower house before inheriting his earldom and had soon lost his awe of its members. "I discovered that, of the five hundred and sixty, not above thirty could understand reason; . . . that those thirty only required plain common sense dressed up in good language; and that all the others only required flowing and harmonious periods, whether they conveyed any meaning or not, having ears to hear but not sense enough to judge." This discovery he carried with him to the House of Lords, and he believed that it accounted for his high reputation as a parliamentary orator.

His gloomy view of human intelligence did not, of course, extend to himself or those he loved. He was an educated man, grounded in the classics, fluent in modern languages, and with a wide knowledge of history and what would be called today political science. He sent his son to the continent for a Grand Tour that lasted for a number of years, to acquire not only polish but information. Over and over again he enjoined Philip to keep up his French, improve his German, learn Italian and someday Spanish, and study the ways and institutions of the countries through which he traveled. A favorite injunction was *approfondissez,* get to the bottom of things: "learn if you can the *why* and the *wherefore.*" This insistence on learning, like the insistence on good manners, had a practical purpose, for Philip was being trained for the diplomatic corps. But the rigor of the training shows that his father, the apostle of the graces, set equal store by a well-stocked and disciplined mind.

Because most people did not have such minds, in Chesterfield's opinion, they were wrong a great deal of the time. But he was strongly averse to telling them so and viewed their mistakes with an almost supercilious pity. Although—or perhaps because—he was quick to recognize and profit from their sloppy thinking, he was tolerant of it and held that persecuting or even mocking it was an egregious breach of taste. No one could help ideas that came from honest muddleheadedness. "The blindness of the understanding is as much to be pitied as the blindness of the eye; and there is neither jest nor guilt in a man's losing his way in either case. . . . I may as well expect that every man should be of my size and complexion as that he should reason just as I do. Every man seeks for truth, but God only knows who has found it."

Chesterfield obviously believed that he had found as much of it as he needed for using others to his advantage. He would have said that he had taken thoroughly to heart Pope's famous couplet:

> Know then thyself, presume not God to scan;
> The proper study of mankind is man.

The earl's study was a cool, detached scrutiny that included, as Pope had advised, his own nature, about which he thought that he was as clear-sighted as about the rest of humanity. "I know myself (no common piece of knowledge, let me tell you); I know what I can, what I cannot, and consequently what I ought to do. . . . My only remaining ambition," he confided to Philip, "is to be the counsellor and minister of your rising ambition. Let me see my own youth revived in you; let me be your mentor, and with your parts and knowledge, I promise you, you shall go far."

But what counsel did he actually have to give? Learn the facts; *approfondissez*. Learn to think. Above all learn to charm men and women in order to manipulate them, for without well-mannered manipulation learning and thinking are profitless. This was no creed to fire the mind, let alone the heart. It was focused entirely on superficialities, as Chesterfield would have been the first to admit, and for that very reason he considered it the only realistic guide to life. "The world is taken by the outside of things, and we must take the world as it is; you nor I cannot set it right."

This world was of course much wider in its tastes and more forceful in its ways than the Chesterfieldian view of it. Those who listened to the music of Handel or bought the engravings and paintings in which Hogarth commented on the passing scene could scarcely be said to have been "taken by the outside of things." Those who were beginning to transform the English countryside, to create through the cabinet a new form of executive, to build an empire overseas, knew their own minds too well to be swayed by anyone's grace of manner. But this is only to say that the oligarchy was too complex to be seen by a single observer, no matter how shrewd. What Chesterfield saw was there: the love of form and style and the surface of life. Much more was there as well, a self-confidence and energy that were carrying the country ahead to new heights of power. These qualities appear, not in an old man's letters to his son, but in the subject matter of the following chapters, the record of what the oligarchs achieved.

5 THE WALPOLE ERA

*F*or the first year of his reign George I sat uneasily on his throne. More than his corpulence made it shake; no one really wanted him for king. The rejoicings that greeted his arrival came from relief and hope, not enthusiasm—relief that the danger of civil war had been averted, hope that the new dynasty might prove to have something attractive about it. As the relief evaporated and the hope proved vain, many wondered whether they had been right to saddle themselves with "King Log."

THE YEARS OF INSTABILITY (1714–1722)

The coronation of George I was scarcely over before Jacobite sentiment was kindling again. The victorious Whigs helped to fan it by their vindictiveness: when George's first Parliament met, in the spring of 1715, they opened an attack on Lord Bolingbroke and his colleagues, purged Tory henchmen from office throughout the country, and so convinced many Tories that rebellion was the only alternative to political extinction. By summer unrest was widespread. Jacobite mobs rioted in the West Country, the Midlands, the North; Scotland was seething. Local magistrates did nothing to stop the disorders or to enforce the measures taken by the government. Central authority seemed to be breaking down. Eight months of Hanoverian rule, wrote the Prussian minister to London, had done more for the cause of James Stuart, the Pretender, than had four years of the Tories under Queen Anne.

But James, like his father, was badly served. He himself had been exiled from France to Lorraine after the Treaty of Utrecht, and at that distance he was powerless. His cause depended entirely on daring leadership in Britain, and this he did not have. Bolingbroke, who had the best chance of rallying the Tories to action, was no more capable of seizing the moment than he had been the year before. At the height of the crisis he bolted across the Channel and took service with the Pretender, and no one of stature replaced him. Risings in the West Country melted away; royal troops seized Oxford. Only in the north of England, where great landlords could still rouse their tenantry in a lost cause as they had in the days of Elizabeth, did a sizable number of "Jacks" turn out to fight for King James.

Their chance of success depended on Scotland, which was the focus of rebellion. There the unpopularity of the union, combined with the magic of the Stuart name, might have touched off a national rising if James himself had been on hand: even without him some 10,000 men took up arms against a force of only 3,300 royal troops. But the Jacobites again had no competent leader. They failed to join hands with their friends across the border and marched aimlessly to and fro until the Pretender finally arrived, just after Christmas. By then his cause was dying, and he was not the man to revive it. "Throughout his life he was, like his grandfather Charles I, a great gentleman, but the virtues of a great gentleman are not by themselves sufficient to regain a lost throne."[1] After six weeks of wandering in the Highlands, more and more the fugitive and less and less the king, James VIII of Scotland and III of England, as he called himself, vanished into the exile's limbo from which he never returned.

The failure of the rising, known to history as the Fifteen (although it actually did not end until 1716), secured the Hanoverian succession at a small price in lives. A few victims, ranging from aristocrats to humble sergeants, were executed for form's sake. Most of the leaders either were pardoned or fled before they could be tried; a few were tried and condemned and then vanished mysteriously just before their executions, to reappear in France. The rank and file of the Scottish rebels melted away into the obscurity from which they had come and kept the cause alive in the Highlands until the final Jacobite effort thirty years later. In England, where the movement was not fed by nationalism and clan loyalties, it rapidly withered away. The country became used to the Hanoverians and was willing to give them its loyalty as long as they looked to its prosperity.

In the years after the Fifteen, prosperity ran wild until it produced in 1720 a financial crisis that endangered the new regime. This was the lurid episode known as the South Sea Bubble. On the surface it was nothing more than an orgy of speculation and bribery, ending in the worst stock-market crash in British history; under the surface it was a political threat of the first order, which bade fair to bring down the government, if not the throne itself. The outcome was quite different: Robert Walpole came to power. During the next twenty years, under his guidance, the dynasty became so firmly established and the political world so well systemized that the tumults of the mid-century—foreign war and Jacobite invasion—could not shake the house of Whiggism.

But in 1720 that house was still under construction, and the bursting of the Bubble shook it badly. The South Sea Bubble deserves to be seen as an example not merely of individual skullduggery and of popular self-delusion but also of the growing pains of a commercial economy. The stock mania resulted in part from the lure of trade with exotic parts of the world. As the chart below demonstrates, the monetary value of trade with the continent was far greater than with Asia or the Americas, and according to modern economic historians domestic trade was far more valuable than all

---

[1]Sir Charles A. Petrie, *The Jacobite Movement: The First Phase, 1688–1716* (1948), p. 195. This and its companion volume, subtitled *The Last Phase, 1716–1807* (1950), are a convenient history of Jacobitism. The facts are reliable, but the conclusions are often eccentric; Sir Charles was unduly addicted to the Stuarts.

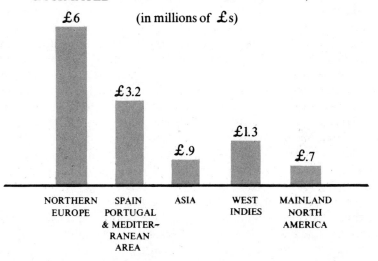

ESTIMATED VALUE OF BRITISH EXPORTS, 1700

£6   (in millions of £s)

£3.2

£1.3

£.9

£.7

| NORTHERN EUROPE | SPAIN PORTUGAL & MEDITER- RANEAN AREA | ASIA | WEST INDIES | MAINLAND NORTH AMERICA |

Adapted from Charles Wilson, *England's Apprenticeship, 1603–1763* (1965), p. 162.

the foreign trade added together. These facts, however, in no way diminished the intoxication with a commercial El Dorado in distant lands.

Because the supply of gold and silver coins was not keeping up with the demands of an expanding commerce at the beginning of the century, business increasingly was transacted by letters of credit, bills of exchange, and other forms of paper money. A still unusual form of business organization, the joint-stock company, was also increasing in importance. In the age of Elizabeth I, a handful of such companies, run by and for the privileged few, had monopolized the kingdom's trade with Russia, the Levant (the eastern Mediterranean), and India. By the beginning of the eighteenth century, the joint-stock principle offered an attractive method of obtaining money for a great variety of projects. The stocks and bonds such companies issued to raise capital constituted in turn a relatively new form of property, which could be bought and sold more readily than land. The "stock-jobbers" who marketed such securities, although they became easy targets for those who made foolish investments, clearly served a need. Since the law was slow to take cognizance of the changing methods of the commercial world, the promoters and investors of the South Sea Bubble era were participants in a game for which the rules had not yet been laid down.[2]

The origins of the specific crisis went back to 1711, when the Tory government, which considered the Bank of England to be an organ of the Whig party, chartered the South Sea Company as a rival to the Bank. One of the

---

[2]The story is told in careful detail in P. G. M. Dickson, *The Financial Revolution in England* (1967). In *The South Sea Bubble* (1960), John Carswell evokes the spirit of popular excitement.

initial purposes of the Company was to trade with the South Seas—the southern Pacific, or in other words Spanish America. The prospect of making money there grew fabulous when Spain, as part of the Utrecht settlement, granted the Company a major concession, the asiento, to run for the next thirty years. The asiento permitted members of the Company to import up to 4,800 slaves a year into the Spanish colonies and to sell there, duty free, such merchandise as could be carried on a single 500-ton ship that was to accompany the annual Spanish treasure fleet from Europe. This trade was confined to the Caribbean (thereby falsifying the name of the South Sea Company), but its merchants had at least an entering wedge with which to break into the Spanish colonial market. They paid little attention to the limits of the asiento and soon developed a significant, if dangerous, trade in smuggled goods as well as in slaves.

The directors of the Company were less interested in trade, however, than in what they could make out of high finance. From the start they engaged in large-scale operations connected with the public debt. The climax of these operations, and the beginning of the Bubble, was a coup of February 1720, in which Parliament empowered the directors to take over that portion of the national debt, more than three-fifths, that consisted of private annuities. The Company agreed to charge the government a lower rate of interest than the treasury was paying on these annuities and to sweeten the bargain with a cash advance of more than £7 million.

As this gigantic payment suggests, the directors looked forward to even more gigantic profits. The operation that they had in mind was complex in detail but essentially simple: to convert the national debt into Company stock. The holders of government annuities were to be persuaded to exchange them for stock, abandoning an assured income from their old annuities for capital gains from the expected rise in market value of their new South Sea shares. Everything depended on this rise. The Company was authorized to issue more and more stock as it took over more and more of the debt, and the greater the worth of its shares the more annuities they would buy. The scheme looked foolproof, granted the one basic assumption that the Company could market its stock at a price that would rise and never stop rising. Of this financial miracle the directors were serenely confident. The Company was as closely tied to the state as the Bank of England was and not only monopolized the South American trade but possessed the largest amount of working capital—some £40 million—ever amassed in England. How could investors resist this opportunity?

For the first few months, they could not. Their scramble for shares drove up the price to almost ten times what it had been in February, and the whole market followed the lead of the South Sea stock in a dizzy upward spiral. New companies burgeoned overnight, with no one caring much whether their aims were real or fanciful; people were buying shares in anything, for everything was going up. By June a few of the more judicious began to sell, and by midsummer the market was leveling off. The South Sea directors were trying to force it higher by every possible means, honest and dishonest, including loans to permit stockholders to buy more shares on credit. But by then the most frantic pump priming would no longer serve.

The crash came in September. The South Sea Company's bankers failed, its stock fell even faster than it had risen, paper fortunes vanished, and those who had bought on credit were faced with ruin. Worse still, the ministry and the court were involved to the hilt: the directors had been lavish in their bribes to the influential and had not neglected even the king's mistresses. The public, disillusioned with its dream of riches, cried for retribution, but almost no one in the government had clean hands. Parliament reassembled in an ugly mood.

This was the opportunity for Robert Walpole. He was a seasoned politician who had been in and out of office for years, but at the moment he held a relatively minor post. He had not foreseen the crash and, like almost everyone else, had lost money in it. But it did not smirch his reputation because he was free from his colleagues' shady dealings with the Company. He also had the means for establishing his ascendancy—a clear idea of what had to be done and the adroitness to get it done. The emergency gave him, for the first time in his career, full scope for his talents.

He had two objectives. One was to avert panic until investors regained their confidence in what was still an essentially sound financial system; the other was to prevent public anger, focused in the House of Commons, from destroying the government and perhaps the dynasty. In both aims he succeeded. He proposed a scheme for salvaging what was left of the South Sea Company with the help of the two remaining giants of finance, the Bank of England and the East India Company. Although the plan was never implemented, it gave time for the market to recover, for people to realize that they could still make money in sane ways. Walpole did not prevent a parliamentary inquiry, but he did manage to keep it within discreet bounds. While the directors' estates were being confiscated and a few ministerial victims thrown to the wolves, the key figures in the government and court were saved from awkward questions. The skill with which Walpole unwound the South Sea Company's tangle of financial fact and fantasy won the admiration both of the king and of "the City" and ultimately helped reconcile the competing interests of land and trade. In the aftermath of the Bubble, admittedly, the prevalent mood of commercial expansion and economic innovation gave way to a spirit of greater caution: the Bubble Act of 1720 forbade all joint-stock companies not authorized by royal charter, and many a landed gentleman vowed in the future to invest in real estate rather than in the stock market. Overseas trade continued to expand, though at a slower pace, and in the course of the 1720s and 1730s the annual value of British exports grew by one-third, and the value of imports by one-fifth.

Luck also took a hand in Walpole's rise to power. Lord Stanhope, George I's chief minister since 1717, in February 1721 in a House of Lords debate defended himself so vigorously against charges linking him to the South Sea fiasco that he burst a blood vessel and died. Walpole detested his principal remaining colleague and rival, the rancorous Lord Sunderland, but for reasons of expediency he defended Sunderland against similar charges. Although the House of Commons, by a narrow margin, voted to acquit Sunderland, George I decided to appoint Walpole in his stead. Thus in April 1721 Walpole became chief minister, and, when Sunderland conveniently died within a year, Britain entered a new era. Politics, which for more than a generation had been so rough-and-tumble a business that no one person or group could long dominate, quickly acquired order and form, and "the country enjoyed a stability of government such as it had not known for a hundred years."[3]

THE WALPOLE MACHINE

Governmental stability derived from a fusion of the two cardinal elements required for administration: support from the king and control of the House of Commons. Walpole had a genius for handling his sovereign, but it was a delicate, time-consuming occupation that required a blend of courage and tact. George was as suspicious as he was stupid. He often had ideas that his first minister would not or could not implement, and rival politicians often insinuated that they, given power, would do exactly as their royal master wished. Walpole had to counter these insinuations, retain the king's confidence, and if need be thwart his wishes. And that was not all. If he hoped for a long tenure of power, he had to serve George I without alienating the Prince of Wales. This assignment was difficult enough to tax even his gifts, but he managed to perform it.

He showed himself equally adept at handling the House of Commons, which he understood as well as any politician of the century. Although he could never afford to neglect the House of Lords, he recognized that the Commons had now become the focus of power: for that reason he refused a peerage and in 1726 became instead a Knight of the Garter. No commoner had received that honor in generations, but neither had a first minister elected to stay a commoner. Sir Robert knew what he was about. He had a hard enough task to control the lower house as a member of it and would have had an infinitely harder one to control it from the House of Lords.

The methods of control that he developed and systematized remained in force for the rest of the century. The office of prime minister did not yet exist in name: the critical position was that of the First Lord of the Trea-

---

[3]John H. Plumb, *Sir Robert Walpole: The Making of a Statesman* (1956), p. 379. This volume and its companion, subtitled *The King's Minister* (1960), are not only a biography but a study of the period in depth. The second volume ends in 1734, and a third volume has not yet appeared. H. T. Dickinson provides a brief but illuminating introduction to the subject in *Walpole and the Whig Supremacy* (1973). Other accounts of the Walpole era include two cited earlier, W. A. Speck, *Stability and Strife, England, 1714–1760* (1977), and Dorothy Marshall, *Eighteenth Century England*, 2nd ed. (1975), as well as Basil Williams's detailed survey, *The Whig Supremacy, 1714–1760* 2nd ed. (1962).

THE HOUSE OF COMMONS IN 1730   Speaker Arthur Onslow points to Sir Robert Walpole. *(The National Trust)*

sury, who controlled vast patronage through the appointment of customs and excise officers. From the treasury Walpole operated his machine. He organized a phalanx of placemen in the House of Commons, who voted as he told them. He distributed favors and honors and preferment in order to maintain and strengthen his political control. He became the key figure, even under the jealous eye of George I, in determining promotion in the army. He exercised a tighter reign over patronage in the Church than any

KING GEORGE I
(1714–1727) *(The
Granger Collection)*

minister had done since 1688. He filled positions in the Civil Service with
men of his personal choice, not with henchmen of his henchmen. He concentrated ruthlessly on a man's present usefulness; anyone who could plead
only past services was likely to lose his pension or his place. This was political realism, because there were never enough plums to go around. For
every one at the minister's disposal, three or four suppliants were clamoring
in the lines outside his doors. He asked himself a single question—how
much each gift would contribute to his power—and made his selection
accordingly.

But even his machine, efficient as it was, could not function without
support from the independent members of the Commons, and he wooed
them assiduously throughout his years in office. Here his background had
much to do with his success. He came of an old Norfolk family, country
squires for generations, and was in some ways the epitome of his breed—
hard-drinking, hard-riding, given to profanity and to womanizing, with
none of the graces that Chesterfield extolled or the aristocratic connections
that most ministers had. He was of his class and made no bones about it:
he in fact made capital out of it. During debates in the House of Commons
he would be nibbling on a Norfolk apple as if to emphasize his origins, and
at the height of the South Sea Bubble he was more absorbed with buying
land than stocks. He took care of his children as so many of the gentry tried
to do, but of course with more success: for his eldest son he obtained a
peerage and an extremely wealthy bride, and for his daughter the heir to an
earldom. The independent backbenchers in the Commons might rail against
him, and often did. But at bottom they understood him, and year after year
they stuck with him.

KING GEORGE II
(1727–1760) *(National
Portrait Gallery,
London)*

He was far from a typical squire or he would not have gotten where he did. In many ways, such as his care for all the details of patronage and his systematic, single-minded pursuit of power, he was less like the gentry of his day than like a modern American political boss: in those ways he was a professional in an age of amateurs. But that was not the whole picture. For all his ostentation and coarseness, he was a connoisseur of wines and had a sure taste in art; the collection of paintings that he amassed was famous throughout Europe. On his Norfolk estate he built Houghton Hall, which is as much a monument to him as Blenheim is to Marlborough—not a palace but a country house, austere on the outside and magnificent within, embellished without thought of cost by the leading sculptors, plasterers, and furniture makers of the day.[4] Sir Robert, in short, was an odd mixture of vulgarity and sophistication.

---

[4]Plasterers may at first glance seem out of place among sculptors and furniture makers, but English plasterwork, from the late Middle Ages through the eighteenth century, was one of the major decorative arts. For a fuller description of Houghton Hall and its contents, see Plumb, *Walpole,* vol. 1, pp. 81–87.

His strength as a politician lay in his common sense, his meticulous attention to detail, and the unerring judgment of people that is the *sine qua non* for manipulating them. His weakness lay in his incomprehension of the subtle, imponderable forces in domestic and foreign affairs. The system he built was singularly unresponsive to the public, even the narrow public of the electorate, except in moments of real or manufactured crisis: he himself was unable to gauge the tide of British opinion and often miscalculated how it was running. His foreign policy suffered from his inability to penetrate the hidden motives, the fear and ambition and prickly concern for national honor, that swayed the courts of Europe. He lacked the sixth sense, in other words, to be a creative statesman.

"I am no saint, no spartan, no reformer," Walpole conceded. He saw himself rather as the defender of things as they were. Someone had to make the creaking governmental machinery work, foster commerce and lower taxes, and buttress a shaky throne: he had supreme confidence that he was the only man who could do it. Perhaps he was right. Britain needed some years of quiet in which the new dynasty could grow roots and a political system could emerge from the chaos of the past. Walpole created the system, less by intent than because he needed it in order to survive. And this limited form of creativity may have been all that the age made possible.

Although his predominance was long-lasting, he could never take it for granted. The first challenge to it came out of the blue in the summer of 1727, when word arrived that George I had died suddenly in Hanover. The political wolves gathered for the kill: Sir Robert's days were numbered, they believed, because a new king meant a new minister. But they did not understand the odd little man who now took the throne. George II had led a wretched life, hated and bullied by his father and hating him in return, and had lost the self-confidence required of kings. He hid his loss behind a violent temper, a restlessness that kept him always in motion and always talking, and an almost insane preoccupation with the minutiae of his daily routine; even his mistress he saw at precisely the same hour each evening. He was a monumental bore to everyone around him, and if he had been a commoner he could have been ignored as a nonentity. On the throne he could not be: his weak, neurotic personality was a fact of politics.

Because he was weak he was profoundly dependent. But he was also that great rarity among his fellow monarchs, one who depended on his wife. Caroline of Anspach was a woman of some charm and much shrewdness; her manners were coarse, but her head was good enough to do her husband's thinking for him. He vented his temper on her, flaunted his infidelities in her face, bored her to distraction, and clung to her. She presumably did not love him as he, in his way, loved her. But she did love power, and through him she possessed it.

She was Walpole's opportunity. Soon after taking office under George I, he had marked out the Princess of Wales as the friend he needed at court. He and Caroline, loving power in equal degree, understood each other. He had no intention of letting her get the upper hand, but he treated her, on almost Chesterfieldian lines, as if she had it: he consulted her assiduously and seemed to defer to her, and soon won her for his staunch ally. She helped him to survive the upheaval of her husband's accession and before long to win a place in the heart of the new king second only to hers. For the next fifteen years, until his fall from office, Sir Robert was not only George II's servant and counselor but also, as nearly as anyone could be, his friend. Their relationship was closer than any between sovereign and subject since the days of Charles I and Buckingham a hundred years before.

THE YEARS OF STABILITY (1727–1738)

Sir Robert was now called "the Great Man," admiringly by his friends and mockingly by his enemies. The mockery rang hollow, for he exercised a kind of power that no minister had ever approximated. He seemed to have a hold on royal favor and on Parliament that was unchallengeable and to stand on an eminence from which only death could topple him. But the appearance was deceptive: the novelty of his position and his way of maintaining it made for insecurity. The oligarchs were unaccustomed to being dominated by anyone, particularly an upstart squire, and for every man he fed with a political plum he left three or four hungry and embittered. The longer his regime lasted and the more completely he controlled all patronage, the more rancorous his enemies became. They railed and mocked at him in the Commons and the Lords and intrigued with undiscourageable hope to turn the king against him.[5] They also used the popular press, then in its brawling infancy, to whip up public excitement by satires, cartoons, ballads, and all the other arts that Grub Street could devise, and so bring outside pressure to bear on the closed world of Parliament. Sir Robert fought back with libel suits, stamp duties on newspapers, and (in 1737) an act requiring the lord chamberlain to give his prior approval to all future theatrical productions. That act was not to be repealed until 1968. Thanks to the efforts of his critics, Walpole felt that he lived from crisis to crisis.

In 1732 he himself, quite unwittingly, provoked one that proved to be more than he could handle. It originated in his attempt to improve the tax structure, one of the few areas in which he was a genuine reformer. He wanted to reduce the land tax, partly because he believed that it put an unfair burden on the country gentry, partly because he needed their support. But he could not reduce the chief source of revenue without finding a substitute, and the obvious area in which to look for one was that of customs and excise. This form of taxation not only increased with the growth of trade but bore on all consumers alike, rich and poor; and Sir Robert had a marked preference, natural in a man of property, for taxing the poor as against the rich.

---

[5]The best modern account of their activities is in Archibald S. Foord, *His Majesty's Opposition, 1714–1830* (1964), chaps. 1–5.

He had long been alive to the need for encouraging trade. He had helped manufacturers by reducing export duties on their goods and import duties on their raw materials; he had simplified the process whereby imports destined for sale abroad passed through the country duty free. He had also experimented, in a few categories of goods imported for home consumption, with shifting from customs to excise—from a duty levied on goods when they entered the country to a tax levied on them when they were released for sale. Tea, cocoa, and chocolate had been admitted duty free and taxed instead through the retailer, and in Walpole's opinion the experiment had proved extremely advantageous.

The advantages of excise were of two sorts. In the first place, eliminating customs duties on the enumerated commodities took the profit out of smuggling them; and smuggling was a vast commerce that cheated the government out of hundreds of thousands of pounds a year. In the second place, collecting a tax from retailers required an army of excise men; and the more jobs Sir Robert could provide, the greater would be his patronage. At the beginning of 1732 he decided to reduce the land tax to 5 percent of assessed value, to reimpose a salt tax that had recently been discontinued (thereby creating still more collectors' jobs), and to extend the excise to wine and tobacco. It would be hard to imagine a proposal that seemed less explosive and turned out to be more so.

In the popular mind customs and excise officers were corrupt tyrants. They had behind them some of the most savage laws on the statute book, which the courts interpreted in their full severity: in one case a man was hanged merely for blackening his face, which was a common precaution of smugglers working at night. The officers themselves were venal and brutal, and against them the citizen had no effective redress. They were hated by high and low, in a society addicted to smuggling and excise evasion, and the hatred mounted as law enforcement became more rigorous. Walpole's scheme was a match to this combustible material; his opponents were ready and eager to fan the flame.

For a year, while the measure took its slow way toward a vote in the House of Commons, excitement rose to a frenzy.[6] The press did its full part; boroughs sent deputations to Westminster; riots broke out; the country seethed as it had on the eve of the Fifteen. But now the pressure was of a different kind: it was on Parliament, to turn against its master and throw out his bill. The Lords and Commons were discovering that they did not always live in a closed world where they could legislate without regard to the public. Elections were impending in 1734. The members of the lower house and the noble borough-mongers in the upper one dared not presume too far on even the most docile constituents.

Walpole had blundered in his timing, but he was unperturbed. Vilification in Parliament was an annoyance, like mosquitoes, that did not de-

---

[6]In *The Excise Crisis: Society and Politics in the Age of Walpole* (1975), Paul Langford provides a detailed account.

flect him; popular anger outside the halls of Westminster seemed to him almost unconstitutional. He ignored the danger signals and held to his course. He was overconfident, after a decade of successfully manipulating kings and Commons, and blind to the fact that his system, unresponsive as it was to the electorate, did rest on that solid earth. Now the earth was quaking, and others felt the tremors if he did not. When Parliament reconvened after the Easter recess of 1733, which its members had spent in their constituencies, Sir Robert was amazed to find his majority melting away. At the last minute he gave in and withdrew the bill. At that price he survived, but his position was never the same again. His opponents had demonstrated the limits of his power. Now that they had forced him to retreat once, they were all the more eager for the next opportunity.

He had survived largely because the king and the coterie of royal advisers had not wavered in their support. The opposition had tried to capture the court through some of the king's favorites in his household, notably Lord Chesterfield, but had run up against the stone wall of George and his queen. Chesterfield had been dismissed from his post, whereupon he and his friends had carried the struggle to the House of Lords. They had come within an ace of winning it there, but the influence of the crown had brought enough wavering peers into line to give the administration a narrow victory.

Walpole could no more take his sovereign for granted, however, than he could the two houses. He lived under the constant danger that the king would insist on a policy that Parliament would not support, a danger that was greatest in the area of foreign affairs. Here George II had distinct and stubborn ideas of his own: he did not see eye to eye with Sir Robert, let alone with the House of Commons. Any crisis in Europe, consequently, might become a crisis at home, and the tumult over the excise coincided with the beginning of just such a crisis—which culminated in the first major European war since the Treaty of Utrecht. The war jeopardized Walpole's foreign policy, and his insistence on keeping Britain neutral strained his relations with the king as they had never been strained before.

Sir Robert's diplomacy was governed by a single-minded desire for peace. His objections to war were, like everything else about him, eminently practical: war would endanger the regime by creating the opportunity for a Stuart restoration and by alienating the landed interest. Walpole was almost obsessed by the threat from the Jacobites, with whose schemings he kept in touch through a wide network of spies. He had no fear that the Pretender, unaided, could raise a successful rebellion; what he feared was rebellion encouraged and aided by France. Any war in which Britain became involved would, he believed, soon bring in France; the way to stop the Jacobites was therefore to keep the peace. Here the future bore him out: Britain's first war did draw in France and did bring a Jacobite invasion with French support.

As for the landed interest, the best way to ensure its loyalty to the Hanoverians—and to Walpole himself—was to keep down the land tax. The only way to do that was to economize, and the only way to economize was to stay out of war. Sir Robert could well remember what had happened in 1710, when disillusionment with a long and costly war had brought a Tory triumph and the resurgence of Jacobitism. He had learned the lesson and did not want to see it repeated.

The core of his foreign policy, in consequence, was a rapprochement with France; and he had the good luck to find circumstances propitious. The death of Louis XIV in 1715 had left the throne to a boy of five, his great-grandson Louis XV, and not until 1726 did French politics become stabilized after the fluctuations of a regency. In that year the young king called to power his tutor, Cardinal Fleury, a man of seventy-three, who directed policy for the next sixteen years. This aged cynic—subtle, crafty, and elusive—was poles apart from the squire of Houghton Hall, but they shared the love of power and the desire to enjoy it in peace. Each was bent on setting his nation's house in order after the wars of the previous generation. Although both had to contend with, and eventually bow to, belligerent factions at home, for more than a decade they worked together in an unavowed and uneasy partnership to prevent a major European conflagration.

One that threatened to be major broke out in 1733, the so-called War of the Polish Succession. Poland, which was approaching dissolution as a state, was a bone of contention among the great powers. A dispute over its elective kingship brought on a brief war between Austria and the Bourbon monarchies, France and Spain. France had an interest in Poland, where Louis XV's father-in-law was a candidate for the throne. Spain had no interest whatever but hoped to regain control of the Italian principalities lost to Austria in the Utrecht settlement. Britain, as Walpole saw it, had not enough concern with either Poland or Italy to warrant intervening.

King George disagreed. For all his faults his viewpoint was more European, less insular, than Walpole's, and he recognized that a decisive defeat of Austria would upset the balance of power. He deeply distrusted France and, as a German prince, had an underlying loyalty to the Holy Roman Emperor, Charles VI, who was also ruler of Austria. For these reasons George wanted to intervene and dreamed of leading his armies himself to the emperor's rescue. But Walpole knew that he could not stir Parliament to war even if he would. Its independent members might have kindled at the prospect of naval hostilities to further British trade but could see no more point than he could in fighting for Poland or Italy or even Vienna. He worked long and hard to convince his sovereign, who eventually, against his better judgment, gave way; Austria got no British aid. Austria was defeated in Italy, where it lost the south to a Spanish Bourbon prince; Louis XV's father-in-law gave up his claim to the Polish throne and received in compensation the duchy of Lorraine, which was to revert to France at his death. The powers finally reached this settlement in 1735, without consulting or even informing the British government. Walpole had chosen isolation at the price of being ignored.

By 1738 his troubles were mounting at home and abroad. Frederick, Prince of Wales, who did what he could to justify his parents' loathing for him, had broken with them completely in 1736 and set up a court of his own, which became the focus of the opposition. In 1737 Sir Robert had lost his most valuable ally by the death of Queen Caroline. Many peers were his avowed enemies, and under their patronage a new generation of would-be Davids were being trained to use their oratorical slingshots on Goliath. The most brilliant of these "boy patriots" was William Pitt, the grandson of "Diamond" Pitt, a merchant who had made his fortune in India and put it to work in English politics. The technique of embarrassing Walpole was highly developed. At one moment a handsome allowance for the Prince of Wales was moved in the House of Commons, and the minister barely managed to defeat this insult to the crown. At another the opposition forced him to fine the city of Edinburgh for a riot in which an English officer had been lynched; the Scottish members of the House of Commons, considering the fine an insult to Scotland's national pride, turned against Sir Robert. So it went. Now by taps and now by blows, now by leverage and now by pouring acid, his enemies were slowly undermining his position.

THE INTERNATIONAL CRISIS (1738–1739)

The opposition could not destroy "the Great Man," however, as long as the country remained prosperous and at peace. Since only a war, if it was unpopular or mismanaged, would enable his foes to pull him down, they consequently worked for war as assiduously as he worked to prevent it. His survival came to depend more and more on his ability to hold to the course he had mapped out in foreign policy, at a time when that course was becoming more difficult with every year that passed. New sources of friction with France were appearing in America and India. The delicate balance that the Utrecht settlement had established in Europe was endangered by the approach of a Habsburg dynastic crisis as menacing as that before the War of the Spanish Succession. A long-standing quarrel between Britain and Spain threatened to explode at any moment into war. Walpole for years had been careful, as he put it, to let sleeping dogs lie. Now all the dogs seemed to be waking at once, and they were growling ominously.

Friction between Britain and France in North America was grounded in geography. France possessed or claimed land to the north and west of the British colonies, extending in a vast arc from the Gulf of St. Lawrence, by way of lakes Ontario and Erie and the valley of the Ohio and Mississippi, to the Gulf of Mexico. The British colonists on the Atlantic seaboard, as their population mounted, inevitably pressed westward across the Appalachians in search of land and furs, trespassing increasingly on what the French considered their preserve. The struggle had already started, for the European wars of William's and Anne's reigns had had their colonial counterparts; but nothing had been settled, and year by year the pressures built up. Although they had little effect as yet on the statecraft of Whitehall and Versailles, where colonial squabbles were still sideshows, the time for a final solution was approaching.

India was the scene of Anglo-French friction of a quite different sort. Here the English East India Company had long been jockeying for position against its Portuguese and Dutch rivals, not as empire builders but as traders. The last thing that the directors of the Company wanted was to extend their territorial jurisdiction beyond Bombay, Madras, and Calcutta, the coastal cities that they controlled as centers for their trade with the interior. But profitable trading was possible only as long as the native government was able to maintain order. By the 1730s the great Mogul empire was falling to pieces, and the rulers of its former dependencies on the coast were struggling with each other for predominance. At the same time the French, with their newly organized Compagnie Perpetuelle des Indes, were beginning to make rapid inroads into the Indian market.

The next inevitable step for both the British and the French companies was from trade to politics. No matter what the directors in London might say about keeping aloof from native affairs, the Englishmen on the spot knew better. They saw the local Indian rajah, to take a concrete but hypothetical example, demanding a higher price each year for maintaining the East India Company's trading privileges, and knew that the French were outbidding them at court. They also knew that the rajah's nephew claimed the throne and with a small investment of British funds could probably get it. To retain the Company's trading position its agents were almost irresistibly tempted to invest in the pretender, install him as rajah, and then protect him, once he became their client, against French efforts to reinstate his predecessor. As long as the Indians were fighting among themselves for power and Europeans were vying for trade, the two forms of competition were bound to mesh, and the Europeans to find themselves fighting through their protégés. The stage was set for one of the great struggles in the history of imperialism, a struggle that ended years later with the ousting of the French and the subordination of all the native states to a trading company that became, despite itself, the paramount power of India.

Neither Walpole nor anyone else, of course, understood the forces that were at work in India and in North America, because those forces were not yet clear. The same was true of Europe, which was Sir Robert's chief concern. There he saw, as did the rest of the world, that a problem was impending for the house of Habsburg, one that promised to strain the resources of diplomacy as they had not been strained since 1701. But he could not guess that diplomacy would fail and that the continent would be plunged into a quarter-century of wars.

The Habsburgs were in dynastic trouble. The emperor Charles VI faced a prospect almost as dismal as that of his Spanish cousin forty years earlier—this time not the extinction of his line but the accession of a woman. His only surviving children were daughters; a woman's inheriting a throne was always dangerous, as Henry Tudor had realized, particularly when her possessions were surrounded by powerful and rapacious neighbors. Charles devoted his life to dealing with the danger. By a document known as the Pragmatic Sanction he arranged for all his hereditary dominions to go to his elder daughter, Maria Theresa. For years he peddled this document around the courts of Europe, offering a variety of concessions until he induced every great power to recognize Maria Theresa as his heir. He hoped that he was living in a world in which kings were gentlemen, even though it was pointed out to him that their promises guaranteed his daughter's inheritance far less effectively than a full treasury and a strong army, neither of which he had. Europe waited for his death, to see which king would be first to forswear himself and plunder Maria Theresa's realm.

THE COMING OF WAR WITH SPAIN

These were some of the dangers to peace that confronted Walpole in the late 1730s. All of them soon materialized, but the one that first occasioned war came from quite a different quarter. While pressures were building up toward bloodshed in North America, India, and central Europe, Britain suddenly found herself fighting Spain. Anglo-Spanish antagonism, which was by then an old story, was so deep-rooted that it perhaps could not have been resolved in the long run by peaceful means; but the issues in the particular crisis of 1738–1739 could certainly have been. Walpole's diplomacy, however, was hamstrung by two factors: an opposition that was eager to bring him down through war, and the mutual suspicion engendered in London and Madrid by years of bickering. Both governments worked hard for compromise because neither wanted a conflict; Walpole lacked the will to fight, Spain the means. The way in which the efforts to keep peace were defeated illustrates how economic and political forces can frustrate the best intentions of diplomats.

The ground of Anglo-Spanish friction was economic, and the war that resulted was more purely commercial than any Britain had fought since the Dutch Wars. Then Britain's goal had been the Dutch carrying trade; now it was the market of Latin America. Spain produced only a tiny fraction of the goods that its colonies demanded. Was the remainder to come from France or Britain? The government of Philip V, if only because he was a Bourbon, looked to France, whose merchants gained a greater and greater share of the legitimate trade between Spain and the Caribbean. Their British rivals responded in the only way they could, by illegitimate trade. Although they had lost the hopes that they had once pinned to the asiento, it still served the South Sea Company traders as a cloak for smuggling, and the merchants of Jamaica and the other British islands smuggled on their own.

The situation was sure to breed trouble and grievances. Spanish authorities in the Caribbean had no way to prevent smuggling except to stop every British ship that came within range and search it for contraband. This right of search was hotly resented, and with reason. A merchant captain en route from London to Jamaica on legitimate business might find himself blown off course into Spanish waters, stopped, accused of being a smuggler bound for Cuba, and ruined by the confiscation of his ship. Worse still, Spanish officials did not have the money for a regular customs service and therefore licensed as a coast guard almost anyone who was willing to work on commission; such men were out for all they could get and were more interested in the value of what they seized than in the legality of the seizure.

Legality, in fact, had little place in the Spanish Main, as the Caribbean was called. In a sea infested with pirates, the smugglers and coast guards who warred with each other were only a short remove from piracy themselves. When British sailors caught a Spanish patrol vessel at a disadvantage, they often gave it rough handling; the Spaniards replied in kind. "It is without doubt irksome to every honest man to hear such cruelties are committed in these seas," a disgusted British admiral wrote home from Jamaica. "But give me leave to say that you only hear one side of the question. And I can assure you the sloops that sail from this island, manned and armed on that illicit trade, has [sic] more than once bragged to me of their having murdered seven or eight Spaniards on their own shore. . . . It is, I think, a little unreasonable for us to do injuries and not know how to bear them. But villainy is inherent to this climate."

The innocent—or at least those who protested their innocence—suffered along with the guilty. In June 1731 Captain Robert Jenkins arrived in London with cargo from Jamaica and a story to tell that curled the hair. Spanish coast guards had boarded his ship while it lay becalmed off Jamaica; they had searched it for contraband, found none, and then begun to look for cash. Three times they hanged him to his foreyard, Jenkins said, and each time dropped him to the deck half dead and demanded to know where his money was hidden. He kept protesting that he had none; they then cut off part of his ear with a cutlass and tried to scalp him, "but his head being close shaven prevented the execution of it. They returned him the piece of his ear again," Jenkins continued, "and bid him give it to King George, uttering some scandalous words. They beat his mate, cut his boatswain, and stripped him and his people of all their clothes, beds, and bedding, leaving them nothing to wear or lay on." Then they let the ship go.

Such atrocity stories as this, repeated from year to year, began to do their work. West Indian traders clamored for redress; the press took up their cause, and by 1738 its campaign was as hot as in the days of the excise crisis. Pamphleteers fanned John Bull's belligerence with talk of preventive war. "No time can be more seasonable for a war with Spain than the present," one of them argued, "since we have the strongest motives to think every year will augment her revenues, her alliances, or territories." The point about revenues was nonsense, and the point about territories trivial: the British believed that Spain was about to claim their newly established colony of Georgia as lying within the borders of Spanish Florida. The point about alliances was more substantial: Spain was angling for a French alliance, which was one of Walpole's chief reasons for not wanting to fight. He feared—and events bore him out—that war against one Bourbon power would sooner or later mean war against both.

Intent as he was on keeping the peace, he could not do it single-handed. The mounting popular pressure for war seemed to him an impertinence, which he was ready to defy. "Are all desires," he asked the House of Commons, "proper to be gratified? Is an inflamed populace to give laws to the legislature?" But pressure from the legislature itself he could not long resist. The opposition was pressing him hard and was raking over the past for material with which to inflame Parliament. Captain Jenkins was called to tell his seven-year-old story and in doing so immortalized himself. When asked what his thoughts had been while his ear was being cut off, he answered that "he recommended his soul to God and his cause to his country." As propaganda this magniloquent balderdash was worth its weight in gold.

The opposition accused Walpole of having no care for the nation's honor. His only way of defending himself, short of war, was to win a tangible diplomatic victory and win it soon. This was difficult enough, because the Spaniards were past masters of evasion and delay. It was doubly difficult because victory had to be won under the watchful eyes of Parliament, "which is in this country a terrible monster," the Spanish ambassador told his government, "and is ruled by private interests under the plausible name of the public good." The situation was too explosive, the ambassador warned, for long and delicate negotiations; Parliament was demanding prompt results. Walpole's diplomacy was working against a deadline imposed on it at Westminster.

The one fact in his favor was that Spain had no more desire for war than he had. The Spanish fleet was in even worse condition than the Spanish treasury, and Madrid was willing to pay a reasonable sum in compensation rather than become embroiled with the leading naval power of Europe. The British negotiators were also reasonable because they needed quick action. They started by demanding £340,000 damages for ships and cargoes illegally seized in the past by Spain but finally settled for £95,000. On this basis the Convention of Pardo was drawn up; it was ratified by both governments in February 1739. Peace seemed assured.

Walpole still had to weather a storm in Parliament, where the opposition now spoke for an infuriated public. Hope had run high that the government would force Spain to pay munificent indemnities, punish guilty officials, formally abandon its claim to Georgia, and above all disavow its right of search in Spanish waters. Instead, all that the Convention provided was a pittance in cash. The settlement, William Pitt told the House of Commons, was "a stipulation for national ignominy, an illusory expedient to baffle the resentment of the nation. . . . The voice of your despairing merchants, the voice of England has condemned it; be the guilt upon the head of the adviser!" But the "adviser" still had the votes; Walpole secured endorsement for his policy. It had been a close battle, in doubt until the last minute, but once more "the Great Man" had won.

It was his last triumph, and it was empty. By now he stood almost alone in his insistence on peace. Key members of his own cabinet were against him, the king was wavering, the country was in a war fever, and the Prince of Wales came out as the champion of the "patriots." Sir Robert might have been able to beat down even this opposition, but the final blow came from Madrid. First the Spanish government refused to pay the damages agreed on until it received compensation for a quite extraneous claim against the South Sea Company, and the Company responded with a counterclaim of its own. Then, while this altercation was heating the atmosphere, Madrid made a further condition: it would not pay until the British fleet was withdrawn from the Mediterranean. At that point hostilities became inevitable.

The developments that culminated in the second Spanish condition show how the fear of war can lead to war. While the Convention of Pardo was being negotiated, the British government had ordered a fleet to Minorca in order to put pressure on Spain. When the Convention was ratified, the ships were recalled. Almost immediately Whitehall began to doubt Spanish good faith and to suspect (wrongly, as it turned out) that Madrid was making an alliance with France. If the two Bourbon kingdoms joined forces, Gibraltar and Minorca would be doomed without naval protection. The Admiralty therefore reversed itself again and ordered the fleet to remain. The reaction in Madrid was immediate and understandable: Britain was acting in bad faith and meant war. If that were so, Spain, already desperately short of cash, would be demented to pay out £95,000 to the power that was about to attack it. The Spanish consequently made payment contingent on withdrawal of the fleet, and the small tragedy of misunderstandings was played out.

Spain, in British eyes, had willfully repudiated the Convention of Pardo. This was what the warmongers had been praying for, a *casus belli*. Even Walpole now had no alternative to war, for he was faced by a revolt within the cabinet led by his chief lieutenant, the duke of Newcastle. All the work of Sir Robert's negotiators, all his arguments for compromise and dragooning of votes in Parliament, had come to nothing. He did not want to fight any more than he had at the beginning, but he had to relinquish either his policy or his office, and he still loved power. On October 19, 1739, the royal heralds at Temple Bar announced Britain's declaration of war. "It is your war," Walpole told Newcastle, "and I wish you joy of it."

WALPOLE'S ACHIEVEMENTS

The beginning of the conflict that was christened the War of Jenkins' Ear marked not only the collapse of Walpole's policy but the end of his era. Although he held on to what was left of his power for more than two years, they were a shabby postscript to a proud career. War was not his element, and the period with which he is properly identified is the quarter-century before 1739, during which Britain was at peace, except for the brief flurry of the Fifteen, and consolidated and developed the gains of the past. In that time the nation's financial system, once it survived the South Sea Bubble, stimulated a prosperity that became the envy of Europe; the parliamentary system took on a new form, with the cabinet recognized as its central mechanism and patronage and influence replacing the old war of parties. Although Walpole dominated these developments, he did so by virtue of his personality and not his constitutional position. He left behind him no tradition of one-man rule—quite the contrary. His power aroused deep and continuous distrust, as witness the virulence of the opposition, and for the rest of the century even the phrase *prime minister* continued to be suspect.

Sir Robert was not a prime minister in the modern sense: he was both more and less. More, because no minister before or since has exercised so much power for so long or put his stamp so deeply on his age. Less, because he had behind him a machine, not a party, and so could never rely on a majority in the House of Commons that would vote as instructed; less, also, because his dependence on the king forced him to guard constantly against intriguers at court and in the House of Lords. He kept his place only by endless manipulation and compromise, and at two critical moments by surrendering the policies for which he stood. If his power was great, so was its price.

In manipulating his world he also served it. He gave it stability, kept it at peace, furthered its prosperity. He has often been accused of debasing its standards of political morality, but the best answer to this charge is to ask which of his opponents had higher standards. They were as prosaic and cynical as he was, with no greater dreams and much less shrewdness; the most that can be said of them is that by the end of the period they sensed, as he did not, the expansive forces in the nation that were urging it on to adventure.

Walpole acted as a dam to these forces, and the Spanish war was the breaking of the dam. From 1739 until 1815 Britain was involved in one war after another and never had more than a twelve-year interlude of peace. Britain was also increasingly involved with economic changes at home, changes that would by 1815 transform the island into the world's foremost industrial power. The quiet days were over, the rest period in which the country had gathered its strength after the upheavals of the Stuart era. Now the strength was being called into play and tested as it had never been before.

6 THE WINNING
OF EMPIRE

*I*n 1739 Britain found itself in a war for which it was unprepared. This was no accident of the moment; unpreparedness is a recurring theme throughout British history, just as it is in the history of the United States, and for the same underlying reason. Both nations have been island powers, strategically speaking, and as such have been immune from any massive invasion at the outbreak of war. Both, therefore, have traditionally tended in peacetime to deny their armed services the equipment, training, and thought required to keep them ready for battle. Both have usually bungled and sometimes been defeated at the start of hostilities and have then set to work to create a fighting machine. Geography has given them time, as it has not given a land power like France, to learn how to fight *after* the declaration of war.

THE EXPANSION OF THE CONFLICT (1739–1740)

At the outbreak of the Spanish conflict, Britain was in an even worse state than usual. The army was negligible, the navy in the doldrums, and Walpole's government inexperienced and inept at military planning. Of these shortcomings the first seemed the least important: everyone expected the war to be a return to the Elizabethan tradition of plundering the Spanish Main, and for that lucrative occupation no great number of troops was required. Even small expeditions, however, proved to be beyond the capacity of the War Office, which could neither organize nor supply them effectively: the soldiers sent to the Caribbean accomplished nothing and died like flies. This was bad enough, but the blundering of the navy was worse. Its officers were better at fighting each other and the generals with whom they were supposed to cooperate than at fighting the Spaniards; the Admiralty had no concept of how to use sea power. The nation, having embarked lightheartedly on what was assumed to be a small and easy struggle, lacked the capacity to win it.

This was a bad augury, for within a year a far greater struggle began in Europe. In 1740 the Habsburg emperor, Charles VI, died, and the accession of his daughter, Maria Theresa, was the signal for neighboring powers to try to partition her territories. This attempt concerned Britain because it threatened to destroy the whole balance of European power. For 200 years continental rivalries had centered on the antagonism between the Habsburgs and the reigning house in France, first Valois and then Bourbon; and for half a century Britain had found in the Habsburgs its counterweight to Bourbon aggression. Now that the troubles of Maria Theresa gave new scope to French ambition, the dictates of self-interest shifted British attention from the Caribbean to Europe.

France was not the first to tear up the Pragmatic Sanction and begin plundering Maria Theresa's dominions. That particular dishonor was reserved for a man known as Frederick the Great, the Hohenzollern who had just ascended the throne of Prussia. His small but relatively compact state in northern Germany, with Berlin for its capital, was emerging into the ranks of the great powers by virtue of its army; Prussia, as Napoleon once said, was hatched from a cannonball. Frederick well knew that he could increase his power only at the expense of the Habsburgs, who had long been the paramount German dynasty, and he found his opportunity in a woman's weak and impoverished inheritance, which he had promised to respect. In December 1740 his troops marched into Silesia, the Austrian province adjacent to his own dominions. As the price of annexing it he offered Maria Theresa an alliance against the rest of the world. She scornfully refused, and war began.

Much more was at stake than Silesia. Frederick was beginning a struggle between Austria and Prussia for dominance of the German states, a contest that went on until 1866. This new theme in the power politics of Europe drowned out before long the old theme of Austro-French rivalry. For the next fifty years, until the coming of the French Revolution, Austria and Prussia were opposed, and until 1763 their opposition was a major factor in Britain's policy. The British ended by conquering India and Canada, in large measure because Frederick began by conquering Silesia.

The connection between wars in Europe and wars outside was almost inevitable. The Austro-Prussian quarrel touched off by the Silesian issue in 1740 developed into a struggle for central Europe, just as the Anglo-Spanish quarrel of 1739 developed into a contest between Britain and the Bourbon powers for empire overseas. These two conflicts, going on at the same time, became the constants around which alliances arranged and rearranged themselves. France was lured by its old ambition of expanding in Europe and aligned itself with either Prussia or Austria in attacking the other; Britain almost automatically took the opposite side, partly to guard Hanover and partly to have a continental ally while fighting the Bourbons at sea and overseas. The two wars of the mid-century were not, like those of Louis XIV, between France and a European coalition led by Britain; they were between coalitions of fluctuating membership. But the fluctuations, however bewildering on the surface, preserved the two fundamental antagonisms: in both wars the Habsburg fought the Hohenzollern, and Britain fought the Bourbon states.

THE NATURE OF EIGHTEENTH-CENTURY WARFARE

Conflicts were conducted like business operations. The wars of religion were things of the past, and the wars of nation against nation were things of the future: calculation and reasons of state took the place of passion. Each belligerent entered on hostilities in the hope of profit, whether in terms of trade or territory, and fought as long as fighting served its ends; then it made peace on the best terms possible and awaited another opportunity. An agrarian state like Prussia coveted new provinces, the revenues and population of which could be translated into additional army corps, while a maritime state like Britain coveted new naval bases and lucrative colonies, which could be translated into dominion of the seas. Alliances were based on expediency and might shift with circumstances, for allies that were concerned entirely with their own interests were unreliable comrades-in-arms. The aims of each were flexible, expanding or contracting as the war went well or badly, but they were always realistic and limited aims.

Land warfare could not be carried to extremes. The officer class of every European state, including Britain, was virtually synonymous with the aristocracy, and had to be as long as the old regimes survived: only men dependent on the crown for their privileges and loyal to it through long tradition could be trusted to command the force on which the social order depended. But no country had enough aristocrats in its population to officer a mass army, any more than it had enough money in its treasury to equip and feed such an army. For social and financial reasons, in other words, the military establishment of even a great power was by modern standards extremely small. The result was that no government had the means, even if it had had the will, to push a war to total victory—to annihilate the enemy's army, seize his capital, and dictate terms of peace. The social system imposed moderation even on war making, man's most immoderate activity.

Campaigns were not only limited in their aims but also, for the most part, inconclusive in their results. A principal reason was that the armies were composed of soldiers who served for pay, not love of their country. Many of the small states hired out their troops to the highest bidder, and even in the national monarchies the enlisted man knew little of nationalism. Such loyalty as he had was to his regiment, a loyalty that was the first meaning of the phrase *esprit de corps*. He came from the lower classes and was often in service because the civil authorities had wanted to get rid of him—

> The youth whose most opprobrious fame
> And clear convicted crimes have stamped him soldier.

Only an iron discipline made troops out of such material, which the duke of Wellington later described as "the scum of the earth." An officer could not trust his men out of his sight for fear they would desert, and consequently could not send them to scout and forage on their own; the army, instead of living off the countryside, had to carry with it virtually everything it needed. It therefore moved at a snail's pace, always concerned for its supply lines, rarely daring to leave an enemy fortress in its rear. Campaigns were largely matters of maneuver, of threat and counterthreat, sieges begun and raised; even the winning of battles might bring victory no nearer.

Commanders had good reason to dread a battle because of the way it was fought. The muskets of the day were not accurate beyond fifty yards; infantrymen were therefore trained to advance in precise and rigid line until they came within range, then fire a volley from the entire line, and then charge with the bayonet—while their opponents, in turn, were firing at them point-blank. The effect was murderous. Casualty rates often ran between 30 and 50 percent of the troops engaged. If those who were left won a victory, in the sense of driving the enemy from the field, they could rarely exploit it by rapid pursuit, which would disorder their line and expose them to counterattack. Most actions, in consequence, produced no gain commensurate with the slaughter involved, and the slaughter in itself was a defeat. The men lost were specialists, hardened by long and rigorous training, and could not be readily replaced; squandering them to no purpose was lunacy. For the orthodox commander a battle, in the words of a German military writer, was "the remedy of the desperate"; and, when both sides were anxious to avoid fighting, campaigns produced results as modest as the casualty lists.

The upshot was that land warfare was slow and inconclusive. Between 1740 and 1763, the great powers fought for fifteen years, and almost the only effect on the map of Europe was to transfer the province of Silesia from Austria to Prussia. While Britain continued to concentrate its efforts on this continental conflict it achieved nothing, except the protection of Hanover. Not until the British shifted their main effort to the ocean and concentrated on a naval war for the expansion of trade and empire did they find the road to victory.

Naval war had, in some ways, much in common with war on land. Neither a navy nor an army could be improvised. The square-rigged sailing vessels that were the warships of the period were costly and slow to build; sailors and naval gunners, like soldiers, were the product of long training; and the backbone of the fleet, the three-decked ship of the line that was the precursor of the later battleship, was too highly specialized and too valuable a unit of firepower to be lightly risked. Actions at sea were commonly fought between two lines, sailing on parallel or opposite courses and firing broadsides at each other like the volleys of soldiers, and the immediate results were likely to be as inconclusive as those of land battles. But there the resemblances ended.

War at sea was different in kind from war on land. A fleet, unlike an army, did not have to stop to besiege a fortress in its path or fritter away its strength in guarding supply lines. Rather, it carried with it what it needed and could go wherever there was blue water. Every enemy ship disabled, every base captured or put out of commission, shifted the balance in some degree and prepared the way for the next advance. Naval war was cumulative in its effect, if intelligently directed, and therefore led in the long run to decisive results.

Its final objective, as the British slowly learned, was not merely to defeat the opposing battle fleet but to drive it from the sea. Ships bottled up in port were at a disadvantage: the crews grew slack from want of practice, and their captains lost their skill in maneuvering with other ships. A blockading squadron, on the other hand, because it had to keep the sea in every kind of wind and weather, tended to increase in efficiency even at the cost of damage to the ships. Hence the longer a blockade was maintained, the greater the disparity was likely to be between the passive and the active navy, and the more complete the predominance of the latter. The fruit of that predominance could be the acquisition of every enemy possession overseas.

So much for the theory of sea power. But theory in war evolves from practice, which is a slow teacher. The British Admiralty, even when it learned the practice of blockade, had little understanding of the theory behind it. The practice was not learned until twenty years after the outbreak of hostilities in 1739 and was forgotten again in the War of American Independence and relearned in the 1790s. Another century elapsed before the theory was formulated—and then by an American.[1]

THE WAR OF THE AUSTRIAN SUCCESSION (1740–1748)

In the long evolution of British strategy the War of the Austrian Succession was a mere preliminary, a process of trial and error in which error predominated. The British had not yet realized the potentialities of sea power, and two factors were chiefly responsible for delaying their realization. One was the traditional emphasis, inherited from the days of Marlborough, on land warfare in Europe, an emphasis now heightened by the need for defending Hanover. The other was developments at home that culminated in a Jacobite rising. These two factors, accentuated by governmental ineptitude, produced one of the most inconclusive struggles in British history.

The war was slow in getting started. France began to intervene on the side of Prussia as early as 1741, and Spain revived its old dream of ousting the Austrians from Italy, but several years elapsed before the Bourbon powers revealed clearly that their aim, like that of Frederick, was to partition Maria Theresa's inheritance. This aim deeply affected Britain, partly because Spain was Britain's open enemy and much more because France intended to conquer the Austrian Netherlands, in which British interests were as closely involved as they had been at the time of the Utrecht settlement. Not until the spring of 1744, however, did the nation formally enter the war.

The reason was in great part the political currents and crosscurrents in London. Early in 1742 the mismanagement of the Spanish war drove Wal-

---

[1] By Alfred T. Mahan in his famous trilogy, *The Influence of Sea Power upon History, 1660–1783* (1890), *The Influence of Sea Power upon the French Revolution and Empire, 1793–1812* (1892), and *The Life of Nelson* (1897). These classics, which are still eminently readable, seem to have a profound influence on thinking about naval strategy during the 1890s and the first decades of the twentieth century. G. J. Marcus, *Heart of Oak: A Survey of British Sea Power in the Georgian Era* (1975), provides a topical summary of more recent research.

pole from office at long last, as his opponents had calculated. The departure of his dominating figure left a political vacuum, and the little men who squabbled for his place had neither the vision nor the support in Parliament to create effective policy. Forced to triple the peacetime military budget, they hired German troops to assist Maria Theresa and safeguard Hanover. George II, acting as a German prince while Britain was still technically neutral, assumed command of an army of Austrians, Hanoverians, and Britons, and in June 1743 at the Battle of Dettingen he had the satisfaction of leading it to an unexpected victory over the French—the last time that a British monarch was to command in the field. But the king's triumph did not still the parliamentary outcry that he was sacrificing British interests to Hanoverian; he was turning the nation, said William Pitt, into "a province to a despicable Electorate."

The king's ministers did not have the wit to devise a coherent offensive strategy, and France saved them the trouble by seizing the initiative. The government of Louis XV, just as Walpole had expected, revived the cause of the Stuarts and massed troops and ships for an invasion of England to coincide with a Jacobite rising. When the plan was abandoned in the face of British naval preparations, the Jacobites decided to go ahead on their own in the hope of forcing the hand of Versailles.

Their leader was no longer James, by now an aging failure, but his son the Young Pretender. Charles Edward Stuart, "Bonnie Prince Charlie," was in some respects the ideal romantic hero: he was strikingly handsome and had a magnetism and charm that recalled the duke of Marlborough; he lacked Marlborough's other gifts as politician and soldier, but he did have courage and a sense of dedication. When he set off from France in a small ship in July 1745, bound for London by way of Scotland to topple King George off his throne, the venture seemed utterly hopeless. Perhaps it was, but in the next few months the Stuart cause came closer to success than at any time since the Battle of the Boyne in 1690.

The Forty-Five, like the Fifteen, began with a Highland rising. Soon after Charles landed on the west coast of Scotland with only seven companions, he had an army of clansmen at his back. He made straight for Edinburgh and by mid-September was installed in his ancestors' palace of Holyrood. Four days later he defeated the only force of British regulars in the country. Meanwhile, far to the south, the cold wind of panic began to blow through Whitehall: the government hastily recalled troops from the Low Countries and summoned King George from Hanover. If the Pretender had been strong enough to invade England at once, he might have had a chance, but he waited for reinforcements until the end of October, by which time armies were massing to bar his road. He eluded them all and marched south to Derby, little more than a hundred miles from London. There he stopped, hesitated, and after bitter argument yielded to his advisers and turned back. Retreat, as he knew, was the end of his bid for a crown.

Yet by then he had no other course but retreat, for events were demonstrating that the name of Stuart, outside the Highlands, no longer had any magic. The years of Walpole had done their work of reconciling the English, and even the Lowland Scots, to the Hanoverian regime. Men would not turn out to fight for that regime, because it did not command a fighting loyalty; but neither would they turn out to fight against it. Without their support the Stuart cause was doomed. Prince Charles and his advisers cared less about the presence of hostile armies than about the absence of the recruits they had hoped for, and, when they found the populace watching their march with indifference, they knew that the game was up. A rabble of kilts and the skirl of bagpipes and a cause from the distant past made no impression on the Whig magnates or the peasants of Derbyshire. Their apathy was as strong a defense for King George as his soldiers were.

The Jacobite army retreated across the border and into the Highlands, where it starved through the winter. The end came in April 1746 when the king's younger son, the duke of Cumberland, destroyed the ragged Highlanders in a battle on Culloden Moor. The Pretender, with a price of £30,000 on his head, wandered between Jacobite households on the mainland and in the Hebrides for the next five months, sometimes disguised as a woman, until in September he finally found a ship to take him to France. He left his followers to the ferocious vengeance of Cumberland, who was known thenceforth as "the butcher". The government also took punitive measures. Many Highland chiefs saved themselves by exile, while the old clan organization was broken up by act of Parliament. The clansmen were forbidden to bear arms or wear kilts, and their leaders were deprived of the right to administer separate law courts and claim military service from their dependents. In the years that followed, a system of army-built roads was extended further into the Highlands, and the Highlanders came to be an integral part of Scotland's economy and society.

As for Bonnie Prince Charlie, he soon ceased to be bonnie. His wanderings after Culloden had driven him to drink. The remainder of his long life was devoted more and more single-mindedly to women and alcohol. When he died in 1788 his shadowy claim passed to his younger brother Henry, a cardinal in the Roman Church, and with Henry's death in 1807 the male line of James II was finally extinguished. Its hopes had died in the Forty-Five, and thereafter its exiled followers flitted through the capitals of Europe with nothing to do but play the game of might-have-been. "It is to no sort of purpose to talk to those people," Lord Chesterfield warned his son, "of the natural rights of mankind and the particular constitution of this country. Blinded by prejudices, soured by misfortunes, and tempted by their necessities, they are as incapable of reasoning rightly as they have hitherto been of acting wisely."

The Jacobites' action in precipitating the Forty-Five was from their point of view unwise, at least by hindsight, because it doomed their cause. From the viewpoint of Versailles, however, it was a godsend. It gave France the initiative in the war. When the British government withdrew its troops from the Low Countries, the French moved into the Austrian Netherlands and part of Holland: all the efforts of the British and Dutch failed to dislodge them. The Austrians were no help, even when Frederick, with Silesia for his prize, withdrew Prussia from the conflict. France, like Prussia, had won a substantial gain on the continent, but overseas its position was precarious. Although in India the French had captured Madras, in America they had lost the fortress of Louisbourg, on Cape Breton Island. Louisbourg, the key to the St. Lawrence Valley, had been captured by an expedition from Massachusetts, supported by a squadron of the Royal Navy; and the whole of French Canada lay open to attack. This was the threat by which the British, in the peace negotiations, pried loose the French hold on the Low Countries.

All the belligerents by now were weary. The business of war offered no assurance of further profit for any of them, and they were ready to bargain. The peace treaty that they hammered out, signed at Aix-la-Chapelle in 1748, was remarkably inconclusive. Spain made minor gains in Italy, but the only major change was that the powers agreed to Frederick's acquisition of Silesia. He alone emerged as a clear-cut victor. Elsewhere the prewar status quo was reestablished—the French back in Louisbourg, the British in Madras, the Austrians in their part of the Netherlands, the Dutch in the border fortresses that they had acquired at Utrecht. Britain made an almost casual peace with Spain: the asiento would lapse in the near future, and the chief issue that had brought on war in 1739, the Spanish right of search, was passed over in diplomatic silence. Walpole was dead by now, but his ghost might have chuckled. Nine years of fighting and spending money—to the tune of some £80 million—had brought his country nothing.

REVERSAL OF ALLIANCES AND RENEWAL OF WAR (1748–1757)

The Treaty of Aix-la-Chapelle left all the basic questions open. In India and America the Anglo-French rivalry was as intense and explosive as ever. In Europe Austria and Prussia were not reconciled but only resting; France was ready to fight again whenever a promising opportunity offered. Before long Maria Theresa provided one. She had no intention of accepting the loss of Silesia as final, and to get it back she needed a more stalwart champion than Britain had proved to be. She began to make overtures at Versailles, to which the British government had only one possible answer—overtures at Berlin. While Austria and France had been at loggerheads, Austria and Britain had been friendly; now that Austria and France were drawing together, Britain had no recourse but to turn to Prussia. This realignment of the powers, particularly in the years 1754–1756, is known as the Diplomatic Revolution.

Though startling to contemporaries, the change of alliance partners is understandable. The War of the Austrian Succession had grown out of two distinct rivalries and had resolved neither one; they continued through a period of uneasy truce. In India the French and British companies encouraged little wars between their client rajahs, while in America the French strengthened their line of forts and trading posts from the Great Lakes to the lower

BRITAIN'S CONTINENTAL
ALLIES AND ENEMIES
Maria Theresa, ruler of the
Habsburg Empire (1740–
1780), and Frederick the
Great, King of Prussia (1740–
1786). *(Library of Congress)*

Mississippi. In Europe the Austrian desire for Silesia gradually led to a much more grandiose project, a coalition of powers to dismember Prussia. To settle the issues left unsettled at Aix-la-Chapelle a new and greater war was in the making, and the only question was where it would first erupt.

The answer proved to be in North America, where the French and British claims overlapped in the great forests of the Alleghenies. Both sides were determined to assert what they considered their rights. When in 1754 an ex-surveyor and colonel of Virginia militia by the name of George Washington led a small expedition of volunteers to the Forks of the Ohio, site of modern Pittsburgh, only to find the French established there in Fort Duquesne, Washington and his whole force were captured. News of this small debacle stirred the British government to act. In 1755 it sent troops under General Braddock to seize Fort Duquesne, and a naval squadron to the mouth of the St. Lawrence to intercept reinforcements for Canada. Braddock was ambushed and killed; most of the French reinforcements got through, but some were captured. This was war, real if undeclared, and within a few months it spread to Europe.

There the opening of hostilities was as much the result of fear as of intent. Britain, drifting into a conflict with France, feared for the safety of Hanover, while France feared a coalition of continental powers and Prussia worried that Maria Theresa would succeed in finding confederates. The old alliance system was breaking apart, and no one knew what kind of realignment would succeed it. Frederick of Prussia was not one to wait on events: as dangers gathered about him, he acted. In January 1756 he formed an alliance with Britain, and in September he invaded Saxony, which he intended to add to his dominions. These moves raised against him a ring of enemies. France, whom he had deserted for Britain, turned to Austria, and this Franco-Austrian combination was promptly joined by Russia. The Romanov empress, Elizabeth, detested Frederick and saw an opportunity to possess herself of eastern Prussia; for these reasons she projected Russia for the first time into the power politics of western Europe. The Seven Years' War was beginning, and it was once more a war of intended partition. Russia, Austria, and France expected to make the Prussian state, which had been the sole gainer from the previous conflict, the victim of the new one.

France immediately seized the initiative. In the spring of 1756, before any formal declaration of war had been issued, France had attacked and captured Minorca with its British garrison; now French armies poured into the Germanies and in 1757 overran Hanover. For the planners at Versailles the electorate was crucial. They accepted Britain's naval superiority as irreversible and realized that it would in all likelihood cost them a good part of their colonies, but they expected to redeem this loss at the war's end in the way that France had recovered Louisbourg in 1748, by surrendering gains in Europe. Hanover, they calculated, would serve them in the peace negotiations as the Austrian Netherlands had served them at Aix-la-Chapelle: by returning it they would win back their overseas empire. They would then be left in possession of whatever other European conquests their armies might make, and Maria Theresa promised them the Austrian Netherlands if she recovered Silesia. Their strategy, in other words, was based on the lesson of the previous war: that Europe was the crucial theater and that gains there would recoup any losses elsewhere.

THE RISE OF WILLIAM PITT

What the French did not take into account, because they did not yet know it, was that they were pitted against the two greatest strategists in the period between Marlborough and Napoleon. One was King Frederick. The crisis that he had helped bring on himself challenged his powers as never before, and he rose to the challenge. Although his army was the best fighting machine in Europe, it faced odds so overwhelming that a lesser man would have succumbed: even he thought at times of suicide. He lost battles and even campaigns; he saw his troops melt away, and the Russians occupy Berlin. But he held on, always fighting, always formidable, and in the end managed to preserve—unfortunately, perhaps, for the world of the future—the Prussia that was hatching from a cannonball.

The other great strategist was William Pitt, who through the critical years of the war directed British policy.[2] Although, or perhaps because, he had little professional training as a soldier, Pitt was impatient with the stolid generals of his day. He grasped military and naval problems intuitively more than rationally, often solving them by unorthodox leaps of the imagination. He had in him much of the poet and, in his arrogance and fits of nervous depression, something of a madman. But he also had indomitable will, a sure judgment of people, and above all the ability to move and inspire the nation. In these respects, as in his imaginative grasp of strategy, he resembled Britain's other outstanding war leader, Winston Churchill.

Pitt, like Churchill, might never have achieved leadership if the war had not begun with calamitous British defeats. The "boy patriot" who had opposed Walpole had made a name for himself by his oratory and, after Sir Robert's fall, a place for himself by his abilities. But King George, remembering Pitt's stigmatizing Hanover as "a despicable Electorate," had kept him from high office and forced him to bide his time for years in a minor position. Between 1746 and 1754 two brothers, Henry Pelham and Walpole's old lieutenant the duke of Newcastle, had reestablished Sir Robert's system and had survived the end of the War of the Austrian Succession and

---

[2]Basil Williams is the author of an authoritative two-volume biography, *The Life of William Pitt, Earl of Chatham* (1913). Stanley Ayling's *The Elder Pitt, Earl of Chatham* (1976) provides an illuminating study of the stateman's complex personality, while Marie Peters's *Pitt and Popularity: The Patriot Minister and London Opinion During the Seven Years' War* (1981) explores the importance of public opinion in his rise and fall. Capsule biographies have been provided by Charles Grant Robertson, *Chatham and the British Empire* (1948), and J. H. Plumb, *Chatham* (1956).

the uneasy peace that followed. The world of the Pelhams felt little need for inspiring leadership.[3]

Henry Pelham's death in 1754 deprived the administration of its manager in the House of Commons and was the beginning of Pitt's opportunity. For two more years Newcastle stumbled on by himself as head of the government, a position for which he was wholly unfit. He had the disadvantage of sitting in the House of Lords, but what principally disqualified him for leadership was his personality. He was a timid, fussy little man, always chattering and fidgeting; and even King George held him in supreme contempt. The duke stayed in office for thirty years, nevertheless, because he knew more about the arts of political manipulation, thanks to Walpole, than anyone else in the kingdom; but he was no man to galvanize the nation in a crisis. As a minister he was indispensable; as first minister he was impossible.

The war opened with defeats, not only on Minorca but in North America and India, and under these blows Newcastle was driven from office in November 1756. Pitt came to power on his own terms, to the king's fury, but in the spring of 1757 George dismissed him and tried to form a ministry of his own choosing. For more than two months the battle raged. Pitt had enormous popularity outside Parliament: once more, as in 1733 and 1739, the pressure of an aroused electorate was brought to bear on Westminster. Yet no amount of pressure could create the political machine that was prerequisite for conducting the business of government; the only man with such a machine was Newcastle, and place had to be made for him. In June 1757 the king, grumbling ferociously, accepted a Pitt-Newcastle coalition; and it remained in office for the next four years. The duke managed the patronage and votes; Pitt managed the war.

They were an odd pair. "The Duke of Newcastle and Mr. Pitt," said Chesterfield, "jog on like man and wife, that is, seldom agreeing, often quarreling, but by mutual interest . . . not parting." They could not afford to part, because both loved power and neither could have it alone. Their views on the war, although widely divergent in theory, were much less so in practice. The focus of Newcastle's interest had always been European, and in particular Hanoverian. Pitt cared no more than he ever had about Hanover in itself: his focus was trade and empire overseas. But he cared a

---

[3]In several areas remote from the heart of politics, the Pelhams did exercise leadership. Their calendar act, strongly pushed by Lord Chesterfield, ended the anomaly of a calendar eleven days out of line with that of most of continental Europe. Britain switched to the Gregorian calendar by eliminating the eleven days between September 2 and September 14, 1752. Since all manner of rents, contracts, and wage arrangements had to be recalculated, the resultant outcry "Give us back our eleven days!" is understandable. The Gin Act of 1751 (see Chapter 3) proved more effective than previous efforts to curb drunkenness in London. An act of 1753 to ease the way for Jews to obtain full citizenship was repealed a year later, however, because of widespread agitation against such a supposed betrayal of the Christian religion.

great deal about keeping the French busy with an inconclusive German war, and it would not be inconclusive unless they were kept out of the electorate. Hence he was as much concerned as his colleague with Hanoverian defense; in the closing phase of the conflict he made his famous remark that "America had been conquered in Germany."

During his first year in office with Newcastle, Pitt was unable to conquer anything. In North America an attempt to take Louisbourg failed, and the French advanced south from the St. Lawrence to threaten the Hudson valley. From India came news that in June 1756 the native ruler of Bengal had captured the British post at Calcutta; after the surrender some of the garrison had been stifled in the notorious Black Hole, the punishment cell of the fortress. In Europe, during 1757, a massive British raid on the French coast, costing £1 million, achieved nothing: the Austrians defeated Frederick in Bohemia, and an Austro-Russian force raided Berlin, while the French occupied Hanover. Only at the end of the year did the tide turn in Germany, when the king of Prussia defeated in quick succession the French at Rossbach, in Saxony, and the Austrians in Silesia. The Austrians recovered, but the French never did. Rossbach blunted their offensive and broke their hold on Hanover. For the next five years they tried to regain the initiative in Germany, and their failure to do so subverted their whole strategy. Rossbach, Napoleon said years later, was the battle that started the Bourbon regime toward its collapse.

THE YEARS OF VICTORY (1758–1760)

Prussia's crisis did not end at Rossbach—far from it. In the ensuing campaigns its enemies pressed harder and harder, until Pitt recognized that British interests required large-scale intervention. He steadfastly refused to commit the bulk of the British army to the continent, but he did send a contingent, which at its peak came to 20,000 men, and he poured out money for hiring Germans. He furnished Frederick a yearly subsidy of £670,000 for his campaigns against the Austrians and Russians in the east and employed some 55,000 mercenaries to cooperate with the British contingent in guarding Hanover and Prussia on the west. This Anglo-German army on the Rhine, commanded by Frederick's chief lieutenant Prince Ferdinand of Brunswick, carried on the work begun at Rossbach and was the means of rendering the German war completely inconclusive for France.

In 1759, Prince Ferdinand won a battle. Out of it came a controversy that had long repercussions in Britain and that illustrates the complex interplay between war making and politics. George II was aging rapidly. His son Frederick had died in 1751, and the heir to the throne was the king's twenty-one-year-old grandson, George, Prince of Wales, who according to family custom was on bad terms with his grandfather. The commander of the British expeditionary force serving under Ferdinand of Brunswick was Lord George Sackville, a favorite of the Prince of Wales and consequently *persona non grata* to the king. Sackville was equally unpopular with his

WILLIAM PITT, FIRST EARL OF CHATHAM (1708–1778), THE ORGANIZER OF VICTORY   In uneasy alliance with the duke of Newcastle, Pitt prosecuted the war vigorously and brought about the defeat of the French in India, Africa, and Canada. *(National Portrait Gallery, London)*

chief, Prince Ferdinand, whom he showered with advice in public and criticized in private. This was the setting for the Battle of Minden.

In the battle, after the Anglo-German infantry had driven the French into retreat, Brunswick ordered Sackville to deliver the *coup de grace* by a cavalry attack. Nothing happened; the moment was lost. Prince Ferdinand, furious, charged his subordinate with disobedience. Lord George answered that the orders had not been clear, but he was relieved of his command and ordered home. The fat was in the fire: Pitt had to choose between turning on Sackville and offending the Prince of Wales, or supporting Lord George and offending the king and Brunswick. He took the former course and sided with the king. Sackville, ostracized, demanded a court-martial, a demand that at least showed courage. A famous court-martial two years before, of an admiral who had helped to lose Minorca, had resulted in his being shot on his quarterdeck. Sackville fared better, but not much. He was found guilty of disobeying orders, declared unfit to serve in any military capacity, and disgraced before the whole army. If ever a career seemed to be blasted, it was his. Yet this was the man to whom the Prince of Wales, as king in later years, entrusted chief responsibility for suppressing the rebellion in America.

Minden was more than an occasion of controversy. It was also a significant victory, even if incomplete, and one of a constellation that made 1759 a year long remembered. "I know that I can save this country," Pitt had said in 1756, "and that no one else can." Now he was making good his words by implementing well-laid plans. He saw the war as an integrated whole and had evolved for it an integrated strategy. The parts were not new but had all been tried before in slipshod fashion; his achievement was to bring them together into a system, much as Walpole, a generation earlier, had created a political system out of ingredients ready at hand. But Pitt's system, unlike Walpole's, produced sensational results.

The new strategy derived from one geographical fact: that Britain was an island and France was not. An insular state can concentrate on its navy, whereas a state with exposed frontiers must divide its energies between sea and land. Pitt exploited this advantage. He raised an army, it is true, of almost 150,000 men, but broke with tradition by sending only a small fraction of it to Europe; for that phase of the struggle he relied primarily on subsidies and mercenaries to contain France, wear down its strength, and prevent the French from taking the offensive at sea. There he intended to defeat the French and, when he had done so, to use the army to gather in their empire.

Sea power and its concomitant, blockading the Mediterranean and Atlantic coasts of France, were the core of his strategy. The test came in 1759, when the French projected an invasion of the British Isles. To cover it, the Toulon squadron broke out of the Mediterranean for a junction with the main fleet at Brest, but was destroyed in a battle off Portugal; the ships at Brest then put to sea for a rendezvous with the transports, only to be annihilated in a second battle. Thereafter the remaining units of the French fleet stayed prudently in port, where the long months of inactivity undermined their crews' morale and seamanship. France lost access to the Atlantic and so to its overseas colonies.

The effect was soon felt from the Ganges to the St. Lawrence. Pitt himself had little interest in India, where the Anglo-French struggle was ostensibly between two commercial companies rather than two governments. But the companies were becoming in effect governments; they had learned to recruit sepoys, Indian troops who served under European officers, and to use them for making full-scale war. Both sides depended on support from home, and the turning point came when Pitt detached a few warships to the scene. The French government, thanks to the British blockade, could send nothing equivalent, and before long the Royal Navy commanded Indian waters. This was the opportunity for Robert Clive, the first of the great proconsuls who served the East India Company. He and his lieutenants reconquered Calcutta, seized the enemy's posts in Bengal, and by 1761 had destroyed French power in India.

Success in America was even more dramatic. In 1758 Louisbourg fell, and Braddock was avenged by the capture of Fort Duquesne; in 1759 General Wolfe won Quebec in a brilliant campaign that cost him his life; in 1760 a fleet and converging armies took Montreal and finished the conquest of Canada. Meanwhile, far to the south in the West Indies, the British were gathering French islands like ripe plums: by 1762 they had Dominica, Martinique, Guadeloupe, and St. Lucia. This surfeit of riches from all parts of the world, which surpassed Britain's fondest hopes and seemed miraculous, was the result of the blockading squadrons that rode the sea in all weather off the coast of France.

VICTORY IN CANADA (1759)   British forces led by General James Wolfe storm Quebec. *(Royal Ontario Museum, Toronto)*

But blockade, even though it produced such victories, did so at the price of alienating the neutral maritime states. Ships of those states could not be permitted to carry French goods under their flags and so maintain the trade between France and its empire. At the start of the war, accordingly, the British government enunciated the Rule of 1756: trade that had been closed to neutrals in time of peace was also closed to them in time of war. Because France had not hitherto permitted them to participate in the commerce with its colonies, in other words, they might not do so now. The rule was enforced not only by the British navy but also by swarms of privateers, licensed by the government to search neutral shipping for contraband and appropriate for their own profit whatever they found. The right of search, which had so infuriated British merchants when exercised by Spain in Spanish waters, was now being exercised in British interests on a vastly larger scale. The neutrals were too weak to fight and could only bide their time for revenge.

Britain's victories were costing the kingdom not only goodwill but also vast sums in cash. The subsidies to Prussia; the cost of the troops that guarded western Germany, of the more than 400 ships in the navy, of combined operations overseas; the £1 million given the colonies in America for raising their own military forces—these and other outlays strained the financial resources of the country to the breaking point. By 1760 the revenue had climbed to £15 million, more than double the figure for 1756, but expenses were still soaring above income and had to be met by loans. The national debt rose between 1756 and 1763 from less than £75 million to almost £133 million. To Newcastle and other conservatives such figures spelled ruin. Even Pitt realized that a nation of roughly seven million, masses of whom were desperately poor, could not pour out gold forever. But he would not make peace until he had led the nation to victory, complete and final.

Whether he could continue to lead it was another question. His colleagues no longer followed him so obediently as they had in the dark days of the war, and were beginning to tire of his arrogance. The public, grown almost blasé about victories, was beginning to tire of his unrelenting demands. Most important of all, he was now serving a new king and could not count on his support. George II, who had begun by detesting his great minister but had fallen under his spell like everyone else, had died in the autumn of 1760, and the accession of his grandson, as Chapter 7 will make clear, changed the whole face of politics. The new king and his advisers were in a position similar to that of the Tories fifty years before: again the nation was wearying of a long war, and the man who dominated the scene was committed to fighting on to victory. That man was as vulnerable by 1761 as Marlborough had been by 1711. Many politicians, Newcastle among them, had ceased to believe that the kind of victory for which Pitt stood was feasible or even desirable. If France were destroyed as a great power, the whole state system of Europe would be disjointed, and no one could calculate the effect. A compromise settlement would be far better, these conservatives believed, than a triumph that would shatter the traditional balance of power. Getting rid of Pitt would be politically dangerous, but giving him his head would be worse.

In 1761 the government learned that Spain was preparing to intervene on the side of France. Intervention, at a time when the Spanish navy was in its usual doldrums and the French navy had been chased from the sea, was such stupidity that some members of the cabinet could not fully credit the news: they hoped that at the last minute Madrid would reconsider. Pitt insisted on immediate attack before Spanish preparations were complete. His colleagues refused and for once would not be bullied. By now he was too autocratic to accept their refusal; he was accustomed to directing every aspect of the war effort and to riding roughshod over the susceptibilities of every department and would not tolerate even the united opposition of the cabinet. "Being responsible," he said, "I will direct, and will be responsible for nothing I do not direct." This was the end. He was no longer permitted to direct, and in October 1761 he resigned.

The next few months saw a rush of events. In January 1762 the empress of Russia died. Her successor, an ardent admirer of Frederick, not only stopped fighting but also threatened to ally with him. Almost at the same moment Spain declared war, and the measures that Pitt had concerted were carried out: British forces seized Cuba and the Philippines. Thus in Europe Frederick was saved from the ring of his enemies and given a chance to triumph over Austria, while overseas the Bourbon powers were surfeited with defeats. The complete victory that Pitt had worked for seemed to be in hand.

THE PEACE OF PARIS

But the British government, like the courts of Madrid and Versailles, had had enough. In May 1762 the old duke of Newcastle was forced from office, and the king installed as first minister his close friend and former tutor, the Scotsman Lord Bute. George and Bute were determined to make peace. They cared little about the German war and less about safeguarding the interests of their Prussian ally, whom they left to shift for himself as best he could. Frederick, thus unceremoniously deserted, was furious, and in the long run Britain paid a heavy price for his anger. Britain also paid a price for Bute's hurry to settle with France, whom he handled as ineptly as he handled his ally. He showed such eagerness for peace that the French raised their terms and extracted concessions to which their defeats did not entitle them. The Peace of Paris of 1763, it is fair to say, was the first good news that France had had since 1757.

Even Bute, however, could not squander all the results of Pitt's strategy, and in the peace Britain made enormous gains. France ceded Canada, Cape Breton Island with its fortress of Louisbourg, and all French holdings between the Alleghenies and the Mississippi except New Orleans; in the whole of North America France retained only its rights in the Newfoundland fishery (supposedly worth £1 million a year) and two small islands in the St. Lawrence for drying the fish. Spain received from France New Or-

BRITISH REDCOATS ON PARADE   Lord George Lennox with men of the 25th Regiment on Minorca in 1771. (*The National Army Museum, London*)

leans and the rest of the vast province of Louisiana, as a sop for Madrid's ill-starred intervention, and got back from Britain Cuba and the Philippines in exchange for ceding Florida and returning Minorca. Britain restored to France Guadeloupe, Martinique, and St. Lucia in the West Indies; the French also returned to India, but with only a shadow of their former power. Thus the treaty, on the surface, was a typical eighteenth-century compromise: everyone got something, and no one got enough to upset the equilibrium.

But the balance of concession and counterconcession was more apparent than real. The war that ended in the Peace of Paris was unlike any other in the century between 1688 and 1792, for one power emerged as the incontestable victor in the world outside Europe; and the peace settlement, for all Bute's errors, confirmed Britain's victory. In the West Indies, it is true, the British sacrificed the strategic position they had won: by returning three islands to France they left the whole question of predominance to be fought out again. But in North America and India that question was settled. The French lost their empire on the American continent, for which they had struggled since the early seventeenth century, and by ceding Louisiana to Spain they showed that their hopes were gone. In India their position was little better: even though French traders returned, the most they could do— and did for years to come—was to stir up local rulers against the British and so contribute to the series of wars through which the East India Company became the paramount power in the subcontinent. The old French empire was finished, and a century elapsed before France gained another of equivalent importance.

The Peace of Paris, in retrospect, was the decisive moment in the second Hundred Years' War. At that moment Britain acquired predominance over France, its only serious rival, in the struggle for dominion of the overseas world; subsequent French attempts to reverse the verdict never came close to success. That verdict determined the future. The Pax Britannica, the oceanic peace enforced by the Royal Navy during the century between the fall of Napoleon and the outbreak of the First World War, was the logical and almost inevitable outgrowth of Britain's triumph in 1763.

Triumph came from sea power, intelligently harnessed and directed for the first time. King Frederick, the greatest soldier of his age, had fought for seven years on land and came out where he started, with Silesia and nothing more. Britain had taken to the sea, gathered in the richest plums of the mercantile world, and then almost contemptuously tossed some of them back to their former owners. The sudden revelation of strength impressed Europe in general and France in particular. Montesquieu, Voltaire, and other French writers had long admired British society in contrast to their own: now the hardheaded realists at Versailles tried to appropriate the secret of British power. After 1760 they began, for the first time in the century, a major effort to build up their navy. The effort was too belated to affect the outcome of the war, but it did affect the future. When the day came for revenge, France had the means.

THE PRICE OF VICTORY

In 1763 Britain was on a pinnacle of its history, and the prospects seemed bright. But a thoughtful observer, looking back over the recent past and studying the example of Prussia, might have wondered whether Britain's very success was not dangerous. Victory bred trouble for the victor, to judge by Frederick's experience, and the British empire was now as tempting an object of partition as Prussia had been a decade earlier. France and Spain were awaiting their opportunity, and it would come whenever the British government began to blunder.

To have avoided blundering entirely would have taxed the wisdom of Solomon, for in the aftermath of war Britain confronted a host of problems. The most immediately pressing was financial. The national debt was staggering, and the recent acquisitions in America promised to increase it: the annual cost of protecting and administering Canada and Florida alone, it was estimated, would come to a quarter of the entire prewar budget. New sources of revenue had to be found, but where? Not by increasing taxes or customs and excise duties at home. These had already been exploited to the limits of public patience, and further demands would be political suicide for any administration. Not by levying internal taxes in the American colonies: only the colonial legislatures could legally do that. Not by asking those legislatures to tax themselves, for experience had shown that they would not respond. The only possible answer was some system of taxing the colonies indirectly, by customs duties and the like, to make them carry their share of the imperial burden. The rudiments of such a system had long existed, but it had never been effective. To make it so, new methods would have to be devised by the British government and rigorously enforced by its agents in America. Increasing the revenue, in short, meant tightening imperial control from London.

There was the rub. The colonists in America had always been hard to control, and the situation in which they now found themselves encouraged them to be headstrong. Hitherto, if they had lost no love on the mother country, they had been unable to afford an open breach. They were divided among themselves, culturally and economically as much as geographically: this lack of cohesion had made them keenly aware of the danger from the French on their frontiers. Protection had been their first necessity and had induced them to put up grudgingly with the arrogance of British officers and the demands of British governors. Now the whole picture had changed. During the war the colonists had learned a little about cooperating with each other and more about quarreling with British regulars; and the Peace of Paris had freed them from their need of the mother country. Few of them, if any, yet dreamed of independence, but for the first time the possibility was there. If Pitt conquered Canada in Germany, he helped to lose the American colonies in Canada.

This generalization, like most in history, much oversimplifies the intricacies of cause and effect. Britain's conquest of Canada was one factor in

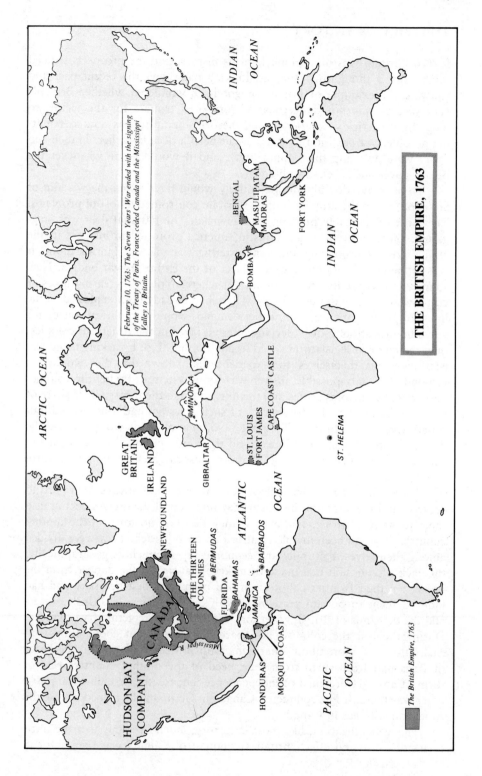

THE BRITISH EMPIRE, 1763

February 10, 1763: The Seven Years' War ended with the signing of the Treaty of Paris. France ceded Canada and the Mississippi Valley to Britain.

INDIAN OCEAN

BENGAL

MASULIPATAM
MADRAS

BOMBAY

FORT YORK

INDIAN OCEAN

ARCTIC OCEAN

MINORCA

GREAT BRITAIN

IRELAND

NEWFOUNDLAND

GIBRALTAR

ST. LOUIS
FORT JAMES

CAPE COAST CASTLE

ST. HELENA

ATLANTIC OCEAN

THE THIRTEEN COLONIES

BERMUDAS

HUDSON BAY COMPANY

CANADA

Mississippi R.

FLORIDA

BAHAMAS

JAMAICA

BARBADOS

HONDURAS

MOSQUITO COAST

PACIFIC OCEAN

The British Empire, 1763

the American problem, and its financial needs were another. The two in conjunction, however, are not enough to explain what followed. To turn the American colonists' resentment into rebellion something more was required, and that was ineptitude in Whitehall. If wise counsels had prevailed there, the government might conceivably have found an acceptable method of raising colonial revenue without raising colonial tempers, or it could certainly have forgone the hope of revenue for the sake of loyalty, because events proved that the mother country was still a long way from bankruptcy. But in the years after 1763 no wise counsels were heard. A series of short-lived ministries alternated between concession and coercion in America and, instead of producing a consistent policy, wobbled toward disaster. Within twenty years of Britain's greatest imperial triumph came its greatest imperial defeat.

IRONWORKS, BARROW, ENGLAND
(Mary Evans Picture Library)

III $\mathcal{F}$ORCES OF CHANGE

1760 to 1789

7 THE AGE OF GEORGE III

*A*lthough the transition from the reign of George I to that of George II in 1727 had—as a result of Walpole's political skill—resulted in continuity rather than change, the accession of the youthful King George III in 1760 meant the beginning of a new and controversial political era. Not only did the new king's personality put its stamp upon the reign, but also his actions gave rise to a historical dispute that has continued into our own time. Was George III, as some of his contemporary critics suggested and as several Victorian historians felt certain, an ambitious man who sought in unconstitutional fashion to restore to the monarchy powers and responsibilities that his predecessors had let slip into the hands of ministers whose primary loyalty lay with Parliament? Was he the tyrant and enemy of free institutions that he is depicted in the American Declaration of Independence? Or, alternatively, was he a victim of the propaganda spread by his enemies? Was he rather a public-spirited and conscientious man anxious to use the accepted constitutional practices of his day in order to advance not his personal interests but those of his nation?[1] Any attempt to provide even tentative answers to these and related questions requires an analysis of both the personality of the new monarch and of the political problems that beset his reign.

---

[1]The role of George III has received a great deal of attention from historians, who are still far from agreed. The traditional and highly unfavorable Whig interpretation is exemplified in the numerous writings of Sir George O. Trevelyan, among them *The American Revolution,* 2nd ed., 4 vols. (1905–1912). The pioneer work of reevaluation was done by Sir Lewis B. Namier in *The Structure of Politics at the Accession of George III,* 2 vols., 2nd ed. (1957) and *England in the Age of the American Revolution* (1933). Richard Pares, *King George III and the Politicians* (1957), provides a balanced assessment. The historiographical controversy is the subject of Herbert Butterfield, *George III and the Historians* (1957), and E. A. Reitan, ed., *George III: Tyrant or Constitutional Monarch?* (1964). Steven Watson, *The Reign of George III, 1760–1815* (1960), touches on all aspects of the era, and John Brooke, *King George III* (1972), is an admirably well-written and authoritative modern biography. Stanley Ayling, *George the Third* (1972), is also reliable.

THE CHARACTER OF THE KING

The future George III became the immediate heir to the throne in 1751, when his father, Prince Frederick, died, and he was educated to become a king. His somewhat rakish father left George an unusual political testament that asked him to resist "the perverseness and bad example of the times," to be pious, to practice personal economy and reduce the national debt, and, as "an Englishman born and bred," to win the love of his people and the respect of foreign powers. "I shall have no regret," Frederick concluded, "never to have worn the Crown if you do but fill it worthily." Frederick's widow Princess Augusta, was at least as eager to have her son equal to the position he was destined to occupy. As a result she kept him cloistered in the schoolroom and deprived him of the company of people his own age, most of whom, she declared, "were so ill educated and so very vicious that they frightened her." George grew into a shy, moody, and lonely boy, and it was not until Lord Bute became his mother's political adviser and his personal tutor in 1755–1756 that George found a friend, a confidant, and an affectionate substitute father. Twenty-five years older than George, the third earl of Bute was a penurious Scottish nobleman with a large family. He had read widely and possessed a worldly air of wisdom, but, except for four undistinguished years as a representative Scottish peer in the House of Lords, he had no immediate experience in British politics.

Bute's impact on his royal friend and pupil had several aspects. He set forth high ideals for the future king, whose surviving schoolboy essays reveal a good constitutionalist in the eighteenth-century sense. "We stand in debt for our liberty and religion to the success of 1688," wrote the youthful George, who went on to exalt freedom of speech as "not only the natural privilege of liberty but also its support and preservation." He wrote of King Alfred's days as a time when "there was scarcely a man in office that was not totally unfit for it, and generally extremely corrupt." Yet Alfred saved his country, and George concluded, "no good and great Prince born in a free country and, like Alfred, fond of the cause of liberty, will ever despair of restoring his country to virtue, freedom, and glory, even though he mounts the Throne in the most corrupted times. . . . " In a firm yet friendly manner Bute discouraged George's infatuation with the youthful Lady Sarah Lennox: it would not do to marry a commoner who was a close relative of several influential politicians of the day. George gave way in a self-sacrificing spirit: "The interest of my country ever shall be my first care. . . . I am born for the happiness or misery of a great nation, and consequently must often act contrary to my passions."

George's upbringing had given him a new attitude toward kingship. He conceived of himself as the chief executive in fact as well as name, ruling through his ministers and a cooperative Parliament. This seemed to be an ambition that he could realize within the existing system: all he had to do was repossess the means of influencing Parliament that his predecessors had largely deputed to the politicians who had ruled for them. In fact, however, his concept of his role struck at the roots of oligarchic power. For half a century the Whigs had been governing, on condition of deferring when necessary to the sovereign's wishes and prejudices, likes and dislikes; they and not he had been the policy-makers. A monarch determined to guide policy himself was profoundly threatening to them, so threatening that conservatives thought the king's intention unconstitutional. Yet they had a weak case. Constitutional theory, as distinct from previous practice, was more on his side than theirs; he was the source of the influence and patronage that they had so long used to manipulate Parliament. The means by which they had hitherto governed, with tacit royal consent, were precisely the means by which the new king expected to reduce them to the status of his servants. The only legal way to stop him would have been to reform the House of Commons by abolishing rotten boroughs and placemen, thereby destroying the system that the Whigs themselves had constructed and by which they had ruled. This they would not at first consider. Neither would they, for the most part, acquiesce in the king's rule. The result was a decade of tension and instability, from 1760 to 1770, and then twelve years in which George largely had his way—and lost the American colonies.

The king's former tutor was instrumental in starting him on this disastrous course. Lord Bute had both constitutional ideas and personal ambitions. He was remote from the give-and-take of everyday politics, but he was fiercely jealous of the leading ministers of the day and clearly hoped, if not to supplant them, at least to become the power behind the throne. He imbued George not only with the ambition to restore his "much loved country to her ancient state of liberty . . . again famous for being the residence of true piety and virtue," but also with the misleading impression that his grandfather had become the veritable prisoner of a bevy of knavish politicians and that Bute alone was a pure spirit in what George described as "the wickedest age that ever was seen." Most of his subjects were exulting in the extraordinary military triumphs engineered by one of the most successful war ministers in British history, but the new king saw the world about him through quite different spectacles. He possessed a profound and admirable sense of duty but no practical experience in government. He found it more difficult to deal with flesh-and-blood human beings than with lofty but abstract ideals.

Soon after mounting the throne, he issued a royal proclamation asking his people "to preserve and advance the honour and service of Almighty God, and to discourage and suppress all vice, profaneness, debauchery, and immorality." The wicked, whatever their social rank, were to be held in contempt, the good to be distinguished by "marks of our royal favour." George did his best to practice what he preached. In 1761 he married Princess Charlotte of the German principality of Mecklenburg-Strelitz, a plain but intelligent and vigorous seventeen-year-old who familiarized herself quickly with the English language and the English environment. The young couple in their large drafty palaces set an example of surprisingly simple domesticity, and they were taken to the coronation ceremony in sedan

KING GEORGE III AS FAMILY MAN   The king, Queen Charlotte, and the
first six of their fifteen children as painted by John Zoffany in 1770. The
boy sitting on the extreme left is the future King William IV, the boy
standing next to him the future Prince Regent and King George IV.
(Reprinted by permission of Her Majesty the Queen)

chairs rather than in an elaborate gilded carriage. They felt happiest in rural
surroundings, and from the 1770s on the king preferred to go to London
for government business but to live at Windsor, where in the role of country
squire he could supervise his model farms and mingle with ordinary people.
He liked hunting and was an excellent horseman; even in his fifties, after a
long day in London, he would ride the twenty miles back to Windsor. In
the morning he would himself light the bedroom fire and spend an hour in
his study before breakfast, a frugal meal because he was fearful of growing
fat. Prayers in the royal chapel would follow. George took religion seriously. When a preacher sought to ingratiate himself by delivering a sermon
highly flattering to the king, George rebuked him by saying: "I go to
Church to hear God praised and not myself."

Though in his own eyes he was a friend to humanity at large, he felt ill
at ease on public occasions. It took him many years to become accustomed
to the levees and drawing rooms that constituted so important a part of the
royal routine. He enjoyed both theater and opera but preferred a quiet evening at home—while he played the flute and Charlotte accompanied him on
the harpsichord—to an elaborate palace function. He favored barley water
over brandy, and at court he abolished Sunday dancing and tried to limit
gambling. One of his favorite hobbies was book collecting, and he eventu-

WILLIAM HERSCHEL'S
TELESCOPE   Built in
1775 under the
patronage of King
George III. *(The Science
Museum, London)*

ally amassed some 65,000 volumes. He also took a keen interest in astronomy and became the patron of William Herschel, the discoverer of the planet Uranus: the king ordered the largest telescope of the day built for Herschel's use. Though theirs was a marriage of diplomatic convenience, George and Charlotte became deeply devoted to one another, and in due course she presented him with fifteen children. Royal mistresses were banned from the court of George III, and there is no evidence that the king ever fathered an illegitimate child. Although he sponsored the founding of the Royal Academy as an exhibition site and training school for British artists, George refused a formal sitting to Thomas Gainsborough, one of the master painters of the age, because he disapproved of the latter's personal morals. In several respects the king and queen were Victorians in a pre-Victorian age, and some of their subjects made fun of the piety, the prudery, the penchant for economy, and the general dullness of the court. Those who did not were all too likely to suspect the king's political designs. It was only in the later 1780s and 1790s, after his active reign was more than half over, that his personal qualities truly won the admiration and even the affection of his people.

THE WORLD OF SAMUEL JOHNSON

Even if George, before he ascended the throne, had been on excellent terms with his grandfather and his grandfather's ministers, the transition from a king of seventy-seven to one of twenty-two would have been profound. Not only youth but also upbringing distinguished the new ruler from his predecessor. Privately George had denounced Hanover, "that horrid electorate," in as vigorous a fashion as might any Whig politician, and in his own hand he inserted in the draft of his speech to his first Parliament the words, "Born and educated in this country, I glory in the name of Britain."[2] That sentiment won the applause of Tory squires, alienated from national politics for two generations, and of Whig factions long suspicious of Hanoverian influence. A case in point was Samuel Johnson, the London author and literary critic who had been born in the small Staffordshire market town of Lichfield back in 1709. Having settled in the capital in his late twenties, Johnson raised himself from poverty and obscurity by his own literary efforts as a contributor to *Gentleman's Magazine,* as an essayist, and in 1755, as the author of a masterly dictionary of the English language. Although he was not England's first lexicographer (an occupation he defined as that of "a harmless drudge, that busies himself in tracing the original, and detailing the signification of words"), Johnson was the most conscientious and the most brilliant man ever to have set himself such a task and the first to illustrate his definitions with quotations drawn from the works of Britain's greatest writers. By the early 1760s Johnson was also coming to be known as a conversationalist who held forth night after night in a London tavern on almost any subject under the sun. Neither Johnson's ungainly manner and appearance nor his slovenly dress was held against him by the members of his informal Literary Club, which from 1764 on met weekly at the Turk's Head Tavern for food, drink, and talk. Its members included Joshua Reynolds, the portrait painter who in 1768 became first president of the Royal Academy, David Garrick, the leading actor and theater manager of the day, Edmund Burke, the youthful parliamentarian, and the yet more youthful James Boswell. Boswell had just arrived from his native Scotland to prepare for a legal career—"Much may be made of a Scotchman," declared Johnson, "if he be *caught* young"—but he found even greater satisfaction in the self-imposed task of writing down verbatim lengthy snatches of Johnson's conversation, jottings that he later used to fashion the most remarkable biography of the age.[3]

Another member of Johnson's club was the poet and playwright Oliver Goldsmith, who dedicated his best-remembered play, *She Stoops to Conquer* (1773), to Johnson, a man who demonstrated—in Goldsmith's words—that "the greatest wit may be found in a character, without impairing the most unaffected piety." The London sage was a devout adherent of the Church of England, although his outlook on the world was tinged with melancholy. His faith and his adherence to a strict moral code went hand

---

[2]So, George's biographer John Brooke points out, reads the original manuscript. In the printed version of the speech, the word reads "Briton."

[3]Boswell's biography, *The Life of Samuel Johnson, LL.D.,* was first published in 1791. As edited and annotated by George Birkbeck Hill and revised by L. F. Powell, it is available in a six-volume edition (1934–1964). Of the modern biographies of Johnson, that by W. Jackson Bate (1977) is the most detailed and that by John Wain (1974) constitutes the most readable introduction.

OLIVER GOLDSMITH, JAMES BOSWELL, AND DR. SAMUEL JOHNSON AT
THE MITRE TAVERN *(The Granger Collection)*

in hand with a hard-headed devotion to common sense. On one occasion
Boswell commented that the theory of Bishop (George) Berkeley that the
physical matter of the universe was not real but only an idea in the human
mind was difficult to believe but impossible to refute. With great alacrity
Johnson struck his foot against a large stone and bounced back, "I refute it
thus."

On another occasion, an associate told Johnson and Boswell that he
was about to set up a school on his estate but that he had been warned that
education might make his tenant farmers and laborers less industrious.

> JOHNSON: No, Sir. While learning to read and write is a distinction, the
> few who have that distinction may be the less inclined to work; but when
> every body learns to read and write, it is no longer a distinction. A man
> who has a laced waistcoat is too fine a man to work; but if every body had
> laced waistcoats, we should have people working in laced waistcoats.
> There are no people whatever more industrious, none who work more,
> than our manufacturers; yet they have all learned to read and write. Sir,
> you must not neglect doing a thing immediately good, from fear of remote
> evil;—from fear of its being abused. A man who has candles may sit up
> too late, which he would not do if he had not candles; but nobody will
> deny that the art of making candles, by which light is continued to us be-
> yond the time that the sun gives us light, is a valuable art, and ought to be
> preserved.
>
> BOSWELL: But, Sir, would it not be better to follow Nature; and go to
> bed and rise just as nature gives us light or witholds it?

JOHNSON: No, Sir; for then we should have no kind of equality in the partition of our time between sleeping and waking. It would be very different in different seasons and in different places. In some of the northern parts of Scotland how little light is there in the depth of winter!

When Oliver Goldsmith put forth the notion that the prevalence of luxury had caused the degeneration of England's people, Johnson took issue once more:

> Sir, in the first place, I doubt the fact. I believe there are as many tall men in England now, as ever there were. But, secondly, supposing the stature of our people to be diminished, that is not owing to luxury; for, Sir, consider to how very small a proportion of our people luxury can reach. Our soldiery, surely, are not luxurious, who live on six-pence a day; and the same remark will apply to almost all the other classes. Luxury, so far as it reaches the poor, will do good to the race of people; it will strengthen and multiply them. Sir, no nation was ever hurt by luxury; for, as I said before, it can reach but to a very few. . . .

By background and by temperament, Johnson was a Tory rather than a Whig. As he often explained, "The first Whig was the Devil," and in his *Dictionary*, Johnson defined Whig simply as "the name of a faction," whereas a Tory was "one who adheres to the ancient constitution of the state, and the apostolical hierarchy of the church of England." Johnson found admirable the piety, the political ideals, and the generosity of King George III, who in 1762 offered him, as England's leading man of letters, the generous pension of £300 a year. A few years later, after Trinity College, Dublin, had surprised Johnson with an honorary Doctor of Laws degree, the king sought him out to ask his opinions on British literary life. When Johnson said of himself that he "thought he had already done his part as a writer," the king replied, "I should have thought so too, if you had not written so well." This, Johnson afterward declared, was a compliment "fit for a King to pay. It was decisive." Johnson was spurred not merely to embark on his last major literary work, *The Lives of the Poets*, but also to write a number of pamphlets defending the policies of George III's ministries during the late 1760s and early 1770s.

THE POLITICS OF THE 1760s

Not all of his subjects were equally pleased with either King George III or his ministers. Many were particularly unhappy with the rapidity with which the king advanced the fortunes of his Scottish friend, Lord Bute. The latter was suspected of all manner of secret and evil designs—not least that of wishing to remove from power the leading Whig politicians of the day, some of whom, like the duke of Newcastle, had held high office for the greater part of four decades.

By March 1761 Bute had been installed as one of the two secretaries of state. In October Pitt resigned, and in May 1762 Newcastle followed suit.

George III had not removed either man, for both had departed on questions of policy, but the king had been eager to see them go, unaware that any successors would have trouble in Parliament without the support of both the greatest orator of the day and the most experienced dispenser of patronage. Bute now became First Lord of the Treasury, and, although the House of Commons gave overwhelming approval to the Peace of Paris, he soon found himself in difficulties. An excise tax on cider, which his ministry felt compelled to impose to balance the budget, was denounced as an example of Scottish tyranny seeking to deprive the English of their liberties. The London populace, which had made a hero of Pitt, pelted Bute's carriage with mud and attempted to overturn it. The blue ribbon of the garter, which the king had conferred on him, was derided in a London street ballad:

> O Bute! If, instead of contempt and of odium
> You wish to obtain universal eulogium,
> From your breast to your gullet transfer the blue string
> Our hearts are all yours at the very first swing.

The cider tax passed, but Bute had become so fearful for his personal safety that in April 1763 he resigned. Parliamentary politics were not his métier. He would have been happy to remain the power behind the throne (and was suspected of being precisely that for many years to come), but George gradually became disillusioned with his "dearest Friend." After 1766 they corresponded no longer.

Bute's resignation returned government to politicians and began a long period of ministerial instability. He was followed for two years (1763–1765) by George Grenville, a Whig of the old school. Although they agreed on policy, the king never learned to like the minister's self-righteousness and verbosity. "When he has wearied me for two hours," the monarch complained, "he looks at his watch to see if he may not tire me for an hour more." George resented Grenville's attempt to monopolize all patronage appointments to gain parliamentary support, even lofty appointments in the army and the Church that the king considered above politics. In 1765 he replaced Grenville with the marquis of Rockingham, whose ministry proved to be weak. In the summer of 1766 George tried the experiment of bringing back the one great figure of British politics, to steer the government out of its doldrums. William Pitt was still the great orator of his age, and, whenever he spoke, he "carried with him unpremeditated," in Chesterfield's words, "the strength of thunder and the splendor of lightning." He was enormously popular in the country, and even the Americans looked up to him. Yet his ministry was a failure. At its start he undercut his position by accepting a peerage and becoming earl of Chatham. Chesterfield expressed the amazement of the political world that any consideration could have induced Pitt to withdraw from the House of Commons, "which procured him his power and which could alone insure it to him, and to go into that hospital of incurables, the House of Lords." Greater wonders were to come. By

December 1766 the new Lord Chatham was in the grip of a severe depression, which for the next two and a half years kept him a recluse; and in his absence the cabinet disintegrated into quarreling factions. In 1768 he gave way to his former lieutenant, the duke of Grafton, who proved to be more devoted to his racehorses and mistress than to public business. After two years the duke's lackluster ministry fell apart.

His successor, who remained in office for the next twelve years, was Lord North. He seemed at first glance the ideal man to implement royal policy. He was easygoing and conciliatory, without long-range plans and uncommitted to any faction, a seasoned politician though not yet in his forties, a superb debater, and deft in managing the House of Commons.[4] His startling ugliness was counterbalanced by charm and wit, but under a polished surface he was neurotically self-distrustful. Decisions were agony for him, and leadership beyond him. The king's search for a servant had brought him more than he had bargained for: a servant who turned to him in crisis not only for guidance but also for willpower. North consulted the king four or five times a week, and George found himself involved in day-to-day direction of policy to a degree not known since the days of William III. Had times been as stable as forty years before, North might have lasted as long as Walpole did, but John Wilkes and his supporters at home, and the colonists in America, had succeeded in raising a host of issues that made it all but impossible to let sleeping dogs lie once more.

THE CASE OF JOHN WILKES

The 1760s were not only a decade of wobbling at the ministerial level. They were also significant for a development that aroused much more attention in Britain than did colonial discontent and had almost as much importance for the future. The ineptitude of successive ministries was bringing the whole parliamentary system into disrepute and, for the first time since the seventeenth century, was awakening the force of political radicalism. The leader of this movement was a remarkable if not estimable man, John Wilkes, who for many years kept the world of Westminster in turmoil. He was as ugly, charming, and witty as Lord North, but there the resemblance ended; Wilkes, even in a period of lax morals and little faith, was notorious as a rake and blasphemer. If the fear of God was not in him, neither was the fear of man. He began by attacking the king's ministers and ended by attacking the king himself and the whole constitutional structure on which royal power rested.

---

[4] To find Lord North in the lower house instead of the upper is confusing, but so are British titles. North was not a peer and hence did not sit in the House of Lords. He was the heir to an earldom, and the eldest son of a duke, marquis, or earl was—and still is—called lord by courtesy during his father's lifetime. The Irish peerage was separate. A member of it, after the Act of Union in 1801, might be elected by his fellows to the House of Lords or by a British constituency to the House of Commons.

Marriage to a wealthy heiress had it made it possible for Wilkes, the son of a distiller, to set himself up as a country squire and in 1757 to gain election to the House of Commons, where he became a protégé of Earl Temple, Pitt's brother-in-law. Temple enabled Wilkes in 1762 to become the owner and editor of a weekly paper, the *North Briton*, which catered to a lower-middle-class London audience; its tone was violently antigovernment, anti-Bute, and anti-Scot. "How far," asked France's Madame de Pompadour, "does liberty of the press extend in England?" "That," Wilkes replied, "is what I am trying to find out." In successive issues of the *North Briton*, Wilkes broadly suggested that Bute was the lover of the king's mother and had bribed the House of Commons to approve the Treaty of Paris. In Number 45 of the journal Wilkes denounced as a lie the passage in the king's speech to Parliament that characterized the peace as "honorable to my Crown and beneficial to my people."

Grenville had Wilkes arrested on a general warrant, an order issued by a secretary of state that named no names; in this case it ordered the arrest, for seditious libel, of all concerned in the publication of the *North Briton* and the confiscation of all their papers. Such exercise of executive power was reserved for emergencies, and its legality was doubtful. So was the question of whether a member of Parliament could be imprisoned for libel. Nevertheless, Wilkes was sent to the Tower of London. When granted a court hearing on a writ of habeas corpus, he dramatically made himself the symbol of English freedom: "The liberty of all peers and gentlemen and, what touches me more sensibly, that of all middling and inferior set of people, who stand most in need of protection," he told the judge, "is in my case this day to be finally decided upon: a question of such importance as to determine at once whether English liberty shall be a reality or a shadow." The court freed him on the ground that a member of Parliament was privileged. He then sued the responsible secretary of state, protesting that general warrants were illegal. He eventually won his case and recovered £1,000 in damages.

This attack on the Goliath of officialdom made Wilkes such a popular hero that the Grenville ministry dared not leave him alone. When, in defiance of the advice of his aristocratic patrons, Wilkes personally republished the libelous articles, the government counterattacked. It induced the House to deny that its privilege covered libel and exposed in the House of Lords *The Essay on Woman*, an obscene parody of Pope that Wilkes had written in part and had printed for private circulation. He was now open to prosecution both for obscenity and for his earlier libel in the *North Briton*. Early in 1764 he fled to France and consequently was expelled from the House of Commons, convicted *in absentia* of libel, and outlawed. Four years later he returned, unrepentant and unafraid, and promptly stood for election to Parliament for the county of Middlesex, an electorate made up largely of London shopkeepers. He canvassed as an independent man persecuted by a costly and inefficient government. When one voter told him, "I'd rather vote for the Devil," Wilkes was quick to reply: "Naturally, but

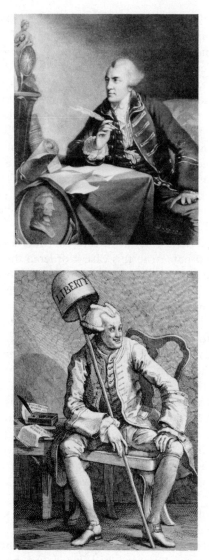

JOHN WILKES: THE ENGLISH
RADICAL AS SEEN IN 1764 BY A
SUPPORTER AND BY A
CRITIC   Engraving based on a
painting by Robert E. Pine;
etching by William Hogarth.
*(Library of Congress;
reproduced by courtesy of the
Trustees of the British Museum)*

if your friend is not standing, may I hope for your support?" He won the election but almost immediately thereafter was imprisoned under his old sentence for libel. He was more dangerous, however, in prison than at liberty. Mobs rioted outside his windows; troops were sent in, fired on the crowd, and killed several people, an action that resulted in coroners' juries bringing verdicts of murder against the military.

It was a time of economic distress in London: weavers, sailors, hatters, tailors, and coalheavers were all intermittently involved in strikes. Such discontented workers were ever ready to cheer Wilkes, not because he advocated a specific economic program but because he, like them, was in revolt.

The threat of revolution was in the city's air, and moderate opinion rallied to the government, then headed by the duke of Grafton. In 1769 the House of Commons quashed Wilkes's election only to see him reelected once again for Middlesex. Time after time the farce of expulsion and reelection was repeated, until at last the Commons declared his opponent, who had received a fifth of the votes, to be the legal member. The defenders of expulsion took their stand on the ground that Wilkes was deliberately flouting the will of the House of Commons, which had in the seventeenth century successfully asserted, against crown and law courts alike, the right to control its membership and to resolve electoral disputes. The opponents of expulsion, with Wilkes's eager encouragement, took their stand on the ground that the House was deliberately flouting the will of the electorate.

While the issue was still in dispute, Wilkes became involved in a related question: Was the House of Commons a private club whose debates could be kept secret, or was it a public institution whose debates might be reported openly in the press? Such disclosure had hitherto been intermittent, and in 1771 several London printers were charged with having violated parliamentary privilege by publishing transcripts of debates. Wilkes, who was by then a London alderman, saved them from arrest, but the government ultimately decided, on the king's advice, to "have nothing more to do with that devil Wilkes."[5] Although the House of Commons continued to reserve the right "to exclude strangers," the reporting of debates soon became customary and the reports were printed with impunity.

THE RADICAL TRADITION

Wilkes in due course rose to be lord mayor of London. He was again chosen M.P. for Middlesex in the general election of 1774 and was quietly permitted to take his seat. Although he gradually faded from the public stage, his followers, who in 1769 had organized the Society of Supporters of the Bill of Rights, set in motion what became a continuous radical tradition in British politics. In their rhetoric they often harked back to the "Country" Opposition of Walpole's day, but their concern was less with the welfare of landowners than with the social status and financial well-being of urban merchants and shopkeepers. They initiated a pattern of organizing and petitioning that was to be emulated in the decades to come. They appealed not only to Londoners but to Englishmen at large to sign petitions upholding Wilkes's cause and asking the king to dismiss his "evil and pernicious

---

[5]*That Devil Wilkes* (1930) is also the title of an informative biography by Raymond Postgate. Louis Kronenberger has provided a more recent account in *The Extraordinary Mr. Wilkes* (1974). George Rudé's *Wilkes and Liberty* (1962) analyzes the social and economic background of Wilkes's supporters, while John Brewer's *Party Ideology and Popular Politics at the Accession of George III* (1976) sets the Wilkite movement in a broader national context. Ian R. Christie, *Wilkes, Wyvill and Reform* (1962), links Wilkes with subsequent reform movements.

counsellors." Their organization reflected and encouraged a widespread sense of disaffection with the government of the day, which seemed to be imposing the burden of taxation primarily on city dwellers. The king was disliked, Bute was feared, and Parliament was considered corrupt and likely to become a tool of the royal will. Wilkes's judicial battles helped to arouse distrust of the executive and of a legislature that, by denying Wilkes his seat, seemed destined to become a self-perpetuating oligarchy. The campaign for the right of the press to report parliamentary debates was elevated into a struggle for the lowliest artisan's right to knowledge of public affairs.

Organizations such as the Supporters of the Bill of Rights and the analogous Constitutional Society gradually put together a radical program of reform. Its demands were all political: the abolition of rotten boroughs; a broader franchise; more frequent elections; members of Parliament specifically pledged to abide by the wishes of their constituents; and the protection of the individual against executive or legislative persecution. A decade later radicalism manifested itself far from London in the so-called Yorkshire movement, headed by the Reverend Christopher Wyvill, which petitioned in favor of strict governmental economy, parliamentary elections each year (or, at the very least, every three years), and the addition of 100 independent county M.P.s to lessen the influence of the magnates who controlled the rotten boroughs.

A considerable number of members of Parliament who were not office-holders played with such reform ideas and supported some of Wilkes's causes. One M.P., Edmund Burke, then secretary to the marquis of Rockingham, set forth in his *Thoughts on the Present Discontents* (1770) the controversial notion that the key to good government was not a ministry above party but organized parties, groups of individuals working together to implement policies on which they were agreed. This notion appealed much more to the conservative Whigs of the day than did the idea of altering the constitutional machinery. Party organization would undermine the king's initiative by restricting his means of influencing Parliament but would leave the system intact. Although major electoral reform was postponed for another sixty years, the agitation personified by Wilkes was the first significant sign of revolt. Some of the unenfranchised were grumbling at their betters, and a strengthening network of public opinion outside Parliament, and even outside London, was becoming critical of a government that could act high-handedly and with doubtful legality. The effect was to call into question the whole idea of an exclusive governing club, composed of a sovereign, his ministers, and the Lords and Commons, that could ignore the will of even the few who voted in elections. The king's threat to the constitution of the club proved transitory, but the threat from below grew intermittently stronger over the years until it produced the upheaval of 1832.

8 THE LOSS OF EMPIRE

*T*he American colonies in general, and New England in particular, had always been difficult to govern. They had quarreled with British officials, civilian and military, and above all had resented British efforts to regulate their commerce. As early as the 1670s Whitehall was complaining to the king that the New Englanders "do not conform themselves to the laws, but take a liberty of trading where they think fit," and that the question to be faced was "what degree of dependency that government will acknowledge to his Majesty." Ninety years later the question was still unanswered; indeed, during those years it had scarcely been confronted.

THE AMERICAN PROBLEM

England had been too much absorbed in domestic and European affairs to pay great attention to the American colonies or to notice that they were growing enormously in population, wealth, and self-confidence. Most of the king's ministers, from the days of Danby to the days of Pitt, cared little about America and knew less; and they had few experts to advise them. The Colonial Office did not yet exist, and until 1768 no single member of the cabinet was charged with American affairs. The only knowledgeable body was the Board of Trade, created in the reign of William III to supervise colonial commerce and the relationship of the various governors with their legislatures; but the board could not act except by recommendations to the cabinet or Parliament. The British government, although it reserved to itself the right to decide imperial policy, was not organized in a way to make statesmanlike decisions.

Neither was it able to implement effectively the decisions that it did make, for its agents in America were unreliable. Customs collectors were notoriously lax, and the few who disapproved of smuggling enough to bring cases to court were likely to see them thrown out by local juries. Governors were in no position to exert royal authority. Most of them were pulled between the need to obey the crown, which appointed them, and the need to placate their assemblies, which paid their salaries. When royal policy and local opinion were at odds, the governor was in a dilemma; but the assemblymen had the whip hand. "I must," said a governor of New York in the 1740s, "either come into their measures—which by doing it may forfeit my governorship—or starve." The constitutional problem was analogous with that in England before the evolution of the cabinet: the various colonial executives were not responsible to their legislatures but depended on them for money, and no legal mechanism existed for resolving a quarrel between the two branches of government. As long as this situation endured, real reform of the imperial system was out of the question.

Ideas of reform had long been under discussion in London and by 1763 had cohered into something approximating a program. It was never precisely defined during the next twelve years, as a sequence of rapidly changing ministries blundered down the road toward Lexington. But behind the alternating ministerial experiments with coercion and conciliation is discernible the outline of a policy, applied in different ways to two very different areas. One was the wilderness west of the Alleghenies, still populated only by Indian tribes, that France had ceded in 1763; the other was the settled colonies of the seaboard. In the first the essential problem was how to keep the peace, while in the second it was how to raise the money required for keeping the peace.[1]

The British government was convinced that strict limits had to be imposed, if possible from London, on white settlement of the wilderness. Otherwise colonial land hunger would continually stir up the hornets' nest of Indian wars, niggardly and irresponsible colonial assemblies would give no help in restoring order, and the resultant demands on the British army and exchequer would become prohibitive. The remedy was to close the frontiers to settlers and police the area with British garrisons at strategic points. The need for such patrolling was demonstrated in 1763–1764 by a widespread Indian rising known as Pontiac's Rebellion. It was suppressed, the military posts were strengthened, and a royal proclamation forbade white settlement in the wilderness. What remained to be seen was whether the seaboard colonies could be made to pay for the garrisons and respect the proclamation.

They would clearly do neither of their own free will. To secure a fixed revenue from them, Whitehall had to devise some form of indirect taxation that was both legal and enforceable. The question of legality was an open one even in Britain, where many shared Pitt's opinion that the powers of the imperial Parliament over the colonists did not include "that of taking their money out of their pockets without their consent." Even if this could be done legally, it could not be done safely, for an enforceable system was necessarily one controlled from London, and any tightening of imperial authority was dangerous. It meant curtailing what the colonists had come through long usage to regard as their rights. If the British used the navy to strengthen the hand of the customs collector, they would be attacking the colonial "right" to smuggle; if they transferred the prosecution of smugglers from colonial courts to their own Admiralty courts—the only way in which

---

[1]For a helpful study of the first problem see Jack M. Sosin, *Whitehall and the Wilderness: The Middle West in British Colonial Policy, 1760–1775* (1961). In *Empire or Independence, 1760–1775: A British-American Dialogue on the Coming of the American Revolution* (1976), Ian R. Christie and Benjamin W. Labaree provide a concise consideration, on the basis of modern scholarship, of the numerous roots of the conflict that was to break out in 1775.

they could secure convictions—they would be assailing the colonists' idea of judicial process. If they found the means to give each royal governor the financial independence that he had to have to carry out the king's commands, they would deprive the colonial assemblies of one of their most cherished weapons. Money could not be raised, in other words, without raising a host of issues—economic, legal, and political. Once those issues came to the fore, as they did in the 1760s, they proved impossible to resolve by peaceful means.

THE DECADE OF WOBBLING (1761–1770)

Consistent pressure on the colonies might conceivably have been effective, but the administrations of the 1760s could not be consistent. Ministers did not stay in office long enough to learn from experience how ignorant they were of colonial realities, let alone to become knowledgeable: they came and went as the Whig old guard struggled to resist royal influence and the king struggled to assert it by choosing his own servants. In this conflict the American issue was a factor, but one that was more often exploited for partisan purposes than considered on its merits.

The 1760s had fatal effects on the empire. The question of imperial revenue was gradually converted into a constitutional issue, in which the colonists' appeal to their rights and liberties as the king's subjects became an overt challenge to the authority of the crown in Parliament. Grenville opened this Pandora's box, first by readjusting import duties in America and tightening the methods of collecting them, then by the famous Stamp Act of 1765. The act required the purchase of government stamps for a variety of paper articles, from newspapers to legal documents; the money so raised was to go toward defraying the expenses of the military garrisons. The best political forecasters, in America as well as in the mother country, had no inkling of the storm that ensued—resolutions from colonial assemblies, a general congress to petition for redress, mobbing of those who distributed the stamps, a boycott of British goods. The American issue was at the forefront of British politics when Grenville fell, and the Rockingham ministry had to decide whether to retract or face the threat of civil war. British opinion was as much aroused as that of the colonists in America, but far more divided. The division expressed itself in Rockingham's solution, which was to repeal the act. To muster the votes for repeal, however, he added a declaratory act that proclaimed the right of Parliament to tax the colonies. The ministers, as a critic drily remarked, "have relinquished the revenue but judiciously taken care to preserve the contention."

This was the situation that Chatham inherited. In the two years that he left the government leaderless, matters went from bad to worse. His chancellor of the exchequer, Charles Townshend, followed a policy of his own, which was designed to buttress royal authority by a series of integrated measures—strengthening customs collection, adding new duties on imports into America, and using the resultant revenue to free governors and other officials from dependence on the colonial assemblies. The colonists regarded this as a revival of the policy behind the Stamp Act, in a more effective and therefore more dangerous guise, and reacted accordingly. The Massachusetts assembly took the lead in denouncing the Townshend duties as taxation without representation and was promptly dissolved by the governor. But the Boston mob, not he, had effective power, and soon he could no longer govern. Whitehall took the only possible course short of evacuating the province: it ordered in troops. Then, as if to cloud the whole issue, in 1769 Grafton's ministry retreated on the financial question and repealed all the Townshend duties except a symbolic levy on tea. Again, as in 1766, Parliament relinquished the revenue and preserved the contention.

How it could have ended the contention at that stage is difficult to see. The argument about money had been transformed into an argument about the right of the mother country to exercise any control over the colonies, a point that could not be resolved by argument. Few on either side of the Atlantic were yet thinking of the extreme solution, independence, or were ready to go to the other extreme and hold the empire together by force. But the quarrel had grown so far by the time North took office in 1770 that a mutually acceptable compromise between the extremes was probably out of the question. This was the fruit of the decade of wobbling.

THE COMING OF WAR (1770–1775)

By 1770 rebellion at home seemed almost as likely as rebellion in the colonies. North had no thought of yielding to the reformers. His central purpose was to allow the crown to exercise the powers that it rightfully possessed according to his concept of Whig theory—to permit the king to guide policy through ministers who depended on his favor. At the price of alienating many old-guard politicians, North intended to found his administration on the support of a group known as the King's Friends, those members of Parliament whose loyalty or self-interest made them willing to give the sovereign his way. At a time when the whole parliamentary system was in bad odor with the public, this was a dangerous course.

A critic of the government, who signed himself with the pen name of Junius, pointed out the danger in no uncertain terms. "One particular class of men," he wrote, "are permitted to call themselves the King's Friends, as if the body of the people were the King's enemies. . . . Edward and Richard the Second made the same distinction between the collective body of the people and a contemptible party who surrounded the throne. The event of their mistaken conduct might have been a warning to their successors." If his readers had forgotten the deposition and murder of those two Plantagenets, he reminded them of the more recent past. Now that the royal prerogative was being exercised *through* Parliament, he declared, it was even more dangerous than when the Stuarts had exercised it against Parliament; and the remedy was the same. King George, "while he plumes himself upon the security of his title to the crown, should remember that, as it was acquired by one revolution, it may be lost by another."

Junius, like so many who use the past for predicting the future, was disappointed in his expectation; George did not provoke revolution at home. But he did provoke a bitter struggle there, and one that affected the coming revolution in America. His attempt to control Parliament and his ministers' attempt to retain Parliament's control over the colonies were necessarily interrelated: those who opposed one tended to oppose the other and to see in American resistance the best hope of maintaining the traditional British constitution. Chatham subsequently expressed this point in his famous comparison of the colonies with Samson: "America, if she falls, will fall like the strong man; she will embrace the pillars of the state, and pull down the constitution along with her."

North had no more intention of subverting the constitution than he had of reforming it. He looked on himself as a conservative, and the last thing he wanted to do was to rouse popular passions on either side of the Atlantic. At the start of his administration the coming crisis in America was only a small cloud on the horizon. Grafton's repeal of the Townshend duties appeared to have soothed contention with the colonies, but the appearance was deceptive. Both the troops that still garrisoned Boston and the one remaining duty, that on tea, were symbols of the basic issue that had been raised—an issue that no government could ignore for long. North soon persuaded himself that he had found a way to resolve it to the satisfaction of all concerned. The East India Company was compelled by law to ship its tea to England for reexport to America; if it were permitted instead to ship directly from the Orient, the reduced cost of transportation would more than offset the surviving and symbolic duty on tea. The Americans would then buy cheaper tea and in the process be painlessly taxed. This seemed to be the way to kill three birds with one stone—to make a profit for the East India Company, to conciliate the colonists by lowering the price of tea, and to induce them to accept the principle of indirect taxation. The proposal was well meant, and it led straight to war.

North, like most of his predecessors, was ignorant of colonial realities. Cheaper tea threatened not only the powerful smuggling interest in America but also legitimate dealers, who would have to dispose of their unsold stocks at a loss. Far more important, the colonists were quite able to recognize Greeks even when bearing gifts—to discern the principle of a tax, no matter what saving it might bring. Tea had become a symbol in Whitehall. It now became a symbol in Boston, when raiders dressed as Indians boarded the East India Company ships and dumped their cargoes into the harbor. The Boston Tea Party was open defiance, and the quarrel entered a new phase. Few had foreseen the challenge, fewer still had desired it, but, once it was made, Lord North's government had no alternative to meeting it.

Events marched fast to a climax. What the colonists called the Intolerable Acts closed the port of Boston until compensation was paid for the tea and remodeled the charter of Massachusetts. These actions had to be backed by force, and the only available troops were those that had been garrisoning the wilderness. Ever since 1768 they had been moving eastward to curb the growing discontent on the seaboard, and now Whitehall had to find another way of keeping peace among the Indians and—the other side of the same coin—excluding the land-hungry colonists. Its solution was the Quebec Act of 1774, which had a dual purpose: to detach the French Canadians from their southern neighbors by concessions to Roman Catholicism, and to give control of the wilderness to the only authority on the spot that had shown some aptitude for the job, the government of Quebec. The effect was to intensify antagonism in the thirteen colonies, which again felt themselves encircled on the north and west by their old enemies, the French.

The Intolerable and Quebec acts, like so many measures that came out of London in those years, constituted a policy that looked well on paper but had no solid foundation. A realistic policy is one that can be implemented, and the means of implementation did not exist. The French Canadians, even if they had the will, lacked the power to police the wilderness, just as the handful of British troops in Boston lacked the power to coerce Massachusetts. And Massachusetts, it soon became clear, was not alone. In September 1774 representatives of all the colonies except Georgia met in the First Continental Congress to concert means of resistance. Now that North's government had taken the strong line in words, the logic of events forced it to back up the words.

That logic the cabinet would not see. General Gage, commander in chief in America and governor of Massachusetts, was insisting that he needed an army. He was in a panic, the ministers concluded, and really needed only a few stalwart subordinates to strengthen his nerve. Consequently they sent him, along with a handful of reinforcements, three major generals—William Howe, John Burgoyne, and Henry Clinton—who were destined to play crucial parts in losing the war that London still hoped to avoid. When the three landed in Boston in May 1775, that war had already begun. Gage's unsuccessful attempts to seize the colonists' supplies at Lexington and Concord had raised an impromptu army against him, and he was cooped up in the peninsula of Boston. In June the rebels occupied an adjacent peninsula, from which their guns could have made the town untenable. General Howe, sent to dislodge them, showed as much courage as stupidity in leading his troops directly against their breastworks; by the time he won the Battle of Bunker Hill it had cost him almost half his force. These "banditti," as British officers called the enemy, knew how to shoot.[2]

---

[2]Three modern studies of the British side of the struggle that began at Lexington and Bunker Hill are Piers Mackesy, *The War for America, 1775–1783* (1964), William B. Willcox, *Portrait of a General: Sir Henry Clinton in the War of Independence* (1964), and Franklin and Mary Wickwire, *Cornwallis: The American Adventure* (1970). For a full history of military operations see Christopher Ward, *The War of the Revolution,* John R. Alden, ed., 2 vols. (1952), and for a briefer and more readable account Willard M. Wallace, *Appeal to Arms: A Military History of the American Revolution* (1951).

THE CIVIL WAR (1775–1778)

In the aftermath of Bunker Hill, royal authority crumbled throughout the colonies. Royal governors either took refuge on shipboard, where the navy could protect them, or fled home to England. The war thus opened with a massive British defeat, much as the American Civil War, eighty-six years later, opened with a massive Union defeat: in both cases the rebels secured, at a stroke, control of virtually the entire area of rebellion. Lord North's government, like President Lincoln's, had to reverse a verdict already rendered, by attacking the enemy on their own ground, evoking support from those who were loyal but cowed, splitting the rebellion into parts, and extinguishing it piecemeal. The only possible British road to victory was to take the offensive and drive it home.

Britain began with some great advantages. The available British army, although small, was an effective fighting machine: the notion that rebel Minutemen and militia, fired by the Spirit of '76, could stand up to British regulars in a pitched battle in the open is one of the myths about the war. Britain had vastly greater financial resources than the colonists, and a functioning governmental system, in contrast to the improvised and discordant authorities in the states and the Continental Congress. Last and perhaps most important, for the first three years the Royal Navy had unchallenged command of the coast. The British were consequently able to blockade, to move their troops by sea faster than the rebels could move theirs by land, and to attack when and where they pleased. Exploiting this advantage might well have won them the war.

But they were also laboring under a host of difficulties. The most insidious was the fact that they had no logical war aim. Military victory in itself is not such an aim, because the only reason to win a war is to produce a more favorable postwar situation; and here the British had little hope. If they suppressed the rebellion, what then? Garrisoning the colonies in perpetuity promised intolerable and purposeless expense; an empire held by force would not be worth holding. Whitehall was therefore compelled to seek some form of compromise peace, and hence to combine military pressure with conciliation. But a general instructed to fight with one hand and to negotiate with the other was unlikely to succeed with either, for the aims were incompatible. There was, furthermore, no real basis for negotiating. If the British gave up their claim to authority they would give up what they were fighting for. On the other hand, if they refused to surrender effective authority they would preclude any compromise. The outbreak of hostilities, in short, plunged the British government into a dilemma that was logically insoluble.

The way to wage the war was almost as hard to determine as the purpose of waging it. The effort to relieve the British taxpayer's burden by increasing colonial revenue had brought on the rebellion, which could not be quickly suppressed without adding greatly to the tax burden to support a large army and navy. The various groups of the opposition in Parliament were either against the war or lukewarm about it, and the surest way to weld them together and provide them with allies was to demand new taxes. Hence the ministry, in order to survive, had to make war economically. But economy meant at least a slow decision, which was dangerous for quite another reason: the likelihood of foreign intervention increased with every month that hostilities lasted, for France and Spain were waiting to learn whether the rebellion was serious enough to offer them a reasonable chance of revenge on Britain. With a restive Parliament on the one hand, and the menace of the Bourbon powers on the other, the government was caught between the devil and the deep blue sea.

A strong cabinet, strongly led, might have silenced the peacemongers and rallied the waverers at home, as President Lincoln's administration did in 1861, and steeled the country to fight a civil war. But Lord North was too timid and self-deprecating to keep his subordinates in hand: they went their own ways while he begged repeatedly and in vain for the king's permission to resign. George, rather than North, held the government together, although he knew even less than his minister about how to run a war. Responsibility for its conduct therefore devolved largely on two officials, the earl of Sandwich and Lord George Germain. Sandwich was the First Lord of the Admiralty, the civilian head of the navy; Germain, in the recently created post of secretary of state for the American colonies, made himself the civilian head of the army. Between them they were a gift without price to the American cause.

Lord Sandwich, a rake and a former friend of John Wilkes, had had long experience of naval administration. But it had taught him neither strategic sense nor how to discover and promote fighting admirals; he was content with humdrum ideas and timorous commanders. Germain, the American secretary, had taken a new name since the Seven Years' War: he was the Lord George Sackville who had been court-martialed and cashiered from the army after the Battle of Minden.[3] The officers who now served under him remembered his past disgrace, and he did little to earn their respect. His principal talent in directing military operations was that of evading responsibility for those he suggested. He had slightly more taste than Sandwich for aggressive strategy, but no more gift for finding aggressive commanders. Both men played favorites and contributed to spreading the factionalism of Whitehall throughout the armed services.

Generals and admirals were gentlemen even before they were officers, and many of them did not scruple to put their dignity or political opinions ahead of their professional duty. Some refused to serve because they disapproved of the ministry or the war or both; others served so half-heartedly that they were suspected of "opposition principles," which meant sympathizing with the enemy. Commanders frequently asked to resign; if the government felt compelled to let them do so, they were likely to reappear at home, often as members of Parliament, to air their caustic criticisms. The

---

[3]For Germain's disgrace see Chapter 6.

oligarchy was a house divided, and the division ran from London to the army's headquarters and the admiral's quarterdeck.

By the spring of 1776 the administration had at last realized that it faced a full-scale war and had made preparations accordingly. British troops were inadequate in numbers for the job ahead; they had been augmented by mercenaries from various German states, whom the Americans lumped together under the hated name of Hessians. General Howe had replaced Gage as commander in chief in the autumn of 1775; he was now provided with a force of some 30,000 men, the largest that Britain had ever sent overseas, and was supported by a strong fleet under his older brother, Viscount Howe. The objective was New York. Boston, threatened by artillery that the Americans had captured at Fort Ticonderoga and carried across New England, had already been evacuated; in the coming campaign the Howes intended to seize Manhattan as a base for controlling the lower Hudson, while General Carleton, the governor of Canada, advanced south from the St. Lawrence by way of Lake Champlain to the upper Hudson. New England would thus be cut off from the rest of the rebel colonies.

General Washington, the new American commander in chief, decided to defend Manhattan by immuring his army on it. The decision should have been fatal to him: his troops were hopelessly inferior to their opponents in quality and numbers, and Lord Howe's ships commanded the surrounding water. But General Howe was a slave to orthodoxy. After the lesson of Bunker Hill he dreaded risking his precious regulars in battle, and in any case he was much more interested in gaining territory at low cost than in destroying the enemy force. He did destroy a part of it in August 1776 in the Battle of Long Island, but a subordinate had planned the action, and Howe had only grudgingly fallen in with the plan. He then maneuvered Washington out of New York, into Westchester, and eventually across the Hudson, all without serious bloodshed. Meanwhile a small American flotilla on Lake Champlain, improvised by the energy of Benedict Arnold, had turned back Carleton's advance from Canada. This was scarcely the way to achieve a quick decision.

The rebel army, almost in spite of its commander, remained intact; the king's army, thanks primarily to its commander, won an island and lost the best chance it was ever to have of winning the war. The results of the campaign reflected little glory on either side and bore out the acid comment of a British observer: "Any other general in the world than General Howe would have beaten General Washington, and any other general in the world than General Washington would have beaten General Howe."

Yet in the week before Christmas 1776, British victory seemed only a matter of time. Washington's army, even though it still existed, had been driven into Pennsylvania, surrendering New Jersey and lower New York to the enemy. To protect his new gains Howe had established posts, manned by Hessians, along the Jersey shore of the Delaware, but he was too confident to be cautious, and it never occurred to him that Washington could be dangerous. Washington himself thought that the game might well be up, but he had one more play. On Christmas night he ferried his ragged troops across the Delaware and captured the Hessian garrison of Trenton. On January 2, 1777, the British counterattacked and pinned him against the river, but during the night he slipped away to Princeton, destroyed a British force there, and vanished into the New Jersey hills. This was a different Washington from the general of the previous summer. In little more than a week he had revived a dying cause, and so changed the face of the war.

But the British were undeterred by their small taste of defeat. Their main forces were unimpaired, and for the summer campaign of 1777 they planned an even greater effort—in two parts. One was an advance from Canada to the upper Hudson under the command of General Burgoyne, the dapper soldier-playwright known as Gentleman Johnny. The other part should have been, according to all the dictates of common sense, a move by Howe with the main army from New York up the Hudson to meet Burgoyne, but it was nothing of the sort. Sir William (the commander in chief had recently been knighted) determined instead to leave only a small detachment on Manhattan under his second in command, Sir Henry Clinton, and take the rest of the army by sea to the Chesapeake for an attack on Philadelphia. Burgoyne, he airily supposed, could look after himself. Germain agreed; instead of listening to those who tried to warn him that such dispersion of force was stupid, he adopted Howe's and Burgoyne's mismatched plans without a thought for their incongruity.

Howe's campaign was a thorough success. Washington tried to defend Philadelphia, to no better effect than when he had tried to defend New York. By late autumn his army, soundly defeated, was forced into winter quarters at Valley Forge. But meanwhile the British suffered a disaster on the Hudson that outweighed their gains in Pennsylvania. Burgoyne's invasion ignored the fundamental requirements of supply: as he advanced southward his communications with Canada were stretched to the breaking point, and he could not establish communication with New York by way of the Hudson; an American army stood in his path, and American forts barred the river. By early October he was marooned at Saratoga, unable to continue, to retreat through the wilderness, or to exist where he was. Sir Henry Clinton, on Manhattan, learned of his plight and made a desperate effort to fight his way up river to save him. But the odds were insuperable, and Burgoyne was by then beyond help. On October 17 he surrendered.

Saratoga was decisive, not in America but in Europe. For some time the court of Versailles had been giving the rebellion surreptitious aid and watching its progress with calculating eyes; did it or did it not provide the opportunity for revenge that the French had been craving since 1763? Even if it did, would intervention be wise? "The spirit of revolt, wherever it breaks out," said one of Louis XVI's chief ministers, "is always of dangerous example." Ministerial policy, nevertheless was moving steadily if hesitantly toward intervention; Burgoyne's surrender was only the final inducement. The rebels by then had proved that they were able to maintain themselves, and the chance of recouping French prestige by helping them seemed to outweigh the menace of their ideas. In March 1778 Versailles announced the signing of a treaty with the infant United States.

THE WORLD WAR (1778–1783)

French intervention changed the whole character of the struggle. What had been a civil war fought on the American seaboard became a world war, fought from India to the Caribbean. Spain was expected to join France, and did so in 1779, leaving Britain for the first time faced with a coalition but without an ally of its own. The crux of the fighting was no longer on land but at sea. There the British, thanks to the revival of the French navy, faced formidable opposition in their task of guarding the outposts of empire and supporting the armies in America. Their best chance of victory was to revive Pitt's earlier strategy of blockade in European waters, but the numerical odds made this far more difficult than it had been twenty years before. Everything hinged on whether daring and skill could compensate for too few ships of the line.

The first months after the French announcement proved that daring, and even clear thinking, were in short supply at Whitehall. The Admiralty permitted the French Mediterranean fleet to sail from Toulon, pass the Straits of Gibraltar unopposed, and make for North America; the British commanders there were not sent timely reinforcement or even timely warning. Instead the cabinet made two moves. It dispatched a commission to America to negotiate peace at almost any price short of independence; it commanded the army to evacuate Pennsylvania and retreat to New York by sea, and did not bother to alter this plan when it learned that a French fleet was arriving off the coast. The government did everything possible, in short, to arrange for failure. It told the Americans, by the retreat from Pennsylvania, that its peace overture was based on weakness. It ordered the army to sea, in vulnerable transports, when enemy ships of the line were in the offing. It did nothing to forewarn, let alone forearm, the responsible commanders.

Sir William Howe had recently resigned, and the army was in the hands of Sir Henry Clinton. Although he was a far more contentious and difficult person than the easygoing Howe, Clinton was fully his equal as a tactician and far abler as a strategist. Sir Henry's naval colleague was still Lord Howe, who was waiting for his successor's arrival from England before following his brother into retirement. The admiral's presence was a lucky accident: he was the one competent naval chief who served in America during the war. He and Clinton between them saved what was left of the British position.

Sir Henry took liberties with his instructions. He marched the army overland to New York, engaging Washington en route in an inconclusive battle, and joined Howe and the fleet at New York just when the French arrived off the harbor. The enemy commander refused to attack in the face of Howe's naval dispositions and sailed off instead to capture a British post in Rhode Island. Howe thwarted him there, by a mixture of determination and good luck, and soon afterward the French left for the West Indies. The campaign had produced no gain for either side, but the British were left in possession of New York and Rhode Island. Their peace overture was contemptuously rejected. The commissioners, with such little dignity as they could muster, sailed home from their fool's errand.

The next year, 1779, was equally inconclusive. Clinton planned an elaborate campaign around Manhattan, which came to nothing because his promised reinforcements did not arrive from England in time; the French fleet reappeared, this time off Georgia, which the British had recently garrisoned, and was repulsed in an attack on Savannah. Meanwhile Clinton was gathering his meager strength for a new move. He was convinced that the war could be won only by organizing support from the American loyalists, or Tories, although every effort to find such support in New England and the middle colonies had failed. The one area where loyalist sentiment had not yet been seriously tested was the South, and there he decided to go. In order to obtain the necessary troops he evacuated Rhode Island, leaving the British nothing in the north except Manhattan, and on Christmas Day he sailed with his army for South Carolina. He thereby opened the phase of the war that ended at Yorktown.

His decision to go south was a dangerous gamble. It meant dividing his forces between New York and the Carolinas at a time when enemy sea power might cut his waterborne communications. He knew that the Admiralty could not or would not confine the French to European waters and prevent their sending fleets overseas. The most it would do, when such a fleet sailed, was to detach what it hoped was an equivalent squadron, in what it hoped would be sufficient time, to what it hoped was the point of danger. This slapdash method of defense had failed to protect New York in 1778 or Savannah in 1779. Whether it could now protect armies separated by hundreds of miles of seaboard remained to be seen.

Clinton opened his campaign for South Carolina with a brilliant victory in May 1780, when he surrounded and captured Charleston and its garrison. But immediately afterward he learned that another French squadron, this time accompanied by troops, was about to establish a base in Rhode Island. The news, which came to him from Benedict Arnold, who was already planning to betray the colonists' cause, necessitated Sir Henry's returning at once to New York. He had to turn over the southern operations to his second in command, Earl Cornwallis, whom he neither liked nor trusted. The earl was popular in the army, and as brave as he was ambitious. But he was also headstrong and had no more strategic sense than a charging bull; to leave him in virtually independent command was an invitation to trouble.

Clinton and the naval chief who had succeeded Howe, Admiral Arbuthnot, returned to a summer of frustration at New York. First they learned that the French had landed troops in Rhode Island, commanded by the Comte de Rochambeau. Then, when the admiral left to reconnoiter the enemy position in Narragansett Bay, he and Sir Henry spent two months quarreling about what they were going to do. In the end they did nothing. Next came the climax of Benedict Arnold's conspiracy to betray West Point, the new fortress guarding the Hudson. The colonists discovered the plot by accident and captured and hanged Clinton's emissary and close friend, John André; Arnold escaped to New York and was commissioned a British brigadier general. Although Clinton thus acquired one of the ablest commanders on either side, he could never make good use of him because Arnold was distrusted. British regular officers had little love for loyalists as colleagues, and none at all for a turncoat.

In December, nevertheless, Clinton gave Arnold command of an expedition to the Chesapeake. The progress of the southern campaign necessitated establishing a post on the bay, where a small body of troops supported from the sea could cut overland communication between Washington's army in the North and American forces in the Carolinas. Arnold established himself at Portsmouth, Virginia, and in March 1781 he was almost captured there in a combined attack by Washington and the French fleet from Rhode Island. The latter was defeated at sea by Admiral Arbuthnot, and the Franco-American operation collapsed. But seven months later it was repeated on a larger scale against Cornwallis.

By the spring of 1781 Cornwallis was turning his eyes toward Virginia, for he had had more than enough of campaigning further south. After securing what he thought was control of South Carolina in 1780, he had embarked on an offensive through the back country of North Carolina, where, out of touch with the sea, he had to live off the countryside and hence had to move his army from place to place. He could never stop long enough in any one area to organize loyalist support and so consolidate his gains. He could only strike blows in the air, like Burgoyne on his march to Saratoga; and the earl was pitted against a far abler opponent than Gentleman Johnny had met. Nathanael Greene, the American commander in the South, had a gift for winning campaigns by retreating. Cornwallis chased him to the border of Virginia, defeated him in battle in March 1781, and then, desperate for supplies, fled to the coast. His retreat left Greene free to move against South Carolina, which he promptly did. The earl, instead of following him, marched with the wreck of his army to join Arnold in Virginia.

This move was foolhardy. It endangered all that the British had won in the South, greatly increased their commitment to the Chesapeake, and for the first time brought Cornwallis within striking distance of the Franco-American forces in the North. The earl insisted that Virginia was the key to the war, and he made it so. He did it without even consulting his chief, who was furious but dared do nothing. The government, Clinton believed, was grooming Cornwallis to succeed him, and the prospect paralyzed Sir Henry's will; he would neither resign to the man he detested nor exert authority over him. This failure of leadership, like Pitt's in 1766, had serious consequences. For the remainder of the campaign, which was the crisis of the war, the army had no unity of command and therefore of purpose.

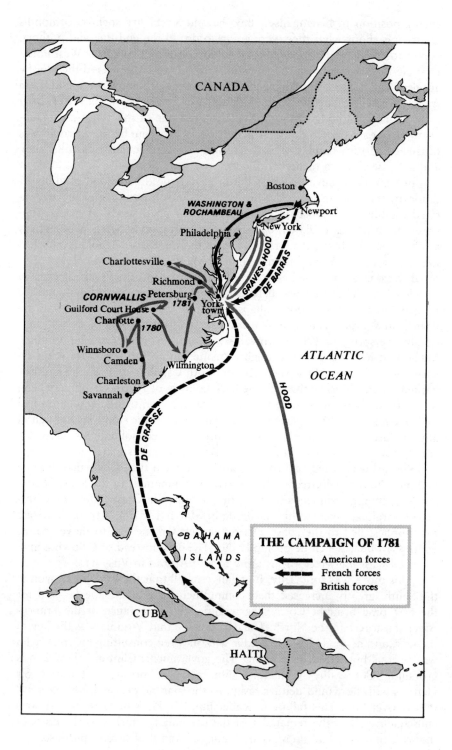

CANADA

Boston

WASHINGTON &
ROCHAMBEAU

Newport

New York

Philadelphia

Charlottesville

Richmond

CORNWALLIS Petersburg

Guilford Court House

Charlotte

1781

York-
town

1780

Winnsboro

Camden

Wilmington

Charleston

Savannah

GRAVES & HOOD

DE BARRAS

HOOD

ATLANTIC
OCEAN

DE GRASSE

BAHAMA

ISLANDS

THE CAMPAIGN OF 1781

American forces
French forces
British forces

CUBA

HAITI

In August 1781 Cornwallis grudgingly obeyed an order from Clinton to establish a post at Yorktown. By that time the British forces were divided into three widely separated contingents: in South Carolina, at Yorktown, and on Manhattan. Greene was threatening the first, and Washington and his French ally, Rochambeau, had the choice of attacking the second or the third. They chose Yorktown and proceeded to capture it by one of the most brilliant combined operations of the eighteenth century.

Its success rested on French sea power. Admiral de Grasse had recently reached the West Indies from France with a fleet that outnumbered the British West Indian squadron, and he now offered to bring his entire line of battle to the Chesapeake. Washington and Rochambeau eagerly accepted. They prepared to march overland to Virginia, while the small French squadron at Rhode Island sailed to join de Grasse and give him an overwhelming superiority. French ships would close the mouth of the Chesapeake and cut off Cornwallis from the army at New York, thus sealing his fate.

De Grasse sailed from the West Indies at the beginning of August. Admiral Sir Samuel Hood followed him with what he thought—quite mistakenly—was an equivalent force, to join the much smaller British squadron at New York. The commander of that squadron was no longer Arbuthnot, who had recently sailed for home, but Admiral Graves, a pleasant nonentity who was senior to Hood and therefore outranked him. At the end of August, when Hood arrived at New York, he persuaded Graves to sail with

THE SURRENDER OF GENERAL CORNWALLIS (1781) A contemporary French engraving shows the British commander handing his sword to George Washington. *(Library of Congress)*

him at once for the Chesapeake. The two admirals reached the entrance to the bay, and there they had a nasty shock: French ships came out to meet them in a seemingly endless line. Graves nevertheless attacked. Even though he was badly outnumbered, the battle was tactically no more decisive than most engagements of the period. Its strategic effect, however, was momentous. The British fleet fell back on New York and left Cornwallis to his fate.

The earl had still several weeks of grace before the enemy army arrived from the North to besiege him. In that time he might have escaped, but instead he did nothing except appeal to Clinton for help. At the beginning of October the siege began. Cornwallis made one abortive effort to break out and then on October 17—four years to the day since Burgoyne's capitulation—asked for terms; on October 19 he surrendered. After all his activity in marching and countermarching through the Carolinas and Virginia he had allowed himself to be caught in a trap, and his behavior in it had been, as Washington said, "passive beyond conception." That passivity brought the war in America to a close.

DISUNION AT HOME

The reason why the British now sought peace with their former colonies was not that they lacked the means to fight, but that they no longer had the will. For many months before Yorktown war weariness had been growing. Not since the news of Charleston had there been any real taste of victory, and troubles were pressing in four separate areas closer to home: Ireland was in turmoil; in Yorkshire a new movement for political reform was being organized; in Parliament itself North's opponents boldly attacked the power of the crown; London suffered the worst riots of the century.

Three generations of ascendancy in Ireland had imbued the Protestant Anglo-Irish landlords with a strong sense of self-confidence, yet the government in London continued to appoint their rulers and to manage their parliament. They were no longer fearful of their Roman Catholic tenants and neighbors, and they were willing in 1778 to modify the onerous laws against Catholic landholding if, in the process, they could obtain more self-government for Ireland. In part they were emulating the American rebels, in part they were responding to the economic problems the war had caused them. No longer could they export textiles or foodstuffs to France or to North America. After the Bourbon powers entered the war and London withdrew much of the army ordinarily stationed in Ireland, the Anglo-Irish leaders organized a volunteer force to defend the island against a possible enemy invasion and against American privateer John Paul Jones, who was capturing ships in Irish waters. Yet the army of eight thousand volunteers proved to be a double-edged sword: at a time when Irish merchants threatened a boycott of British goods, on the American model, the volunteer force could undermine British authority as readily as it could uphold it. Irish leaders like Henry Grattan now sought free trade as well as greater legislative independence, and they obtained substantial concessions. In 1780 the

British government opened the colonial and the Mediterranean trade to Irish merchants, while in 1782 it gave up the right to pass laws that bound Ireland or to amend those passed by the Dublin parliament. It also acknowledged the independence of Irish courts. For the moment only the monarch and the lord-lieutenant of Ireland (who served as both Irish chief-executive and as a member of the British cabinet) continued formally to link Ireland with Great Britain.

In the closing years of the war, North's parliamentary critics were increasingly willing to risk accusations of lack of patriotism. The true patriot, they insisted, opposed an unnecessary and unsuccessful war. They revived talk of the excessive power of the crown over the House of Commons and of ministers who fashioned majorities by corrupt means. In distant Yorkshire, squires inspired by an Anglican clergyman, Dr. Christopher Wyvill, organized county committees linked by a general assembly to petition Parliament on behalf of a reform program similar to that of John Wilkes in the 1760s. It featured lower taxes, annual parliamentary elections, and the addition of one hundred independent county members to the House of Commons. North's opponents in both houses, little as many of them liked such proposals, were encouraged by the discontent. In April 1780 a defiant House of Commons endorsed John Dunning's resolution "that the influence of the Crown has increased, is increasing, and ought to be diminished." Lord North seemed to be on the ropes, but there was no widely acceptable substitute; the influence of the crown remained sufficient to keep him in office.

The most violent example of domestic discord in 1780 was also related indirectly to the war. In order to encourage the enlistment of Scottish and English Roman Catholic soldiers, Lord North's government had permitted the passage in 1778 of a Roman Catholic Relief Act. Those Catholics who took an oath of loyalty to the king were permitted not merely to serve in his army but also to purchase and to inherit land. Meanwhile, an old statute, no longer enforced, that made Roman Catholic priests and schoolmasters subject to life imprisonment was also repealed. Parliament accepted these limited measures of toleration with little debate or fanfare, but within two years they aroused a ground swell of "No Popery" fears. By the spring of 1780, a group known as the Protestant Association was holding rallies petitioning for the repeal of the act of 1778. The organization was led by the eccentric younger son of a Scottish duke, the twenty-nine-year-old Lord George Gordon, who had long dreamt of spearheading a popular cause. When Parliament refused an immediate hearing to Gordon's anti-Catholic petition with its supposed 120,000 signatures, the crowd assembled outside the Palace of Westminster began to jostle peers, bishops, and some commoners. Within hours the "Gordon Riots" were spreading to various parts of the metropolis. Five days later, according to one observer, "London offered on every side the picture of a city sacked and abandoned to a ferocious enemy."

Although religion was clearly a pretext for many of the apprentices, petty criminals, and thrill seekers who were drawn into the riot, there was a pattern of sorts to the destruction that ensued. The first targets were the Roman Catholic chapels attached to the houses of foreign ambassadors; burning and looting then spread to the section of the city occupied primarily by Irish immigrants resented for their willingness to work for lower wages than English laborers. Next on the agenda were the homes of well-to-do Catholics, such as the owner of one of the city's largest distilleries, and the homes of public figures favorable to the Catholic cause or active in attempting to suppress the riot. The occasion was also taken to burn the Blackfriars Bridge tollbooths, at which those who crossed the Thames had to deposit half a penny each time. Newgate Prison was stormed and set afire and hundreds of prisoners set free. Other prisons were attacked as well, as were the homes of two symbols of authority: William Markham, the Archbishop of York, and Lord Mansfield, the Lord Chief Justice. A bonfire was made of Mansfield's unique legal library.

City magistrates soon lost all control of the situation. They were indeed fearful of instructing the army to shoot lest their own homes be sacked in turn. The tide turned only after the king had spurred Lord North's government to take a stand and after the attorney-general had formally ruled that army commanders had the right to use force whenever they witnessed law-breaking. After the army had fired on the rioters who were trying to attack the Bank of England and the London homes of Lord North and the Archbishop of Canterbury, the rioting soon died down. Suspicions were voiced against Americans and Frenchmen and members of the parliamentary opposition, but no evidence could be found that anyone had planned the riots as such. Although the youthful Charles James Fox insisted that he would "much rather be governed by a mob than by a standing army," even those members of Parliament most eager to oust North and most accustomed to speak in the name of "the people" were horrified by the consequences of popular frenzy. On this occasion even John Wilkes sided with the forces of order. The half-mad Lord George Gordon spent several months in the Tower of London but was ultimately found innocent of high treason. Some 160 rioters were eventually brought to trial, and twenty-five of these were hanged—for an outburst that had brought death to more than 300 Londoners and injury to many hundreds more.[4]

The Gordon Riots failed to topple Lord North's government, but the American war ultimately did. In 1780 the neutral maritime states formed an armed league to enforce against the Royal Navy their right to trade where they pleased; Britain's old friend the Netherlands had been goaded into entering the war against the British; the king's prestige was sinking, and his adamant refusal to consider American independence was coming to

---

[4]The story of the Gordon Riots is vividly recounted in Christopher Hibbert, *King Mob* (1958). Hibbert's account may be supplemented by Part III of George Rudé, *Paris and London in the Eighteenth Century* (1973).

THE GORDON RIOTS (1780)   *Top:* The Anti-Catholic petitioners march to the House of Commons on the afternoon of June 2; *bottom:* Newgate Prison is set aflame four nights later. *(Reproduced by courtesy of the Trustees of the British Museum)*

be more and more widely regarded as folly. The news of Yorktown was the last straw. North's government staggered on for a few more months, with the opposition in full cry. In March 1782 the House of Commons resolved that offensive war in America should end; a few weeks later North resigned. The king prepared to abdicate but then thought better of it. His policy was repudiated, however, and with it his dream of governing by manipulation. Defeat in America led to the decline of royal initiative at home.

THE PEACE SETTLEMENT

In September 1783 the peace treaties were signed at Paris and Versailles. Britain acknowledged the independence of the United States and its sovereignty as far west as the Mississippi; Florida and Minorca were ceded to Spain, and minor possessions in the West Indies and Africa to France. From the viewpoint of Versailles these gains were little to show for five years of fighting, but the Anglo-French war had been indecisive, and France was in a weak bargaining position. The French strategy had been inept. Instead of providing just enough assistance to keep the American war going and to distract the British with it until France had gathered in conquests of its own, the French had brought it to an end before they had anything to show for their efforts. The result was triumph for the United States but not for

"BLESSED ARE THE PEACEMAKERS" (1783)   A contemporary British engraving shows the belligerent powers in procession: Spain; France holding a rope tied around the neck of George III; Prime Minister Shelburne holding the preliminary articles of peace; America, holding a scourge; and Holland. (*Reproduced by courtesy of the Trustees of the British Museum*)

France. The French acquired little prestige, a burden of debt, and the virus of revolutionary ideas.

The acknowledgment of American independence was of course a schism in the old British empire, but it was not such a complete break with the mother country as it appeared to be at the time. In the fifteen years after the peace treaty, 1783–1798, Anglo-American trade doubled. The tradition of hostility between the two countries, born of the war and soon to be nourished by a second war in 1812, lasted for another century. Yet during that time the United States grew to nationhood within a framework of British power. The Royal Navy, after the War of Independence even more than before, controlled the egress from Europe and discouraged European states from gaining new footholds on the American continent. The United States was consequently free to expand westward without hindrance and, when the time became ripe, to acquire land from Florida to Louisiana and from Texas to California that had formerly been claimed by France and Spain. Expanding northward was another matter. Canada long remained a temptation to the growing republic and after 1814 produced periodic crises in Anglo-American relations. But the very fact that the crises did not produce war indicates that they were no more than surface turbulence.

Underneath that turbulence the United States and Britain had more in common than either one cared to acknowledge. Between the Canadian frontier and the West Indies Britain had no vital interest. London never seriously considered reconquering the former colonies or encircling them on the west as France had once tried to do, and it had no intention of permitting a rival to subjugate them in its stead. British command of the Atlantic acted as an effective, if often inadvertent, barrier against European interference in America and insulated the United States from outside dangers so effectively that it grew into a great power without possessing, except in its Civil War, the large army and navy that were the hallmarks of all other great powers. The British not only acknowledged a new republic in 1783; they also took on its protection, quite unintentionally, while it steadily inched its way westward into the empty space that stretched to the Pacific. Just as the failures of the Royal Navy contributed to the birth of the new nation, so the power of that navy was its mainstay in childhood and adolescence.

9 THE ONSET OF INDUSTRIALIZATION

*T*he years between the beginning of the American and the French revolutions witnessed a notable quickening in the pace of economic change. Such change in European history may be discerned from the tenth century on: in international trade fairs, the growth of medieval cities, the beginnings of transoceanic commerce in the fifteenth and sixteenth centuries, and the development of medieval and early modern textile weaving, shipbuilding, and coal mining. Yet changes in technology and methods of production came so imperceptibly that the average person rarely had the sense of being propelled from one economic world to another. Britons who were born in the 1750s or 1760s and lived into the 1830s, however, were acutely aware of change, so much so that historians have dubbed the era the Industrial Revolution.

Although that revolution involved no single event that corresponds to the Battle of Lexington or the fall of the Bastille, the metaphor has stood the test of time. It is a capsule description of the process whereby new methods of production and new sources of power enabled a given worker to produce an ever greater quantity of goods and through which a largely agricultural society transformed itself into one composed primarily of producers of manufactured goods and providers of services. In nineteenth-century England the quantity of goods and services per capita multiplied four times over. There was no precedent for the development of such self-sustaining growth: the process has been compared to an airplane that slowly gathers speed on the runway until it takes off and flies.[1]

The purposes of this chapter are to outline some of the explanations that have been advanced as to why the "takeoff" began in England and to call attention to both the characteristics and the consequences of industrialization during the late eighteenth and the early nineteenth century. First, however, it is necessary to describe the demographic conditions of the age.

THE EIGHTEENTH-CENTURY POPULATION EXPLOSION

In traditional accounts of the Industrial Revolution, the growth of population is discussed on the assumption that it was a side effect of economic

---

[1]Although W. W. Rostow's *The Stages of Economic Growth* (1960) has been criticized in detail, his notion of "the takeoff" has won widespread acceptance.

growth. Demographic historians of our day have become skeptical of that assumption. For one thing, they have realized that the mid-eighteenth-century onset of rapid population growth coincided with, rather than followed, industrialization. For another, they have noted that rapid population growth, regional variations notwithstanding, was a Europewide phenomenon and that in certain areas (like Ireland) it took place in a clearly unindustrialized society. This population explosion appears to have been the third period of significant growth during a thousand years of European history. The first, during the twelfth and thirteenth centuries, was followed by a decline in the fourteenth and fifteenth as a result of repeated epidemics of bubonic plague. The second period of population expansion, from the late fifteenth to the early seventeenth century, was followed by another century-long period of stagnation or even of decline.

The hard data on which population estimates rest tend to become less reliable the further into the past that demographers venture from 1801, the year of the first national census. Ever since the era of Henry VIII, Anglican vicars had been recording baptisms, marriages, and deaths, but many of their parish registers have not survived and not all have proved equally reliable: the births of the unbaptized and the deaths of non-Anglicans often went unrecorded. Demographers are in general agreement, however, that the population of England and Wales increased by at most 15–20 percent between 1695 and 1750, by 50–60 percent between 1750 and 1801, and by almost 100 percent between 1801 and 1851 (a half-century for which reliable census data do exist).

There is far greater agreement on the reality of this growth than on the reasons for it. A few historians have sought the solution in a rise in the birthrate because some women married earlier and had a larger number of children, yet a majority have found the answer primarily in a fall in the death rate. But why the fall? An earlier generation of historians suggested the decline of the "gin mania," better food, greater use of soap, and better medical care. More recent scholars have cast doubt on the reality of such improvements, at least for the mass of the population, until well into the nineteenth century. The "gin mania" probably did not affect all of Great Britain. Eighteenth-century medical advances made some people more comfortable but appear to have prolonged few lives; the practice of "bleeding," a remedy that only the well-to-do could afford, clearly did more harm than good, and hospital care was as likely to kill as to cure. The rapid growth of cities was as likely to create public health problems as to solve them.

Part of the answer may lie in the greater availability of food and more specifically in the introduction into the British diet of the potato, which Adam Smith characterized as "being peculiarly suitable to the health of the human constitution." The potato clearly stimulated Irish population growth and may have had a significant effect in England as well. Part of the answer also may lie in the widespread practice of inoculation against smallpox. Though the actual injection of smallpox virus was more dangerous than the method of vaccination developed by Dr. Edward Jenner in the 1790s, inoculation had by then prevented the death of thousands of Britons from the most dangerous infectious disease of the age. The taming of smallpox, the disappearance of bubonic plague from the British Isles after its last major outbreak in the 1660s, and the declining virulence of other infectious diseases, for reasons still unclear, meant that cumulative increases in population were no longer wiped out by epidemics. The consequent survival of just a few more infants per thousand people per year readily accounts for the overall increase that resulted.

The process of industrialization may therefore have had little to do with the beginnings of the eighteenth-century population explosion, but it had a great deal to do with the fact that, during the decades that followed, an era of decreasing mortality was not again followed by a period of rising mortality. What happened instead was the gradual working out of a two-century-long process now generally known as the demographic transition, during which there developed a wide gap between a still high birthrate and a much lower death rate. Before the change began in the mid-eighteenth century, birthrates and death rates ranged between thirty and forty per thousand per year. Birthrates were high despite the fact that the poor were encouraged to marry late or, if they were domestic servants or army recruits, not at all. Death rates were high because a majority of children failed to reach adulthood. A woman who lived to the age of forty-five might produce eight children in the course of a typical marriage, but only two or three of them could expect to survive infancy or childhood. By the time the demographic transition ended in Britain and much of Europe in the mid-twentieth century, both birth and death rates had dropped to between ten and twelve per thousand per year. Average life expectancy was sixty-five or more (rather than twenty-five to thirty), and a married woman with but two children might feel reasonably sure that both would reach adulthood.

A slowly growing population provides industrialists with workers for their factories and consumers for their products, whereas a population rising too rapidly can, as twentieth-century "third world" experience has demonstrated, handicap rather than encourage the accumulation of investment capital and the utilization of labor-saving devices. The population of late-eighteenth-century Britain was apparently growing at 1.5 percent per year, slowly enough to encourage industrial development but fast enough to pose a real challenge to the economy. A society with many more people to be fed, housed, and clothed may require a change of economic methods merely to maintain its standards. If it seeks to improve individual living standards while expanding in numbers, the challenge becomes greater still. The population explosion and the Industrial Revolution were at the outset independent phenomena, but they clearly became closely intertwined.[2]

---

[2]M. W. Flinn, *British Population Growth, 1700–1850* (1970); and H. J. Habakkuk, *Population Growth and Economic Development Since 1750* (1971), provide helpful brief introductions to the subject.

INDUSTRIALIZATION: THE PREREQUISITES

Historians may never resolve the problem of what particular factor triggered the eighteenth-century economic takeoff. What they do agree on is that a number of conditions had to be present to make possible the onset of industrialization: a supply of natural resources; a system of agriculture flexible enough to feed an increasing proportion of workers divorced from the land; a market sufficiently large and accessible to make the concentration of industry and large-scale division of labor worthwhile; the necessary capital to finance both the new industries and the roads and waterways on which products were transported; a social structure sufficiently elastic to permit large groups of people to shift occupation; and a social environment favorable to technological innovation and new enterprises.[3]

The natural resources most important for industrialization were coal and iron, and Great Britain was blessed with sizable deposits of both. Their location did much to determine the geography of industrial growth. At the same time the British Isles completely lacked what proved to be a highly significant natural resource: raw cotton. It had to be imported in increasing quantities from the American South.

A British population that doubled between 1750 and 1821 obviously required twice as much food to keep pace with mid-eighteenth-century dietary standards. It was during the late eighteenth and early nineteenth centuries that more land was brought into grain production and the methods of improvement outlined in Chapter 3—planting of turnips and clover rather than leaving arable land fallow, greater use of fertilizer, improved drainage—came into extensive use. One of the principal techniques for promoting more efficient production was the enclosure of the open fields in which the strips of different owners and tenant cultivators had been intermingled since time immemorial. The process of enclosure, which from Tudor times had been primarily of pastureland, during the 1760s and the half-century that followed was applied vigorously to the open fields used to grow grain: hundreds of private acts of Parliament empowered commissioners to cut through the tangle of property rights and, in effect, redistribute the land to its owners in compact rather than scattered parcels. The result could be beneficial to all who held valid title, though the expenses of enclosure (such as legal fees and the cost of hedge planting) tended to fall more heavily on the small landholder than the large. Cottagers without legal title to the land lost their accepted right to pasture pigs, cows, and geese on the manorial common, which their betters had appropriated.

> The law locks up both man and woman
> Who steals the goose from off the common,

---

[3]Until recently, historians seem to have been more concerned with the consequences than with the origins of the Industrial Revolution, but M. W. Flinn provides a compact introduction to the subject in *Origins of the Industrial Revolution* (1966), as does Peter Mathias in part I of *The First Industrial Nation* (1969).

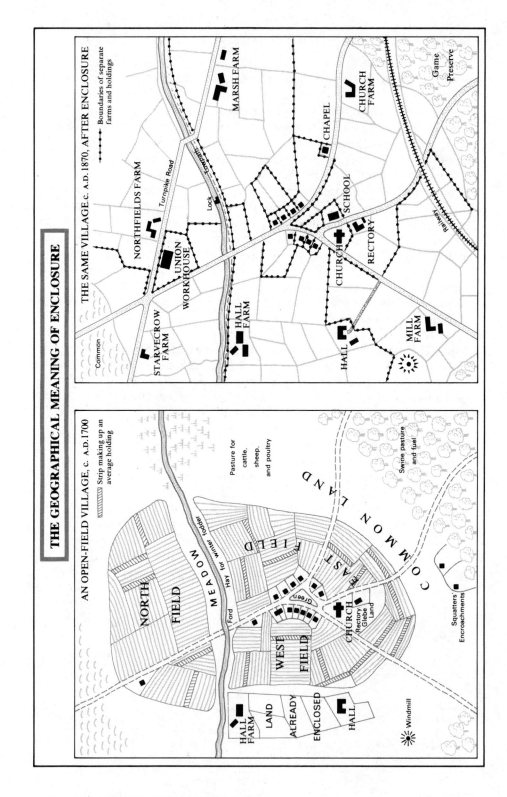

THE GEOGRAPHICAL MEANING OF ENCLOSURE

AN OPEN-FIELD VILLAGE, c. A.D.1700

Strip making up an average holding

NORTH FIELD

MEADOW

Hay for winter fodder

Ford

WEST FIELD

EAST FIELD

Green

CHURCH

Rectory Glebe Land

COMMON LAND

Pasture for cattle, sheep, and poultry

Swine pasture and fuel

Squatters' Encroachments

HALL FARM

LAND ALREADY ENCLOSED

HALL

Windmill

THE SAME VILLAGE c. A.D. 1870, AFTER ENCLOSURE

Boundaries of separate farms and holdings

MARSH FARM

CHURCH FARM

CHAPEL

Game Preserve

NORTHFIELDS FARM

Turnpike Road

Lock   towpath

SCHOOL

RECTORY

Railway

UNION WORKHOUSE

STARVECROW FARM

Common

HALL FARM

CHURCH

HALL

MILL FARM

But lets the greater felon loose
Who steals the common from the goose.

The long-term effects of enclosure were to increase the size of land-holdings and to concentrate them in fewer hands. Enclosure also helped make agriculture more efficient: the average yield per acre for English wheat was fifteen bushels in 1750 and twenty-seven a hundred years later. No mass depopulation of the rural areas occurred before the middle of the nineteenth century, but, as the number of people grew, so did the number of landless laborers, and their existence remained a bleak one. They worked long hours for little return, with scant hope of improving their lot; in times of distress they had to rely on the goodwill of the local overseers of the poor. The children of such laborers were increasingly likely to try bettering their status, either in London or in a growing number of factory towns.

At a time when transportation by water was far more economical than by land, it was an invaluable advantage for Great Britain to be an island. Adam Smith once estimated that 8 men sailing a ship between Edinburgh and London could transport as large a load as 50 wagons, with 100 men and 400 horses, could carry overland. The coastal seas by mid-century were supplemented by 1,000 miles of river that had been made navigable, and between 1760 and 1800 a network of 3,000 miles of canals was added, linking coal mines to ports and factories to customers. By 1790 London, Bristol, Birmingham, Liverpool, and Hull were all connected to one another by canals.

The canals were built mostly by joint-stock corporations, each authorized by a separate act of Parliament. Hundreds of roads also were constructed or improved by local turnpike trusts that were granted the authority to collect a toll from each driver. The typical eighteenth-century main road had been impressive only in name—the "king's highway." It was usually no more than a strip of cobblestone flanked on each side by dirt tracks. The parish had the responsibility to maintain roads, but, according to one pamphleteer, the condition of most had been "what God left them after the Flood." In contrast, as Lord Byron observed in Don Juan,

What a delightful thing's a turnpike road!
So smooth, so level, such a mode of shaving
The earth, as scarce the eagle in the broad
Air can accomplish, with his wide wings waving.

The largest actual market for industry was at home, but eighteenth-century Britons did not overlook the potential market beyond the seas. A mid-century boom in overseas trade that gave way to stagnation in the 1760s and 1770s—in part because of the American War of Independence—was followed by a new era of growth; the value of British exports doubled during the final fifteen years of the century.

Industrialization required not merely a large and accessible market; it also required capital. Funds could be derived both from profits on land—

THE CANAL AGE,
EARLY 19th CENTURY

INLAND NAVIGATION

BY CANAL AND RIVER AT ITS
GREATEST EXTENT

50   0   50
MILES

50   0   50   100
KILOMETERS

Inverness

Inverurie

Aberdeen

Caledonian Canal

Fort William

Edinburgh

Glasgow

NORTH

SEA

Newcastle

Carlisle

Kendal

Malton

IRISH

SEA

Preston

Leeds

York

Huddersfield

Manchester

Liverpool

Sheffield

Lincoln

Louth

Chesterfield

Chester

Nottingham

Grantham

Llangollen

Derby

Oakham

Shrewsbury

Leicester

Stamford

Nene R.

Norwich

Newtown

Wolverhampton

Birmingham

Bury St.
Edmunds

Northampton

Cambridge

Worcester

Bedford

Stratford

Colchester

Hay

Hereford

Brecon

Gloucester

Oxford

St. George's Channel

Newport

Thames R.

London

Swansea

Bristol

Reading

Cardiff

Rochester

Bath

Basingstoke

Croydon

Andover

Guilford

Tonbridge

Taunton

Glastonbury

Winchester

Torrington

Tiverton

Southampton

Exeter

ATLANTIC

OCEAN

Launceston

Liskeard

Tavistock

ENGLISH CHANNEL

which some landowners invested in canals and mines rather than in the enlargement of country houses—and from profits in commerce. The capital needs of the early factory owners were relatively modest, and in the course of the century more money was invested in roads, bridges, and canals than in factory buildings. Many late-eighteenth-century captains of industry plowed back much of their profit into the family business; others depended on a growing number of country banks to lend them operating capital.

The process of industrialization had noneconomic roots as well. A social environment that encouraged rather than discouraged innovation was essential, and the Royal Patent Office, which issued less than a dozen patents a year during the first half of the century, granted 36 in 1769, 64 in 1783, 107 in 1802, and 250 in 1825. Although the Enlightenment in England was accompanied by widespread complacency, many Englishmen and Scotsmen welcomed new inventions. Groups such as the Society for the Encouragement of Arts, Manufactures, and Commerce (1754) gave prizes to successful inventors, and even Parliament occasionally voted its thanks in monetary terms. Though a considerable gap often separated popular mechanics from theoretical science, it was as an instrument maker for the University of Glasgow that James Watt, the inventor of the first rotary steam engine, learned his trade.

Equally important was an environment favorable to an entrepreneur prepared to put new inventions to work and to mobilize capital and labor in new forms of organization. English society, hierarchical as it was, proved sufficiently adaptable to permit the wealthy merchant to buy a country seat and to have his children intermarry with the squirarchy; a fledgling industrialist might hope to do the same. Protestant dissenters, moreover, who

THE REGENT'S CANAL IN THE 1820s   A sketch by Thomas Shepherd.
(BBC Hulton Picture Library)

constituted less than 10 percent of the mid-century population, provided half of the notable inventors and entrepreneurs of the Industrial Revolution. Part of the reason was doubtless the relatively high quality of education provided by their academies, part the drive to excel economically in a society that tolerated religious minorities but did not grant them full social equality.

Entrepreneurs, whatever their religion, lived in a society in which many internal economic restraints had fallen into abeyance. British guilds were less powerful than on the continent, though sometimes powerful enough to cause industrialists to set up shop in rural areas outside guild control; in part for this reason, a relatively new industry like cotton developed more rapidly than an old industry like wool. Within Great Britain there were no tariff barriers and no chartered monopolies, a circumstance that explains why Adam Smith made free enterprise a formal philosophical condition for economic prosperity in his *Inquiry into the Origins and Nature of the Wealth of Nations* (1776). It was "the highest impertinence" for kings and ministers "to pretend to watch over the economy of private people." Let them cease imposing restrictions on commerce and industry, he argued, and limit themselves to providing for the national defense, the administration of justice, and the construction of large public works beyond the powers of individuals.

The British government was not completely isolated from the process of eighteenth-century industrialization, to be sure, but in contrast to most twentieth-century efforts to industrialize it took a passive role. The tariffs that formed part of the mercantilist tradition did provide protection from foreign competition for certain industries like cotton, linen, and shipbuilding. Patent laws might hamper economic growth by granting temporary monopolies to successful inventors, but they also gave publicity to new ways of doing things and a financial incentive to those who wished to support industrial research. The Bubble Act of 1720 continued to confine industrial enterprise to individual owners or partners, and the state clearly could have done more to provide the small-denomination coins that manufacturers needed to pay wages to their workers; it could also have imposed a minimum of public services on rapidly growing industrial towns. Yet it did, despite occasional rioting, foster a general sense of internal security in which new enterprises could develop. The legislation that made the parish responsible only for the poor who were born there tended to restrict the mobility of labor, but the Poor Law itself provided a safety net of sorts to those who became the victims of economic change.

INDUSTRIALIZATION: THE PROCESS

The availability of natural resources, the expandability of farm production, the presence of a sizable market and investment capital, a social environment favorable to innovation, and a government that served as a benevolent policeman—all helped to account for the late-eighteenth-century industrial

AN EARLY NINETEENTH-CENTURY ENGLISH COAL MINE The Boulton and Watt steam engine in the center is being used to lower miners into the mine and to raise coal out of it. *(Walker Art Gallery, Liverpool)*

"takeoff." The process itself is difficult to grasp, however, because almost every change influenced and was influenced by every other.[4] Take coal and iron and steam, for example. In mid-century an effective way was found to use coal, instead of wood, for smelting iron; until then, depletion of the forests had threatened to extinguish the iron industry. Coal mining also was threatened by water that leaked into the mines, and the deeper the mines went, the worse the problem became. The solution, as will soon be seen, proved to be steam pumps, which were eventually developed into steam engines. Thus steam helped to provide coal for the iron foundries, which in turn provided the metal for steam engines, while the coal mines provided fuel for the foundries and engines alike. Coal production increased from 3 million tons in 1700 to 10 million tons in 1800 and 25 million tons in 1830 (three-quarters of all the coal then mined in Europe), and the number of blast furnaces grew from less than 20 in 1760 to 372 in 1830. The three industries grew in such intimate relationship with each other that describing any one by itself is meaningless.

The process of change, nevertheless, can be most easily understood by concentrating on a single industry. The best focus is not coal or iron or steam engines or even the wool trade, which had so long been at the center

---

[4]The classical treatment of early industrialization is Paul Mantoux, *The Industrial Revolution in the Eighteenth Century in England,* rev. ed. (1928). Phyllis Deane, *The First Industrial Revolution,* 2nd ed. (1979), is a judicious up-to-date survey, while T. S. Ashton, *The Industrial Revolution, 1760–1830,* rev. ed. (1964), remains a concise and lucid modern account.

of the nation's economy, but an upstart—the manufacture of cotton cloth. Largely because it was an upstart, the cotton trade took an early lead in the race to industrialize and kept it for generations.

Cotton cloth of a sort had been manufactured by hand since the late seventeenth century in Lancashire, on the western slope of the Pennines. The primary reason why the industry grew up in that backward part of England was water: the prevailing winds from the Atlantic with their burden of rain, which make the west coast one of the wettest parts of the island, ensured both a reliable source of waterpower in the Pennine streams and a moist atmosphere in which the fragile cotton threads could be worked without breaking. Lancashire therefore became the cotton kingdom, with Manchester for its capital and Liverpool for its port.

The earliest incentive to cotton manufacture was cloth imported by the East India Company, which caught the fancy of the British public. The Company, intent on protecting its market from domestic competition, had the alliance of the wool trade, which wanted no rival textile industry. Early in the century these powerful vested interests secured legislation to discourage domestic cotton manufacture; but the industry throve in spite of laws that soon became dead letters. The early years of the cotton trade went far to determine its character. It attracted men of daring, who were tough and unconventional and ready to seize every opportunity for increasing their output. They had to be adventurers to make headway against the conservative woolen interest, which the state had monitored and cherished for centuries. They were self-made men, nurtured on open and even cutthroat competition, and wanted from the government neither regulation nor protection. By the 1780s they were already showing the spirit of what became Victorian free enterprise.

They were also beginning to challenge the economic predominance of wool. By now they had most of what they needed to increase production—market, capital, labor, and a food supply. The principal obstacle was technological: machines were not available for the entire manufacturing process, which at some stages was held to the snail's pace of the hand laborer. Just as a chain is no stronger than its weakest link, so the output of cloth is no faster than the slowest operation involved.

The revolution in the cotton trade was the progressive mechanizing of four main operations in producing cloth: harvesting and transporting the cotton; combing its matted fibers and spinning them into thread; weaving the thread into cloth; and lastly finishing and bleaching and dyeing the cloth for market. The first major improvements were made in weaving, and their introduction there revealed a basic characteristic of industrialization: accelerating what has been the slowest operation removes that bottleneck and accelerates the whole manufacturing process, but only up to the point where some other operation becomes a new bottleneck. The focus of improvement therefore shifts from one to another and back again in a never-ending battle for more output.

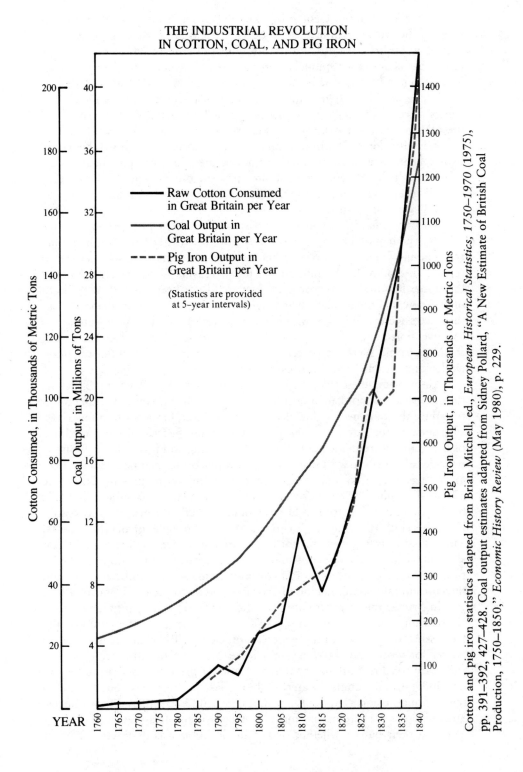

THE INDUSTRIAL REVOLUTION
IN COTTON, COAL, AND PIG IRON

Raw Cotton Consumed
in Great Britain per Year

Coal Output in
Great Britain per Year

Pig Iron Output in
Great Britain per Year

(Statistics are provided
at 5-year intervals)

Cotton Consumed, in Thousands of Metric Tons

Coal Output, in Millions of Tons

Pig Iron Output, in Thousands of Metric Tons

YEAR

Cotton and pig iron statistics adapted from Brian Mitchell, ed., *European Historical Statistics, 1750–1970* (1975), pp. 391–392, 427–428. Coal output estimates adapted from Sidney Pollard, "A New Estimate of British Coal Production, 1750–1850," *Economic History Review* (May 1980), p. 229.

At the accession of George II, when the cotton trade had still been confined to the workers' houses, the bottleneck had been weaving. The invention of an improved shuttle by John Kay in 1733 increased the productivity of the looms until four spinners were required to keep one weaver in thread. Spinning then became the bottleneck, and inventors tackled the problem of a spinning machine. By the time of the American Revolution two such machines driven by waterpower—one the brainchild of James Hargreaves and the other of Richard Arkwright—were in common use. They were far too expensive for domestic workers, and even capitalists could afford them only if they kept them in continuous operation: they therefore put them in factories to which the workers came in shifts. Before the end of the century hand laborers were an anachronism in cotton spinning, and the factory system was well established.

Weaving again became the bottleneck, but here progress was much slower. The hand loom, as improved by Kay, was vastly more complex than the spinning wheel; years passed before an effective machine was devised to replace the loom. In the interim the hand weavers were the aristocrats of the trade: for the very reason that they could not keep up with the output of the new spinning mills, their services were everywhere in demand. But their days were numbered. Manufacturers were becoming more clamorous for inventions, and inventors were becoming more adept. Before the end of the Napoleonic Wars the power loom was in operation for all but the finest cloths, and weaving was in transformation as spinning had been.

Mechanizing these two operations stimulated change elsewhere. Bleaching the cloth was temporarily a bottleneck, but by 1800 chemists had managed to reduce the time needed for bleaching from several months to a few days. The demand for raw cotton exceeded the supply because the old methods of harvesting were inadequate, until the New England inventor Eli Whitney provided the answer with his cotton gin. Raw cotton then poured into Britain in ever increasing quantities: less than 8 million pounds a year in the 1770s; 37 million in the 1790s; 100 million in 1815; 250 million in 1830, by which time the cotton industry employed 500,000 people, and cotton yarn and cloth constituted 40 percent of the total value of British exports. Thus, by the strange ramifications of cause and effect, the needs of Lancashire mills in the 1790s contributed to an American invention, which in turn contributed to the spread of cotton growing in the southern states and the concomitant strengthening of slavery—and so to the Civil War of 1861.

In Britain the transformation of the cotton trade was intimately associated with other changes in industry, of which the most dramatic was the harnessing of power. Until the reign of George III available sources of power for work and travel had not increased since the Middle Ages. The sources were three: animal or human muscles; the wind, operating on sail or windmill; and running water. Only the last of these was suited at all to the continuous operating of machines, and it had great disadvantages. Streams flowed where nature intended them to, and factories had to be located on their banks, whether or not the location was desirable for other reasons; even the most reliable waterpower, furthermore, varied with the seasons and disappeared in a drought. The new age of machinery, in short, could not have come into being without a new source of power that was both movable and constant.

The source had long been known but not exploited. Early in the century a pump had come into use in which expanding steam raised a piston in a cylinder, and atmospheric pressure brought it down again when the steam condensed inside the cylinder to form a vacuum. This "atmospheric engine," invented by Thomas Savery and vastly improved by his partner, Thomas Newcomen, embodied revolutionary principles, but it was so slow and wasteful of fuel that it could not be employed outside the mines for which it had been designed. In the 1760s James Watt perfected a separate condenser for the steam, so that the cylinder did not have to be cooled at every stroke; then he devised a way to make the piston turn a wheel and thus convert reciprocating into rotary motion. He thereby transformed an inefficient pump of limited use into a steam engine of a thousand uses. The final step came when steam was introduced into the cylinder to drive the piston backward as well as forward, thereby increasing the speed of the engine and cutting its fuel consumption. At long last the new source of power was fully harnessed.

Watt's steam engine was soon showing what it could do. It was liberating industry from dependence on running water: the factories did not have to go to the streams when power could come to the factories. The engine was eliminating water in the mines by driving efficient pumps, which made possible deeper and deeper mining. Iron manufacture, which had been starving for fuel while it depended on charcoal, now fed on a wealth of coal, while blast furnaces with steam-powered bellows were turning out more steel and iron for the new machinery. Steam was the motive force of revolution, as coal and iron ore were the raw materials. Matthew Boulton, Watt's partner in manufacturing steam engines at the great Soho Works near Birmingham, well understood the importance of his product. "I sell

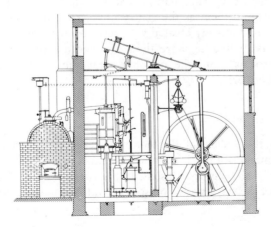

WATT'S STEAM ENGINE
A plan of the engine as perfected by 1787. *(The Science Museum, London)*

here, Sir," he proudly remarked to James Boswell, "what all the world desires to have—*power*."

By 1800 more than a thousand steam engines were in use in the British Isles, and Britain retained a virtual monopoly on steam-engine production until the 1830s. Steam power did not merely spin cotton and roll iron; it also promised to eliminate a transportation problem not fully solved by either canal boats or turnpikes. Boats could carry heavy weights, but canals could not cross hilly terrain; turnpikes could cross the hills, but the roadbeds could not stand up under great weights. Still another solution was needed, and the ingredients for it were close at hand. In some industrial regions heavily laden wagons, with flanged wheels, were being hauled by horses along metal rails; and the stationary steam engine was puffing in the factory and mine. Another generation passed before inventors succeeded in combining these ingredients, by putting the engine on wheels and the wheels on the rails, so as to provide a machine to take the place of the horse. But the railroad age was a logical, almost an inevitable, result of what had already happened in the eighteenth century.

At the close of that century industrialization was in no more than its initial stages. Canals were being built and roads improved; coal mining, iron manufacture, and the cotton trade were booming; and in some industrial processes, such as cotton spinning, machines were replacing hand labor, steam engines were replacing waterpower, and the factory system was firmly established. But only certain areas of the economy were affected as yet, and much of what the Victorians took for granted was still undreamed of in 1800. Steel, in contrast to iron, was a luxury because it could not yet be cheaply produced. The stationary steam engine was of limited efficiency, and the locomotive and steamship were unknown. Weaving, even in cotton, was done on the hand loom. Last but not least, the wool trade was scarcely touched by machinery and steam for a generation to come. Throughout the Napoleonic Wars, with bustling innovation on all sides—in the furnaces of the Midlands, the collieries of South Wales and Northumberland, the mills of Lancashire—wool spinners and weavers of Yorkshire and East Anglia went their old ways undisturbed. They had almost as little to do with the industrial world rising around them as the gentry of Jane Austen's novels. And yet industrialization had already created vast new economic resources, out of which Britain was to finance more than two decades of war and grow stronger in the process, until the nation emerged in 1815 with a power felt throughout the world.

THE SOCIAL CONSEQUENCES

Historians have viewed the Industrial Revolution as everything from an economic triumph that made Britain, for a time, the most influential country in the world to a social disaster that fastened "the curse of Midas" and "the moral atmosphere of the slave trade" on society and that in the process entailed "suffering and the destruction of older and valued ways of life."[5] The disagreement results in part from the fact that for some historians "the Industrial Revolution" refers to anything that happened in Great Britain between, say, 1760 and 1830, while for others, it involves only those conditions directly affected by the growth of industry—and many aspects of British society clearly had not been, even by 1830.

The most obvious consequence of industrialization was the growth of large factory towns like Manchester, the cotton capital, Liverpool, which was rapidly becoming the nation's second port, and Birmingham, the chief center for metal wares. Such communities all grew from villages to large cities in the course of a few decades in a manner for which there was no precedent in earlier eras, and Greater London attained a population of 1,100,000 by 1801 and 1,600,000 twenty years later. Cities that expand so rapidly are unlikely to develop civic amenities and the necessary public services at a comparable pace, and many a factory town became a drab and smoky place where redbrick rowhouses stretched mile after mile about the town center.

Factory organization necessarily required not merely a high degree of division of labor—found on occasion in domestic industry but rarely in farming—but also a clear-cut separation of roles and functions between employers, foremen, and employees. An economic relationship that, whatever its reality, could be looked back on as benevolently paternal often became coldly institutional. Factory life also required a psychological adjustment for the first generation of workers in industry. The factory whistle and the factory clock exerted a type of discipline and an emphasis on punctuality for which the eighteenth-century church bell provided no precedent. Artisans once independent were now guided by the rhythms of a machine, and the fact that the factory operative was paid better and more regularly than the worker in domestic industry or the rural laborer may not have provided sufficient recompense. Industrialization, furthermore, while enhancing the

[5]The first two quotations come from J. L. and Barbara Hammond, *The Rise of Modern Industry* (1925), one of several frequently reprinted volumes that portray the lower classes almost solely as victims rather than as beneficiaries of industrialization. The third quotation comes from E. P. Thompson, *The Making of the English Working Class* (1963), a compendious attempt to see the Industrial Revolution from the vantage point of the articulate or semiarticulate artisan and laborer. Enlightening as it is, the evidence fails to confirm the book's thesis: that by 1830 there existed a single quasirevolutionary English working class. Nor do Thompson and his disciples explain how a nation whose population was tripling in size during less than a century could house, clothe, and feed so many more people while preserving its old "moral economy" and retaining its old artisan traditions. Another "pessimist" is E. J. Hobsbawm, the author of *Industry and Empire* (1968). The first volume of J. H. Clapham's *An Economic History of Modern Britain*, 3 vols. (1930–1938), and the books by Ashton and Mathias cited earlier, take a far less gloomy view of the social consequences of industrialization. P. A. M. Taylor, ed., *The Industrial Revolution in Britain: Triumph or Disaster?*, 2nd ed. (1970), and A. J. Taylor, ed., *The Standard of Living in Britain in the Industrial Revolution* (1975), provide introductions to the historical controversy.

opportunities of skilled artisans like mechanical engineers, devalued the traditional skills of others like the hand loom weavers, who were demoted in both status and well-being once the power loom had been perfected.

In a factory atmosphere a sense of class-consciousness began to develop among some workers. Francis Place, the London tailor who became a noted political reformer in the 1820s, complained in 1834 of the tendency to jumble together, "as the 'lower orders,' the most skilled and the most prudent workmen with the most ignorant and most imprudent labourers and paupers, though the difference is great indeed, and indeed in many cases will scarce admit of comparison." The vast majority of factory workers could read and a majority could write,[6] and large workplaces fostered the exchange of ideas and, on occasion, the formation of large trade unions. Writing about the cotton industry in the 1820s, R. Guest took note of this sharpening of wits among factory operatives: "from being only a few degrees above cattle in their scale of intellect they became Political Citizens."

For the social reformers of the 1830s, child labor in the factories was the greatest blot on the face of industry. Such labor in the cotton mills was common: in 1835, 40 percent of the mill workers were under eighteen, 16 percent under thirteen. Some children worked there because as pauper orphans they had been apprenticed by their parish overseers; a majority were employed because their parents found the children's wages, which were paid to the parents, a useful and often necessary addition to the family income. Child labor in workshop or farm was not a nineteenth-century novelty but a powerful eighteenth-century tradition adapted to new circumstances. Reformers were as much troubled by the presence of women workers as by that of children of both sexes and feared the danger to morals as much as to health. Yet many young women found factory work a liberating experience that freed them either from the supervision of parents, in the overcrowded cottages in which lace making, glove making, straw plaiting, and similar domestic industries were still carried on, or from the authority of master and mistress in domestic service.[7]

The new industrial system was not solely responsible for the cyclical periods of boom and depression that may be charted throughout the nineteenth century. The eighteenth century was equally well acquainted with such cycles, determined in the first instance by the abundance or paucity of the most recent harvest, and the size of the harvest continued to have a major impact well into the nineteenth and even the twentieth century. Mass unemployment was, however, a phenomenon far more concentrated and therefore more readily visible in an industrial society than in the rural one that it displaced. In times of distress the workers' discontent became highly vocal.

---

[6]See E. G. West, "Literacy and the Industrial Revolution," *Economic History Review* (August 1978).

[7]Ivy Pinchbeck, *Women Workers and the Industrial Revolution* (1930).

CHILD LABOR IN A MANCHESTER COTTON MILL   One of a series of
instructional prints prepared in the 1840s. *(Manchester Public Library)*

The available statistics cannot quantify relative happiness or unhappi-
ness, but they can and do measure the wages earned and the prices paid
both for food and for the slowly increasing number of consumer goods.
These statistics indicate that in the course of the last three decades of the
eighteenth century and the first five decades of the nineteenth, the average
standard of comfort of the lower ranks of British society improved—not
rapidly, not steadily, and not uniformly throughout the working class; but,
on balance, the supply of food, clothing, and shelter was greater (for a very
much larger population) after the Industrial Revolution than it had been
before.[8] This tendency was not operating, however, during the war period
discussed in Chapter 11, when the government utilized the kingdom's growing resources for military rather than domestic purposes. In the years 1793–
1815 the position of the average wage earner stagnated or in some cases
deteriorated.

The era of the Industrial Revolution was thus a complex one that involved a unique historical "takeoff" into self-sustaining economic growth,
the utilization of steam power and of new forms of industrial organization,
a rapid growth of population, a widespread reorganization of agriculture,
and a generation accustoming itself to the discipline of the factory whistle.
At the same time, such older phenomena as the alternation of good harvest

[8]The evidence is summed up by M. W. Flinn in "Trends in Real Wages 1750–1850," *Economic History Review*, August 1974, pp. 395–413.

and bad, of peace and war, continued to influence the manner in which human beings lived. As Thomas Ashton has concluded:

> If harvests had been uniformly good; if statesmen had directed their attention to providing a stable standard of value and a proper medium of exchange; if there had been no wars to force up prices, raise rates of interest, and turn resources to destruction, the course of the industrial revolution would have been smoother, and its consequences would not have been, as they are, in dispute.[9]

[9]*The Industrial Revolution,* pp. 107–08.

10 PAUSE BETWEEN STORMS

One characteristic of the 1780s was a quickening in the pace of economic change. Another was a growing preoccupation with political and social reform, a concern that reached a climax in the early 1790s when the French revolutionaries imposed a choice on English reformers: were they to regard the French as models for emulation or as prophets of disaster? Until the Revolution in France was well under way, however, concern with reform aroused more ripples than storm waves on the surface of an era of relative calm. The great issues of the past were settled: the Bourbon powers had tried and failed to regain what they had lost overseas in 1763; the problem of how to govern the thirteen American colonies no longer existed; the king's attempt to dominate the ministry had ended with North's resignation, and after two years of ministerial uncertainty, a balance of power between the sovereign and the oligarchy had been in essence restored. The aristocrats were able to set their house in order again, and it stood, like the country palaces of the magnates, as if it would last forever.

THE OLIGARCHY

For the few who had money and position, life was a delight. Society moved with a seasonal rhythm from town to country and back again, congregating in London for the winter when Parliament met, dispersing in summer to its members' country estates. In the dog days of July and August no one of fashion wanted to be in town, and least of all in Parliament; men's light summer clothing had not yet been dreamed of, and the heat of Westminster could be intolerable. In winter, on the other hand, the great country houses were likely to be frigid; most of them were designed for grandeur rather than warmth, and the wood that burned in their monumental fireplaces made little impression on the chill of the rooms. Town houses, being smaller and more compact, were better suited to cold weather. Political and social life, which served the comfort of the oligarchs, consequently moved through a yearly cycle of urban and rural, a cycle that was to continue until the early twentieth century. Lord Byron, a product of the Georgian aristocracy, satirized the annual exodus from London in these lines:

'Tis perhaps a pity
When nature wears the gown that doth become her

> To lose those best months in a sweaty city,
> And wait until the nightingale grows dumber,
> Listening debates not very wise or witty,
> Ere patriots their true *country* can remember;—
> But there's no shooting (save grouse) till September.

Comfort and hunting were not the only reasons for the exodus from London. The rulers of Britain were still as deeply rooted in the countryside as their grandfathers had been, but they were also more urbane, both figuratively and in the literal sense of being habituated to the city. Their social position as magnates in their localities was intimately connected with their parliamentary position as boroughmongers and manipulators of county elections and with their economic position as landlords; their influence on the national scene derived from their rural power. Yet they were much less earthy than the blue-blooded country bumpkins of Walpole's day, for time had eroded their provincialism. Many of them had been polished in youth by the Grand Tour, kept up their knowledge of Europe through frequent travel, and spoke and read French as a second language. They might regard foreigners with the scorn of Samuel Johnson or the humor of Laurence Sterne, but their opinions were likely to be based on firsthand experience, and they were achieving a level of sophistication that would have delighted Lord Chesterfield. At heart they were still uncompromisingly British; on the surface they were cosmopolitan.

Their taste had improved, and the change shows most clearly in the monuments that they were building to their own grandeur. A typical ex-

BLENHEIM PALACE: THE MAIN ENTRANCE   The work of John Vanbrugh during the 1710s. *(A. F. Kersting)*

ample, just as Blenheim Palace was typical of an earlier period, is Kedleston Hall in Derbyshire, which is largely the work of a famous Scottish architect and decorator, Robert Adam. A comparison of the façades of the two structures shows that they have much in common: they are symmetrical, in that the flanking wings are balanced on each side of the central building; and there is a rhythmic alternation of such decorative motifs as columns and pilasters, round-arched and square-headed windows. But there the resemblance ends. Vanbrugh's work at Blenheim reveals an almost obsessive concern with variety and mass. The design has so many constituent parts that it is a busy jumble, with no surfaces of plain wall on which the eye can rest; and the elaboration of obelisks on the skyline looks like the headgear of a crowd of overdressed dowagers. Adam, by contrast, achieves his effect through restraint. The flanking wings are subordinated to the central block, though tied to it by the repetition of window motifs; the columns are concentrated on a single point of emphasis, and the moldings of doors and windows and stringcourses are set off against unadorned stonework. The silhouette is clean against the sky. Kedleston, though on a smaller scale than Blenheim, is equally monumental but much quieter. It is self-assured, where the other is self-assertive.

A great house such as Kedleston was a hub of county society. Guests were constantly coming and going, to stay for a meal or a weekend or a month; hospitality was mixed with business. The selection of local candi-

KEDLESTON HALL, DERBYSHIRE   The work of Robert Adam in the mid-1760s. *(A. F. Kersting)*

dates for Parliament, the choice of a new vicar or justice of the peace, the planning of an enclosure act or of how to pull down a cabinet minister were discussed and often settled over the after-dinner port and madeira. The country house, in other words, was more than a building or even a way of life: it was a political institution that endured as long as the governing class endured. The leaders of that class were not, like their counterparts in eighteenth-century France, drawn away from the countryside to the court in order to win favors from the king. Courtiers they were in season, and adept at scrambling for governmental plums, but they were never mere courtiers. The sources of their power and the centers of their lives were in their counties, and above all in their estates.

No estate of any size could be maintained without a vast number of servants. Horses and carriages, the only means of conveyance, required an army of stable boys and grooms; a similar army of parlor maids wielded the dusters and polishing cloths and brooms that were the only means of housecleaning. The formal garden, then coming into vogue, needed a staff of its own. A kitchen large enough to serve twenty or thirty guests, and body servants to attend to their needs, meant an additional horde of cooks,

THE LIFE OF THE COUNTRY GENTRY *The Drake-Brockman Family at Beachborough, 1744–46* is the subject of this painting attributed to Edward Haytley. *(National Gallery of Victoria. Everard Studley Miller bequest, 1963.)*

scullery maids, footmen, valets, lady's maids, each with status and functions strictly defined by custom, and all presided over by the head butler and housekeeper, the monarchs of the world below stairs. It was a world that the gentry took for granted, but on which their whole way of life depended. These servants were by modern standards incredibly ill-housed, over-worked, and underpaid. Yet they gained from the advantages, and were compelled to abide by the restraints, of a paternalism from which workers in industry were beginning to escape. For the time being, indeed, their way of life was scarcely affected by the Industrial Revolution.

THE RELIGIOUS REVIVAL

The surface calm of the 1780s was ruffled not merely by economic change but by an increasingly widespread revival of religious feeling. In the late 1730s a new outburst of Christian faith had come from a small group of Anglican clergy, and by the 1780s their work was having a profound impact on the working classes and affecting other groups in English society as well. No movement could have been more unexpected, either in its origin or its impact. The eighteenth-century Church of England was an institution in the doldrums: its gospel was rationalized and diluted to fit a secular age, and its clergy were more concerned with teaching how to be good than how to be saved. Although they preached that charity to the poor was part of Christian duty, with the poor themselves they had little concern. Neither, for that matter, had the dissenters, for the Puritan tradition had never been involved with the mass of the people. Organized Christianity was of and for the propertied classes, as it had been since the Restoration, and did not dirty its vestments in the poorhouse and the slum, whose inhabitants consequently had little more contact with religion than if they had been living in the Dark Continent.

But the Church of England was not completely absorbed with being respectable. A few of its members still held to the concept expressed by its last famous archbishop, William Laud. The Church, as Laud had envisaged it, was the whole of society—in Saint Paul's phrase "the Body of Christ"—of which rich and poor alike were parts; salvation through Christ was open to all the faithful rather than limited, as the Calvinists held, to a narrow circle of the elect. This Anglican concept survived, if dimly, in the intellectual torpor of the one-time stronghold of Laudianism, the colleges of Oxford. Out of Oxford came the beginnings of a spiritual revolution.

On a May evening in 1738 John Wesley, a former fellow of an Oxford college and a High-Church Anglican priest, had an overwhelming experience. "I felt my heart strangely warmed, I felt I did trust in Christ, Christ alone, for salvation; and an assurance was given me that he had taken away *my* sins, even mine, and saved me from the law of sin and death." Wesley became convinced that everyone to whom this experience of conversion came was saved, and that everyone to whom it did not come, no matter how good or pious, was in a state of damnation. His duty, therefore, was to open human hearts so that God might invade them—to preach hellfire on the one hand, repentance and salvation on the other. This was a startling message to a rationalistic age, for it meant that God was not a set of percepts or an abstraction, but a Person concerned with redeeming every one of His creatures.

Wesley and his companions, a small group called Methodists, began to carry their gospel to all who would listen. They went from parish to parish, asking and sometimes demanding to be heard from the pulpit. They held out to their listeners the choice of heaven or hell, Christ or Satan, and denied them the comfortable middle ground between belief and unbelief. They preached with a passion and crude power that left some convulsed with repentance, some with anger. The workings of grace, which the Methodists hailed, more skeptical Christians stigmatized as mania, and this clash of views could not be arbitrated. The parish clergy, understandably enough, resented the itinerant missionaries who troubled their peace, and began to bar them from their pulpits. The Methodists then took to the highways and byways, speaking wherever they could gather a crowd. They still considered

JOHN WESLEY (1703–1791) The organizer of Methodism is characteristically seen preaching in the open air. A painting by Nathaniel Hone. *(National Portrait Gallery, London)*

themselves Anglican priests, but when their church excluded them they found their congregations out of doors.

Their greatest preacher was George Whitefield. He reached the hearts of the humble, and they gathered in the hundreds, thousands, and even tens of thousands to listen to him. He was a man of passion and intuition, not logic, who cared as little for theological niceties as for the disapproval of his bishop. His one overmastering purpose was to save souls, wherever and however he could reach them; and he, more than anyone else, was responsible for transforming Methodism from a revival within the established church into a mass movement outside it. John Wesley was deeply reluctant to accept this transformation. He had an almost superstitious reverence for Anglican ritual and usages, and if he could have had his way he would never have left the ecclesiastical fold. But that fold was not for him and his followers, and they were inexorably forced out of it.

Two worlds were in conflict. One was the cool and decorous world of the established clergy and the society to which they ministered; the other was the primitive, stormy world of the lower classes, steeped in superstition and half-believing in witchcraft, which the Methodists were kindling with their talk of miracles and demonic possession and redemption open to all. These ardent spiritual egalitarians took at face value Christ's teaching about rich and poor, and they therefore seemed to the rich to be social as well as religious firebrands. "Their doctrines," wrote an irate duchess, "are most repulsive and strongly tinctured with impertinence and disrespect towards their superiors, in perpetually endeavoring to level all ranks and do away with all distinctions. It is monstrous to be told that you have a heart as sinful as the common wretches that crawl the earth." The duchess and her ilk would have nothing to do with the new movement for the very reason that the common wretches embraced it.

By the 1780s Methodism was to all intents and purposes a separate denomination. Wesley, in many ways the most conservative of revolutionaries, was being forced against his will to ordain his own clergy and even consecrate his own bishops; and in organizing his flock he showed an administrative genius at least equal to his power of touching human hearts. His followers were mostly uneducated, drunk with what the period called "enthusiasm," and convinced that they were inspired by the Holy Ghost; hence they were in danger of falling apart, like the Puritans before them, into numberless splinter groups. But Wesley held them together. Tactfully and patiently and firmly he imposed on them an ecclesiastical structure and so gave them the cohesion and corporate discipline that the Puritan sects had lacked. Chapel life also provided rituals, festivals, education, and entertainment, and for many lowly born laymen it presented an opportunity to exert leadership. By the time Wesley died in 1791, Methodism had clearly become a force to be reckoned with.

The institution that had cast out the Methodists was soon affected by them. The Church of England, unreceptive as it was to change, still considered itself Christian, and it could not remain impervious to the new evangelism. Before the end of the century a leaven was working in many Anglican rectories and even some episcopal palaces. It showed itself in a heightened stress not only upon the experience of individual conversion and Bible reading but also upon the social implications of the Gospels expressed through good works. This so-called evangelical movement gained ground within the Established Church, just as Methodism gained ground outside it, and in the next sixty years the two in conjunction helped to alter the whole tone of British society. For evangelical converts like William Wilberforce what was needed most of all was a change of behavior, and he helped found a new Society for the Reformation of Manners.[1] That organization derived much encouragement from the example of piety and simplicity set by King George III and Queen Charlotte—though not from the example set by their sons—and it applauded the Royal Proclamation of 1787 against vice. The monarch urged magistrates to punish all persons operating public gambling houses, profaning the Lord's Day, or publishing "loose and licentious" books. Gradually the aristocratic code of the Georgian era, with its emphasis on reason and detachment and the Chesterfieldian graces, yielded to the earnest and muscular Christianity of the Victorians.

One humanitarian movement toward which a number of evangelicals showed sympathy was that of prison reform. Either capital punishment or "transportation" to distant colonies remained the preferred eighteenth-century antidote to serious crime, but by the middle years of the century imprisonment for debt had become common, and prisons were also increasingly used to hold convicts until a final punishment had been determined. During the 1770s and 1780s prison reform became the special province of John Howard, a Protestant dissenter whose experiences as a French prisoner of war in 1756 caused him to devote his life both to the study of prison conditions and to the advocacy of a program of reform: the provision of adequate food, water, and fresh air; an end to the indiscriminate herding together of men and women, children and adults, hardened criminals and first offenders. As high sheriff of Bedfordshire, he was able to put such proposals into effect. For many magistrates even the best-run jails remained a dubious mode of punishment. For Sydney Smith, jails were merely "large public schools, maintained at the expense of the county for the encouragement of profligacy and vice." Smith preferred to see convicts plod hour after hour on a treadmill, a form of punishment he deemed efficient, economical, and exemplary.

Other Britons of the 1780s continued to regard "transportation" as the proper punishment. Now that convicts could no longer be sent to the North American colonies, they sought a new destination. Fortunately the voyages of exploration and scientific discovery that Captain James Cook had carried on in the South Pacific during the 1760s and 1770s provided an answer.

---

[1]The movement for reform of manners during the late eighteenth and early nineteenth century, its successes and setbacks, is well described in M. J. Quinlan, *Victorian Prelude* (1941).

Cook had charted the coast of New Zealand and had both explored and claimed on behalf of Britain the fertile southeast coast of Australia. There at Botany Bay in 1788 a British penal colony was founded, the first of a trickle of settlers that by the 1820s had become a flood. Among them voluntary immigrants soon exceeded convicts by a ratio of five to one, but "transportation" as a form of punishment was not to end until the 1850s.

A reform movement into which many evangelicals (as well as Quakers and Methodists) threw themselves even more vigorously than the treatment of crime at home was that of opposition to the slave trade abroad—as a first step toward the eventual abolition of slavery within the British empire and the wider world. For several generations most Britons had taken for granted the trade whereby English shippers sent vessels to the West African coast in order to exchange textiles and manufactured goods with native chieftains for black slaves to be transported to the Caribbean and to mainland North America. During the middle years of the eighteenth century, the port of Liverpool had come to dominate a trade that involved the annual dispatch of thirty thousand or more human beings across the Atlantic Ocean. By the 1780s more than a million and a quarter had been shipped to Jamaica, Barbados, and the smaller West Indies "sugar islands" to serve as plantation laborers, and almost 300,000 had been unloaded and sold on the North American mainland. The trade had proved both moderately profitable and dangerous: the net profit per voyage averaged 10 percent, but one voyage in three brought no gain whatsoever. The anti–slave trade organizers, joined by William Wilberforce, had become by the 1780s a powerful pressure group. They criticized not only the horrors of the "middle passage" for the enslaved victims (of whom 10 to 20 percent perished at sea) but also the hazards the trade posed for British sailors. Of every ten crewmen who left Liverpool, two were likely to die by accident or of some tropical disease, three were likely to jump ship, and only five returned to their home port. The slave trade, Thomas Clarkson insisted in 1788, was not the nursery but the graveyard of the British navy.[2]

The anti–slave trade movement had won initial encouragement from the Sommersett Case of 1772, in which Chief Justice Mansfield had ruled that a slave brought to England by a West Indies planter was automatically free because slavery was not sanctioned by the laws of England. Although the anti–slave trade lobby did not ultimately succeed in gaining a parliamentary triumph during the 1780s, it did transform a state of affairs that had long been taken for granted into a subject of keen controversy: both the West Indies planters and the Liverpool merchants found themselves thrown on the defensive.

The religious revival clearly helped alter standards of behavior and affected questions of public policy. It may also have helped to contribute in two ways to strengthening Britain for the coming wars against France. One

---

[2]See Roger Anstey, *The Atlantic Slave Trade and British Abolition, 1760–1810* (1975), and Philip D. Curtin, *The Atlantic Slave Trade: A Census* (1969).

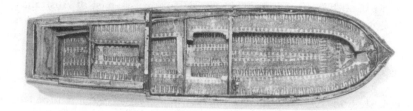

WILBERFORCE'S MODEL SLAVE SHIP   The anti–slave trade crusader used the model to show his parliamentary colleagues how 300 slaves or more could be crowded into a 130-ton vessel. *(Wilberforce House, Kingston-upon-Hull City Museums and Art Galleries)*

was by turning the workers against the atheism of the French Revolution, the other by inculcating in them a sense of order and discipline that was antithetical to the spirit of revolutionary violence.[3] This argument, like most generalizations from history, cannot be proved. The only proof would be written testimony, from innumerable workers who professed themselves Christian, on how they regarded the social order; and the testimony does not exist. "The short and simple annals of the poor" are in fact neither short nor simple, but neither are they written: laborers left virtually no written records. Hence historians lack the evidence to clinch their case and can at best advance conclusions that are plausible but not demonstrable.

PITT AND REFORM

While some Englishmen thought of reform as religious conversion and change of heart, and some as the legislating of proper behavior, yet others worked for the reform of the constitution. In the aftermath of the American Revolution, the parliamentary opposition added three laws to the statute book designed to lessen the influence of the crown on the makeup of the House of Commons: customs and excise officers were disenfranchised; government contractors were ruled ineligible for election to Parliament; and numerous sinecure positions through which the ministry influenced members of the House of Commons were abolished. These measures had only a modest effect, however: they removed a few excrescences, but the system of

---

[3]William E. H. Lecky, *A History of England in the Eighteenth Century*, 8 vols. (1878–1890), vol. 3, pp. 145–146; Elie Halévy, *England in 1815*, vol. 1 of *A History of the English People in the Nineteenth Century*, 2nd ed., 6 vols. (1949), pp. 424–426. Lecky's monumental work, which first appeared in 1877, is by now antiquated. But he was a talented historian writing in a leisurely age, and his volumes contain a wealth of information, lucidly presented, on every aspect of the period. Halévy was a French scholar who knew British history better than most Englishmen. His treatment of the nineteenth century is as exhaustive as Lecky's treatment of the eighteenth, and his judgments are always interesting and often provocative.

patronage remained largely intact. What did much more to curtail royal influence was the emergence of a leader strong enough to stand on his own political feet.

In December 1783, after a year and a half of ministerial turmoil following the fall of Lord North, the king called on William Pitt, the second son of the earl of Chatham, to head his government. The young man was already a seasoned politician at the age of twenty-four, and he had a gift for using the support of the crown without becoming its tool. He was also a superb administrator who had as shrewd a head for finance as Walpole himself, and a greater taste for experimenting. The experiments were primarily of two sorts: attempts to liberalize commercial policy and measures to improve Britain's antiquated fiscal system.

In his commercial policy Pitt was influenced by Adam Smith, the pioneer Scottish economist, whose *Wealth of Nations* had publicized the doctrine that unfettered private enterprise operates to the public good. Governmental control of the economy, according to Smith, was an artificial and therefore undesirable interference with the natural laws of supply and demand; what was needed was not control but freedom for everyone to follow the dictates of self-interest. That interest was assumed to be enlightened and intelligent, so that the conflict of individual interests in open competition would redound to the benefit of all. The wealth of a nation rested on the production of consumable goods, Smith argued, and the way to increase production was to leave each producer of goods or services "free to pursue his own interest his own way." The machinery of governmental regulation created over the years ought to be dismantled, and state interference be limited to those areas, such as education and public works, that could not be supported by private capital alone. Because Smith also placed great stress on national defense and hence on sea power, he commended the navigation acts that were designed to encourage the British merchant marine at the cost of foreign competitors, but with this exception he believed that the rule in commerce, as in industry, should be uninhibited competition. He was thus the chief source of the later classical economists, who preached laissez-faire, or free enterprise, at home and free trade abroad.

William Pitt, said Smith, "understands my ideas better than I do myself." The compliment was not only exaggerated but irrelevant, for Pitt as a politician was much less interested in theory than in what would work. Although he was willing to lower tariffs if he could thereby increase trade, and let industry manage itself unless he saw good reason to interfere, he was even less of a doctrinaire believer in free trade and laissez-faire than was Adam Smith. The young prime minister's tentative experiments in the 1780s, nevertheless, did foreshadow those two sacred principles of Victorian economics.

The first experiment, to reduce tariffs between Britain and Ireland, proved unsuccessful. The Dublin Parliament had recently regained a high degree of legislative independence, and Pitt hoped to continue the process of conciliation by agreements that would amount to a commercial union.

WILLIAM PITT THE YOUNGER ADDRESSES THE HOUSE OF COMMONS   Detail of a painting by Karl-Anton Hickel. *(National Portrait Gallery, London)*

But a complex of forces was working against him. Now that Irish manufacturers were recovering from the doldrums of the early Hanoverian era, conservative British industrial interests dreaded to see the domestic market flooded with Irish goods. Pitt's political opponents made the most of these fears and also stirred the apprehensions of the Irish that commercial union would subvert their newly won political autonomy. The prime minister abandoned his measure, and one more chance was lost of a rapprochement between the two countries.

Pitt was undiscouraged. In the following year, 1786, he opened negotiations for a treaty with France to effect a mutual reduction of tariffs. This overture to Britain's oldest, most inveterate rival showed both his courage and his clear-sightedness. "To suppose that any nation can be unalterably the enemy of another," he said, "is weak and childish. . . . It is a libel on the constitution of political societies, and supposes the existence of diabolical malice in the original frame of man." He had to contend with the "weak and childish" not only in Parliament but among leaders of the older industries, like the wool trade, that had been nourished on protection. Such industrialists formed a pressure group, known as the General Chamber of Manufacturers, to impress on the business world that the principle behind the treaty was one of "serious and awful importance . . . comprehending a prodigious change in the commercial system of this country."

But Pitt found influential allies among leaders in the new industries, who believed, as he did, that the treaty would benefit both sides. France exported primarily such products as wine, they argued, which did not compete with British manufactured goods; an agreement between the two nations would be mutually profitable and would usher in an era of good feeling. When Pitt succeeded in concluding the agreement, known from the name of his chief negotiator as the Eden Treaty of 1786, the point was clearly put in a jingle celebrating the occasion.

> May kingdom 'gainst kingdom no more be at spite;
> For both 'twere much better to trade than to fight;
> And whilst mutual friendship and harmony reign
> Our buttons we'll barter for pipes of champagne.

Pitt's economic reforms were not confined to the Eden Treaty, and those he made at home proved to be more important because they were more lasting.[4] He attacked smuggling by reducing and simplifying import duties and by extending the excise (as Walpole had tried and failed to do) to tobacco, wines, and other articles on which smugglers had hitherto made their profit.[5] He improved the tax structure, abolished numerous sinecures, established a Consolidated Fund in which all revenues were deposited and from which all governmental expenses were paid, and created the so-called Sinking Fund, which he hoped would eventually yield enough interest to pay off the public debt. This last experiment was not a success, but the others were. Pitt did more than anyone else in the eighteenth century to curb bureaucratic peculation and bring order and efficiency into the finances of the state, and he accomplished his goals in the nick of time. Although his reforms bore little relation to the work of the new manufacturers, he, like them, was strengthening the nation for the ordeal to come.

In other areas his efforts at improvement were halfhearted and unsuccessful. In 1785 he proposed reforming the House of Commons by gradually abolishing a number of rotten boroughs. When he encountered strong parliamentary opposition and found that even his eloquence could not kindle a lethargic public, however, he abandoned his measure. Three years later he championed the movement led by his close friend, William Wilberforce, to wipe out the slave trade throughout the empire. Pitt denounced the trade as a "noxious plant . . . under whose shade nothing that is useful or profitable to Africa will ever flourish or take root," but he had no wish to stake the future of his ministry on the measure; when it failed to attract a

---

[4]The Eden Treaty vanished, like most of the rest of the eighteenth-century world, in the explosion of the French Revolution. Between 1785 and 1793 Pitt made numerous unsuccessful attempts to secure similar treaties with other powers; see John Ehrman, *The British Government and Commercial Negotiations with Europe, 1783–1793* (1962), and, for all aspects of the administration in those years, his *The Younger Pitt: The Years of Acclaim* (1969).

[5]For Walpole's failure to extend the excise see Chapter 5.

parliamentary majority, he let it drop. Pitt was no crusader. For his own career he would fight hard; for a worthy cause he would fight only up to the point where he began to jeopardize that career.

Pitt's character was squarely at odds with that of his great rival, Charles James Fox. Fox, who had entered Parliament a decade before Pitt, had been one of the most vocal of North's opponents during the American war and one of the most inveterate enemies of royal influence. He had inherited from his father, Lord Holland, a personal grievance against George III, whom he spoke of privately as a "blockhead" and even as "Satan," and he insulted the king publicly by proposing a toast to "His Majesty—the People." The king disliked Fox in turn not merely because of his politics and reputation as a rake, but also because his friendship with the king's eldest son, the Prince of Wales, seemed to be encouraging that young man's rebellion against parental authority. For a time in 1782 and 1783 the king had to accept Fox as a minister, but thereafter, for more than two decades, he used his influence to keep him out of office. Politically Pitt and Fox had much in common: they both believed that the American war had been a

CHARLES JAMES FOX (1749–1806)   William Pitt's great parliamentary rival in the late eighteenth century. *(The Granger Collection)*

mistake; they wanted to reform Parliament, end the slave trade, and conciliate the Irish; they were experts in the thrust and parry of debate and were powerful orators. But as people they were poles apart. Pitt wrapped himself in a lofty and chilling virtue and never unbent except to a few intimates. He was a Puritan of politics, hardworking and incorruptible, who won from his contemporaries vast respect and little love. Fox was just the opposite. He embraced great causes, often with more passion than wisdom; he drank and gambled excessively and with gusto; he threw himself into political battling with everything he had and yet retained enough sense of humor to be unembittered when victory time and again eluded him. Although in his long career he never achieved more than momentary power, he was probably better loved than any other man in the history of Parliament. He was big, both in girth and in personality, and what a friend called his "negligent grandeur" left its mark on the age.

EMPIRE IN INDIA

One of Pitt's major achievements was to find an answer to the question of how to govern India. Ever since the Seven Years' War that question had played an increasing role in British politics, as the East India Company had become more and more deeply involved in the affairs of the native princes. Political involvement was as far removed as ever from the intent of India House, the Company's headquarters in London, for the directors were still interested in trading, not governing. But their hands were forced by their own servants. The men on the spot realized that the only way to safeguard trade was to assume political power, and they carried on the process begun during the Seven Years' War of transforming the Company into a sovereign state. By the time Robert Clive left India in 1767, the Company had establishments at Bombay on the west coast and Madras and its environs on the southeast coast, and, most important, it had become the paramount power in Bengal, the area around Calcutta. There it held extensive territory and controlled, through native puppets, the revenue of the entire province. Bengal was the cornerstone of the empire that India House was inadvertently acquiring.

The government at home could not long remain indifferent to what was happening. Company officials, Clive among them, were returning with great wealth gained by dubious means. These "nabobs," strutting their way through British society, aroused both anger and envy—anger because they were accused, often with good reason, of having shamelessly exploited the natives; envy because the golden fruits of exploitation were not open to all the greedy but only to those with influence at India House. Two factors combined, in other words, to attract the attention of Parliament: the moralist's desire to ensure at least some minimal standards of good government in Bengal, and the politician's desire to share in the Company's vast and growing patronage.

Lord North attacked the problem in his Regulating Act of 1773, which was the first clear assertion of Parliament's supremacy over India House. The act created a governor-general in Bengal, gave him authority over Bombay and Madras, provided him with a council, stipulated who he and the councillors were to be for the next five years, and settled on them handsome salaries to be paid by the Company. This attempt to solve the problem had serious drawbacks. It made the directors of the Company responsible for agents whom they had not chosen and over whom they had no more than limited control. It established the position of governor-general only to circumscribe its occupant. His supremacy over Bombay and Madras was ill defined; he could not override his council, in which he had only a single vote, and the councillors did not have clearly demarcated powers of their own. The resultant system was so cumbersome that only a genius could have made it work at all.

The Company's service produced such a man. For the next twelve years the governor-general was Warren Hastings, one of the great proconsuls in the history of empire. During the crisis occasioned by the War of Independence, when Britain was fighting with its back to the wall and the French were stirring up trouble throughout India, Hastings almost single-handedly saved the Company and extended its power. His chief enemy was neither French nor Hindu but one of his own councillors, Philip Francis, a man with vast ambition and a program of his own. The Company should continue to rule Bengal, Francis believed, without responsibility for justice or effective administration or anything but moneymaking, and should leave the rest of India to its own devices. Hastings, in contrast, was convinced that the Company must become the paramount power in the whole subcontinent, ruling directly in Bengal through a governor-general in whose hands authority was centralized, indirectly elsewhere through princely dependents and allies, and must slowly permeate the whole complex of native institutions with British concepts of justice and good government. Francis worked to perpetuate the old order, Hastings to create a new one.[6]

The governor-general won by a narrow margin, by means that were sometimes none too scrupulous, and in 1780 Francis left for home to engineer his revenge. By then Hastings was at war against a coalition of princes in central India who had been induced by French intrigue and their growing fear of the Company to do what they had never done before: unite to drive out the British. They almost succeeded. Hastings's small armies of sepoys were overwhelmingly outnumbered, and he was so desperate for money that he resorted to what his enemies regarded as high-handed extortion. But

---

[6]Even Hastings was far from envisaging the way in which the new order would develop. For a vivid modern sketch of him see Philip Woodruff, *The Men Who Ruled India: The Founders* (1954), pp. 122–132. This volume, the first of two, deals with the period from 1600 to 1858; it is an unorthodox collection of portraits of men who served the Company, famous and obscure, good and bad, by an author who himself had a distinguished career in the Indian Civil Service. He is familiar at first hand with the kinds of problems that his predecessors faced and describes them with a freshness and professional appreciation that most historians lack.

by a mixture of hard fighting and shrewd diplomacy he managed to break up the coalition, and the advent of peace in Europe saved him in the nick of time from a French naval threat. By 1784 his work was done, and in India the position of the Company was stronger than ever before.

But in Britain its position was under attack. Recent events had made clear that North's Regulating Act left room for great irregularities, and rumor painted Hastings as a monster of rapacity. India House was split by factions, each of which had parliamentary support; and the quarrels in London were reflected in Bombay, Madras, and Calcutta. Both the Company and its governor-general needed surveillance by the state, but how was this to be achieved? If the Company lost all power to appoint officials in India, who would appoint them? The obvious answer was the crown. But Whig politicians like Fox, who had long fought the king's influence, had no intention of giving him such a vast increase in patronage. For Parliament itself to appoint, as it had in 1773, would turn the Company's service into a grab bag for politicians. There was no feasible alternative to leaving India House autonomous in selecting its personnel.

Nor was there any alternative to an autonomous governor-general. The Whigs were opposed by long tradition to the concentration of power in the executive, but the realization was slowly dawning on them that their tradition made no sense in the alien world of Bengal. London could not in any case exert effective control over a governor-general in Calcutta. The attempt to circumscribe him by a council had not worked, and he could not be circumscribed directly from Britain if only because of communications: to send him a dispatch and receive his answer might take as much as a year. He had to be given great leeway in order to function at all. Hastings himself might deserve to be called to account, but the power of his office could not be impaired.

Pitt met the problem by dividing authority at home between the Company and the government and by demarcating the relationship between London and Calcutta. His India Act of 1784 created the pattern of British rule for the next seventy-four years and was as much a constitutional landmark as Hastings's governorship had been a political landmark. The essence of the new system was a partnership between the Company and the state: the former continued to direct commercial affairs, and the latter took responsibility for governmental affairs. A board of control, composed in part of cabinet ministers, was set up in London; to it the Company directors submitted proposals for political or military action, and from it they received their orders. The Company appointed all officials except the highest, but the board had power to remove them. The crown appointed the governor-general, to whom Bombay and Madras were subordinated, and he was soon made commander in chief and empowered to override his council. Thus was established a mixed authority. The Company retained a sphere of action and its patronage, the government assumed responsibility for Indian administration, and the governor-general acquired the free hand that he needed.

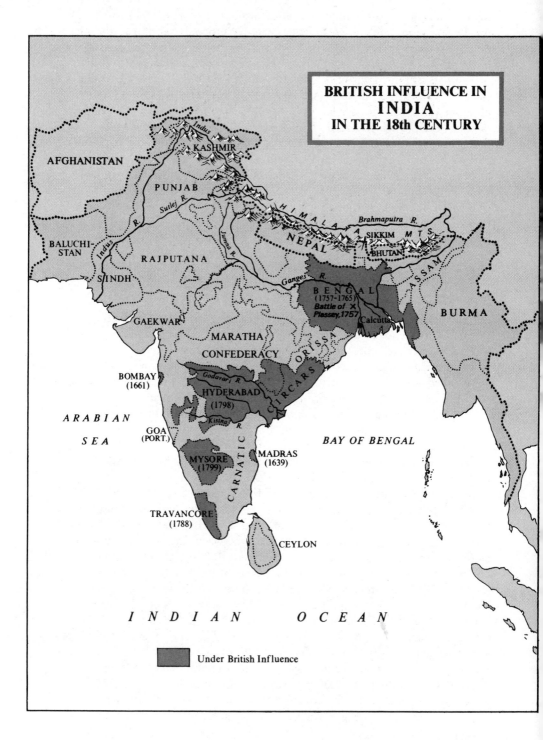

BRITISH INFLUENCE IN
INDIA
IN THE 18th CENTURY

AFGHANISTAN

KASHMIR

PUNJAB

Indus R.

Sutlej R.

HIMALAYA

Brahmaputra R.

BALUCHI-
STAN

Indus R.

Jumna R.

NEPAL

SIKKIM M T S

BHUTAN

ASSAM

RAJPUTANA

SINDH

Ganges R.

B E N G A L
(1757-1765)
Battle of X
Plassey, 1757

Calcutta

BURMA

GAEKWAR

MARATHA
CONFEDERACY

ORISSA

BOMBAY
(1661)

Godavari R.

HYDERABAD
(1798)

CIRCARS

Krisna R.

ARABIAN

SEA

GOA
(PORT.)

CARNATIC

BAY OF BENGAL

MYSORE
(1799)

MADRAS
(1639)

TRAVANCORE
(1788)

CEYLON

I N D I A N   O C E A N

Under British Influence

While the India Act was creating the future, it also tried to perpetuate the past by condemning territorial conquest and intervention in the affairs of the native states. Hastings correctly interpreted these provisions as reflecting on his policy, and in 1785 he resigned and came home. Three years later he was impeached for misconduct as governor-general. Philip Francis had poisoned the minds of Edmund Burke and others in Parliament, until they saw in Hastings the epitome of all the evil, extortion, and ruthlessness that had stained British rule for generations. He was the scapegoat more than the epitome, for he had committed fewer and more venial sins than most of his predecessors while fighting against heavier odds, but even he was not above reproach. For seven years his trial dragged on, draining his fortune, until at last he was acquitted on every count.

He deserved vindication, but his impeachment was more significant than the rights and wrongs of the charges against him. For many years the conduct of the Company's servants had troubled even the tough consciences of British politicians, who were coming to realize slowly and grudgingly that political authority in India meant responsibilities to the governed. The state, now that it had assumed the authority, could not in honor shirk the responsibilities and join in the game of exploitation. Burke persuaded himself that Hastings had done exactly that and should be called to account for it. "I impeach him," he said in closing his indictment, "in the name of all the commons of Great Britain, whose national character he has dishonored. I impeach him in the name of the people of India, whose laws, rights, and liberties he has subverted. . . . I impeach him in the name and by the virtue of those eternal laws of justice which he has violated."

The charge was as intemperate as the oratory suggests, and the victim was unfairly selected, but the underlying idea was valid. A principle cannot be judged by the use to which it is put, for good causes frequently lead to mistaken persecutions. Burke, for all his partisan blindness, could at least see that the crown, in assuming a new role, had also acquired a new duty—to provide a framework of order within which the Indians could enjoy their "laws, rights, and liberties."

The India of the nineteenth century was already beginning to take shape. Britain, on the way to being the major power of the subcontinent, was developing a form of rule that was at best paternalistic but that remained in essence dictatorial. Hastings's successors governed in what seemed to them the best interests of the governed but remained as aloof from them as the early Stuart kings had been from their people. Although such a concept of sovereignty might seem anachronistic at the end of the eighteenth century, Hindus and Moslems knew nothing of representative institutions or of constitutional curbs on executive power. British rule at its worst promised domestic peace and therefore a lessening of oppression, inefficiency, corruption, and bloodshed.

As Indians adapted to the British and the British to them, the effect on both sides was profound. The new rulers from the west had to break out of the constitutional traditions that had long been bred into them and learn the kind of autocratic paternalism that would work in an alien culture. Throughout the nineteenth century they continued to learn by trial and error, while the Indians began to learn from them novel ideas of liberty and parliament and nationhood. The system that Hastings had foreshadowed, the British raj or government of India, began in response to the country's needs, much as the strong Tudor monarchy had begun in England three centuries before. It ended, as that monarchy had done, by educating its subjects to the point where they could dispense with it.

British dominion rested from beginning to end on the Indians themselves. They provided the sepoys, the soldiers of the army, by which first the Company and then the British crown gained military predominance—thereby making India the outstanding example in modern history of a country brought by its own inhabitants under the rule of a foreign state. But the importance of the sepoys did not end there. They eventually became the means of British expansion outside India, and even a factor in the power politics of Europe. Until the First World War Britain never maintained at home a military force comparable with those of its rivals, but in India it did; and the Indian army strengthened Britain's hand in international affairs. Danger to India or to the Indian sea routes always touched a sensitive nerve at Whitehall, for a threat to the raj threatened the heart of Britain's imperial position.

When Hastings was acquitted, the fantastic growth of the raj was still hidden in the future. But the elimination of the French and the weakening of the princes had prepared the way. Even though those old enemies were not yet ready to admit defeat and crises aplenty lay ahead, the means of weathering crises were at hand in the sepoys and in a workable system of government. Moreover, a new sense of responsibility, in London and Calcutta, ensured that the worst exploitation was over and that power in the future would be soberly used. The foundations of the nineteenth-century empire were securely laid.

CONCLUSION

Britain was also preparing at home for its nineteenth-century role. The nature of government was changing: Pitt was modernizing the fiscal system and experimenting with new economic policies, and the king, as his prime minister gained firmer control, was almost imperceptibly moving away from the center of the political stage. Great aristocrats still dominated local and national affairs from their country palaces and the House of Lords and were at the peak of their sophistication and splendor, but it was the splendor of approaching sunset. Landholding was no longer the sole hallmark of the wealthy. Iron and coal and steam and cotton textiles—as well as banks and insurance companies—were creating a new class of plutocrats, who would soon demand political and even social recognition and who were already challenging the traditional concepts of what economic policy should be. The old cohesiveness of the ruling class was beginning to give way, and a growing tension between landed and industrial magnates presaged a struggle for power that eventuated, a half-century later, in a vast readjustment.

The chief reason why this struggle took another fifty years to work out was Britain's wars against the French Revolution and Napoleon. For the better part of a generation, a continuous military crisis distracted the nation from the need for domestic reform, whether of Parliament, the Poor Law, or trade policy. The new need grew steadily more urgent. Industrialization developed with enormous speed under the pressure of war, but the development was so lopsided that it spawned problems and tensions: when the country emerged from twenty-two years of fighting in 1815, its economy and society were badly askew. The traditional ruling class was unable to restore the old order and keep its power intact; those who led the nation to victory abroad were compelled to adapt to the forces of change at home.

NELSON FALLING, BY D. DIGHTON
(National Maritime Museum, London. Photograph from American Heritage Publishing Co., Inc.)

IV   **WAR AND ITS AFTERMATH**

1789 to 1830

11 THE STRUGGLE AGAINST THE FRENCH REVOLUTION

On the afternoon of May 6, 1789, King Louis XVI opened the first session of the French Estates General that had been held in 175 years. Events thereafter moved rapidly. The *ancien régime* was literally and metaphorically bankrupt, but the nation was not: France had the resources of money, manpower, and ideas to fashion a new order for itself and for much of the continent. By the autumn of 1789 the medieval Estates had been converted into the National Assembly, and Paris, the center of radicalism, had captured from Versailles the legislature and the royal family. Three years later, France was a republic, waging war against Austria and Prussia. French troops had thrown back the enemy armies and were pouring into Savoy, central Germany, and the Low Countries. The Revolution had Europe in its grip.

FRENCH REVOLUTIONARIES AND BRITISH REFORMERS

The British were slow to realize what the upheaval meant. At its start different observers read different things into it: patriots predicted the disintegration of Britain's most dangerous rival, reformers the conversion of absolutism into a parliamentary system modeled on that at Westminster; and both groups looked on in complacent approval. Only the radicals were enthusiastic, for they dreamed that the collapse of one regime of privilege would usher in a new day of freedom for all people. This dream was given enduring expression by the young William Wordsworth, for whom the French were the heroes of humanity:

> a people from the depth
> Of shameful imbecility uprisen,
> Fresh as the morning star. Elate we looked
> Upon their virtues; saw, in rudest men,
> Self-sacrifice the firmest; generous love,
> And continence of mind, and sense of right,
> Uppermost in the midst of fiercest strife. . . .
> Bliss was it in that dawn to be alive,
> But to be young was very Heaven!

The poet was voicing, in his exclamatory way, a sense of human kinship that was widespread among intellectuals of the period. They were interested in the rights of all people, not merely the English or the French or the Germans. It was this cosmopolitan interest, reflected in the acts and words of the National Assembly, that gave the early phase of the Revolution its appeal outside France. The Assembly spoke of the powers inherent in one particular people, as Thomas Jefferson had spoken earlier in the Declaration of Independence; but both used terms so ultimate that they could apply to every people. The American proclamation of popular sovereignty had been a faint and distant challenge to the privileged orders of Europe; the French proclamation was a trumpet at the gates.

The supranational character of the ideas enunciated by the National Assembly can be seen most clearly by contrasting them with the ideas enunciated by Parliament in the Glorious Revolution. The contrast lies in the language of two constitutional documents exactly a hundred years apart: the English Bill of Rights of 1689 and the French Declaration of the Rights of Man and the Citizen of 1789. The Bill of Rights opens with a recitation of past history, then declares illegal certain practices of King James that have violated the "undoubted rights and liberties" of his subjects and of Parliament; it then settles the crown on William and Mary. The document is a terse, prosaic bit of lawmaking, intended to remedy specific grievances of the English and provide for the future of the monarchy, not to theorize about the nature of humankind. The French Declaration, on the other hand, speaks to the world in sweeping terms. "The ignorance, neglect, or contempt of the rights of man," it begins, "are the sole cause of public calamities and of the corruption of governments." Those rights, which are liberty, property, security, and resistance to oppression, belong to all people by virtue of being citizens and can be limited only by law that is applicable to everyone and is made by the citizens through their representatives; without such law society has no constitution. The Declaration is not primarily legislative, like the Bill of Rights, but a statement of political philosophy that has no limits of time or place.

Wordsworth was not alone in believing that the Revolution was the dawn of universal freedom. People prominent in many walks of life shared the young poet's enthusiasm. It was widespread among the new industrial leaders, such as James Watt and his partner, Matthew Boulton; Charles James Fox hailed the fall of the Bastille as the greatest and best event in history; Joseph Priestley, a famous chemist and freethinking theologian, wrote to a friend that "I feel myself becoming all French, both in chemistry and politics." Priestley, a nonconformist, detested the established Church of England and consequently applauded the revolutionaries' assault on the French equivalent, the Roman Catholic Church: he believed that "the time is approaching when an end will be put to all usurpation in things civil or religious, first in Europe and then in other countries." Many dissenters shared his views and saw in the Revolution their best hope of full religious emancipation.

In the autumn of 1789 Richard Price, a well-known nonconformist minister, published a sermon in which he adapted to the British scene the philosophy of the Declaration of the Rights of Man. "A king," he declared, "is no more than the first servant of the public, created by it, maintained by it, and responsible to it. . . . His authority is the authority of the community; and the term *Majesty*, which it is usual to apply to him, is by no means *his own* majesty, but the *Majesty of the People*." King George and those who governed under his aegis derived their power from the people, to whom they were answerable and by whom they could be ousted for misconduct. This was the logic of the Declaration of Independence, of the National Assembly, and, Price believed, of the future: the light of liberty that had first appeared in the freeing of the United States was now "reflected to *France,* and there kindled into a blaze that lays despotism in ashes, and warms and illuminates *Europe!* Tremble, all ye oppressors of the world! . . . Restore to mankind their rights; and consent to the correction of abuses before they and you are destroyed together."

BURKE AND THE NEW CONSERVATISM

Such fire breathing made the oligarchs uneasy. Many of them did not know precisely why, because as Whigs they considered themselves friends of liberty. They were soon given reasons, however, when Price's sermon evoked an answer from the leading political theorist of the day. Edmund Burke had

A SMUG BRITISH VIEW OF THE DIFFERENCES BETWEEN BRITAIN AND FRANCE *(Reproduced by courtesy of the Trustees of the British Museum)*

been strongly opposed to coercing the American colonies, but he refused to agree that the French Revolution was an extension of the American. To his mind France was busily subverting everything on which social order depended, and Price's implication that Britain should follow suit drove him to answer. His rebuttal was more than mere polemic, more even than is suggested by its title, *Reflections on the Revolution in France*. He went beyond reflection on a particular revolution to a consideration of the basic questions that it raised about the relationship of the citizen to the state. His treatise left its mark on all later conservative thinking.

Burke was no slave to the status quo. He recognized the truth of the old adage that times change and we change with them, and he had made his name as a reformer, but he insisted that reform must not be the means of eliminating the good with the bad. He was too much pervaded by a sense of the past to be a revolutionary. The social organism was for him not a thing of the moment, to be reconstituted according to the dictates of abstract philosophy; it was the product of a slow and infinitely complex process of historical development, "a partnership not only between those who are living, but between those who are living, those who are dead, and those who are to be born." The revolutionary would dissolve the partnership and destroy the organism in the hope of creating something better in its place. The French, to take the immediate example, were denying their past for the sake of an untried future, and their faith that reason alone could create utopia struck Burke as madness.

Their watchwords, liberty and equality, left him unmoved. Liberty in itself was no virtue: as he dryly pointed out, if we permit individuals to do as they please "we ought to see what it will please them to do before we risk congratulations. . . ." The liberties of the English were not their abstract rights as members of the human race, but special privileges acquired and passed down to them by their forebears, privileges that did not include, as Price contended, any right in the people at large to choose or change their governors. As for equality, it was a dangerous myth. In any society some are always at the top, some at the bottom, and those who try to level do not equalize but merely turn the social order topsy-turvy. To give power to the unpropertied masses would turn them against the propertied few in a scramble for spoils and in the end would give each of them an infinitesimal share in the plunder of the wealthy.

A government subservient to the popular will, as expressed through universal suffrage, would be heading for disaster, Burke argued, because wise public policy cannot be determined by the simple arithmetic of counting votes. "Absolute monarchy is tyranny," Bolingbroke had said a generation earlier, "but absolute democracy is tyranny and anarchy both." Burke would have agreed. He saw the French revolutionaries in their zeal for abstract liberty and equality busily tearing down all intermediate corporate bodies—guilds, provinces, churches—that stood between the individual and the state. The result of wiping the slate clean, he warned, would be to leave the individual defenseless against the power of the all-encompassing state that might speak in the name of, but that could never be controlled by, the public. Burke had no faith in the democratic dogma that the people best know their own interests. They frequently do not, he claimed, and when their will conflicts with their good they must, for their own sake, be restrained by an authority that is independent of them.[1] Otherwise they will use their freedom to destroy themselves. "The restraints on men, as well as their liberties, are to be reckoned among their rights. . . . Men have no right to what is not reasonable, and to what is not for their benefit."

Burke, in other words, attacked the first principle of the Revolution— that sovereignty resides in the entire body of citizens and is expressed in the law that their representatives make. The people may arrogate to themselves the *power* of governing, but, he said, that does not give them the *right* to govern. "Government is a contrivance of human wisdom to provide for human *wants*," and such wisdom comes only from long ages of experience. No individual or group has a right to flout experience and destroy a constitution that has been centuries in the building, for no one has the sagacity to create a better one from whole cloth. The rationalists argue that they have such sagacity, but their "new conquering empire of light and reason" is an illusion: they misconceive the nature of society and government and try to apply a logic of human rights that is "the offspring of cold hearts and muddy understandings."

Burke revered history as the medium of divine creation. In his own way he had as deep a religious conviction as Whitefield or John Wesley; he saw in the social order, fashioned through countless generations, the handiwork of God and regarded those who would jettison it as infidels. The value of humanity's historical heritage needed to be stressed in a time of revolution. The *Reflections*, it is true, had dangerous seeds, which sprouted in later Toryism into an idolatry of the past, a belief that whatever had stood the test of time was good and that innovation was *ipso facto* bad. But seeds of the future did not concern the conservatives of the 1790s. What mattered to them was that Burke provided an articulate credo with which to defend their threatened world.

By the time this credo appeared in 1790, the upheaval in France was dividing British public opinion. Britons were having to examine what they believed and to take a stand on the issue of reform. Many stood with Burke. Others, such as Charles James Fox, insisted that true Whiggism was dedicated to the cause of liberty and that the Revolution, whatever its mistakes and even its crimes, was furthering that cause. These factions were relatively moderate, but on each side of them were extremists. To the right of Burke were the arch conservatives, who identified reform with treason. To the left of Fox were radicals, even republicans, who sent addresses and del-

---

[1]The same question of popular sovereignty posed by the French Revolution had also been to the fore during the Puritan Revolution, and Burke's stand had been foreshadowed by that reluctant revolutionary, Oliver Cromwell. The people were bent on doing as they pleased even if it meant their destruction, Cromwell decided; and his answer was to force on them "what's for their good, not what pleases them."

EDMUND BURKE (1729–1797) AND THOMAS PAINE (1737–1809) In the 1790s and for decades thereafter, Burke and Paine were the rival prophets of conservatism and radicalism. *(Library of Congress)*

egations to the National Assembly in Paris and worked to promote French principles at home. The views of one of these Francophiles were thus parodied by a contemporary:

> Whatever is in France is right;
> Terror and blood are my delight;
> Parties with us do not excite
>   enough rage;
> Our boasted laws I hate and curse,
> Bad from the first, by age grown worse;
> I pant and sigh for univers-
>   al suffrage.

The most famous of the republicans was Tom Paine. He had already made a name for himself in 1776 by his fiery pamphlet, *Common Sense,* supporting the American Revolution, and he now threw his heart into supporting the French. He answered Burke in 1791 by publishing *The Rights of Man,* a violent and uncompromising attack, in the name of democracy, on the whole nature of British oligarchical society. Monarchs for Paine were no more than the descendants of robber chieftains; no one was more noble by birth than another. Parasitical courtiers, placemen, pensioners, and unnecessary soldiers and sailors riddled society; if they were eliminated, £4 million a year might readily be devoted to children's allowances, old-age pensions, and education. The pamphlet, both provocative and inexpensive, had an enormous circulation—partly subsidized by democratic clubs—among artisans and small tradesmen; during the next half-century it had a greater impact on British working-class radicalism than any other work. The government's immediate reply was to indict Paine for seditious libel. He fled to France, where he was first elected to the legislature and then condemned as an enemy of the Revolution whose virtues he had so ardently extolled. Having barely escaped the guillotine, he spent his final years in the United States.

The fear of a popular rising in Britain, which underlay the government's prosecution of Paine, proved to be unfounded. The common people were as much divided as their betters. Agitators wandered the country, preaching that a republic was at hand and that all property would be divided equally; in some areas mobs responded by rioting against the established order. But in other areas the riots were against reformers, among whom Joseph Priestley was the most prominent victim. His house in Birmingham, with his manuscripts and scientific instruments, was sacked and destroyed, and he too, like Paine, was eventually forced to find refuge in the United States. The old days of embattled factions, of political trials and forced exile, seemed to be returning.

THE WAR IN EUROPE (1793–1797)

For almost four years after the outbreak of the Revolution, Pitt tried to keep peace at home and abroad. He hoped to contain the agitation of domestic radicals without resorting to stringent repression and to avoid a conflict with France that would undo all the progress he had made in financial retrenchment. But by November 1792 the second hope was fading: French armies had turned back the Austro-Prussian invasion in the previous summer, had overrun the Austrian Netherlands, and were menacing Holland. In Paris the monarchy had given place to a republic and the National Assembly to a new legislature, the Convention, that was increasingly dominated by its most radical element, the Jacobins. The Convention had proclaimed that "France will grant her help to all peoples who desire to recover their liberty." The Jacobins, as the only judges of who these desirous peoples were, could use the proclamation as ground for conquering any part of Europe that they pleased.

With this kind of threat the British were familiar. Since the days of Marlborough they had fought French expansion into the Low Countries, into Germany, across the Alps; and French armies were no less a threat under the new tricolor of the Republic than under the Bourbon lilies. Pitt had no desire to fight the Revolution while it remained within the frontiers of France, as Austria and Prussia had done, but no responsible British prime minister could sit by while the French established their hegemony in western Europe. The Convention was launching an idealistic conflict, spiced with the hope of aggrandizement. Whitehall, which cared little about the ideals and a great deal about the aggrandizement, was being drawn into a struggle to defend the old balance of power.

In February 1793 France declared war on Britain, Holland, and Spain, and so added them to a coalition that already included Sardinia, Prussia, and Austria—a ring of enemies that would have done credit to Louis XIV. Their aims, in which even Pitt now acquiesced, were to despoil France of border provinces and overseas colonies and to reimpose on the French people the regime that they had shaken off. To the Revolution the allies opposed a stark negative, with no hope for the future. They intended to crush French power along with French ideas; if they had succeeded, as Fox said, they would have given "all the kings of Europe a perpetual guarantee against all peoples who might be oppressed by them in any part of the world."

The allies seemed to have every chance of succeeding. The War of the First Coalition, on the face of it, should have crushed the Revolution in its infancy. The bureaucratic and military system of the Bourbons was in ruins; factions in the Convention struggled for power and for their own lives, under the periodic threat of the Paris mob; the royalists of northwestern France were in arms in a counterrevolution. Yet a nation that seemed to be disintegrating won the war with ease. In 1795, when the Jacobin Republic gave place to the bourgeois regime of the Directory, Holland was conquered and Prussia and Spain were forced out of the war; only Sardinia, Austria, and Britain continued to fight. In 1796–1797 a young French general from Corsica, Napoleon Bonaparte, eliminated Sardinia and Austria by a whirlwind campaign in the Po Valley. Britain was left alone. France annexed Belgium, turned Holland into a satellite republic, extended its eastern frontier to the Rhine, and dominated northern Italy. What the Bourbons had dreamed of the Directory achieved.

The military force that the Revolution generated in France deserves explanation, or it remains as mysterious as it was to its victims in the war. French armies, first under the Republic and then under the Directory, defied all the rules and went from triumph to triumph, producing such a military overturn as had never been seen before. It was only a foretaste of what was to come. Small wonder that contemporaries were bewildered. They could not grasp the fact that a military revolution, growing out of the social revolution within France, was producing a new kind of warfare. Change of such magnitude is seldom fully understood even by those who initiate and profit from it, let alone by those who are beaten and demoralized by it.

The War of the First Coalition was a conflict between two kinds of society, and the contrast between them was mirrored in their armies. Those of the *anciens régimes* were products of a world sharply divided between the privileged and unprivileged: officers were gentlemen; common soldiers were mere canaille, creatures to be insulated from contact with civilians, supplied with their needs by the commissariat, and controlled by rigorous discipline.[2] An army in consequence moved and fought under a tight rein, and the premise that its individual soldiers could not be trusted to act on their own affected both tactics and strategy.

This premise disappeared in France as a result of the Revolution. When the Jacobins had to improvise a military system in 1792, they called the country to arms in a *levée en masse,* which was in itself a major act of revolution. It created a new kind of army, which had to fight in a new way if it was to fight at all. The army was huge and was largely composed of recruits who had little training and great enthusiasm. Because these citizen soldiers were numerous and ill trained, they were expendable, for the government could draw on the manpower of the nation to replace them in short order. Because they were enthusiastic, they did not need to be tightly controlled to prevent desertion; they could forage on their own. The army therefore needed to carry fewer supplies, moved at a speed that its opponents could not match, and, even more important, had the capacity, which its enemy lacked, to exploit a victory to the full. These raw troops were formidable.

The nature of battle changed to match the changed nature of the fighting man. The French relied on mass more than specialized training, fervor more than discipline, and could afford much heavier losses than the enemy. French soldiers soon learned how to utilize their advantages on the battlefield, flowing around the static lines of regulars, and how to turn their opponents' retreat into a rout. Battle began to yield them rich dividends. It ceased to be "the remedy of the desperate" and became the means of winning a campaign, a province, an empire. The old days of limited war for limited ends were over: the Jacobin military revolution had opened almost unlimited possibilities of conquest.

THE IMPACT OF WAR AT HOME

These conquests, which began the disintegration of the old order on the continent, staggered the ruling classes in Britain and forced them, though slowly, to mobilize the nation's resources as they had never been mobilized before. In the days of Queen Anne the government had spent some £5 million per year for military purposes, and in the days of the elder Pitt it had spent £15 million; the expenses of the quarter century of war that began in 1793 were to average £40 million per year. No government could raise such sums without unprecedented taxation and a great increase in the debt. The amount derived from customs and excise duties—the normal source of rev-

---

[2]For a discussion of eighteenth-century warfare see Chapter 6.

enue for the state—quadrupled during the war years, and that derived from the land tax doubled. Even so, these sums proved insufficient, and in 1797 William Pitt persuaded Parliament to impose an income tax on those who earned more than £60 a year. All these taxes combined failed to match expenses, however, and by the time the war was over Britain had tripled its national debt.

The needs of war distorted the development of the economy in other ways. For shipbuilders and munitions makers the war constituted a boon; for overseas merchants the vicissitudes of the conflict closed some traditional avenues of trade and opened others. Consumer industries like brewing were handicapped by high excise taxes, while the construction of roads, canals, and ordinary houses was severely curtailed by a sharp rise in interest rates. In 1797 the Bank of England stopped redeeming its notes in gold on demand, an action that spurred an inflationary trend that was already well under way. Eighteenth-century Britons were accustomed to price fluctuations resulting from the harvest, but these ups and downs tended to average out over the years, and long-range price stability had been the rule. The inflation of the 1790s came therefore as an unexpected shock.

Wartime inflation and the poor harvests of 1794 and 1795 accentuated the problem of poor relief. In 1795 in the Berkshire village of Speenhamland, the justices of the peace initiated a novel form of aid for workers whose wages had not kept up with rising prices. Their wages were supplemented with contributions from the poor rates, in accordance with a sliding scale tied to the price of bread. The so-called Speenhamland system came to be applied in much of the country during the decades that followed; it helped bring about the tripling of poor rate expenses by the end of the Napoleonic Wars. The system has been praised for its humanity and condemned both for its high cost and for its effect in deterring the employer from raising wages and the laborer from working harder. Whatever the limitations of the system, and of a related one of allowances for low-paid workers with more than two children, the working poor received some measure of protection in a period of critical economic change; the cost was the price of assuaging what might otherwise have been explosive discontent. At a time when much of Europe was torn by revolution spreading outward from France, most British laborers remained loyal to a society that, for all its shortcomings, was concerned in keeping them alive.[3]

In the early years of the war the oligarchs were, however, far from certain of that loyalty. They saw in every critic of the status quo a Francophile conspirator, and their alarm infected the government and the judiciary. Any attempt at change came to be regarded with suspicion: a motion to reform Parliament, for example, which had won 174 votes in the House of Commons in 1785, mustered only 41 when it was reintroduced in 1793. Pitt's ministry, reflecting this changed mood in the ruling class, began to adopt repressive measures. Aliens were put under severe restrictions in 1793, and

---

[3]J.D. Marshall, *The Old Poor Law, 1795–1834* (1968), provides a succinct introduction to the subject.

the government was authorized to expel them at its discretion. From 1794 to 1801 habeas corpus was suspended, so that suspects could be—and were—held in prison for years without trial. In 1795 the Treasonable Practices Act broadened the law of treason to cover any writing or utterance that incited to contempt of the sovereign, the authorities, or the constitution. In the same year the Seditious Meetings Act required the license of a magistrate for any gathering of more than fifty persons; this drastic interference with freedom of assembly broke up most of the radical clubs that had been flourishing since 1789. Freedom of the press was as drastically curtailed: cheap newspapers were forced out of business by stamp duties, and printers were held strictly accountable for publishing anything that displeased the government. The rights of the citizen, in short, no longer included the right even to grumble at the established order.

The judges enforced the new legislation with a rigor of their own. They were trained in conservatism, like all the legal fraternity. They also shared the general belief that a conspiracy was afoot to subvert the constitution, of which they considered themselves the guardians, and they rallied to its defense. Whoever preached the necessity of reform, one of them said, was guilty of sedition. Whether or not this was good law was beside the point; what mattered was not how the law read but how it was interpreted from the bench. The government needed only to bring him prisoners, declared a Scottish judge, and he would find the law to hang them. In Scotland this was no idle boast, for the bench selected the members of the jury and instructed them in their findings; against such a system the accused had little protection, and treason was likely to be whatever the court said it was. English jurymen could on occasion be more independent, as they showed in 1794 by acquitting the shoemaker Thomas Hardy and eleven other leaders of the London Corresponding Society who were being tried together for treason. But this was a rare exception: for the most part the judges stretched the law to serve their purposes, and no one gainsaid them. An extreme example was the trial of some journalists in 1799 for criticizing Russian tariff regulations as detrimental to British trade, at a moment when a Russo-British alliance had just been formed. The astounding charge against the accused was that they had libeled the Russian tsar, and if the libel went unpunished, the judge solemnly informed the jury, the tsar might call Britain to account for insulting him. Judge-made law, working in such preposterous ways as this, became a gag for every form of opinion that the government disapproved. "God help the people," said Charles Fox, "who have such judges."

But the people at large feared and hated French Jacobinism so much that they gave little thought to what was happening to their liberties. The panic that gripped the upper classes spread to the rest of the nation and grew, as such hysteria often does, by feeding on its own fancies. Magistrates all over the country were unearthing what they considered proofs of sedition; spies and informers were turning up the lurid tidbits that they were paid to find; and a voluntary association of snoopers was gathering "evidence" from the gossiping servant, the disgruntled peasant, the drunken innkeeper, and other similarly reliable sources. Fear of the traitor and the foreign agent was rampant.

But fear was only one of the factors that united the country behind its government. Another was the growing hostility to the Revolution on religious grounds. The Jacobins in Paris were moving not only toward greater radicalism but also toward more and more open atheism and were thereby alienating all British Christians; the Methodists in particular, with their vast lower-class membership, were discovering in Jacobinism the figure of Antichrist. The common people had a traditional antipathy to the French, which was now heightened by apprehension and religious antagonism. In the grip of these emotions the masses, restive as they were under the hardships that beset them, followed the lead of their rulers and accepted the idea that only a traitor would want to change the established order. The reform movement, which had been so active before the war, was forced underground for a generation to come.

One man stood out almost alone against official repression. Charles James Fox continued to insist, in the teeth of misrepresentation and obloquy, that the true strength of the nation lay in the citizen's freedom to think and speak and criticize. He himself showed the way. Year after year he proclaimed in Parliament the virtues of the French Revolution and the iniquity of fighting it, and flayed the government with all the power of his oratory. When most of the former opposition was supporting Pitt's ministry, Fox was forced to pay for his courage by political ostracism. But he served his country well. At a time when Pitt was allowing conservatism to become identified with curtailing popular rights, a policy based on fear, Fox kept alive a liberalism based on confidence in the people. The legacy of Pitt's regime was the narrow, ossified Toryism of 1815–1830; the legacy of Fox was the reforming spirit of Whiggism that triumphed in the years thereafter.

Pitt and his colleagues had much reason to be fearful. The adjustments imposed by industrialization were aggravated by the burden of wartime taxation as well as by bad harvests and agrarian unrest—and only partly alleviated by the prevailing system of poor relief. Ireland was in ferment. From Paris and from domestic crackpots came talk of invasion supported by insurrection. The war, above all, was going from bad to worse. The government concluded that drastic measures were needed to save the nation, and the error behind the conclusion is apparent only by hindsight. The British people, for all their grievances, were far from insurrection. Their provincialism insulated them from the ideas of the Revolution, as geography insulated them from its power. They were therefore largely immune to the moral and physical forces that were reshaping the continent and deserved more trust than their rulers put in them.[4]

---

[4]Albert Goodwin, *The Friends of Liberty: the English Democratic Movement in the Age of the French Revolution* (1979), provides a comprehensive narrative account of the reformers whom the British government feared as revolutionaries. In *Threats of Revolution in Britain, 1789–1848* (1977), Malcolm Thomis and Peter Holt evaluate the significance of those threats.

THE NAVAL WAR (1793–1797)

The triumphs of France on land in the War of the First Coalition had no counterpart at sea. The Revolution that put new power into the hands of France's generals did not help its admirals, for their problem was different in kind. Although they too had numerous and enthusiastic recruits, they could not recreate the old Bourbon navy on revolutionary lines. The reason was simple. The square-rigged ship of the line, which was the mainstay of the fleet, was so complex that her crew needed years of training in discipline and seamanship before she was an effective fighting instrument, let alone a smoothly functioning part of a squadron. A general could soon fashion an army out of inexperienced men and officers promoted from the ranks; an admiral who put to sea with ships so manned was inviting disaster. The factors that made military innovation possible and successful did not apply to war under sail.

From the beginning of hostilities, in consequence, Britain had the wherewithal for naval predominance. The expeditionary forces that she sent to the continent suffered as humiliating defeats as the armies of her allies, and she squandered some 80,000 troops on useless expeditions to the West In-

A COMMEMORATIVE PANEL (1794) The panel is surrounded by portraits of four naval commanders. The British lion at the top radiates light. The royal coat of arms is shown in the middle. The word *commerce* is engraved at the bottom. *(Sutcliff-Smith Collection)*

dies; but her power at sea was beyond challenge throughout the War of the First Coalition. In 1793 she had half again as many serviceable ships of the line as the enemy, with far better crews; and her naval administration, by comparison with that of the French, was a model of efficiency. If she had immediately capitalized on her strength to establish a tight blockade, she could probably have brought France to starvation.

Instead she frittered away her chance, and the principal blame lay with the naval command. The senior admirals were an undistinguished lot, most of whom had helped to lose the American war; they were still governed by the notion that a battle should be fought between two parallel lines firing at each other, and such tactics were bound to be inconclusive.[5] The Admiralty had no more idea of how to plan a blockade than it had had in 1778; in winter it recalled its fleets to port to protect them from storms, and permitted the enemy to come and go as they pleased. British naval predominance was consequently used to little purpose while it lasted; and it did not last long.

In 1797, when the collapse of the First Coalition left the British to fight alone, they faced the same ring of enemies at sea that had nearly ruined them in the War of Independence. France had gained the Dutch navy by conquering Holland and had bullied Spain into alliance; the British, faced by these combined fleets, were forced onto the defensive. They withdrew entirely from the Mediterranean, and even their hold on the Channel was endangered. To add to their troubles came mutiny in their navy and rebellion in Ireland. Their worst crisis in the whole quarter-century of war was in the years 1797–1798, when they were in greater peril than ever again until the dark days of 1940–1941.

They might not have weathered the crisis if the new generation of admirals rising to high command had not contained, at long last, some men of genius. One of the best of the new school was Sir John Jervis, the commander in chief of the fleet that had withdrawn from the Mediterranean. He was a cold, awesome disciplinarian with a fighting spirit. In February 1797 he encountered off Cape St. Vincent, the southwestern tip of Portugal, a large Spanish fleet sailing to join the French and cover an invasion of the British Isles. Jervis, outnumbered by almost two to one, attacked with a confidence that was justified in the event. At the decisive moment of the battle one of his officers, who commanded the smallest ship in the line, left his post without orders and interposed his vessel between the divided segments of the enemy to keep them from uniting; he then boarded and captured two of the huge Spaniards. Jervis acknowledged this bold initiative in his sub-

[5]For a discussion of traditional naval tactics see Chapter 6. The classic study of the British navy during the period covered in this and the following chapter is Alfred T. Mahan, *The Influence of Sea Power upon the French Revolution and Empire*, 10th ed., 2 vols. (1898). For more modern accounts, briefer and eminently readable, see William O. Stevens and Allan Westcott, *A History of Sea Power* (1944), chaps. 10–12; and E. B. Potter and Chester W. Nimitz, eds., *Sea Power: A Naval History* (1960), chaps. 6–9.

ADMIRAL HORATIO
NELSON (1758–1805)
A painting by Friedrich
Heinrich Fuger, ca. 1800.
*(With acknowledgments
to the Royal Naval
Museum, Portsmouth)*

ordinate, who had flouted the time-honored principle of holding the line
and had thereby converted an indecisive action into a triumph. London was
soon buzzing with the officer's name: Horatio Nelson.

The Battle of Cape St. Vincent shattered the Franco-Spanish plan of invasion, and in the autumn of 1797 a defeat of the Dutch ended the threat
from that quarter. But between these two victories the Royal Navy had to
meet and surmount a greater danger that came from within itself. In April
mutiny broke out in the Channel Fleet at Portsmouth and soon spread to
the squadrons guarding the Thames against the invasion that was then mo-
mentarily expected from Holland. For weeks the nation was stripped of its
defenses. The spirit of disaffection seemed suddenly to be everywhere, and
even the army was suspect.

The mutiny had nothing to do with French revolutionary ideas but was
the spontaneous outburst of men tried beyond endurance. The sailors were
the roughest and toughest members of the king's service. Some had been
forced into it by the press gangs that roamed port towns in search of likely
victims, some by parochial authorities who wanted to be rid of them; some
were foreigners, some Irish jailbirds. The great majority were loyal and
grumblingly accepted their cramped quarters, abominable food, and ferocious discipline. What they would not accept, and what finally touched off
the explosion, was their rate of pay. Wages in the merchant marine had

risen, under pressure of demand and of wartime inflation, to four times the naval rate. Although soldiers had recently received a slight raise, sailors were paid what they had been for more than a century and rarely got even that when it was due. They had families to feed. When wages were in arrears and prices were soaring, the families starved.

The Admiralty had ignored petitions from the Channel Fleet, which on Easter Sunday, 1797, took matters into its own hands. The men pushed their officers politely aside, seized the ships, and then waited for the government to redress their grievances. The Admiralty for once acted with speed and good sense: the First Lord hurried to Portsmouth and conceded the substance of the men's demands, subject to parliamentary approval. The crisis seemed to be resolved. But the mutineers' taste of power was intoxicating. Parliament acted too slowly for them, and they again took over the ships; the contagion spread to the fleets at Plymouth, Yarmouth, and the Nore, off the mouth of the Thames. The navy was paralyzed.

When Admiral Duncan sailed from Yarmouth to watch the Dutch coast, all but two of his ships deserted him. With those two the indomitable old man took up his blockading station, and to keep the enemy from attacking him he signaled over the horizon to his nonexistent fleet. For some days his bluff succeeded, until one by one his mutinous ships rejoined him. For the Admiralty had managed to pacify all the malcontents except those at the Nore, where trouble continued for weeks. When supplies to the fleet were cut off, the mutinous sailors retaliated by seizing every ship that tried to enter or leave the Thames. But before long they began to realize the futility of their defiance, which the public regarded as treason, and by the middle of June the last resistance at the Nore fizzled out.

Twenty-nine ringleaders were executed and others variously punished, but the men in general profited from what they had done. They had taught their superiors a salutary lesson: that obedience could not be taken for granted. Sailors were men, and if driven too far they would, like the Frenchmen they despised, assert their rights. The most pressing of their grievances were redressed and the worst abuses remedied. Slowly but surely conditions in the fleet began to improve, and with them morale, until within a few years the Royal Navy was the finest fighting instrument that Britain had ever known.

THE EGYPTIAN EXPEDITION (1798)

In the spring of 1798 all signs pointed to an imminent French invasion of England, the one unconquered enemy. General Bonaparte, fresh from his triumphs in Italy, commanded an army massed on the Channel coast of France, where the ports were bustling with preparation. Pitt called the people to arms, and thousands of volunteers responded; plans were made for laying waste the countryside and fortifying every tenable point. "The nation had not yet learnt to know its own strength or its resources," wrote a foreign observer. "The government has taught it the secret and inspired it with an unbounded confidence almost amounting to presumption."[6] Presumption indeed it was, for yeomanry armed with fowling pieces would have been no match for Bonaparte's veterans.

But the Corsican had no idea of attempting invasion, which he knew would be suicidal as long as the Royal Navy held the Channel. His preparations were disguise for a quite different plan—to attack Egypt. He intended to open the Mediterranean and Near East to French influence, cut the British route to India by way of Suez, and perhaps eventually move against India itself. The Directory supported him with an enthusiasm born of self-interest: his success would bring wealth and glory to a shaky regime, and his failure would rid it of a general who was too popular for comfort. In May, Bonaparte sailed from Toulon for Alexandria.

His Egyptian expedition was the first sign that his genius, dazzling as it was, had a serious limitation. No leader in history had greater gifts for commanding an army or organizing and administering a state, but Napoleon was inferior to many of his pedestrian contemporaries in his understanding of sea power. He expected to establish on the Nile a base for operations against the Near East, but that base would depend on waterborne communications with Europe. If those communications were cut, his army would sooner or later be imprisoned between sea and desert. He was acting on the assumption that Britain would not or could not regain control of the Mediterranean—an assumption that was fallacious.

Pitt realized that Britain could not make headway alone and that its best chance of creating a new coalition lay in reasserting British naval power in the Mediterranean. He had consequently weakened the fleet at home, despite the threat of invasion, in order to reinforce the squadron at Gibraltar under Admiral Jervis—now Lord St. Vincent in honor of his victory—and permit him to reenter the inland sea. St. Vincent thereupon sent most of his battle line to join Nelson, who was cruising off Toulon to observe the French preparations. The Royal Navy was resuming a blockade in force.

On May 19 Bonaparte sailed from Toulon, convoyed by thirteen ships of the line. On June 6 Nelson, joined by his reinforcement, set off in pursuit with thirteen ships of the line and one heavy frigate but without light frigates for scouting. On June 22 he learned that the French had captured Malta from the Knights of St. John, who had long possessed it, and had then sailed eastward; he guessed that their destination was Egypt, and in a fever of impatience set sail to overtake them. On the night of June 22 Nelson passed the French fleet in the darkness. The enemy heard his signal guns and made off, and by sunrise were safe over the horizon. He soon outdistanced them and, on reaching Alexandria, found to his chagrin no signs or

---

[6]Quoted by Arthur Bryant, *The Years of Endurance, 1793–1802* (1942), p. 228. This is a vivid and lively account of the first phase of the war. See also Clive Emsley, *British Society and the French Wars, 1793–1815* (1979) and the relevant chapters of Asa Briggs, *The Age of Improvement, 1783–1867* (1959).

rumor of them. Immediately he left to hunt along the Syrian coast. As Egyptian observers watched his sails disappear over the eastern horizon, they saw other sails rise from the sea to the west. Bonaparte was arriving; sheer luck had saved him for his future.

He landed his army, crushed native resistance, and was soon secure in the mastery of Egypt. Yet his fleet was far from secure. The coast offered it no refuge, no fortified harbor like that of Toulon, and Nelson was hunting blindly but indefatigably. He had no more idea of the enemy's whereabouts after a month of cruising than he had had at the start: "the Devil's children," he said, "have the Devil's luck!" He beat back westward to Sicily, turned east again, and on July 28 learned that the French had gone to Egypt after all. Once more he pressed for Alexandria. He was a master of teamwork, and he had trained his captains—whom he called his band of brothers—to cooperate by instinct.

On the afternoon of August 1 the fleet sighted the enemy ships moored in Aboukir Bay, near one of the mouths of the Nile to the east of Alexandria. The French admiral had anchored in line ahead, facing the mouth of the bay; shoal water to port seemed to preclude attack from that side, and only the starboard batteries were cleared for action. The wind blew from the sea, and the British ran before it as they bore down on the enemy van. Their tension was at fever pitch. They knew that their chief was determined on victory at any cost. "If we succeed," asked one of his captains, "what will the world say?" "There is no *if* in the case," Nelson answered. "That we shall succeed is certain; who will live to tell the story is a very different question."

The only way to complete success, when the enemy had almost as many ships as the British and larger ones, was to concentrate in full force on one part of the French line after another. Nelson gambled on there being enough room to pass between the line and the shoals without running aground; his five leading ships got through, by superb seamanship, and anchored on the west side of the van while the rest of the fleet assaulted the other side. Darkness fell, and the battle raged on. Nelson himself was dazed and disabled by a flying splinter, but his captains knew their job. The French were caught between two fires and could reply to only one because their port batteries were useless. Their ships in the van surrendered one by one; the attack moved on to the center, where their huge flagship caught fire and blew up with a glare that lighted the bay and a shock felt for ten miles. All night the cannonading waxed and waned until both sides were too exhausted to man the guns. At dawn two enemy ships at the rear of the line slipped their anchors and escaped to sea, the lone survivors of thirteen. No conflict between fleets of comparable strength had ever before produced such an overwhelming victory. Nelson's novel approach to naval warfare was to attempt to destroy every ship that he could reach, and he pursued this aim with whole-souled concentration, undeterred by fear of damage to his ships, of casualties in his crews, of wounds or death for himself. The

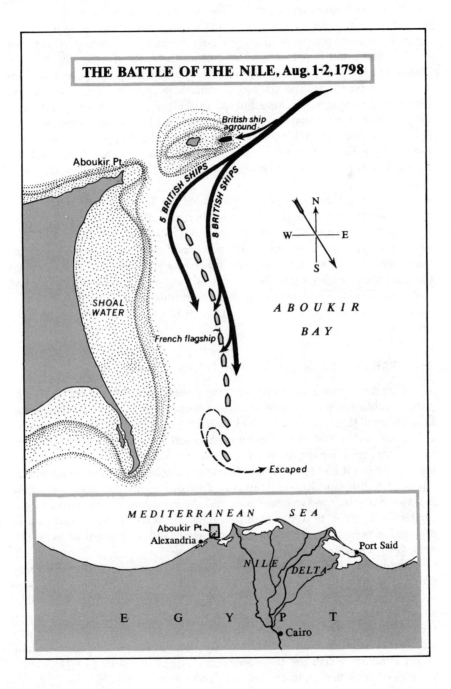

THE BATTLE OF THE NILE, Aug. 1-2, 1798

British ship aground

Aboukir Pt.

5 BRITISH SHIPS

8 BRITISH SHIPS

N
W — E
S

SHOAL WATER

French flagship

A B O U K I R

B A Y

Escaped

MEDITERRANEAN   SEA

Aboukir Pt.
Alexandria

Port Said

NILE   DELTA

E   G   Y   P   T

Cairo

kind of victory that he sought justified all losses. His goal, like Bonaparte's, was a battle of annihilation; and at the Nile he achieved it.

The results were far-reaching. The Corsican and his army were cooped up in Egypt, the prisoners of his miscalculation. In the spring of 1799 he tried to break out by moving into Syria to attack the Turks, who had declared war on him: he dreamed of emulating Alexander the Great by conquering the Near East and advancing from there against India, or of moving on Constantinople and taking Europe in the rear. These grandiose fancies evaporated before the city of Acre, when a small British squadron captured his siege artillery and landed it to strengthen the Turkish garrison. The French were repulsed, the invasion collapsed, and Bonaparte fell back on Egypt. For the first time in his career he had, thanks to sea power, met defeat.

In August 1799 he and his staff sailed for home in two frigates. He evaded British cruisers and in early October landed in France, where he was received as a savior. His skillful propaganda had magnified his triumphs and concealed his underlying failure, whereas the failure of the Directory at home was all too apparent. In November he overthrew it and established the Consulate, with himself as first consul; and where he was first no one else was second. The Revolution had come full circle. It had destroyed a decrepit absolutism only to create in its stead an efficient one: a military dictatorship.

THE WAR OF THE SECOND COALITION (1799–1801)

The Egyptian expedition impressed the French people, thanks to Bonaparte's publicity, but did not impress Europe. The Powers saw in it the long-awaited sign that France had overreached itself. Its ambitions were clearly insatiable: France had occupied Switzerland and the Papal States before Bonaparte's departure for Alexandria and had mulcted them to pay for his expedition; it had seized Malta from the Knights of St. John, whom Tsar Paul, the half-insane Russian autocrat, regarded as his particular protégés; it was infiltrating the German states and the Kingdom of the Two Sicilies, the feeble Bourbon power in southern Italy. The French nation was undermining the political structure of the continent, and only proof of its weakness was needed to rekindle armed opposition.

The Battle of the Nile was staggering proof. In its aftermath the French position in the Mediterranean began to collapse. The British seized Minorca, which they had lost in 1783, and so regained their base for blockading Toulon; their troops strengthened the fragile Bourbon hold on Sicily; their fleet encouraged a revolt on Malta and blockaded its French conquerors. This reversal of fortune persuaded Austria and Russia that the time had finally come to overthrow the Revolution, and by the spring of 1799 they were allied with Britain in the Second Coalition.

At first the allies swept everything before them. A Cossack general, Suvorov, stormed through Italy; the Austrians defeated the armies of the Directory in Switzerland and Germany; a French fleet that had ventured into the Mediterranean retreated ignominiously; rebellion again broke out in western France; an Anglo-Russian expeditionary force invaded Holland. In that summer of 1799, when Bonaparte was still in Egypt, the French empire was tottering. A concerted push might well have brought it down, but the allies lost their opportunity by bickering among themselves. The eruption of Suvorov into Italy disturbed the Austrians, who had no desire to see the peninsula pass from French to Russian dominance: they were glad when he was transferred to Switzerland, and they failed to support him there. Anglo-Russian cooperation in Holland was little better, and the expedition failed dismally. By autumn the French had suppressed rebellion at home and regained control of Holland, Switzerland, and western Germany. The Austrians held Italy, but at the price of infuriating Tsar Paul. In the autumn he withdrew from the war, just as Bonaparte was seizing the reins in Paris.

The next two years were disastrous for Britain. The First Consul justified his coup d'état to the French people by dealing promptly with the Austrians, in a campaign that broke their grip on Italy and forced them, in February 1801, to make peace. Meanwhile Bonaparte had courted and won the favor of the mercurial tsar, who was persuaded to turn against Britain and put an embargo on its ships; Russia also joined Sweden, Denmark, and Prussia in a new League of Armed Neutrality, like that of 1780, to enforce its members' right to trade as they pleased. This defiance of Britain's blockade revealed how low its stock had fallen. The British had been deserted by their allies; their navy had done nothing of moment since the Battle of the Nile except force the surrender of Malta; their troops had been ferried around the coasts of Europe on a series of pointless and fruitless expeditions. The strategy of Whitehall was at its nadir.

But the main instrument of strategy, the fleet, was stronger than ever before. Between 1795 and 1800 it made ready for its central task of blockade by conquering what had hitherto been its most lethal enemy. This was not the French but scurvy. The disease is caused by a deficiency of vitamin C, found in fresh fruits and vegetables, both of which were lacking in the sailor's diet; prolonged cruising without some source of vitamins had always meant that scurvy would decimate the crew. Although nothing was known about vitamins, since the early seventeenth century lime juice had been recognized as an antiscorbutic, or corrective of scurvy; during the War of the Austrian Succession a way had been found to concentrate and preserve the juice. Not until 1795, however, did the Admiralty order a regular issue of this remedy throughout the fleet. The effect within the next five years was virtually to eliminate the disease in the navy. Crews might remain healthy at sea for indefinite periods; the ships of a blockading squadron no longer needed to be replaced in alternation by ships fresh from home, but could hold their station month after month. The result was an enormous increment in naval power.

The navy had also learned the techniques of effective blockade. They were extremely arduous, but Lord St. Vincent, now in command of the

Channel Fleet, enforced them with a ruthless disregard for wear and tear on ships or men. He cruised in all weather and seasons off the western approaches to the Channel, where he was in touch by frigates with smaller squadrons masking the exits from Brest; if the enemy dared to come out, one of these detachments would summon help from the main fleet. The enemy did not dare. Their ships of the line were penned into the roadstead of Brest like helpless sheep, and the First Consul's repeated orders to put to sea were not obeyed. He was having his second lesson in the uses of sea power.

By the spring of 1801 he had a plan for circumventing that power through the League of Armed Neutrality. If the Baltic states combined their navies against Britain, they would be enough of a threat so that the Channel Fleet, to meet it, would have to relax its stranglehold on Brest. But Whitehall had no intention of waiting passively for this plan to mature. The keystone of the neutral coalition was Denmark, and Pitt resolved to demonstrate to the Danes, and so to their would-be allies, the futility of their designs. He prepared in great secrecy to deliver an ultimatum to Copenhagen, backed by what Nelson called "the best negotiators in Europe"— twenty ships of the line.

The Admiralty, with the obtuseness it often showed in choosing men, entrusted the mission to an incompetent old admiral, Sir Hyde Parker, but had the good sense to name Baron Nelson of the Nile as his second in command. Nelson had done almost nothing since his victory except acquire a glamorous mistress. He had returned home with her and her complaisant husband and had broken with his own wife and been snubbed by the king; his career seemed to be over. But in a crisis the Admiralty wanted his talents, whatever the shortcomings of his private life, and gave him a second chance.

The Danes rejected the ultimatum. The only way to coerce them was to destroy their fleet, moored in Copenhagen harbor under strong shore defenses, and Parker was most reluctant to do so. To conquer the enemy Nelson had first to conquer his superior; this he did, and received permission to attack as he pleased. But in the middle of the battle Parker, watching from a distance, lost his nerve and signaled the ships to retire. They could not have done so if they would, and Nelson would not. He put his telescope to his blind eye and said that he saw no signal. His coy disobedience might have earned him a court-martial; instead, after he had battered and bluffed the Danes into submission, he superseded Parker and sailed to negotiate with the Russians. Tsar Paul had been assassinated. His successor, Alexander I, agreed to reopen his ports to British trade and admit the Royal Navy's right of search.

The League of Armed Neutrality had dissolved at the touch of force, and the British had made clear that they could at will control the Baltic. Meanwhile they had reemphasized their control of the Mediterranean by landing an army in Egypt to begin the reduction of the French garrison there. The long arm of their sea power now reached around Europe from the Gulf of Finland to the mouth of the Nile. Although Britain was once more alone and France was stronger than ever before, the effective limit of French ambitions was the water's edge.

THE IRISH CRISIS (1797–1801)

Pitt was no longer in power by the time the operations he had planned in the Baltic and Egypt came to fruition. He had been unseated, after having been in office almost eighteen years, by a complex of developments growing out of the Irish problem. He had tried and failed to deal with that problem in time of peace, and almost inevitably it returned to plague him in time of war. The pattern has been repeated over and over in British history, from the days of Elizabeth I to the days of Lloyd George: Irish grievances have gone unredressed until Britain has entered into a conflict at home or abroad, when the Irish have seized their opportunity for making trouble. They revolted against Elizabeth during her war with Spain. They revolted against Charles I on the eve of civil war in England and went on fighting until Cromwell crushed them. They rose in the cause of James II as King William was beginning his struggle with France and again were crushed. They threatened revolt when Britain had its back to the wall in the War of Independence, and this time succeeded in winning both economic and political concessions. But they were far from satisfied, and in the 1790s the story was once more repeated.

The legislative "independence" they had acquired in 1782 was proving illusory. Even by British standards the Irish Parliament was corrupt, and old religious tensions were reviving. Although Grattan's Parliament had restored the right to vote to Presbyterians and the right to hold land and to become lawyers or schoolmasters to Roman Catholics, a small Anglican clique continued to dominate the Irish executive. This clique was appointed by and dependent on the British government, and was adept at manipulating a legislature to which it owed no constitutional responsibility.

The 1780s brought a temporary economic boom to Ireland, and in Dublin impressive public buildings and private town houses were built. The French Revolution and the French Wars disrupted that boom, and Presbyterians and Roman Catholics alike were soon agitating once more for reform. Pitt, wishing to conciliate upper-class Catholics, secured for them in 1793 the right to vote for members of the Dublin Parliament, though not the right to be members themselves; the bogy of a legislature dominated by Catholics terrified most Protestants. The radicals of Ulster were beyond conciliation: their Society of United Irishmen wanted to transform the island into a democratic republic, and the means seemed ready to hand.

Emissaries had assured the French government that Ireland, if given a stiffening of troops, would chase the British into the sea. At the end of 1796 a strong French expedition sailed from Brest, eluded the fumbling British blockade, and appeared off the Irish coast. A storm prevented the soldiers from landing, but their coming at all stirred wild excitement in Ulster, which by the spring of 1797 was ripe for revolt. The Dublin government acted with the brutality of panic. Troops, largely Protestant militia, were sent to disarm the province, and what little discipline the men had soon vanished in an orgy of looting and burning and killing. The principal victims were Catholics, who were intermingled with the Presbyterians; refugees, with their tales of rapine, fled in thousands to the south. The harrying of Ulster had crushed disaffection there and ended the dream of a united Ireland, but it rekindled the religious furies of a hundred years before. The Orange and the Green, Protestant and Catholic, were at each other's throats as they had been on the Boyne. By the spring of 1798 Catholic Ireland was seething and, like Ulster the year before, looking to France for deliverance.

Again deliverance did not come. Pitt had weakened the fleet guarding the coast in order to send reinforcements to the Mediterranean; when he heard of Bonaparte's departure from Toulon he assumed that the enemy were bound for Ireland, where at the moment the southeastern counties were at the mercy of 30,000 peasants, bent on loot and massacre. But the French sailed instead for Egypt, while the British poured troops into Ireland and savagely suppressed the rising; a few French soldiers did land during the summer and autumn but were promptly rounded up. Whether the Directory could have exploited the crisis is an open question, like all historical might-have-beens. The stakes were high: landing an army in Ireland would have been hazardous in the face of the Royal Navy, but would also have been a knife in Britain's back, whereas landing in Egypt turned out to be a blow in the air. France first encouraged the Irish and then left them to their fate.

By the late summer of 1798 Ireland was again a conquered nation. The Dublin clique had destroyed the fragile union of Protestants and Catholics, had then provoked the latter to revolt, and had crushed them with almost the brutality of Cromwell's Ironsides. Dublin had only one policy—repression—and considered voices of moderation as treasonable. But this narrow, frightened executive had at last overreached itself. Pitt was no Cromwell: he would not govern through an army of occupation, and in any case he could not afford one during a European war. He was determined on a more lasting solution, which meant one that would be acceptable to Catholic Ireland—and therefore unacceptable to Dublin Castle. His worst troubles were beginning.

He had a solution in two parts that were integrally connected. One was a political union of Ireland and Great Britain, akin to the union of England and Scotland in 1707, with a single parliament in which the Irish would have proportional representation. The other was Catholic emancipation—in other words, the admission of Roman Catholics to the newly enlarged Westminster Parliament. They could not feasibly be admitted to the existing Dublin Parliament, as he had discovered, because the Protestant interest feared their domination. At Westminster they would be a small and unthreatening minority in a legislature overwhelmingly Protestant, but they would have a voice in government. The scheme had great advantages for both sides. The Irish would for the first time have members of Parliament of their own choosing, commercial barriers between the two countries would disappear, and the British would be rid of a governmental system that was artificial, antiquated, and unworkable. But the scheme could succeed only as a whole. Neither half by itself was viable: Protestant Ireland would never accept emancipation without union, and Catholic Ireland would never accept union without emancipation.

Pitt, with his orderly mind, decided to tackle the two halves of his problem separately—to achieve first legislative union and then Catholic emancipation. Union met little resistance in Britain but much in Ireland, where the Dublin Parliament was understandably reluctant to pass an act that would end its own existence. Pitt's Irish agents resorted to a campaign of corruption such as the eighteenth century had never witnessed, buying votes with peerages, honors, and simple bribes. Meanwhile the cabinet agreed informally to emancipation, and the prime minister's assurances of it won Irish Catholic support for union. In the summer of 1800 both Parliaments passed the Act of Union, which went into effect at the beginning of 1801. Twenty-eight Irish peers, elected for life, and four Irish bishops took their places in the British House of Lords, and a hundred Irish members in the House of Commons.[7] Virtual free trade was established between the two countries, along the lines that Pitt had tried and abandoned in 1785. The cross of St. Patrick was superimposed upon those of St. George and St. Andrew to form a new flag, the Union Jack, symbolizing the United Kingdom of Great Britain and Ireland.

The symbolism was hollow. The kingdom had not been united by the voluntary agreement of two nations acting through their representatives, as England and Scotland had been, but by the British government's imposing its will on a Parliament that did not represent either Protestant or Catholic Ireland. Pitt had achieved a settlement with the only means at hand, unsavory as they were; and nothing but success could make anyone forget the corruption out of which union had been born. Success, furthermore, was problematical. The prime minister had won only half a victory, and that by itself was not enough. Because Ireland could not be saved without union, one of his lieutenants remarked, "You must not take it for granted that it will be saved by it."

Pitt had not laid the groundwork for completing his victory. He had no binding pledge from his colleagues to support Catholic emancipation, and on this crucial point he had failed to convince the king. The blunder proved to be irretrievable. Supporters of the old order in Dublin and London were adamant against any concession to Catholics, and they could always appeal to the bigotry latent in the British electorate. But it turned out that they had

---

[7]The act allowed an Irish peer, if not elected by his fellow peers to the House of Lords, to stand for election to the House of Commons from a British constituency. This provision accounts for the continuance of titled Irish members in the lower house, some of whom, such as Lord Palmerston, played prominent roles in nineteenth-century politics.

no need to: they appealed instead to the bigot on the throne. George III, at his coronation, had taken an archaic oath to uphold the supremacy of the established Anglican Church; he believed, as he had long since made clear to Pitt, that permitting Catholics in Parliament would violate that oath. "I shall reckon any man my personal enemy," he said, "who proposes any such measure." He was in an excitable frame of mind, which threatened to lapse into the insanity that had already attacked him twice during his reign. But, if his mental balance was unreliable, his conscience was not.[8] His stubbornness produced a major crisis. The cabinet refused to press for emancipation, and Pitt was impaled on the horns of a dilemma. Because he could not fulfill, but would not repudiate, the assurance he had given the Irish Catholics, he took the only honorable course and submitted his resignation. The king reluctantly let him go, after extorting from him the promise that while his sovereign lived he would not reopen the Catholic question.

Pitt had staked his ministry on an equitable solution to the Irish problem, and he had lost. The Act of Union could not satisfy the Irish. They had surrendered the symbol of their own Parliament in order to be governed from London, on the understanding that they would be represented in that government; and what they were left with was a travesty of representation. The men who ostensibly guarded their interests in Westminster, the Irish members of the new House of Commons, were part of the same Protestant clique that had misgoverned Ireland into rebellion in 1798. To the old grievances that had produced rebellion was now added a sense of betrayal, of having been hoodwinked into union under false pretenses.

Many of the Irish detested their new status and went on detesting it for almost thirty years until, with the threat of a new rebellion, they forced emancipation. By then the harm had been done, for they had come to look on union as a British contrivance. What Pitt intended as part of a larger reconciliation became a mere political bond, which galled the Irish more and more as time wore on. Under a different king the problem might have been settled at the beginning of the nineteenth century; instead it grew for more than a hundred years, and in the end brought the United Kingdom to the verge of civil war. This was the price paid for George III's conscience.

THE PEACE OF AMIENS (1802)

Pitt's resignation came at a time when the country's will to fight was at low ebb. Twice Britain had joined in coalitions to stop French aggrandizement, and twice had seen them destroyed; now the kingdom was on its own and could no more hope for victory on land than France could at sea. After eight years of war the burden of the national debt was staggering: it had more than doubled since 1793 and stood at over £530 million. Prices were

---

[8]Some medical historians of our day tend to attribute the king's insanity to a hereditary metabolic disorder, porphyria, which was then unknown. See Ida Macalpine and Richard Hunter, *George III and the Mad Business* (1969).

rising far faster than wages, so that by 1800 some farm laborers were receiving in real wages less than half of what they had at the start of the war. Village mobs threatened to hang farmers who would not cut the price of their grain. Trade and industry, it is true, were booming: between 1796 and 1800 the value of British exports and imports increased by £12 million. But the spread of machinery in the manufacturing areas was throwing manual laborers out of work and creating bitter discontent, which was further heightened by a succession of calamitously bad harvests. Continuing the war seemed pointless, when rich and poor alike were longing to be free from the burden of what promised to be an interminable conflict. Their views were summed up by an admiral in the blockading squadron off Brest, who wrote that "nothing good can ever happen to us short of peace."

If Pitt had remained in office he might have opened peace negotiations, but he would not have conducted them as his successor did. The new prime minister, Henry Addington, was an amiable nonentity unversed in foreign affairs, and he had the gentleman's illusion that Bonaparte would behave like a gentleman. All began smoothly. The First Consul was ready to negotiate; he needed a breathing space to consolidate his position at home, to organize France's conquests and satellite states, and to create an effective navy. But his need did not make him easy to deal with. First he bullied Whitehall into an armistice that removed the pressure of blockade; then he haggled over terms for months, using bluff, threat, and deception, and ended by driving a hard bargain. In March 1802 the treaty of peace was signed at Amiens.

The British people went wild with rejoicing, but they had little to rejoice about. The government had returned virtually everything conquered overseas to France and its satellites, Holland and Spain; it had agreed to restore Malta to the Knights of St. John under a flimsy international guarantee, and to evacuate both British and French troops from Egypt; and it had done nothing to secure British trade with Europe. Most humiliating of all, Whitehall had accepted the First Consul's haughty insistence that the affairs of Germany, Switzerland, and Italy were not subject to negotiation; in those areas he considered his will to be sovereign. For him the peace was a substantial triumph, short-lived as it proved to be. He ceded nothing of moment, marked out western Europe as his preserve, and regained access to the world overseas. The French people hailed this success by making him First Consul for life, and he now began to call himself Napoleon.

The Peace of Amiens marked the end of an era during which Britain had been groping for security. The nation had entered the war in 1793 with little idea of how its armed forces should be used, with public opinion deeply divided, and with no overriding purpose to steel its will. Pitt had hoped that, after a quick victory, Britain would rearrange the affairs of the continent to its liking. When the hope had faded, he had made abortive efforts to negotiate peace with the Directory, and he favored renewing the negotiations with Bonaparte. The war was for Pitt not ideological but essentially defensive, to curb the expansion of France rather than destroy it as a power or undo the Revolution; the British public, by and large, took a similar view.

But over the years Pitt had come to see, more clearly than many of his contemporaries, the scale of the threat inherent in French aggression. Shortly before his resignation he was asked in Parliament to define his war aims without the qualification of any *but*'s or *if*'s. "In one word," he answered, "security, security against a danger the greatest that ever threatened the world. . . . Peace is most desirable to this country. *But* negotiation may be attended with greater evils than could be counterbalanced by any benefits which would result from it. And *if* it afford no prospect of security, *if* it threaten all the evils which we have been struggling to avert, *if* the prosecution of the war afford the prospect of attaining complete security, then I say that it is prudent for us not to negotiate. These are my *but*'s and my *if*'s. This is my plea, and on no other do I wish to be tried by God and my country."[9]

The Peace of Amiens did not make the British secure, for Napoleon had no intention that they should be; instead it ended their hope of finding security as long as he ruled western Europe. For the British the uncertain phase of the war with its periodic gropings for a settlement was drawing to a close. During that phase they had slowly and painfully learned how to use their strength, particularly their sea power, but had not recognized the need to fight through to final victory. In the second phase, which opened in 1803 and lasted with one brief intermission until 1815, there was an early, abortive attempt to negotiate peace, but thereafter the British settled down to the job of destroying the French empire, whatever the effort might cost and however long it might take.

This later phase, like the previous one, was replete with military stupidity, bright chances lost, allies defeated. Yet in it the British harnessed their power as never before and exerted it with more and more effect. When Napoleon rejected his opportunity to make a lasting peace with them, he evoked a force that contributed, perhaps more than any other, to driving him step by step down a long road. The road led from Paris to Moscow to Leipzig to Elba, and from Elba to Waterloo and St. Helena.

---

[9]Winston Churchill, just after he became prime minister in May 1940 at the start of Britain's great crisis in the Second World War, dealt with the same question of war aim, and his words bore a striking resemblance to Pitt's. "You ask, what is our policy? I will say: It is to wage war . . . against a monstrous tyranny, never surpassed in the dark, lamentable catalogue of human crime. That is our policy. You ask, what is our aim? I can answer in one word: Victory— victory at all costs, victory in spite of all terror; victory, however long and hard the road may be; for without victory, there is no survival." Winston S. Churchill, *The Second World War*, vol. 2 (1949), p. 22.

12 THE NAPOLEONIC WARS

*T*he Peace of Amiens had much in common with the Munich settlement that the British reached with Hitler in 1938. In both cases the dictator, whether French or German, had no intention of keeping faith or desire for a lasting accord but was playing for time to prepare further aggression. The British public, by accepting the offer of peace at face value, exerted pressure on the government to come to terms; and the government acted in the hope, though not in the conviction, that real peace could be bought at the price of concessions. The year that followed the settlement put an end to hope, roused anger instead, and so kindled in the nation a will to fight that had been lacking.

Napoleon, like Hitler after Munich, soon showed his hand. He drastically restricted British trade with his dominions, tightened his control of Holland and Italy, made Switzerland into a satellite, sent French agents to stir up trouble in India and Ireland and even to survey British ports, renewed his active concern with Egypt, and brushed aside all protests as impertinent. Addington's government, by the standards of traditional diplomacy, might claim compensation for the increase of French power in Europe; and the First Consul's continuing interest in Egypt meant that a British naval base in the Mediterranean was vital. Addington decided that Britain would compensate itself, despite the terms of the Treaty of Amiens, by holding on to Malta. Napoleon was furious. "Woe to those who do not respect treaties," he burst out at the British ambassador. "They shall answer for it to all Europe." For his own actions, presumably, he saw no need to answer.

He spurned several last-minute efforts to compromise the quarrel, and in May 1803 the British government renewed the war. The First Consul's high-handedness had defeated his own ends. He wanted peace in order to prepare for more effective war, particularly at sea, and had ordered a 50 percent increase in ships of the line. With the shipyards of the Low Countries, France, and northern Italy at his command, he might have had this great increment within another year or two. Instead he provoked the British before he was ready, and they promptly reestablished a blockade that he was powerless to break. His naval plans evaporated, and with them his dreams of reconquering Egypt and moving against India, and even his hope of retaining a colonial empire.

The renewal of the war had an immediate impact on the United States. In 1800 France had regained, by a treaty with Spain, the territory of Louisiana that the French had ceded in 1783; this vast tract had indeterminate frontiers, but it stretched from the Mississippi to the Rockies and from the Gulf of Mexico to Canada. The prospect of its passing from the frail hands of Spain into the grip of the First Consul roused angry excitement in the United States. Napoleon realized that he could not reassert French control without war against the United States and that he could not fight such a war if the British closed the Atlantic to him; their navy insulated the young republic from his power. As soon as he understood that Whitehall was about to renew the struggle, he concluded that Louisiana was as worthless to him as it was valuable to the Americans, and offered to sell it to them for fifteen million dollars; in May 1803, just when London declared war, the transaction was completed. Thus the United States, with the quite inadvertent help of the British government and navy, almost doubled its territory.

THE WAR AT SEA (1803–1805)

Napoleon was as thoroughly resolved to destroy Britain as the British were to destroy his empire, and he had only one sure way to do so—to invade. The prerequisite was the same for him as it had been for the Spaniards in 1588—to secure control of the Channel. Unless he had control, invasion was out of the question. A few regiments might get across under cover of night or fog, or by rowboats in a calm that immobilized sailing ships; but his troops when landed could not be supplied. To supply them he had to concentrate in the Channel a fleet strong enough to beat back whatever the British brought against it and to keep position until the invaders had crushed resistance ashore. Here the Spanish Armada had failed, but Napoleon was not accustomed to failing. He was approaching the zenith of his career, for in 1804 he had himself made emperor of the French; and his one sure way to secure his empire was by breaking the islanders' will to fight.[1]

While awaiting his chance for a naval concentration, he prepared small craft and drilled the soldiers that they were to carry. The shipyards of western Europe were mobilized and turned out a flotilla of some 2,000 flat-bottomed boats, propelled by sail and oar, to ferry the elite of the French army across thirty-odd miles of water from Boulogne to the beaches of Kent. As the boats were completed they moved, under protection of shore batteries, to the points of concentration near Boulogne. There Napoleon had massed 100,000 men, and he trained them month after month until

---

[1]For works dealing with Britain's role in the Napoleonic Wars see, in addition to those cited in the previous chapter, Carola Oman, *Britain Against Napoleon* (1942), Richard Glover, *Britain at Bay: Defense Against Bonaparte 1803–14* (1973), and Arthur Bryant, *The Years of Victory, 1802–1812* (1945), the sequel to the same author's *The Years of Endurance, 1793–1802* (1942).

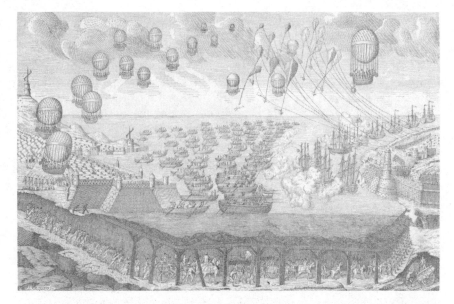

A FANCIFUL FRENCH PLAN TO INVADE ENGLAND IN 1805—BY TUNNEL, SEA, AND AIR   *(The Mansell Collection)*

they became as superb a fighting force as any general ever commanded. This was the *Grande Armée* with which the emperor subsequently overawed the continent. But that army, fine as it was, could not march on the water, or be carried in boats, until the French navy mastered the Channel.

Mastery for six hours, Napoleon said, would make him master of the world. But he presumably knew that this was grandiloquent nonsense, for by the spring of 1804 he faced formidable British defenses on land as well as at sea. Addington was no man for the crisis; it swept Pitt back into office, and he quickly saw to it that the country was prepared. Light vessels and fortifications protected the coast; regulars and militia numbered 180,000, and in reserve were 400,000 volunteers armed with a variety of crude weapons. The southeastern counties were denuded of any supplies that invaders might use, and plans were made for defending the Midlands if London fell. The island was a tough nut to crack, and Napoleon could not have cracked it without weeks of undisputed naval control. British admirals knew that such control was impossible. They had finally learned the business of blockade, after years of fumbling; and they held the enemy in a grip that could not be broken for long.

But the newly crowned emperor was determined to try. He had naval forces for his purpose that were superficially imposing: Spain had recently joined France in the war; and the Dutch, Spanish, and French fleets, if they could combine, were roughly equal to the British in numbers though in nothing else. Combining them all was out of the question, for they were scattered in ports from the North Sea to the Mediterranean. Concentrating even a substantial part of them in the Channel would be difficult—and pointless as well unless the British fleet could somehow be removed from the scene.

In the spring of 1805, when the final campaign opened, the disposition of forces was that shown on the map. The main French fleet, twenty-one ships of the line, was cooped up in Brest by Admiral Cornwallis, cruising in the western approaches to the Channel with twenty-five of the line; Admiral Keith, with eleven, guarded the Channel itself. A minor French squadron at Rochefort and Franco-Spanish contingents at Ferrol and Cadiz were contained by small British forces. The French Mediterranean fleet at Toulon, eleven of the line under Admiral Villeneuve, was watched by Nelson with thirteen. Although the geographical focus of the impending campaign was the Straits of Dover, the naval elements involved were dispersed along the whole coast of western Europe.

Napoleon planned to disperse them more widely. He hoped that his fleets, if they escaped from port and eluded British pursuit, could then converge on the Channel while the enemy was still hunting them blindly across the ocean. He misunderstood his problem. He could not depend on decoying the British, whatever the bait, away from the Straits of Dover for the time he needed; the only way to secure his army's communications was to defeat the Royal Navy and drive it from the seas. But he believed that its *absence*, not its destruction, would be enough for his purpose.

The French emperor nevertheless attempted to carry out his daring and imaginative plan. Villeneuve would slip out of Toulon past Nelson's guard, pick up the Franco-Spanish squadron at Cadiz, and make for the Caribbean; the fleet at Brest and the Rochefort contingent would escape simultaneously and sail for the same destination. The British would have to pursue, to save the West Indian islands on which the "nation of shopkeepers" set such store; the French would join forces in the Caribbean before their enemy arrived and then double back to the Straits of Dover to convoy the invading force. Britain would be conquered while its fleet was half a world away.

This design rested on two premises, and both were ridiculous. One was that the Royal Navy would behave as Napoleon expected; the other was that the French navy would. The emperor assumed that the British would relax their guard on Toulon, Brest, and Rochefort simultaneously, to allow his squadrons to escape, and would then follow them to the West Indies and stay there, bemused, while the French returned to Europe. The British blockade, it is true, was not completely effective; with sailing ships it could not be. A storm might blow a covering squadron off station and allow the enemy to come out and disappear in the waste of ocean, or a frigate with a crucial dispatch might miss the admiral to whom it was addressed. Yet, for all the accidents of wind and weather, the noose of sea power that the British had drawn around the continent was far stronger than Napoleon supposed, and the Admiralty far more resourceful. He was predicting a weakness and incompetence that were not there.

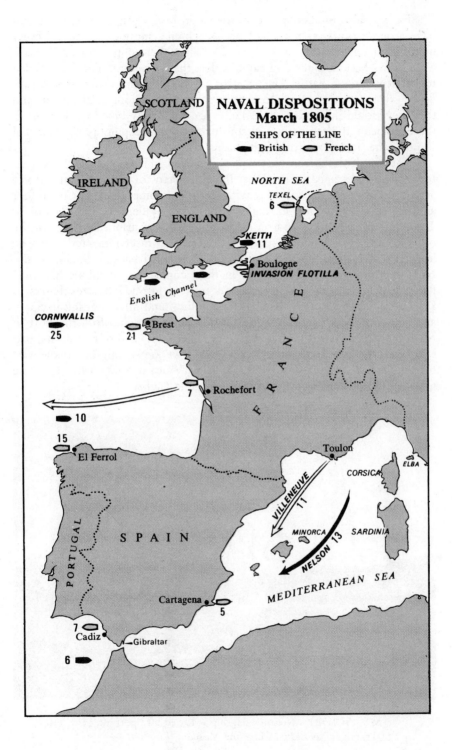

NAVAL DISPOSITIONS
March 1805

SHIPS OF THE LINE

British   French

SCOTLAND

IRELAND

ENGLAND

NORTH SEA

TEXEL
6

KEITH
11

Boulogne
INVASION FLOTILLA

English Channel

CORNWALLIS
25

21 ● Brest

● Rochefort
7

10

15

El Ferrol

F R A N C E

Toulon ●

CORSICA

ELBA

VILLENEUVE
11

MINORCA   SARDINIA

NELSON 13

P O R T U G A L

S P A I N

Cartagena ●
5

● Cadiz
7

Gibraltar

6

MEDITERRANEAN SEA

He was also predicting a competence in his own navy that it did not have. For years its strength had been declining, morale sapped by every month that passed with nothing to do. When their ships rode idly at anchor, crews became slack and captains lost the sixth sense that they needed for maneuvering in battle. The emperor assumed that his orders would suddenly galvanize these men into breaking out of their long confinement and that they would then cross the Atlantic for a precisely timed rendezvous in the Caribbean and return in a victorious armada sweeping up the Channel to Boulogne. It was a glittering dream.

The wonder is that any part of it materialized. In January 1805 the Rochefort squadron escaped to the West Indies, waited for support that did not arrive, and then returned in May with nothing accomplished. The main fleet at Brest stayed prudently in harbor. In March, Villeneuve did get out of Toulon, evaded Nelson, and set off in turn for the Caribbean. None of the other contingents that he expected was there to meet him, and when he learned that Nelson was hot in pursuit he doubled back to Spain. So did Nelson. Napoleon's chief purpose in the campaign, to combine his three fleets, had failed; but Villeneuve's was now of formidable size, thanks to French and Spanish ships that had joined him, and after refitting in Spain and gathering additional ships the admiral put to sea in a forlorn effort to reach the Channel. His morale was gone. He complained of bad masts, bad sails, bad officers and seamen, bad tactics; "we know only one maneuver, to form line, and that is just what the enemy wants us to do." In August he gave up, turned southward, and took refuge in Cadiz.

H.M.S. *VICTORY* Nelson's flagship is towed into port after the Battle of Trafalgar. *(National Maritime Museum, London)*

His armada of more than thirty sail of the line was wasted there, however, and he was badgered by the emperor to justify its existence. When the admiral continued to do nothing, he was superseded. News of this disgrace was the last straw for Villeneuve: he felt impelled to make a sortie, if only as a gesture, before he was replaced. In his heart he may have known it for a gesture of despair, because Nelson had now taken command of a blockading force that numbered twenty-seven ships of the line. On October 19, 1805, the Franco-Spanish fleet put to sea and headed southward from Cadiz.

At dawn on October 21 it sighted the British. In the darkness far to the west lay Cape St. Vincent, where Nelson had first made his name; to the eastward the surf rolled against the cliffs of Cape Trafalgar. The British approached from the west with a light wind behind them; Villeneuve, as they drew near, reversed course and headed back for Cadiz. "We know only one maneuver, to form line, and that is just what the enemy wants us to do." Indeed it was: Nelson intended to tear the line apart. He divided his force into two divisions, one to break through the allied rear and his own to break through the center. As he led his column he flew the famous signal, "England expects that every man will do his duty." A sailor supposedly responded, in words that ring true even if they were never spoken, "Does the old bitch think we shan't?"

Battle was joined at noon and raged for the next four hours, but the issue was never in doubt. Early in the action Nelson was mortally wounded, and he died at the moment of victory. Partly in consequence, the British did not achieve a battle of annihilation as they had at the Nile, but they did break the back of French sea power. They captured or destroyed roughly half of Villeneuve's fleet; thereafter Napoleon had no force of any consequence except the squadron at Brest, which dared not venture out. For the rest of the war—in fact for the next hundred years—the British were free not only from threat of invasion but from any serious challenge at sea. Their power extended as far as the tides ran. After Trafalgar they used their naval preponderance to contain and destroy Napoleon, and after Waterloo they used it to maintain the Pax Britannica throughout the maritime world.

THE WAR OF THE THIRD COALITION (1805–1807)

Napoleon's attempt to invade Britain did not end at Trafalgar; it had ended months before. Since the spring of 1805 he had realized that he faced a renewal of the continental war: his expansion in Germany and Italy was alienating Sweden, Russia, and Austria; and British diplomacy was bringing them into alliance against him. The emperor had waited until late August to see whether Villeneuve's fleet might yet open the Channel to him, and then, deciding that it would not, he had turned to a campaign on the Danube. Two months before Trafalgar, in other words, he had tacitly admitted the bankruptcy of his naval plans, and the battle itself was a mere postscript to their failure.

PITT AND NAPOLEON CARVE UP THE GLOBE   A cartoon by George Cruikshank (1805). *(The Mansell Collection)*

Napoleon's genius and army were at their peak, and he launched the greatest offensive of his career. He marched from the Channel to the Danube, like Marlborough a century before, with a speed that his enemies thought impossible; on the day before Trafalgar he captured an Austrian force of 60,000 men. He pressed on to Vienna, occupied it, and in December moved north to annihilate an Austro-Russian army at Austerlitz. Austria for the third time made a humiliating peace, and the Russians fell back toward their frontiers.

In London, during these catastrophes, Pitt was dying; the strain of the war years had worn out his frail body. When the news of Austerlitz reached him, he recognized what it meant: the old map of Europe, he said, would not be needed for another ten years, a prophecy that was fulfilled almost to the letter. He died in January 1806, murmuring, "my country, how I leave my country!" He certainly did not leave it triumphant, but he did leave it indomitable. It was sufficiently united, thanks in great part to his leadership, so that it carried on the struggle for the next nine years without any single leader of his stature.

The next administration had an optimistic name, the Ministry of All the Talents, which included at last those of Charles James Fox. But the talents were largely wasted. Fox promptly put to the test his long-standing sympathy for the French Revolution, and for Napoleon as its heir, by opening peace negotiations. The emperor encouraged them with one hand, and with the other tightened his grip on Europe. Even Fox became disillusioned. The French, he concluded, did not want peace and were not to be trusted; they "fly from their word." In September 1806 he also died, only nine months after the death of his lifelong rival, Pitt; the negotiations virtually died with him.

In his brief tenure of office Fox did achieve one aim that had been as dear to him over the years as the cause of peace. Just before his death he secured the consent of Parliament to abolish the slave trade throughout the empire, and the measure was formally passed into law in the spring of 1807. Although slavery itself remained legal in the colonies for another quarter-century, and only the importation of slaves was forbidden, this prohibition was recognized at the time for what it was—the crucial step in abolishing the whole institution of slaveholding. The statute was not the work of Fox alone. For nearly twenty years William Wilberforce had been waging the parliamentary campaign for abolition, and in the country at large the cause had won the support of many prominent people, among them John Wesley, Samuel Johnson, and Adam Smith. But Fox led the final phase of the battle, and the victory that he assured before he died is a fitting tribute to his indomitable spirit.

The Ministry of All the Talents, which did not long survive the loss of Fox, resigned in the spring of 1807. It failed in its central task, for it neither made peace nor showed any talent for making war. The British apparently knew no more about how to cooperate with allies than they had in 1793. Pitt's successors continued his long-established policy of subsidizing any power that would fight France on the continent, so that Britain maintained its role as "the paymaster of Europe." But the millions of pounds that the British poured out were largely wasted, because they had no real plan for integrating their efforts, by land or sea, with those of Napoleon's faltering opponents. Britain's strategic influence on the War of the Third Coalition was consequently negligible, and by 1807 that conflict was drawing to a close in a way that was peculiarly threatening. In the previous autumn Prussia had joined Russia against the French emperor, who was more than a match for them both; in June 1807 he defeated them with finality. Prussia was conquered, Russia ready to come to terms; and the terms he offered the Russians were directed against Britain.

Napoleon met the young Alexander, who was dazzled by him; a series of interviews between them produced the Treaty of Tilsit. This settlement, signed in July 1807, was a landmark in the Napoleonic Wars. It was an alliance betweeen the two emperors, by which the whole continent was divided into French and Russian spheres of influence. Prussia was temporarily reduced to impotence, and Austria was in eclipse. The emperor of the French had become emperor of the West, dominating Germany and Italy; and in the east the tsar ruled the only other great power that was left. "What is Europe, where is it," Alexander exclaimed to Napoleon, "if it is not you and I?" He was melodramatic, but for the moment he was right.

The two sovereigns bound themselves at Tilsit to cooperate in any war that either one might undertake in Europe. As a result, when the British refused to come to terms, Alexander changed sides and turned against them. By now he detested them, and they had given him cause: in the recent war they had done nothing effective to aid him, either by arms or subsidies, and had even seized some of his merchant marine. To his proud and mercurial temperament the only answer was to join Napoleon and bring Britain to its knees.

Once more the islanders stood alone, with no hope of creating another coalition like those of the past. They seemed to have only enemies left in a Europe more solidly united against them than ever before. The climactic phase of the struggle was beginning, and it brought into sharp relief both the strengths and the shortcomings of British society. One source of strength was industrialization, which was advancing at a forced pace under the impetus of war: the British supplied the continent with much of its manufactured goods, and even their enemies were compelled to buy from them. War also stimulated the enclosure movement, as did the rising population that had to be fed; even bad harvests did not halt the increasing productivity of the land. But foreign imports still had to supplement domestic foodstuffs, because the British by now insisted on their coffee, tea, and sugar. Their merchant marine, despite the best efforts of French privateers, retained the lion's share of the European carrying trade. Mines, factories, farms, and ships created the wealth that the government converted, by taxation and borrowing, into the sinews of war.

"A nation that by her activity and the genius of her citizens," wrote an admiring German observer, "manufactures its numberless articles of merchandise infinitely finer, in much superior workmanship, in far more exquisite goodness than all other nations without exception, and that is able to sell them infinitely cheaper, owing to her admirable engines, her machines, and her native coal; a nation whose credit and whose capital is so immense as that of England—surely such a nation must render all foreigners tributary; and her very enemies must help to bear the immense burden of her debt and the enormous accumulation of her taxes."[2]

But the shortcomings were also apparent. Both industrialization and enclosure dislocated the economic order and consequently bred unrest. Artisans who could no longer compete with the products of machinery, such as the hand loom weavers, were not ready to be docilely unemployed; some of them much preferred to smash the machines. Villagers who lost their rights in the common, or found that their small holdings had been filched from them in the process of enclosing, were as angry as the weavers, and discontent among the lower ranks of society remained potentially explosive. The well-to-do were also unhappy. The Speenhamland system had significantly raised poor rates, and that galling invasion of personal liberty, Pitt's

---

[2]Quoted in William Cunningham, *The Growth of English Industry and Commerce in Modern Times* (1892), pp. 516–517; I have modernized spelling and punctuation. Cunningham's work, although long out of date, contains much useful detail.

income tax, appeared to be becoming a permanent fixture of government finance. Although the war stimulated the expansion of grain growing and boosted the sales of particular manufacturers, the propertied classes were keenly conscious of the burden of taxation that the war had imposed on them.

Yet many members of those classes, to judge by literary evidence, lived as if there were no war. The great novelist of the period was Jane Austen; her books deal with middle-class county society, which she saw with an amused and keen eye and described in lucid detail. Her characters are entirely absorbed with their own affairs and those of the neighborhood. They move through their daily rounds, flirting, drinking tea, making delightful conversation, with never a hint that the country is in the grip of economic revolution and is standing at bay against Napoleon. Though Miss Austen's two brothers were in the navy throughout the war, the world of her novels is untouched by anything outside itself: it is tranquil and timeless. This tranquillity is not the aberration of a single author, but the reflection of a significant truth. War, even on the Napoleonic scale, was still limited in its impact, and so was economic change. Every inhabitant of the British Isles was in some way and to some degree affected by what was happening, but the effect was often too subtle to be perceived. Britons continued in the traditional frame of their society, almost unaware that they were living through upheavals that would fascinate historians.

If Jane Austen reflected the myopia of many of her contemporaries, William Wordsworth spoke for others who were passionately involved in the struggle against France. The poet had changed his tune. The young man who had regarded the French as heroes was now a middle-aged patriot who regarded them as "slaves, vile as ever were befooled by words," and who gloried in Britain's isolated stand against the enemy.

> Another year!—another deadly blow!
> Another mighty Empire overthrown!
> And We are left, or shall be left, alone;
> The last that dare to struggle with the Foe.
> 'Tis well! from this day forward we shall know
> That in ourselves our safety must be sought;
> That by our own right hands it must be wrought;
> That we must stand unpropped, or be laid low.
> O dastard whom such foretaste doth not cheer!

Rational calculations gave little cause for cheer. Although the tsar's *volte-face* meant almost nothing to Britain in military terms, because his fleets were insignificant and his armies no more amphibious than the French, it meant a great deal in commercial terms. He closed the ports of Russia to British goods and agreed to bully the other Baltic states into doing likewise. He thereby enabled Napoleon to implement on a large scale a project with which the emperor had already been experimenting—to cut off Britain's entire trade with Europe. Out of the Tilsit settlement came the far-reaching design for economic warfare known as the Continental System.

Economic weapons were the only ones left that could be effective. The French naval offensive had failed, and with it all chance of invading Britain. The French military offensive, on the other hand, had given Napoleon direct or indirect control of a large part of the European coastline, and the adhesion of Russia accounted for much of the rest; the few holes that remained did not seem difficult to plug. The emperor intended to answer the British naval blockade by a blockade on land, enforced in every port of the continent and extending like a gigantic dike from the Baltic to the Black Sea. This dike, he reasoned, would accomplish two purposes simultaneously. On the one hand, by eliminating France's greatest competitor it would give French products a virtual monopoly of the European market. On the other hand, by damning the flow of British manufactures it would turn the islanders' greatest strength into a fatal weakness. Britain was already so far industrialized, the emperor believed, that it was highly vulnerable. The nation could not exist unless the factory system continued to function, because it must either export or starve. Once its markets were cut off, the machinery of mass production would break down. As it did so, factory owners would rage, hungry workers would riot, and the pressure on Whitehall would mount until the government was forced to capitulate. This was the design, and it determined the whole future of the war.

The Continental System could succeed only on two conditions. One was the continuance of the accord with Alexander, for only his collaboration made the dike complete and kept central Europe docile. The other was that Napoleon could make his power effective along the vast stretch of European coast that lay outside the Russian orbit. Either his system was truly continental, or it was nothing. In order to develop its full force he had to make sure that it operated in every saltwater harbor that had good communications with the interior. Balkan and Scandinavian ports were relatively unimportant because of the poor communications between these peninsulas and the landmass of Europe, but all the rest of the coastline, from northern Germany to Naples, was Napoleon's concern.

The implications for him were enormous. He soon discovered that he could almost never enforce a strict embargo through satellite governments because they were too weak, even if they were willing, to suppress the smuggling of British goods. He was compelled to bring in his own bureaucracy of customs officers, backed by troops, which meant extending his dominions; this he did over the next four years. The attempt to make his economic system work involved him in more and more expansion of his political system, until in the end even he overreached himself.

RESULTS OF THE CONTINENTAL SYSTEM (1807–1809)

The ink was scarcely dry on the Tilsit agreement before Napoleon was planning further moves. They were directed at two corners of Europe that were far apart but vital to his schemes. One was Scandinavia, where he intended to revive the old idea of a naval coalition, with Denmark for its focus, to seal off the Baltic from British penetration. The other was the Iberian peninsula, where Portugal was in his bad graces because of its traditional friendship with Britain, and Spain seemed ripe for absorption into his system. If British goods were excluded from the Baltic and from Portugal and Spain, as they already were from the Low Countries, France, and Italy, the blockade would be complete, at least in theory. The islanders would face a choice of ruin or surrender.

London recognized the danger in the Baltic and responded at once. In September 1807 a powerful British expedition attacked Copenhagen for the second time, bombarded the city into surrender, and sailed away with the entire Danish fleet. This act, whatever its justification as self-defense, was almost Napoleonic in its brutality; but it did accomplish its purpose, for the Baltic remained open. In November, when Napoleon's troops were at the gates of Lisbon, another British squadron convoyed the Portuguese fleet and royal family to refuge in Brazil. The Royal Navy was becoming adept at filching fleets from under the emperor's nose.

Almost simultaneously London counterattacked on another front by tightening the operation of its blockade. A series of orders in council redefined to Britain's benefit, and therefore narrowly curtailed, the right of neutrals to freedom of the seas. The complex provisions of the orders were not designed to ruin neutral commerce, which was vital to the British themselves, but to control and profit by it while diverting it from the enemy. Neutral ships were encouraged to trade with Britain and were prohibited, unless they had first called at a British port and received a license, from trading with any continental state that excluded British ships and goods. The principal impact of the restrictions was on the United States, the only remaining neutral that had a large carrying trade. American merchant captains were in a dilemma. If they disobeyed the restrictions, they risked capture by British men-of-war; if they obeyed them, they were fair game for French privateers at sea and customs officials on land. United States opinion was incensed against both sides, and the only queston was which was the greater enemy.

To the peoples incorporated into the Continental System the answer to that question became clearer with every month that passed. For them Napoleon was the enemy. Britain had what they wanted, the products of the Industrial Revolution and the produce of the overseas world—silk and sugar and coffee and spices and a thousand others; these imports were in such demand that the black market flourished even as prices soared. Britain offered European consumers the satisfaction of their material wants. Napoleon offered them, in return for tightening their belts and foregoing their wants, the benefits of the French Revolution enforced by French arms; and the benefits he conferred at bayonet point were not popular. "We come to give you liberty and equality," announced one of his marshals to a newly subjugated people, "but don't lose your heads about it. The first person who stirs without my permission will be shot." Before this kind of pronouncement the sins of the Royal Navy paled into insignificance.

A year after Tilsit, Napoleon was challenged for the first time by a people in arms. His troops crossing Spain, ostensibly to subjugate Portugal, were actually intended to win him the entire peninsula. In the spring of 1808 he kidnapped the Spanish royal family and elevated his brother Joseph to the vacant throne. This kind of procedure was almost routine with him, but he did not reckon on the nature of the Spaniards. They had no taste for the reforms that King Joseph dangled before them; they wanted their own despicable monarchy, obscurantist church, and moth-eaten aristocracy, and were ready to fight for them. Revolt germinated almost overnight. In June a French army of 20,000 men surrendered, and the shock was felt throughout Europe. King Joseph was discovering what the British had learned a century earlier from their attempt to install Archduke Charles in Madrid—that foisting a regime on the Spanish against their will was a dangerous game.

Napoleon was incensed at Spanish resistance. But, having no idea of the hornets' nest he had roused, he supposed that suppression would be easy: he knew that the Spanish irregulars, or guerrillas, could not stand up to his troops in the field. He did not know that those troops faced difficulties that would prove in the end insuperable. Communications with France, thanks to the British navy, were almost entirely by land; and the roads south from the Pyrenees ran over a series of mountain ranges where guerrillas could take a heavy toll of men and supplies. Left to themselves, the French would have been hard put to hold down a people ferociously determined to oust them—but they were not left to themselves. The Spaniards appealed to the British, who responded at once. So began the Peninsular War, which lasted for the next five years.[3]

The war gave Britons two new opportunities to use their resources. One was commercial. The collapse of the Bourbon regime at Madrid loosened Spain's hold on its American empire, which began to disintegrate. Spanish colonists, hungry for manufactured goods, opened their ports to the British and so gave them, at the moment when Napoleon's blockade was beginning to produce serious economic repercussions at home, the market that British merchants had coveted for a century. It was too limited a market to end their difficulties, but it did help to tide them over the most critical phase.

Britain's other opportunity was strategic. After years of landing expeditionary forces on the continent and having them chased back into the sea, the British had the chance to use their army effectively. Control of the Span-

---

[3]The classic history of the Peninsular War, written by a historian who was also a participant, is Sir William F. P. Napier, *History of the War in the Peninsula and in the South of France, from the Year 1807 to the Year 1814,* 5 vols. (1828–1836). For an equally full modern account see Sir Charles Oman, *A History of the Peninsular War,* 7 vols. (1902–1930). The standard work on British military operations as a whole, up to 1870, is Sir John W. Fortescue, *History of the British Army,* 13 vols. in 20 (1899–1930). Fortescue handles his subject in almost overwhelming detail, as the number of volumes suggests, but his judgments on men and campaigns are often open to question.

ish coast enabled them to strike where they pleased, supply their troops, and evacuate them if need be; the Spaniards' hatred of the French gave the British a base of popular support. The redcoats alone, or the Spanish irregulars alone, might have been crushed, but not the two in conjunction. The French could not concentrate against the former without opening their communications to the latter, or disperse over the countryside to hunt down guerrillas without exposing their detachments to the British army. For the first time since 1793 that army was able to prove itself.

It was a different kind of army from the French. The British, untouched by social revolution, had maintained their eighteenth-century military structure; but since the beginning of the war they had taken great pains to overhaul it. The pay, drill, and equipment of the troops had been improved, and their administration reorganized; riflemen and rangers had been introduced, to operate on their own as scouts and skirmishers; the artillery had adopted Major Shrapnel's new explosive shell; the infantry had become so skilled in marksmanship that the volley of a British line was devastating. The result of all these changes was still an eighteenth-century army, small, professional, and highly trained; but it was a more effective instrument than that century had ever developed.

A reformed army with unreformed leaders would have been useless. "In war *men* are nothing," wrote Napoleon in the summer of 1808; "it is a *man* who is everything." The British hitherto had not produced a man worth mentioning; their generals, in contrast to Nelson and his "band of brothers," had been almost uniformly incompetent. But by the beginning of the Peninsular War a commander was on the scene, though not yet in command, whose talents were comparable with Marlborough's a century before. Just as the navy had had the luck of finding genius at the climax of its struggle against France, so now the army in its struggle had the same luck.

Arthur Wellesley, the younger son of a minor Irish nobleman, had his way to make in the world like most younger sons. He elected the army and in 1796 was sent with his regiment to India. There fortune smiled on him, for in 1797 Pitt appointed his older brother, by then Lord Wellesley, to be governor-general. In the next eight years the two Wellesleys made names for themselves. The French were everywhere, stirring up trouble among the native princes; and the governor-general, despite the lamentations of the East India Company's directors, promptly took the offensive. He waged a series of wars that shattered the princely coalitions and affirmed the supremacy of the British raj, and in them his younger brother performed brilliantly and rose to high command. By the time the two men returned home in 1805 Britain's position as the paramount power, which Hastings had established, was expanding into the empire of India. Lord Wellesley's work was done, but his brother's was only beginning.

In August 1808 Arthur Wellesley landed in Portugal with a small army. He defeated a French force guarding Lisbon and might have annihilated it if he had not been superseded by a blunderer who threw away most of the fruits of victory. Wellesley and his inept superior were recalled; the command in Portugal devolved on Sir John Moore, who advanced into Spain to aid the insurgents. But Napoleon by now had crossed the Pyrenees with 250,000 men. He destroyed the Spanish levies and reached Madrid, where he heard that a British army of only 27,000 was on his flank. The prospect of capturing it turned him away from his plan for reducing the rest of Spain, and he set out on one of his lightning pursuits. But Moore, racing to the sea and the waiting transports, moved even faster, until the disgusted emperor turned over the chase to a subordinate and returned to France. Moore reached his destination, Corunna, early in January 1809; there he turned on his pursuers and repulsed them in an action that cost him his life. But he had saved his army and distracted Napoleon from the best opportunity the French ever had to conquer Spain.

The emperor's reason for returning to France had been news that Austria was again preparing for hostilities. He had defeated the Austrians three times, but they were not yet crushed; now that he was embroiled in Spain and the exactions of his Continental System were making him more and more unpopular in Germany, the Austrians hoped that the time had come for revenge. They fought alone, however, and Napoleon brought them to heel in a single campaign. Yet it was not easy; he met tougher resistance than ever before, because he was now fighting a people as well as a government. When the two together defied him, they gave pause even to the *Grande Armée*.

As Napoleon's involvement in Spain had encouraged Austria to turn on him, so his consequent involvement on the Danube gave new life to the Spanish rising. It also gave an opportunity to Britain, which the government botched with an ineptitude reminiscent of the 1790s. Instead of assisting either the Austrians or the Spaniards in the summer of 1809, it sent 40,000 men to capture Antwerp, which Napoleon had transformed into the most important French naval base in northern Europe. The question of how the city could be held, once captured, did not arise because the expedition was an ignominious failure. The troops would have been invaluable to Wellesley, who had returned to Portugal in the spring as commander in chief. Without them he had only 25,000 regulars and could make no lasting impression. He advanced on Madrid and won victories that earned him a peerage as Lord Wellington, but his Spanish allies proved unreliable, and he barely managed to extricate himself and retreat to Portugal. There he waited to be attacked, for in the autumn Napoleon, having crushed Austria, began to pour troops back across the Pyrenees. It was the dismal end to a dismal year.

THE BRITISH COUNTERATTACK (1810–1811)

Fortunately for Lord Wellington, the French elected to conquer Spain before moving against him, so that he had many months in which to prepare his defense. He put the time to good use, for he knew that the crisis of the war was approaching. His plans were based primarily on food: he set out to prove the Napoleonic dictum that an army marches on its belly. The French lived off the countryside, he reasoned, and could not long remain stationary; they had to move like locusts from region to region, stripping each one of everything edible. The British, in contrast, lived off the sea; if they held Lisbon for access to waterborne supplies and maintained their communications with the city, they could exist anywhere. Their two necessities were an impregnable base and the means of supplying the army from it; Wellington attended to both by fortifying the approaches to Lisbon and by creating an effective transport service. He also built up an excellent staff and medical corps, drilled his troops until they were the equal of any in Europe, and trained an army of more than 10,000 Portuguese that gave a good account of itself. His gift for military organization was what Thomas Carlyle defined as genius, "the transcendent capacity for taking trouble." Nothing that concerned the smooth functioning of an army escaped his eye. He was never popular with his men, or cared to be, but he was as meticulous in watching over their needs as he was remorseless in his demands on them.

The test of his preparations came in September 1810, when Marshal Masséna began his long-heralded invasion of Portugal with more than 60,000 French veterans. Wellington fell back on Lisbon, fighting as he went, while the Portuguese peasants laid waste their farms in the invaders' path. In October Masséna's advance halted abruptly. Before him were the lines of Torres Vedras, fortifications that ran across the neck of the Lisbon peninsula for almost thirty miles, from the Atlantic to the Tagus River. The Marshal was helpless. The lines were too strong to be carried by assault, and the defenders could not be starved out while their navy commanded the sea. The French, on the other hand, could starve and did. The land offered them no subsistence, and only a trickle of supplies from Spain got through the swarms of Portuguese irregulars operating in their rear. Masséna held out until the spring of 1811, while his army dwindled; then he retreated by a route already picked bare of food during his advance. Wellington harassed his rear, and guerrillas hung on his flanks. He lost 25,000 men and returned to Spain with an army of scarecrows.

His retreat had large repercussions. With his usual public fanfare, Napoleon had ordained that the British should be swept into the sea, but instead the emperor had suffered a disaster to his arms and prestige. French morale in Spain sank, and Spanish morale was toughened; the tide of war in the peninsula had turned. The subject peoples of Europe began to hope again, and the Russian tsar took a more independent tone than he had since the Treaty of Tilsit. What Napoleon later called the Spanish ulcer was draining the health of his empire.

Not the least important effect of Wellington's success was at home, where good news was sorely needed. By the beginning of 1811 Britain was in a parlous state. The king had lost for good his sight and his sanity; his eldest son, the Prince Regent, was popular only with the sycophants around him; the prince's younger brother the duke of York, commander in chief of the army, had been driven from office by a noisome scandal; and the country was governed by a ministry with no discernible talents. After the death of Pitt and Fox only two men of real ability were left—Lord Castlereagh at the War Office and George Canning as foreign secretary. The public distrusted them both, they loathed each other, and in 1809 their quarreling forced them simultaneously from office. For the next three years the government, run by mediocrities and riven by factions, had no clear-cut policy at home or abroad.

The immediate danger by 1811 was at home, for Britain was at last feeling the full effect of the Continental System. Commerce was little impaired, but the industrial population was suffering almost the hardships that Napoleon had anticipated. Raw materials were in desperately short supply, and prices soared accordingly; the market value of silk almost quadrupled, and wool, timber, and hemp were not far behind. An unusually poor harvest caused food prices to shoot up as well; in 1812 the price of wheat in some areas rose from ten to twenty-five shillings a bushel, and famine stared the country in the face. Bankruptcies were coming thick and fast, unemployment was rife, and riots were a commonplace. A worker's job was a life-and-death matter; a smoldering resentment of machines, which were blamed for curtailing employment and depressing wages, finally broke into violence.

At the end of 1811 organized bands of men, masked and working at night, began to destroy knitting frames and other types of textile machinery throughout the Midlands. Local opinion supported the rioters, and their activities spread. Their leader was said to be a mysterious "General Ned Ludd," who may or may not have existed; and from him they took the name of Luddites.[4] At first they abstained from bloodshed, but before long, when some of their men were shot by the soldiery, they retaliated with murder. The government sent 12,000 troops into the disordered counties, and in a mass trial at York in 1813 seventeen leaders were sentenced to hang and six others to be shipped to Australia. The movement then disintegrated, although it revived briefly after the war. The Luddites were not revolutionaries, because they had no motive except the blind fury of the dispossessed, no aim except to return to a bygone era before machines had complicated life; they were the old England protesting against the new. The protest was hopeless, but for the moment they terrorized employers and scared the government. How long, many wondered, would the common people endure their miseries?

Most politicians took a gloomy view. They knew that the popular hardships were real and dangerous and that radical agitation was making the most of the danger. The nerve of the ruling class began to falter, and defeatism was in the air. The nation seemed to be too close to ruin to dare continue the war. And why continue it? Many believed in their heart of

---

[4] Malcolm I. Thomis, *The Luddites* (1970), provides a reliable account.

hearts that Napoleon was invincible on land and that the British army would go on repeating in Spain the failures that had dogged it since 1793; the struggle, they argued, was hopeless. This mood was so strong in Westminster that Wellington, during his campaign against Masséna, expected at any moment to have his army called home. But the government carried on doggedly, and he justified its doggedness. By the close of 1811 the British public was realizing that its cold and taciturn general had a gift for victory.

While the army was redeeming itself in Spain, the navy was gathering in new conquests. Guadeloupe and Martinique in the West Indies, Java in the East Indies, Mauritius and the Cape of Good Hope—all over the world the colonies of France and its satellites fell into British hands. Around the European coast—on Heligoland in the North Sea, on Malta, Sicily, and the Ionian Islands in the Mediterranean—bases were established for blockading squadrons and for the smuggling of British goods into the continent. Napoleon had no answer but wider and more stringent control. He annexed to France a strip of territory on the northeast, running through the Low Countries and the North Sea coast of Germany to Lübeck on the Baltic, and on the southeast he incorporated Piedmont, the Papal States, and the eastern coast of the Adriatic; his brother-in-law Murat, king of Naples, ruled such of Italy as was not annexed. The French grip on the coastline seemed to be secure.

But by the end of 1811 it was less secure than ever, because each time the emperor tightened his grip he added to his enemies. Annexing the Papal States roused against him a power that he could not understand—that of a gentle and unbending old man who excommunicated him and became his prisoner; the sight of the pope at the imperial chariot wheels was an insult to Catholic Europe. Napoleon's intrusion into Germany, and his increasingly overt domination of his satellites there, waked in opposition to him a new sense of German nationalism, particularly in the young, while in Italy, integrated for the first time since the days of Rome, nationalistic dreams were also stirring. The emperor had forcibly disseminated the ideas of the Revolution through Europe, and now they were working against him.

THE AMERICAN AND RUSSIAN WARS (1812)

While the Napoleonic system was stretching French power toward the breaking point, Britain was also paying a price for its method of making war. The British were embroiled in a second Anglo-American conflict, which from their viewpoint was merely a regrettable and minor by-product of the great struggle in Europe but from the viewpoint of the United States was momentous. The War of 1812, the first on which the new republic embarked, confirmed the emotions in which the United States had been born: hatred of Britain became part of orthodox American patriotism. That hatred, and the reciprocating British resentment, obscured the fact that the two countries had common interests and poisoned their relationship for generations to come.

The war grew directly out of the struggle in Europe, even though for many years that struggle was a chief source of American prosperity. As European neutrals disappeared into the maw of the French empire, Britain swept their flags from the seas; the United States inherited the bulk of the continent's carrying trade. But the Americans inevitably fell foul of the navy that was bringing them their business. They needed more and more ships, hence more and more seamen; and they offered high wages. Soon they were attracting deserters from the Royal Navy, which was also expanding and was desperate for sailors. British press gangs gathered in Americans who could not prove their citizenship, while British men-of-war stopped and searched American vessels and appropriated any of the crew who were thought to be deserters. The United States protested, but Whitehall would not mend its ways because, for the British, manning the fleet was a matter of self-preservation.

Both of the great European belligerents imposed more and more restrictions on neutral trade, which roused a resentment in the United States that brought it to the verge of war in the 1790s, first against Britain and then against France. But the crises passed, partly because American commerce was thriving despite all trammels, and primarily because the European struggle was not yet focused on economic warfare. After 1806 it was. Neither Britain nor France would permit a neutral to give comfort to its enemy; each aimed at manipulating American trade to its own advantage and exerted increasing pressure to that end. Here Britain was at a disadvantage. Sea power, usually far less conspicuous than land power, was more so for once: while Napoleon was confiscating American merchantmen in the distant ports of France, British warships were invading American territorial waters and outraging national pride.

The United States, caught between the upper and the nether millstone, at first attempted to escape by putting an embargo on all foreign trade, but the effect at home was ruinous. The next move was to inform France and Britain that American trade would be open to whichever one abandoned its restrictive policy, and closed to the other. Napoleon pretended to rescind his decrees in compliance; he duped President Madison, who believed that the French were acting in good faith and that the British would not act at all. Whitehall did act, by repealing the orders in council. But a few days earlier the United States, antagonized beyond endurance, had declared war against Britain.

It was a needless conflict, provoked by prickly emotions on the American side and haughty ineptitude on the British: neither contestant had an intelligible war aim. The Americans had the will to conquer Canada, but not the power. Neither did they have the power to achieve their ostensible goal: the right to trade as they pleased. For Britain, fighting for existence, would not compromise the effectiveness of its blockade unless compelled to do so, and the United States Navy of that day could not compel anyone. As for the British, they had no goal: they lacked both the will and the power to conquer the United States and could ill afford a contest that further

"JOHNNY BULL IN A FRET" During the War of 1812, an American cartoonist gloats over the manner in which the world's largest navy has been stung by American ships like the Wasp and the Hornet. *(The Historical Society of Pennsylvania)*

strained their resources, already spread thin, and that offered them nothing in return.

The conduct of operations was as faulty as the logic that had caused them. An American attempt to invade Canada was a fiasco. A British raid on the Chesapeake had no results except to burn public buildings in the new capital at Washington, thereby further embittering the Americans, and to inspire *The Star-Spangled Banner*. The infant United States Navy won a number of minor actions, on inland lakes and at sea, that jolted British complacency and elated the American public but had little effect on the outcome of the war. A British attack on the mouth of the Mississippi had no effect at all; veterans of Wellington's Peninsular army were defeated in the Battle of New Orleans, which started Andrew Jackson on his road to the White House but which was fought after the war was over. Peace was concluded in December 1814 in the Treaty of Ghent. As if to emphasize the pointlessness of the conflict, the treaty kept discreetly silent on all the issues out of which hostilities had grown.

For the United States the war had great significance, but in Britain it was little regarded at the time and has long since been forgotten.[5] It was a

---

[5]The present place of the War of 1812 in British history is suggested by the anecdote—whether true or not makes no difference—of a modern Englishman's reaction when told that his compatriots had once burned Washington. "Really? I knew of course that we burned Joan of Arc, but George Washington—?"

sideshow, played out just when the great drama on the continent reached its climax. In the years 1812–1814 Napoleon made his supreme gamble for the mastery of Europe, and by the time the Treaty of Ghent was signed his empire had shrunk to a Mediterranean island. Small wonder, then, that events in the United States received scant attention overseas.

The declaration of war by the United States in June 1812 coincided almost to the day with the opening of Napoleon's gamble, which was his invasion of Russia. It was forced upon him, he believed, by a change in Russian policy. Soon after the Tilsit agreement Tsar Alexander's enthusiasm for his new ally had begun to cool, as conflicts of interest between the two had become more and more apparent. Napoleon's activities in Germany disturbed the tsar, because they were undermining the influence of Russia in an area with which the Russians had been concerned for half a century. Still more disturbing, because closer to home, was Napoleon's encouragement of Polish nationalism: in the eighteenth-century partitions of Poland, Russia had absorbed vast territories that might be lost if the Poles reasserted themselves. Last but not least, the tsar's embargo on trade with Britain was losing him popularity at home and straining the Russian economy. For political and economic reasons he was ready to break the Tilsit accord, and in 1811 he issued a series of decrees that reopened his ports to British goods.

This defiance jeopardized the whole structure of the Continental System. Napoleon could not understand what was happening. Russia, he had thought, was a planet revolving about himself, but now it was moving into a new course. Either he could let it go and abandon his method of war against Britain just when it seemed to be succeeding, or he could force Russia back into orbit. For him this was no choice. Both his nature and his position precluded retreat; he had to go on.

He did not delude himself that coercing Russia would be easy, and for the task he gathered the greatest army that Europe had ever seen. Its core was 250,000 French veterans, but large contingents of Germans, Italians, Poles, and other nationalities brought the total to 600,000; Prussia and Austria, bullied into alliance, provided another 50,000 to guard the flanks of the invasion. In the whole of continental Europe only one small power stood out: the Napoleonic Marshal Bernadotte, whom his master had recently installed as crown prince of Sweden, defied him and allied with the tsar. But Sweden was in no position to give effective help, and neither was Britain; Russia stood alone against a continent in arms.

In June 1812 Napoleon's vast horde crossed the Russian frontier and rolled eastward. It failed by a narrow margin to encircle the defending army, which fell back before it and, like the Portuguese, laid waste the countryside. In mid-September the French entered Moscow, and there they stayed for a month. They were in much the same position that Masséna had been in before Lisbon: the enemy hung on their flanks, their lines of communication were stretched to the limit, and they faced starvation. Napoleon's overtures for peace were met by silence. He had to retreat. As soon as he did so his whole supply system disintegrated, and his nightmare began. In December he reappeared in the west, and only then did Europe learn what was behind the rumors that had been circulating for weeks. Out of the host that had entered Russia some 20,000 men returned, and they were more dead than alive. Half a million had disappeared, and with them had gone the foundation of the Napoleonic empire.

THE FALL OF NAPOLEON (1813–1815)

Even the catastrophe in Russia did not break Napoleon's hold on his people. He hurried back to Paris and by the spring of 1813 had succeeded in raising a new army of 200,000 to meet the onslaught that he knew was coming. Alexander had not halted on his frontiers but continued westward, and his advance roused the Germans to a national war of liberation from their oppressor. Prussia joined the tsar, Crown Prince Bernadotte crossed from Sweden, and in the summer of 1813 Austria, thanks in part to British pressure and loans, threw in its lot with the allies. Napoleon won several battles, but with his raw troops he could not win the campaign; never had he so sorely missed the 200,000 veterans who were fighting in Spain. In October Swedish, Russian, Austrian, and Prussian armies converged upon him at Leipzig and in the three-day Battle of the Nations broke his hold on central Europe. With the remnants of his forces he fell back behind the Rhine; his empire was gone, and only France remained.

Meanwhile Wellington, after two years of fluctuating success and failure against greatly superior numbers, had finally expelled the enemy from Spain. At the close of 1813 he crossed the Pyrenees in the first invasion of French soil since 1792. His adversary, Marshal Soult, put up a skillful and dogged defense, but with fewer and fewer troops as Napoleon called for reinforcements to hold the eastern frontier. By April 1814 the British were in Toulouse. There they learned that the war was over. During the spring Napoleon, in eastern France, had fought one of the most brilliant campaigns of his career, but against odds that even genius could not overcome. On March 30 his capital surrendered, and on April 11 he abdicated; in return for giving up the crowns of France and Italy he was made sovereign of the minuscule island of Elba. Bourbon rule was reestablished in France under the late king's brother, who was proclaimed as Louis XVIII; in the autumn the powers convened at Vienna to make peace.

It was a staggering task. The reactionaries who had "learned nothing and forgotten nothing" imagined that the world of 1789 would reemerge with all its trappings of monarchy and privilege, and that the map of 1789 would be recreated; but that world and that map were gone. New concepts of nationalism, of representative government and individual rights, had been carried through the length and breadth of the continent; they could be contained, perhaps kept from growing rapidly, but not rooted out. The crazy-quilt pattern of little states in Germany and Italy had been destroyed, the partition of Poland undone. Neither Russia, Austria, nor Prussia wanted to restore the old map in its entirety, for each hoped to aggrandize itself.

THE DUKE OF
WELLINGTON (1769–
1852) The portrait is by
Sir Thomas Lawrence,
ca. 1814. *(Victoria and
Albert Museum, London)*

The peacemakers were confronted with two problems, each of which was a challenge to their statesmanship. The first was how to protect the new order that they were establishing, of which France would necessarily be a part, from the subversion of French revolutionary ideas. The second was how to adjust the spoils of victory among the continental powers without precipitating another war. Prussia, Austria, Russia, and Britain had bound themselves together in the Quadruple Alliance, to arrange the settlement and then to cooperate in maintaining the peace, but soon after the sovereigns and plenipotentiaries met at Vienna, peace was hanging by a thread. Russia and Prussia wanted to make annexations in central Europe that Britain, Austria, and France threatened to oppose by force. War was averted through compromise, thanks largely to the skillful diplomacy of Klemens von Metternich, the minister who had directed Austrian policy since 1809. But the shrewd observer on Elba had taken note of the crisis.

Napoleon concluded that his enemies were about to fly at each other's throats and that France would welcome his return. From all over Europe his veterans, released from captivity, had come home to find themselves cold-shouldered by the Bourbon government; many of them longed to have him back, and with them he could build such an army as he had not had since 1812. The reduction of France to its pre-Revolutionary frontiers, furthermore, outraged French patriots and endangered the regime of Louis XVIII, who had only the humdrum virtues of peace and retrenchment to offer a nation that had so long lived on glory. The king was unknown to his people after his years of exile and looked to them like a pigmy replacing a giant. Some were eager to have the giant again; few would lift a finger to oppose his return.

In March 1815 Napoleon landed in the south of France. Three weeks later he was installed in the Tuileries, while the Bourbons fled again into exile. But the emperor knew that he was not yet master of the country: the people, he said, "have let me come just as they let the others go." To win support he had to prove himself, again by the sword. His return had united the quarreling allies, who had outlawed him as an enemy to the peace of the world; their forces began to converge on France. He had the material for rebuilding the *Grande Armée,* but he did not have the time. For 170,000 Russians and 250,000 Austrians were lumbering slowly but inexorably toward the eastern frontier, while close at hand in Belgium were 120,000 Prussians under Marshal Blücher and to the west of them, barring the road to Brussels, a polyglot force of 100,000 men in British pay. These allied armies determined in outline Napoleon's plan of campaign. He had to strike into Belgium, divide and destroy the enemy there, and then deal with the Austrians and Russians.

Wellington, now a duke, had been Britain's representative at the Congress of Vienna; he was hastily recalled and put in command of the improvised forces guarding Brussels. They were a far cry from his Peninsular veterans, most of whom had been shipped to the United States and had not yet returned. Every soldier available in the British Isles was sent to him, but he had only 30,000 of them. The remaining 70,000 were a scratch collection of Dutch, Belgians, and Germans, some raw recruits, some veterans of Napoleon's armies; their fighting spirit and even loyalty were doubtful. The Iron Duke needed all his imperturbability.

Napoleon moved at top speed. He had to, because each of the two armies before him was roughly equal to his in size. His only hope was to outmarch them, get between them and drive them apart, and then crush each in turn. His first target was Blücher. On June 16, while a French detachment under Marshal Ney held off the British at Quatre Bras, the emperor with his main force fell on the Prussians at Ligny and cut their army in two. Napoleon assumed that it was shattered and would retreat eastward; he sent a corps under Marshal Grouchy in pursuit and then turned to destroy Wellington. The duke barely managed to extricate his army and retire hastily northward from Quatre Bras, hunting a position strong enough to defend. On June 17 a torrential rain slowed his pursuers, and that evening the British commander found what he wanted: a low ridge south of the village of Waterloo. There he turned at bay.

Wellington knew, as Napoleon did not, that the entire Prussian army was nearby and coming to his aid. It had not been demoralized by the Battle of Ligny, and it had retreated not eastward but northward to Wavre, on a

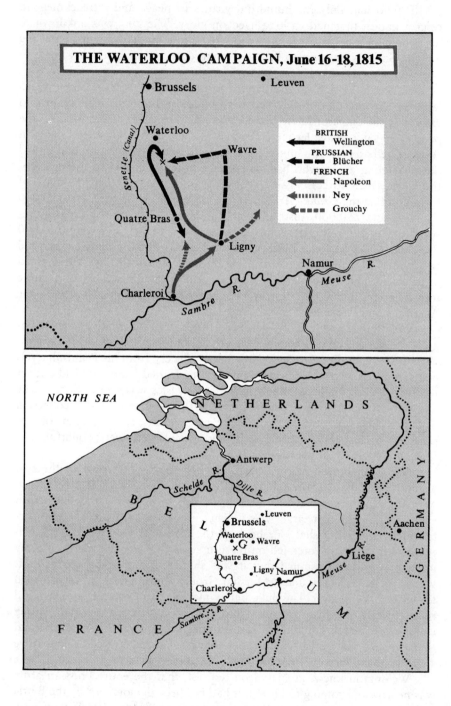

THE WATERLOO CAMPAIGN, June 16-18, 1815

Brussels • Leuven

Waterloo

Wavre

Senette (Canal)

BRITISH	
	Wellington
PRUSSIAN	
	Blücher
FRENCH	
	Napoleon
	Ney
	Grouchy

Quatre Bras

Ligny

Charleroi

Namur

R.

Meuse

R.

Sambre R.

NORTH SEA

NETHERLANDS

Antwerp

Schelde R.

Dijle R.

B E L

Brussels • Leuven

Waterloo • Wavre

×G

Quatre Bras

Ligny Namur

Charleroi

Aachen

Liège

R.

Meuse

G E R M A N Y

U

M

F R A N C E

Sambre R.

route roughly parallel to the British; Grouchy had lost touch with his quarry and was miles away. But the Prussians moved slowly—far more slowly, in the event, than Wellington had supposed they would—and everything depended on whether the duke could hold until they arrived. His position was strong and gave scope for the kind of defense at which he was adept: in front he had little protection, for the slope was gentle, but behind, where the ground fell away to the northward, he could maneuver his reserves under cover and out of sight of the enemy. In artillery and cavalry he was much weaker than they, and his chief reliance was on the firepower of the British infantry.

Napoleon, after delaying until almost noon of June 18, put that power to the test by ordering a frontal attack. Marshal Soult had learned from his Spanish experience how costly such an attack could be, and he cautioned his chief. The emperor's reply was both brutal and unrealistic. "Because you have been beaten by Wellington you think him a great general. And I tell you that Wellington is a bad general, that the English are bad troops, and that this will be a picnic for us." He soon learned better, and he did not forget the lesson. "The Duke of Wellington," he confessed a few weeks after the battle, "is fully equal to myself in the management of an army, with the advantage of possessing more prudence."

During the battle Napoleon showed no prudence at all, and little finesse: his one aim was to overwhelm resistance by sheer mass. In the early

THE BATTLE OF WATERLOO Wellington raises his hat to signal the final allied advance. A painting by J. Atkinson. *(Bibliothèque Nationale, Paris)*

afternoon his columns broke through Wellington's center, scattering a force of Dutch and Belgians in wild rout, but were counterattacked and driven back by British reserves. Then the emperor threw in his cavalry, some 15,000 under Marshal Ney, in three waves of assault that, though torn by artillery fire, flowed up the slope and poured through gaps in the enemy line. The defenders formed squares, within which the artillerymen took refuge. French round shot ripped the squares, but they held. The attack broke against them twice, reformed and broke again, until by six in the evening it was spent. Wellington had committed his last reserves. Napoleon had not; although his right was by then heavily engaged against the Prussians, who at long last had arrived from Wavre, he made one more effort in the center with the Guards, the elite of his army. They too failed, and the last tide of the empire ebbed down the hill.

Wellington ordered his whole line forward. As it swept into the valley and the Prussians broke through on the flank, the French army dissolved in rout. All night the panic-stricken mob fled down the roads toward France. The British were too exhausted to follow, but the Prussian cavalry took up a relentless pursuit. The emperor, his face streaked with tears, tried time and again to make a stand. But his authority was gone, and at last he gave up and led the race to Paris.

Although he had no thought of surrender, his compatriots had; his own legislature forced him to abdicate. The French provisional government threatened to arrest him if he did not leave the country at once, and the Prussians were hunting him in order to shoot him. He fled to the port of Rochefort, hoping to escape to the United States, but the wind was against him, and the British were waiting for him. Their blockade, which had done so much to bring him to the end of the road, now claimed his person. He surrendered to the captain of H.M.S. *Bellerophon*, and with supreme effrontery wrote to the Prince Regent, as "the most powerful, the most constant, and the most generous of my enemies," to claim asylum in England. Instead he was brought to Plymouth but not permitted ashore, then exiled to the small British island of St. Helena, in the south Atlantic more than a thousand miles off Africa. There he lived for six years and died of cancer in 1821.

His second defeat and abdication were essentially a postscript to his first defeat in 1814, as the Battle of Trafalgar was a postscript to the preceding naval campaign. But the Hundred Days of 1815 also determined, as Trafalgar did, much of what came after. Europe was brought together in a new unanimity born of the final, unexpected French aggression. Bonapartism was discredited in France for a generation to come; the fallen emperor of 1814 was a hero to many, but the man who fled from Waterloo to Paris, then from his own countrymen to the *Bellerophon*, was not. Lastly the prestige of Britain was raised to a higher point than ever before.

When Napoleon called the British, as personified in the Prince Regent, "the most powerful, the most constant, and the most generous of my enemies," he was wrong only on the last point. They were not generous to him, beyond frustrating the Prussian hope of putting him before a firing squad, and they had no cause to be: he represented to them the same force of ruthless imperialism that they had fought in the French Revolution. In struggling against that force they had not always been constant or powerful. But they had been more constant than any other people, if only because less vulnerable, and had fought on alone when the future seemed without promise. Their naval power had slowly but surely increased until it held the continent in a vise, and their military power, for fifteen years the laughingstock of Europe, had redeemed itself in the Peninsular War and the Waterloo campaign. The Spaniards had helped in one, the Prussians in the other; but the hero of both was Wellington. He was at the zenith of his fame, and his country was at the start of its greatest influence in the world. The years had amply borne out the prophecy in Pitt's last public speech: "England has saved herself by her own exertions, and will, as I trust, save Europe by her example."

13 THE TWILIGHT OF ARISTOCRACY

While Napoleon was marching toward Waterloo, far away on the Danube the diplomats and sovereigns were winding up their business at the Congress of Vienna, so that after Waterloo all that remained was to make peace with France. This was done in the autumn, as part of the general settlement. French frontiers were reduced to those of 1790, before any of the Revolutionary conquests; the nation was obliged to return to their former owners the art treasures that Napoleon had filched from all over Europe, to pay a large indemnity, and to turn over a number of its border fortresses to allied troops until payment was complete. These provisions were anything but punitive, and with good reason: the victors had no other choice. If they destroyed France, they would once more revolutionize the continental power structure, an unthinkable prospect. If they severely punished but did not destroy France, they would arouse such resentment that Louis XVIII could never be secure on his throne; and instability in Paris meant instability in Europe. The only peace that could endure was one that was tolerable to France.

THE SETTLEMENT OF 1815

The allies did all they could to prevent a recurrence of French aggression. In their territorial arrangements at Vienna they erected barriers across the two principal routes by which France, since the seventeenth century, had invaded central Europe. The first route, and the one with which Britain was deeply concerned, was through the Low Countries. Here the Belgian provinces, which had been under Austria until 1792, were joined with the Dutch provinces, which had been independent before the wars, to form the kingdom of the Netherlands. The peacemakers hoped that this new state would be large and strong enough to repel French attack; to make doubly sure of this they gave to Prussia the Rhenish territory immediately to the eastward, so that, if need be, Prussian armies could again march into Belgium as Blücher had done. The second invasion route from France was into northwestern Italy. Here, in the upper Po valley, the kingdom of Sardinia was enlarged to be an Italian equivalent to the kingdom of the Netherlands; and Austria took on the same supporting role as Prussia in the north by acquiring the provinces of Lombardy and Venetia that occupied the lower valley of the Po. In the rest of the peninsula the old non-Italian dynasties were

THE GREAT HYDE PARK FAIR (1814)   Londoners celebrate the end of a generation of war with France. *(John R. Freeman & Company Ltd.)*

restored. North of the Alps the German states, considerably reduced in number, were joined together in the German Confederation; one of its members was Hanover, enlarged and converted from an electorate into a kingdom, of which the aged and insane George III was king.[1] In the east, Russia gained the lion's share of Poland, largely at the expense of Prussia; and the latter was compensated with part of Saxony and the Rhineland.

These arrangements, relatively minor as they seemed on the map, affected the future of Europe. Sardinia became the only Italian state that both was ruled by a native Italian dynasty and was strong enough to be a factor in the affairs of the peninsula. Austria, the dominant power there, by shifting from the Netherlands to the Po relinquished its old role of protecting

---

[1]The Hanoverian crown, unlike the British, descended only in the male line. At the accession of Queen Victoria in 1837, consequently, the Hanoverian throne went to her uncle, the younger brother of King William IV, and the long dynastic connection between the two countries was broken.

Good general works dealing with the period covered by this chapter are the first two volumes of Eli Halévy, *A History of the English People in the Nineteenth Century,* 2nd ed., 6 vols. (1949–1952), E. L. Woodward, *The Age of Reform 1815–1870* (1938), and Asa Briggs, *The Age of Improvement, 1783–1867* (1959). The most up-to-date synthesis, Norman Gash's *Aristocracy and People: Britain, 1815–1865* (1979), and Boyd Hilton's study, *Corn, Cash, Commerce: The Economic Policies of the Tory Governments, 1815–1830* (1978), are particularly helpful in making the policies of the national government understandable.

the German states against France. Prussia assumed that role by acquiring the Rhineland, where the Prussians also gained, quite inadvertently, the area that was to be crucial for the future industrialization of Germany. Russia advanced westward into the heart of the continent and subsequently played a more important part in its power politics than ever before.

Britain had little direct concern with most of these territorial adjustments and so could afford to be detached. Its principal aims in the peacemaking were less controversial than those of the land powers. The British wanted security for the Low Countries, with which their own security was involved; they wanted a lasting, and therefore an equitable, settlement with France; and they wanted an end to the international slave trade. (At Vienna Castlereagh obtained international agreement on a statement condemning that practice; and he subsequently put pressure on the Dutch, the French, the Spaniards, and the Portuguese to abide by their pledges.) Their final objective at Vienna was to safeguard Britain's communications with India. At the end of the war the British occupied the colonies of almost all the maritime states and therefore had strong means of persuasion during the peacemaking: only if British wishes were met could the former owners be sure of regaining their possessions. The British had their way on almost every point and gave up the bulk of their conquests. In the West Indies they retained a few small islands won from France, in the North Sea Heligoland, and in the Mediterranean Malta and a protectorate over the Ionian Islands. To guard the route to India Britain kept the former French island of Mauritius, off the coast of Africa, and two erstwhile Dutch possessions, Cape Colony and Ceylon, for which the British paid compensation to the kingdom of the Netherlands.

That compensation was nothing to what Cape Colony would cost them in the long run, for there they were buying trouble. The Cape of Good Hope was a valuable possession, largely because it grew the fruit and vegetables that were the standard preventive of scurvy: ships on the long voyage to or from India made Capetown a port of call in order to preserve the health of their crews. But the colony was populated by Boers—Dutch who had been settling there since the seventeenth century and had preserved their old ways; and they soon proved to be among the most intractable inhabitants of the British Empire. Cromwell or William III might have known how to handle them; Victorian administrators did not, and the South African problem developed until it produced, in the 1890s, the greatest imperial crisis since the American War of Independence.

If the Vienna settlement had in it seeds of trouble for the British Empire, it also had seeds of European trouble. The latter sprouted fast, and in the postwar years the problems of the continent influenced British history almost as much as they had during the war. Those problems arose primarily from the conflict of two forces—the revolutionary idea of nationalism that the French had sown, particularly in Germany and Italy, and the determination of the continental powers to maintain peace by suppressing any revolution anywhere. Britain at first cooperated with its allies and then defied them, and its policy is comprehensible only in terms of the conflicting forces in Europe.

The arrangements made at the Congress of Vienna betrayed the dreams of patriots in many countries. Napoleon's armies had destroyed the *anciens régimes* all over Europe, much as the Japanese armies in the Second World War destroyed the European colonial regimes all over southeast Asia. In both cases, after the conquerors had gone, the attempt to reconstruct the Humpty Dumpty of the past touched off a series of revolts by peoples who wanted to determine their own affairs. To German nationalists, who had dreamed that the War of 1813 would lead on to unification, the loosely structured German Confederation was a poor sop; to Italian nationalists the change from French to Austrian hegemony was no sop at all. This was not accidental: one powerful man at Vienna had designed it that way. Prince Metternich, the Austrian chancellor, was a Rhinelander by birth but a Viennese by policy; and the policy of Vienna was necessarily opposed to unification in Germany or Italy. The Austrian Empire, composed of Germans, Hungarians, Poles, Czechs, and a host of smaller minorities, was the living denial of nationalism. A united Germany would deprive the Habsburgs of the influence that they had exerted there since the fifteenth century, and a united Italy would deprive them of Lombardy-Venetia. Those losses would only be the beginning: the end would be the breakup of the empire itself into its constituent national parts. The French virus menaced the existence

THE CONGRESS OF VIENNA (1815)   A painting by Jean-Baptiste Isabey. The Duke of Wellington stands at the extreme left. Austria's Prince Metternich is pointing towards the seated Lord Castlereagh. France's Prince Talleyrand is seated at right with arm on the table. (*Bildarchiv der Osterreichischen Nationalbibliothek, Wien*)

of the state over which Metternich presided, and for more than thirty years after the Congress of Vienna he tried to guard against the danger, until it materialized in the great explosion of 1848.

His attempts to stop national risings, like Napoleon's attempts to stop British imports, involved him in every corner of Europe. A rising anywhere might be contagious and spread to Italy or Germany and thence to Vienna and Prague and Budapest: the only protection was to intervene at the start. This Austria could not do alone, but it was not alone. All the great powers, in varying degree, feared a resurgence of French Revolutionary ideas; and the fear brought them together. They were aware as they never had been before that they were parts of a single community, which they described as the Concert of Europe. Whenever a threat to the peace arose, they agreed to assemble in a congress like that at Vienna and there to concert action against the danger.

This so-called congress system scarcely deserves the name of system. It had no formal organization, no agreement on methods of coercion or even of procedure; it committed its members to nothing except to meet. In international relations, nevertheless, it was an advance from the anarchic world of the eighteenth century because it recognized the principle that all the powers had a common stake in maintaining peace. "The immediate object," said Lord Castlereagh, the British foreign secretary, "is to inspire the states of Europe with a sense that the existing concert is their only perfect security, . . . and that their true wisdom is to keep down the petty contentions of ordinary times and to stand together in the support of the established principles of social order."

Tsar Alexander attempted to Christianize this new spirit of unanimity. In the autumn of 1815 he announced that he had formed with the emperor of Austria and the king of Prussia a Holy Alliance, the members of which bound themselves in indissoluble fraternity to act according to the precepts of Christ, and that they invited the adhesion of other sovereigns. "Sublime mysticism and nonsense" was Castlereagh's comment, and the Prince Regent politely declined to join, as did the pope. The other European heads of state, with tongue often in cheek, accepted the tsar's invitation. But only Russia, Austria, and Prussia ever took the alliance seriously, and for them it soon became more reactionary than holy. Britain was still tied to them, however, in the Quadruple Alliance formed against Napoleon in 1814; and in 1818 France, after a probationary period, was admitted as a fifth partner. These were the powers at the center of the congress system.

BRITAIN'S BREACH WITH THE CONCERT (1815–1823)

A concert is as a concert does, and the fundamental question was how the new order would operate. This question of what means to employ in keeping peace is inherent in any such international collaboration and has since arisen in the League of Nations and the United Nations. It has no easy answer. A threat to peace is most difficult to assess correctly at just the moment when it is easiest to deal with—its early stages. At that moment the collaborating powers are in danger of doing either too little or too much—too little if they allow a real threat to grow until it gets out of hand; too much if they regard every alteration of the status quo in any country as a threat that justifies intervention to reestablish "principles of social order," for their policing to maintain peace then becomes a tyrannical suppression of change.

Castlereagh and his colleagues were aware of the difficulty. They regarded the Concert of Europe in its early years much as President Wilson regarded the League of Nations—as an international framework within which change could take place. The Concert could not be more than that. It was unable, they argued, to "secure and enforce upon all kings and nations an internal system of peace and justice," and until it could ensure equitable government within a country it had no right to intervene in that country's affairs; to do so would be to buttress whatever power was established there, "without any consideration of the extent to which it was abused." Keeping the peace was one thing, supporting misrule quite another; and Britain's collaboration with its allies depended on whether they preserved the distinction between the two.

At first all went smoothly. But after 1818, when the Congress of Aix-la-Chapelle withdrew allied troops from France and admitted their former enemy to full standing in the Concert, the mood of the continental powers began to change. Liberals, restive under their static regimes, were resorting to sporadic violence; Tsar Alexander had posed for three years as their champion, but was wavering erratically; Metternich was turning to repression as the only security. In 1819 the Spanish army, with which the king of Spain had hoped to regain his American colonies, revolted against him and touched off a revolution that spread from Spain to Portugal, the Kingdom of the Two Sicilies, and Sardinia. Metternich responded by convoking the Congress of Troppau, where in November 1820 the Holy Alliance got down to work. Prussia, Austria, and Russia bound themselves to intervene in any state where a revolution endangered its neighbors, and a few months later Austrian troops moved against the two Italian culprits. This action was based on sound logic, for revolution had in fact proved itself highly contagious; and the spread of contagion had demonstrated the force of Metternich's argument that the peace of Europe was indivisible and that the only way to preserve it, and with it the social order, was to intervene before trouble got out of hand.

But Castlereagh strongly dissented. He took much the same stand that his mentor, Pitt, had taken toward France before 1793 but carried it further; he denied that the Holy Alliance had the right to interfere in the domestic affairs of independent states. In taking this position, it may be argued, he could not help himself. The Spanish and Italian revolutionaries were moderates who demanded the kind of constitutional, parliamentary regime of which Britain had long been the chief exemplar; and no minister responsible to the Mother of Parliaments could well have agreed that such a regime menaced the social order. In the 1820s, nevertheless, revolution of any sort was disturbing. Castlereagh and his colleagues, who sometimes feared it at home, needed the courage of their convictions to defend it abroad and to take a stand that tacitly admitted a people's right of revolution. But for the moment their stand was merely verbal, and, while they protested, the continental powers acted. Austrian arms made Italy safe for reaction; the Congress of Verona, in 1822, authorized France to do likewise in Spain, whereupon a French army crossed the Pyrenees, restored the despicable king, and kept guard while he wreaked his vengeance on his subjects.

Many Britons welcomed the prospect of weakening diplomatic ties with the continent. Sydney Smith, a prolific contributor to the prestigious Whig journal, the *Edinburgh Review,* expressed such isolationism in a private letter in 1823:

> ... For God's sake, do not drag me into another war! I am worn down, and worn out, with crusading and defending Europe, and protecting mankind; I *must* think a little of myself. I am sorry for the Spaniards—I am sorry for the Greeks—I deplore the fate of the Jews; the people of the Sandwich Islands are groaning under the most detestable tyranny; Bagdad is oppressed; I do not like the present state of the Delta; Tibet is not comfortable. Am I to fight for all these people? The world is bursting with sin and sorrow. Am I to be champion of the Decalogue, and to be eternally raising fleets and armies to make all men good and happy? We have just done saving Europe, and I am afraid that the consequence will be, that we shall cut each other's throats. ... If there is another war, life will not be worth having.[2]

George Canning, who succeeded Castlereagh at the Foreign Office upon the latter's suicide in 1822, was a different kind of isolationist from Smith. The change in foreign ministers influenced the style of British policy more than its underlying direction. Canning had a gift for drama, in words and actions, that his predecessor had lacked; and, where Castlereagh had regretted Britain's alienation from its allies, Canning welcomed it. He did not believe in the Concert of Europe; "it will necessarily involve us deeply," he had said, "in all the politics of the continent, whereas our true policy has always been not to interfere except in great emergencies, and then with a commanding force." Early in 1823 he was encouraged to think that the Concert was breaking apart and that international relations were reverting to a wholesome state—"every nation for itself, and God for us all."

France was certainly acting for itself by invading Spain and seemed to Whitehall to be behaving uncomfortably like the France of Louis XIV. The ascendancy of the French in Madrid was bad enough; worse still was the possibility that they would go on to regain for their new protégé the Spanish American empire, in which Britain had so long been interested. The Holy Alliance considered the Spanish colonists as revolutionaries whose vi-

---

[2]W. H. Auden, ed., *The Selected Writings of Sydney Smith* (1956).

FASHIONABLE LONDON DURING THE REGENCY ERA   A drawing by
George Cruikshank.

rus had once infected the mother country and might again; the sooner they
were brought to heel the better. The British government, in contrast, considered them as independent *de facto* and held that Spain had lost its claim
to them and France had none.

The crisis revealed a strong community of interest between Britain and
the United States, for Washington was as much opposed as London to European intervention. The Americans wanted to loosen the ties between the
New World and the Old: they had recently recognized the colonies as independent, as Britain had not, and were determined to do all in their power
to keep them so. The physical power of the United States, with no army or
navy worth the name, was negligible, but Britain did possess the "commanding force" of which Canning had spoken. While repression had been
confined to Europe he had been limited to protests; now that it threatened
to reach across the Atlantic he could act. In October 1823 he brusquely informed the French government that intervention in America would not be
tolerated. This ultimatum was decisive because it was backed by the force
of the Royal Navy.

Meanwhile in Washington, as the trend of British policy became unmistakable, President Monroe recognized and rose to a great opportunity.
On December 2, before he knew of Canning's ultimatum to Paris, he delivered to Congress the message known ever since as the Monroe Doctrine. It
proclaimed that the United States would not interfere in the internal affairs
of any European state or of an existing colony in America and would oppose both European interference in any independent American state and future European colonization on either American continent. The doctrine was
a bold gesture. The United States seemed to be throwing the mantle of its
protection, by fiat, over the entire hemisphere; but in fact the president had

no mantle to throw. Instead he appropriated, by dexterous timing, the mantle of British sea power. For the rest of the century, with one brief interlude, the Royal Navy rather than the American gave teeth to the Monroe Doctrine.

The British were delighted with the president's message. They had little wish to gain more colonies themselves in the Americas, and less wish to see European powers do so; and they were glad to share with the United States the onus of defying the Holy Alliance. The crisis evaporated, for the French did not dream of challenging Monroe's words when backed by Canning's threat. Reaction was stopped, as the Napoleonic system had been, at the water's edge.

British withdrawal from the Concert of Europe resembled the defection of the United States from the League of Nations a century later in that it destroyed the unanimity on which the experiment depended; but the *kind* of unanimity that Britain repudiated in the 1820s was more dangerous than hopeful. The Great Powers were high-handed as well as repressive. They were ignoring the wishes of the smaller powers, one of whose kings accused them of exercising "the influence arrogated by Napoleon"; and, if they had held together, their control might have become as tyrannical as the emperor's and even more stifling. By defying them, it may be argued, Britain served the best interest of Europe.

Its action was dictated, of course, not by such considerations but by British interests and tradition. Britain had been accustomed, as Canning said, to interfere on the continent only in great emergencies growing out of overt naval or military threats. Its interests were worldwide, as those of Prussia or Austria were not, and Britain was deeply involved only when European developments touched the security of its home islands, its empire, or the routes of empire. The British accepted for a time the idea of collective security, but it remained to them essentially alien. When their reactionary allies used the idea to further their own ends, Britons had no reason to cooperate and every reason not to. Their past history and present concerns worked to draw their homeland away from the Concert and, as Thomas Jefferson said in 1823, to "bring her mighty weight into the scale of free government."

THE TORY REACTION (1815–1822)

The ministry that carried out this momentous shift in British foreign policy was, ironically enough, notorious for its opposition to freedom at home. Since Fox's death the reform impulse that was coming to be known as liberalism[3] had been in eclipse. Under the pressure of war, economic disloca-

---

[3]Although the word *liberal* had long been used as a synonym for "unrestricted" or "generous," it was only after 1815 that it became identified—by its opponents—with a particular political point of view or party. Spaniards resisting the reactionary King Ferdinand called themselves the *Liberales,* and members of the Tory government came to apply the label to Whigs and Radicals. Not until the mid-1840s did many Whigs themselves begin to accept the label. By then it had entered the political vocabulary of much of Europe.

tion, and popular unrest, the mood of the ruling classes had become increasingly apprehensive and averse to new ideas. The Whigs who remained faithful to the tradition of Fox had dwindled to a small minority, doomed to what seemed to be permanent opposition; divided among themselves, they offered a wide range of criticism but no coherent program. The shifting groups of politicians who held office during the war years had set their faces against reform and come to stand for a rigid, repressive conservatism. By 1812, when Lord Liverpool formed an administration that lasted until 1827, these conservatives were assuming the name of Tories. A two-party system was more clearly perceptible than it had been at any time since the Hanoverian accession a century before. Party labels again had meaning, although the meaning had changed since the days of Queen Anne. The Whigs, little as they could agree on specific measures, insisted on the need for change. The Tories denied the need; they clung to the status quo as the only safeguard against revolution, and, as long as they heeded those groups in society most strongly represented in Parliament, they were able to stay in power.

The heyday of this static conservatism was the first decade of the Liverpool ministry, from 1812 to 1822. The prime minister himself was colorless and undistinguished and acted more as umpire than as leader. Three men in his cabinet were chiefly responsible for governmental policy: Lord Eldon, a diehard conservative who was Lord Chancellor; Henry Addington, now Lord Sidmouth, who was home secretary; and Lord Castlereagh, the foreign secretary and chief government spokesman in the House of Commons. Under the leadership of this triumvirate the cabinet, particularly between 1816 and 1819, followed a repressive policy almost worthy of Metternich. The liberties of British citizens were more drastically curtailed than in any other peacetime period of modern history. The government acted from fright, as it had in the 1790s, and this time the fright infected the Whigs and paralyzed their opposition. Charles James Fox must have turned over in his grave.

The postwar problems that beset the country, it is true, might have frightened any government. The sudden curtailment of wartime expenditures helped throw the economy into depression, while the debt contracted to conduct the war cast its shadow over peacetime budgets for many years. Since 1793 the net annual revenue—from customs and excise, various forms of taxation, crown land rents, and so on—had increased more than fourfold, thanks in part to the introduction of the income tax in 1798; and by 1815 this revenue was just under £83 million. In 1816 the Liverpool government bowed to public pressure and abolished the income tax, which had been an emergency war measure, and the annual revenue soon fell off to a mere £58 million. The struggle with France had cost Britain, in subsidies to its allies and the expenses of its own operations, more than £830 million, a sum that was almost four times the total outlay for all the nation's wars between 1739 and 1783. The money had been raised in large part by loans, with the result that the national debt had more than tripled during the twenty-two years of fighting. By the time of Waterloo the debt had climbed to £860

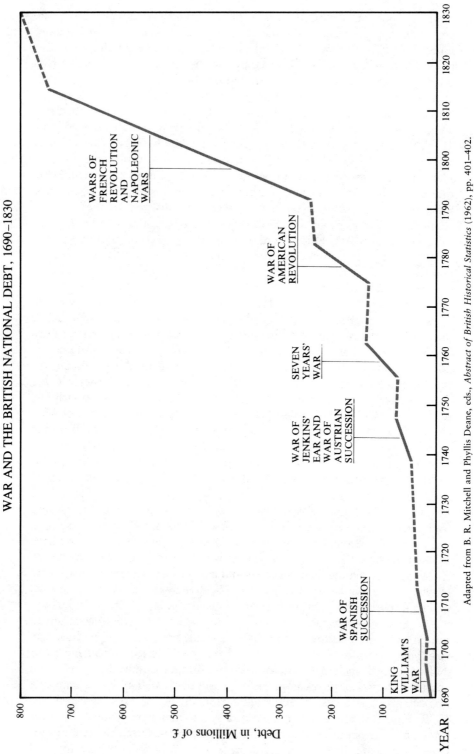

WAR AND THE BRITISH NATIONAL DEBT, 1690–1830

Adapted from B. R. Mitchell and Phyllis Deane, eds., *Abstract of British Historical Statistics* (1962), pp. 401–402.

WARS OF FRENCH REVOLUTION AND NAPOLEONIC WARS

WAR OF AMERICAN REVOLUTION

SEVEN YEARS' WAR

WAR OF JENKINS' EAR AND WAR OF AUSTRIAN SUCCESSION

WAR OF SPANISH SUCCESSION

KING WILLIAM'S WAR

Debt, in Millions of £

YEAR

million. The carrying charges on this sum remained virtually constant when the revenue declined; before long, therefore, more than half the annual budget was absorbed in servicing the debt, and another £5 million went to veterans' pensions. What Castlereagh called an "ignorant impatience of taxation" caused the government's financial position to be more difficult in peacetime than it had been during the war.

The Bank of England had long since suspended payment in gold and was issuing only paper currency. Bank notes were also put out by a host of country banks that had recently sprung up, some with shaky assets. The effect was twofold: to debase the value of the currency and hence encourage inflation, and to produce great financial instability. The worth of the paper notes, even those of the Bank of England, fluctuated from month to month, and prices rose and fell accordingly. Business was a gamble for all concerned, until an act of Parliament in 1819 ordered the Bank of England to resume the payment of gold and silver for bank notes on demand. The immediate effect of this step was deflationary, and critics condemned it as a discouragement to trade. On balance, however, it promoted financial stability: the gold standard soon became a tenet of Victorian orthodoxy.

The private sector of the economy was as badly strained as the public. During the war the problem of the food supply, with European imports greatly reduced, had become acute. The only way to feed the nation had been by more efficient farming, and in consequence British landlords had enclosed some three million acres. For this group peace was a disaster because imported grain, or "corn" in British parlance, sent domestic grain prices tumbling. The landed interest had long used Corn Laws to maintain a stable market in grain, but the Corn Law of 1815 introduced the novel principle of prohibition: no foreign grain was to be imported at all unless the domestic price rose to ten shillings a bushel.

The result was tumult. Mobs ranged London, insulting members of Parliament and threatening cabinet ministers; the young Lord Palmerston, secretary of war, defended his town house by arming the servants with shotguns. More significant if less dramatic opposition to the government came from the manufacturers. They protested that the high price of grain, and hence of bread, would inflate wages and thereby raise the cost of production and the price of the finished goods, which had to be marketed abroad in competition with foreign products; British industry, therefore, would be penalized for the sake of the British landlord. Parliament held to its course. The landed interest was deaf to argument and had as yet no inkling of the future. The great struggle over the Corn Laws was still thirty years away, but already the lines were being drawn. On one side were the industrialists and the workers in town and country who were the chief consumers of bread. On the other side were the landlords and the farmers.

When the harvest was good, as it was in 1815, even the most stringent of Corn Laws could not prevent the domestic price of grain from falling. Prices shot up again during the next three years; a violent volcanic eruption in the East Indies led indirectly to the coldest summers (and the worst grain harvests) that either England or continental Europe had experienced in several generations. English laborers had good cause therefore to lament the high price of bread. They had many other grievances as well. Despite Napoleon's best efforts, during the war Britain had come to supply the needs of much of the outside world for manufactures: its exports in the year before Waterloo were more than three times as great as in 1792. In the same period, furthermore, the British population had risen by some 35 percent. Peace brought a rapid decline in the European demand for goods, the termination of governmental war contracts, and the return to civilian life of more than 330,000 soldiers and sailors. The result, inevitably, was massive unemployment and destitution.

The government was ill prepared to cope with a sudden increase of paupers. It regarded Corn Laws and Currency Acts as within its domain but did not dream of a nationally administered program of demobilization and industrial reconversion. The consequences of a return to peace were, to officialdom, the concern of the counties and the localities. And there the problems were legion. The justices of the peace were responsible for dealing with a great many more of them than they had fifty years before. They had played a major role in military recruiting during the war with France and had also been given responsibility for the welfare of soldiers' wives and families. A sharp wartime and postwar increase in crime, especially among juveniles, had forced them to devote more time to the apprehension and trial of suspects and more money to the enlargement and maintenance of jails (for example, the county jail of Warwick, which had housed forty-one prisoners back in 1775, had to accommodate 351 sixty years later). Whitehall, furthermore was imposing more and more administrative duties on each county: the registration of savings banks and friendly societies, supervision of turnpike trusts, annual reports on assignments performed.

The poor law system came under increasing attack during the years after 1815. Its cost was staggering, and the effect of the Speenhamland system (described in Chapter 11) of supplementing wages out of public funds seemed, where it operated, to be pernicious: the employer who did not have to pay a living wage was liberated from whatever social conscience he might have, and the laborer had no incentive to work when the lazy and diligent were treated alike. The wage earner, who received an extra dole for each child, was invited to be fruitful and multiply. Modern demographic historians have found scant evidence that families were largest where the poor law allowance was most generous, but for contemporaries the forebodings of Thomas Malthus in his *Treatise on Population* (first published in 1798) seemed to be amply confirmed: the population was still growing as rapidly as the food supply; state intervention, however humanitarian its intent, was simply encouraging the poor to multiply; the ratepayer was financing this population explosion. Between 1803 and 1818 the cost of poor relief rose by more than 400 percent, from £4.25 million to £18 million, yet the agricultural laborer, in the regions where the Speenhamland system operated, became almost synonymous with the pauper.

The eighteenth-century working classes had not been supine but had aired their grievances in riots and other forms of direct action. Industrial laborers, particularly in the wool trade, had combined in associations to hinder the introduction of machinery and keep up the wages of hand labor. These associations, the ancestors of the modern trade unions, had petitioned Parliament, conducted strikes, bargained with employers, and in general made such a nuisance of themselves that they had precipitated a series of repressive statutes. The most important of these was a wartime measure, the Combination Act of 1799, which gave capitalists a powerful weapon: any group of laborers who collectively refused to work for a reduced wage, or any unemployed individual who refused an offer of work in his trade, could be prosecuted and imprisoned.[4] Workingmen's associations continued despite the law and during the war years had some notable successes. But in the postwar depression, with wages falling and jobs scarce, the employer had the whip hand. Laborers could not look for redress to their trade or to the magistrates: they either accepted their lot or turned to violence.

The government had no way of knowing which the workers would do. It is difficult, in today's era of mass communications, to realize how little communication existed a century and a half ago between the rulers and the ruled. The masses had few ways to communicate. The popular press was still in its infancy; petitions to Parliament, even if they were read, seldom revealed a consensus among the petitioners. Riots were not a tactful way of making a point to authority, but they remained almost the only way. The government, in turn, had no reliable method for feeling the pulse of the masses. Spies and informers, widely used as they were, tended to produce what they thought their employers were looking for. Investigations by parliamentary committees and commissions were at best a ponderous and limited procedure. Reports from local magistrates were distorted by the reporters' upper-class prejudices and fears. The amateurs who still governed Britain had far better means of gathering information than their grandfathers had had.[5] But, when they tried to gauge the will of the unrepresented and mute majority, they had to rely on their instinct.

That instinct, though experienced, was fallible—all the more so when dulled by apprehension. The men of Whitehall and Westminster had to read such signs as came their way and then guess what was going on in the workers' hearts and minds. When the signs were ominous, as they were in the postwar years, the danger was easily exaggerated: a plot concocted by

---

[4]Combinations of employers, either to reduce wages or to blacklist troublesome workers, were also forbidden, but these practices continued without hindrance from the magistrates. See Graham Wallas, *The Life of Francis Place, 1771–1854*, 4th ed. (1925), pp. 198–199. Place was one of the leading radicals of the period and was chiefly responsible for the repeal of the Combination Acts in 1824, for which see later in this chapter.

[5]A major example is the census of population, which was first taken in Britain in 1801. Another is the reports of parliamentary commissions, which in this period became more detailed and circumstantial than ever before: the commissioners took voluminous testimony, from witnesses called from all over the country, on the subject under investigation.

a few hotheads, a riot with a few fatalities, or a mass meeting with a few wild speeches became a portent of revolution. And *if* revolution were brewing, the authorities had to nip it in the bud or not at all, for they lacked the force to put down a full-blown insurrection. They had as yet no police in the modern sense, even in London; the regular army at their disposal was extremely small, and they could not rely on the ill-trained volunteers of the militia. Because they did not have the knowledge to evaluate a threatening situation, or the strength to wait and see whether the threat materialized, they could be frightened into precipitate action.

Britain after the war, with its load of debt and a disordered currency, its markets slumping, its unemployment rising to add to the burden of poor relief, was certainly going through difficult times. The misery of the people was obvious, and misery bred violence. The government interpreted the first acts of violence to mean that insurrection was starting, and it reacted, much as the Irish executive had reacted in 1797, with a ruthlessness born of anxiety. The year 1816 saw an outbreak of political agitation. Some of it was lurid: the Luddites again took to smashing machinery in the Midlands; mobs rioted in London, displaying the revolutionary French tricolor, and on one occasion pillaged firearms and invaded the heart of the city. Some of the agitation was respectable: the sober Corporation of London petitioned the Prince Regent for financial retrenchment and parliamentary reform. In the following winter secret committees of both houses of Parliament made alarming reports, whereupon the government suspended habeas corpus, banned seditious meetings, and ordered local magistrates to prosecute authors of dangerous pamphlets. For a time agitation died down—less because of these measures than because of economic improvement—but soon the depression returned, and with it political unrest.

In August 1819 a meeting of some 60,000 people was held in St. Peter's Fields in Manchester. The crowd was unarmed and included many women and children but carried banners demanding annual Parliaments, universal suffrage, "representation or death"; and a well-known rabble-rouser mounted the platform to harangue the concourse. At that point the magistrates panicked and ordered mounted militia—local businessmen in uniform—to arrest the speaker. The men charged in with drawn sabers and were reinforced by regulars; the result was pandemonium. Several people were killed and hundreds wounded—sabered or trampled in the crowd.

The shock of the "Manchester Massacre," which was also derisively nicknamed from St. Peter's Fields "the Battle of Peterloo," was felt through the country and beyond. From the safe distance of Italy the young republican Shelley sent a call to revolution.

> Rise like Lions after slumber
> In unvanquishable number—
> Shake your chains to earth like dew
> Which in sleep had fallen on you—
> Ye are many—they are few.

THE "PETERLOO MASSACRE" (1819)   An engraving by George
Cruikshank. (*City of Manchester Art Galleries*)

At home even moderate opinion was outraged. But the government was profuse in its thanks to the soldiers and inflexible in the line of action that had produced their handiwork. In the autumn of 1819 Parliament passed the notorious Six Acts, which were the highwater mark of repression. They returned to Pitt's policy in the late 1790s, but this time without the excuse of war. The acts banned unauthorized military drilling and provided for the seizure of firearms, muzzled the cheap press by imposing a stamp duty not only on newspapers but also on political pamphlets, and limited freedom of assembly in the open air to meetings held under official auspices. This legislation, much of which expired or was repealed within a few years, served its purpose of silencing the radicals. Whether the purpose was worth the price is another matter.

The events of 1816–1819 revealed as never before the distance between the propertied classes and the masses. The former, smelling revolution in the air, closed ranks in self-defense. In Parliament the Whigs, with few exceptions, were acquiescent; party labels meant nothing when oligarchy itself was threatened. Outside Parliament the businessmen and magistrates, if Peterloo is a fair sample, eagerly supported the government. A Lancashire merchant boasted to a radical leader about how the people had been kept in their place: "the sons of bitches had eaten up all the stinging nettles for ten miles round Manchester, and now they had no greens for their broth. . . . Damn their eyes, what need you care about them? How could I sell you goods so cheap if I cared anything about them?" Economic forces alone scarcely account for such bitter brutality.

The gulf between rich and poor should not be overemphasized, however, because British society was far more complex than such a division implies. Patrick Colquhoun, the London magistrate whose *Treatise on the Wealth, Power, and Resources of the British Empire* (1814) constitutes an early-nineteenth-century counterpart to Gregory King's late-seventeenth-century estimates, had the benefit of official census statistics when he surveyed the social gradations in the United Kingdom. (Colquhoun, unlike King, included both Scotland and Ireland in his calculations.)

Classes	Heads of families	Total persons, comprising their families
Highest Orders		
1st. The Royal Family, the Lords Spiritual and Temporal, the Great Officers of State, and all above the degree of a Baronet, with their families	576	2,880
Second Class		
2d. Baronets, Knights, Country Gentlemen, and others having large incomes, with their families	46,861	234,305
Third Class		
3d. Dignified Clergy, Persons holding considerable employments in the State, elevated situations in the Law, eminent Practitioners in Physic, considerable Merchants, Manufacturers upon a large scale, and Bankers of the first order, with their families	12,200	61,000
Fourth Class		
4th. Persons holding inferior situations in Church and State, respectable Clergymen of different persuasions, Practitioners in Law and Physic, Teachers of Youth of the superior order, respectable Freeholders, Ship Owners, Merchants and Manufacturers of the second class, Warehousemen and respectable Shopkeepers, Artists, respectable Builders, Mechanics, and Persons living on moderate incomes, with their families	233,650	1,168,250
Fifth Class		
5th. Lesser Freeholders, Shopkeepers of the second order, Inn-keepers, Publicans, and Persons engaged in miscellaneous occupations or living on moderate incomes, with their families	564,799	2,798,475

Classes	Heads of families	Total persons, comprising their families
Sixth Class		
6th. Working Mechanics, Artisans, Handicrafts, Agricultural Labourers, and others who subsist by labour in various employments, with their families	2,126,095	8,792,800
Menial Servants		1,279,923
Seventh, or Lowest Class		
7th. Paupers and their families, Vagrants, Gipsies, Rogues, Vagabonds, and idle and disorderly persons, supported by criminal delinquency	387,100	1,828,170
	3,371,281	16,165,803
The Army and Navy		
Officers of the Army, Navy, and Marines, including all Officers on half-pay and superannuated, with their families	10,500	69,000
Non-commissioned Officers in the Army, Navy, and Marines, Soldiers, Seamen, and Marines, including Pensioners of the Army, Navy, &c., and their families	120,000	862,000
Total	3,501,781	17,096,803

The two final groups almost disappeared after 1815, when the size of the army and navy declined by more than four-fifths, and the veterans distributed themselves among Colquhoun's seven classes. But his other estimates, even though they fail to distinguish between agricultural and industrial workers or between the different portions of the United Kingdom, remain a useful guide to the social structure of Britain in the postwar era.

THE PRINCE REGENT AND REGENCY ENGLAND

During this era the head of state in fact, though not in name, was the Prince Regent, who acted for his father from 1811 and became, when the old man finally died in 1820, King George IV. The prince, in typically Hanoverian fashion, had rebelled continually against the king's tutelage, and for the greater part of three decades father and son were hardly on speaking terms. They could not have been more different. George III had been simple in his tastes and financially prudent. Young George loved to gamble and to spend lavishly; he was perpetually in debt and time and again had to be bailed out by his parents or Parliament. George III had been a model of marital fidelity; his son moved from one affair to another, both before and after his marriage in 1795 to his cousin, Princess Caroline of Brunswick, from whom he separated within less than a year. George III was by conviction a political conservative, but his son made a firm friend of George III's keenest political antagonist, Charles James Fox.

When the future regent was a boy, his tutor prophesied that he would become "either the most polished gentleman or the most accomplished blackguard in Europe—possibly both"; the prediction was a shrewd one. George indulged himself on a lavish scale and made no attempt to hide this fact. During the Napoleonic Wars, when most Britons were on short rations, he boasted the best French chef of the day and invited guests to routine meals in which they might choose among 116 different dishes served in nine different courses accompanied by a multitude of wines. (On special occasions the dinners would be even more elaborate.) It is little wonder that even strict limitations on the freedom of the press did not protect the corpulent Prince Regent from savage caricatures and lampoons.

Yet he had another side to him. Unlike his father, he possessed both wit and easygoing charm, and he acquired a sense of royal showmanship that pleased a fashionable society long repelled by his father's court and that attracted even the fickle London populace. George saw to it, for example, that the end of the Napoleonic Wars was celebrated with a state visit by Tsar Alexander I of Russia and King Frederick William III of Prussia to a London brightly illuminated by gaslight. For the occasion he had Hyde Park transformed into a vast pleasure garden: Oriental temples, towers, pagodas, and bridges were erected there; mock naval battles were fought on the Serpentine; balloon ascents were staged; and, in the midst of a tremendous display of fireworks, a specially constructed 100-foot-high Castle of Discord "with all its horrors of fire and destruction" was magically converted into a delightful Temple of Concord. Royal showmanship was not confined to London. George made successful state visits to Scotland and Ireland, which his Hanoverian forebears had studiously ignored for more than a century; in fact, he won a popularity in Edinburgh and Dublin, perhaps because his visits were brief, that he evoked rarely in London. Not all of his showmanship was ephemeral: he was a patron of some of the best architects, authors, and painters of his day. With his encouragement, Henry Holland transformed the prince's London home, Carlton House Terrace, into one of the finest palaces in Europe, while John Nash planned Regent Street, the broad, curving avenue that leads to Regent's Park, which to this day is one of the world's most charming parks. At a cost of many hundred thousand pounds, Nash also rebuilt Buckingham Palace. When a Radical M.P. criticized such extravagance "at a time when bread can scarcely be found for a large portion of our population," the chancellor of the exchequer responded that such censure was peculiarly inappropriate on the day that George IV had presented his father's magnificent library to the nation. The king became the chief patron of Sir Thomas Lawrence, the leading Regency

KING GEORGE IV: ROYAL SHOWMAN OR ROYAL REPROBATE? *Left:*
The fashionable monarch. *(The Granger Collection) Right:* The king as
symbol of decadence. The cartoon by George Cruikshank (1820) quotes
King Solomon: "Give not they strength unto women, nor thy ways to
that which destroyeth kings." *(Graphic Works of George Cruikshank,
selected and with an introduction by Richard A. Vogler; Dover Books,
1979)*

portrait painter, was an admirer of Jane Austen, who dedicated *Emma* to
him, and was a friend of Sir Walter Scott.

He, like Sir Walter, was in his own way a Romantic, and Romanticism
was in vogue. It took many forms. William Wordsworth expounded the virtues of nature and of the unlettered villager; Percy Bysshe Shelley lashed out
at tyranny in politics, religion, and social convention; Lord Byron, one of
the best known literary figures of Europe and the idol of Romantics, celebrated the lonely, melancholy, recklessly passionate hero who sought adventure in exotic climes. These were all part of the Romantic movement. So
too was a revival of the Gothic: in tales of mystery and horror, in the novels
of Scott, in a veneration of the ruins of medieval abbeys, and in the rein-
troduction of Gothic architecture. George, too, felt the appeal of what was
distant in time or space. His Stuart predecessors fascinated him; he had
Windsor Castle restored in what the architects thought was the original
style; he built the Royal Pavilion at Brighton, an Arabian Nights extrava-
ganza with exotic domes even on its stables.

Although George had his Romantic side, some of his actions were un-
romantic and to his critics unregal. In January of 1820 George III, that
"old, mad, blind, despised, and dying King," as Shelley called him, did in
fact die. The prince became king in his own right and immediately precipitated a crisis that shook the monarchy, revivified Whig opposition, and gave

"REFLECTION" George IV, trying on his new crown, admires himself in the mirror only to see instead the dread vision of his exiled wife, Princess Caroline (already attired as queen). A cartoon by George Cruikshank (1820).

the mass of the people a chance to show that their anger was still a force to be reckoned with. George IV's wife, Princess Caroline, had lived on the continent for the previous six years, touring Italy in the company of an entourage headed by an impoverished Italian aristocrat. Her dress and her behavior had given rise to much gossip, and in 1820 she infuriated George by hurrying home to London to be crowned by his side as queen. The king quickly asked his government to bring in *A Bill to deprive her Majesty Caroline Amelia Elizabeth of the Title, Prerogatives, Rights, Privileges, and Pretensions of Queen Consort of this Realm, and to dissolve the Marriage between his Majesty and the said Queen.* Immediately the Whigs took up the queen's cause for its political value, and London rallied to her with wild enthusiasm. If Caroline was vulgar, foolish, and of questionable morals, her husband's morals left no room for question. George IV had followed the example of Charles II and had made no attempt to conceal his profligacy. No matter what his wife had done, he had done worse; in the eyes of the nation she was the injured party.

When the bill for divorce was introduced into Parliament in the summer of 1820, the king was in fact on trial; as the weeks went by it became clearer and clearer what the verdict would be. The most brilliant of Whig lawyers defended the queen, the idol of the populace, and excitement

THE ROYAL PAVILION AT BRIGHTON The pavilion symbolizes Regency romanticism as fashioned by architect John Nash. *(Royal Pavilion, Art Gallery and Museums, Brighton)*

mounted into a threat of revolution. In November the bill was dropped, amid tumultuous rejoicing. For the last time a king had persuaded his ministers to introduce a measure at his personal behest, and he had been defeated by the minority party because it had the people behind it.[6] The lesson was not lost on the Whigs. One of their younger members, Lord John Russell, remarked that "the Queen's business had done a great deal of good in renewing the old and natural alliance of the Whigs and the people, and of weakening the influence of the Radicals with the latter." The Whigs of the 1820s had strayed a long way from the old alliance, personified in Charles James Fox; and they were beginning to realize that renewing it might be politically profitable.

But the profit was delayed, because by 1822 the Tories were showing a new vitality. In their domestic policy they had hitherto followed the injunction attributed to Metternich, "govern and change nothing," and they had almost forgotten the warning of their patron saint Edmund Burke that

---

[6]Though he lost the battle, King George IV won the war. The Privy Council ruled that Caroline, because she had long lived separately from the king, might not be crowned queen. She was excluded from both the elaborate ceremony in Westminster Abbey and the lavish coronation banquet in Westminster Hall, and she died—of natural causes—only a few weeks later. Until the mid-twentieth century, most biographical accounts of George IV were distinctly hostile, but Roger Fulford, *George the Fourth*, rev. ed. (1949), is judicious, and Joanna Richardson, *George IV: A Portrait* (1970), eminently favorable. In *The Prince of Pleasure and His Regency, 1811–20* (1969), the literary critic J. B. Priestley has provided an entertaining and lavishly illustrated survey of the era. Mark Girouard furnishes an informative and richly illustrated introduction to the impact of romanticism on nineteenth-century English society in *The Return to Camelot: Chivalry and the English Gentleman* (1981).

"a state without the means of change is without the means of its conservation." But now new faces were appearing, and with them new ideas. In 1822 Castlereagh's mind failed, and he committed suicide; Canning, his successor as foreign secretary and leader of the House of Commons, was far more open-minded on the need for reforms. Lord Sidmouth, who had taken the odium of enforcing the Six Acts, had resigned as home secretary and been replaced by the son of a Lancashire cotton manufacturer, Robert Peel, who was developing a strong distrust of any Toryism that did not move with the times. William Huskisson, one of the ablest financiers of his day, was the new president of the Board of Trade. The static, repressive period was over, and the state was recovering the means of change.

THE NEAR EAST CRISIS (1821–1830)

After 1822 change appeared in both foreign and domestic policy. Canning's interference with the Holy Alliance in 1823 over the issue of the rebellious Spanish American colonies was only the beginning of Britain's concern with rebels. In 1821 the Greeks had revolted against their rulers, the Ottoman Turks; from this revolt came a crisis that tormented Europe for a decade. Until 1825 the decrepit Ottoman Empire tried without success to regain control of Greece, in a war that was one of grisly atrocities on both sides. But a wave of sympathy for the Greeks swept over Europe. The ruling class of Britain and the continent had been nurtured on the classics and, knowing little or nothing of modern Greece, saw in rough peasants the ancient Spartans and Athenians. The cause not only aroused the sympathy of the classicists; it also appealed, in its exotic wildness, to devotees of Romanticism. Philhellenes, or supporters of the Greeks, were soon found everywhere from Russia to the American frontier.

Lord Byron set his seal on the revolt. He wrote about it in a tone that blended nostalgia for the Greeks' past with anxiety about their future, a combination that was calculated to rouse Philhellenes to frenzy.

> The isles of Greece! the isles of Greece
>   Where burning Sappho loved and sung,
> Where grew the arts of war and peace,
>   Where Delos rose, and Phoebus sprung!
> Eternal summer gilds them yet,
> But all, except their sun, is set. . . .
>
> Fill high the bowl with Samian wine!
>   Our virgins dance beneath the shade—
> I see their glorious black eyes shine;
>   But gazing at each glowing maid,
> My own the burning tear-drop laves,
> To think such breasts must suckle slaves.
>
> Place me on Sunium's marbled steep,
>   Where nothing, save the waves and I,

May hear our mutual murmurs sweep;
    There, swan-like, let me sing and die:
    A land of slaves shall ne'er be mine—
    Dash down yon cup of Samian wine!

Byron not only wrote; he took action. In 1823 he went to Greece to help the revolt, which he did most efficiently, and in 1824 he gave his life for it. He died, not singing on the promontory of Sunium but at Missolonghi from fever, and he proved to be worth even more to the cause dead than alive. He became the hero-martyr of the Philhellenes. They sent money, supplies, and volunteers to the Greeks until the war, like the Spanish Civil War of the 1930s, took on the aspect of an international crusade.

Although the idealism that stirred such excitement put pressure on the great powers to intervene in Greece, they were not accustomed to act on idealism. Their policies rested on calculations of interest, and in this case the interaction of their interests was enormously complex. But the underlying forces at work are clear in retrospect, and they are worth examining. They operated, like forces pressing on a fault in the earth's crust, to produce a series of European upheavals, from the first tremor in the Greek crisis to the Balkan disturbances that began the earthquake of 1914.

The geographical focus of these forces was the Ottoman Empire. For almost 200 years its dominions had been shrinking, and the sultan's government, the Sublime Porte at Constantinople, had been growing more fee-

LORD BYRON (1788–1824) The romantic poet (shown in Albanian costume) called upon his countrymen to help restore the Greece of old. Portrait by Thomas Philips. *(National Portrait Gallery, London)*

ble. By the 1820s Russia had conquered the north coast of the Black Sea and was pressing toward the mouth of the Danube; the Serbs had revolted in the Balkans before the Greek rising and had gained substantial autonomy; and the Sultan's ambitious vassal in Egypt, Mohammed Ali, had an effective army and navy with which to build an empire for himself. The Ottoman state appeared to be on the verge of disintegration.

But the great powers could not allow it to disintegrate before they had agreed on dividing the spoils, and agreement proved impossible. Russia longed for Constantinople and the sultan's Balkan provinces, in order to open the Straits and get access through the Aegean to the Mediterranean. Statesmen in Vienna had good reason to fear such Russian expansion in the Balkans, and statesmen in London had equally good reason to fear the Russians in the Mediterranean; the Ottoman Empire, shaky as it was, served a vital function for both Austria and Britain as a barrier against the tsar. The affairs of the Porte also concerned France, whose government, if only for domestic reasons, needed to reassert its influence abroad; and Napoleon himself had pointed the way to the Near East. Every great power except Prussia, in short, had a stake in the sultan's empire and therefore in the revolt of the Greeks against him.

In the years 1824–1827 the crisis deepened. First the sultan called in Mohammed Ali's army and fleet; the Egyptians set to work, with efficient ferocity, to end the Greek rebellion by exterminating the rebels, whose only hope soon lay in intervention by the powers. At the end of 1825 Tsar Alexander died, and his successor, Nicholas I, made clear that he would intervene alone if need be. In that case Russia would probably make Greece into a satellite and be a long step nearer to realizing its own expansionist dreams. Metternich, who disliked this prospect slightly less than he disliked the principle of intervening to *aid* rebellion, refused to join in concerted action, and Prussia followed his lead. Neither France nor Britain wanted to apply force for fear of bringing down the whole Ottoman edifice, but they dared not let Russia proceed alone. They decided, in order to keep some influence on events, to cooperate with the tsar in whatever measures might be necessary. The Holy Alliance of the three eastern powers gave place for the moment to a new triangular grouping of Russia, France, and Britain.

In August 1827 Canning died; power in Whitehall passed to a group of mediocrities whose one idea was to retreat into what looked like the safety of inaction. But events were out of their control. In October a combined squadron of Russian, French, and British men-of-war, which had been sent to the Greek coast, was observing the Turko-Egyptian fleet in the Bay of Navarino. The allied admirals were uncertain as to what they had been sent to do, but the question became academic when they were fired on. They returned the fire and wiped out the enemy fleet.

The Battle of Navarino saved the Greeks, but it roused consternation in London. At the beginning of 1828 the duke of Wellington became prime minister; he was strongly opposed to any action that would impair Ottoman power, particularly if Russia reaped the benefit, and had the king express to Parliament his hope that the battle, "this untoward event," would not interrupt Britain's friendly relations with its "ancient ally," the Porte. This diplomatic nonsense made no impression in Constantinople, where the sultan called for a holy war against the powers that had destroyed his fleet. Russia responded by doing what Canning had worked so hard to prevent—going to war on its own. British diplomacy was bankrupt. From the beginning it had had two conflicting objectives: to protect the Greeks from being slaughtered by the Turks or dominated by the Russians, and to preserve the integrity of the Ottoman Empire. Canning, when the chips were down, had been willing to compromise the second objective for the sake of the first; Wellington had relinquished the first for the sake of the second; and at the outbreak of war Britain seemed to have failed in both.

Britain was saved from utter diplomatic defeat by an unforeseen factor—the fighting power of the tatterdemalion Turkish army. After the Russian troops had sustained a number of reverses, Nicholas became more amenable. Metternich urged an independent Greece, and Wellington, much against his will, was persuaded to agree. The negotiations between the powers dragged on until the spring of 1832, when at long last Greece was formally established as a sovereign kingdom under the guarantee of Britain, France, and Russia. Meanwhile, in 1829, the Russo-Turkish war had ended in the Treaty of Adrianople, which considerably strengthened Russian influence in the Balkans outside Greece and proportionately weakened Ottoman control. There for the moment the eastern question rested.

It was far from closed. For almost a hundred years it reopened periodically, bringing with it wars and the threat of wars. The settlement of the Greek phase left an uneasy three-cornered balance of power in the eastern Mediterranean between Russia, Britain, and France, which operated for a time to British advantage. When the French became disturbingly ambitious in the Near East in the late 1830s, the British and the Russians drew together to restrain them. When the Russians attempted to dominate the Porte in 1853, the French and the British opposed them, diplomacy fumbled, and the result was the Crimean War. After the eclipse of France in 1870 Austria took its place, and in 1876–1878 Austro-British pressure prevented the Ottoman Empire from becoming a Russian preserve. Not until Russia and Britain came to terms in 1907 could that empire, so long "the sick man of Europe," be allowed to die. Until then the powers kept it alive, not because they relished its existence but because they could not agree on how to divide the inheritance.

THE DISRUPTION OF TORYISM (1822–1830)

The period 1822–1827, when Canning was the leading figure in the ministry, was one of legislative change that foreshadowed the upheaval of the 1830s. The Tories were belatedly realizing that conservatism was doomed if it did nothing. They were not always agreed among themselves on what to do, and they were determined not to budge on the central issue, the constitution of Parliament. But the House of Commons sanctioned so many innovations in administrative and social policy that by 1827, when Canning died, the question was not whether but when the house would consider reforming itself.

The first change, initiated by Robert Peel, was in the criminal code. As early as 1819 Peel had made a name for himself as a rising financier by regularizing the currency and providing for the resumption of specie payments; now, as home secretary, he carried through a massive program to amend the substantive law and the system of law enforcement. The abolition of the death penalty for all but the most serious offenses curtailed the high degree of discretion that judges had previously exercised in sentencing; the average number of executions per year declined within a decade from 108 to 61. That medieval anachronism, benefit of clergy, by which those who could claim clerical status resorted to church courts when accused of a crime, was totally ended. Peel was as much concerned with deterring crime as with altering the criminal law, and in London he created a metropolitan police force. With their distinctive blue uniforms, top hats (later helmets), and truncheons, British policemen are still known as Bobbies in honor of Robert Peel.

The Combination Act of 1799, like the old criminal code, had proved impossible to enforce. In 1824 it was repealed, and masters and men alike were freed to organize as they pleased. The result was an epidemic of strikes and lockouts, which precipitated a new statute in 1825 that continued to permit combinations "for the sole purpose of consulting upon and determining the rate of wages and prices"; such combinations were illegal if they involved violence, intimidation, molestation, or obstruction. Penalties were imposed on employees who used force against their employers or who coerced fellow workers to join what was then called an association and soon came to be known as a trade union. For years to come, the union remained in limbo; it was neither illegal, provided that it was voluntary and uncoercive, nor recognized by the law. Parliament had established one of the principles sacred to Victorians, freedom of contract, whereby an employee might contract with his employer on any terms that were mutually acceptable, without interference from any organization of employees or, in theory, of employers. This was laissez-faire with a vengeance: it was neither the state nor the union but the law of supply and demand that was to determine the rate of wages.

Victorian economic doctrine was also foreshadowed in the reforms instituted by William Huskisson, the president of the Board of Trade. In principle he was for his day an advanced free-trader; and, although in practice he proceeded cautiously, the sum of his achievements was impressive. He relaxed the Navigation Acts, primarily to stimulate the trade of the British colonies and thereby cement their loyalty to the mother country; he changed the Corn Laws to reduce the tariff on imported colonial grain; he also lowered tariffs on foreign manufactured goods and, even more dras-

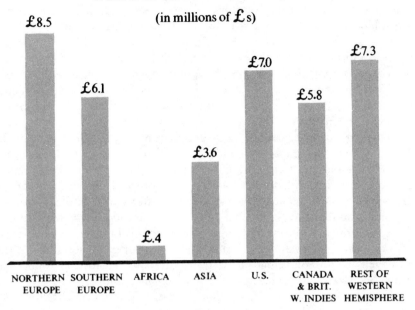

VALUE OF BRITISH EXPORTS, 1825
(in millions of £s)

£8.5

£6.1

£7.0

£7.3

£5.8

£3.6

£.4

| NORTHERN EUROPE | SOUTHERN EUROPE | AFRICA | ASIA | U.S. | CANADA & BRIT. W. INDIES | REST OF WESTERN HEMISPHERE |

Derived from B. R. Mitchell and Phyllis Deane, eds., *Abstract of British Historical Statistics* (1962), p. 313.

tically, on foreign raw materials, and in the process dealt a lethal blow to smuggling. British trade boomed.

The prosperity that followed, however, brought a wave of speculation almost as wild as the South Sea Bubble, and a crash in 1826 that was almost as shattering as that when the Bubble burst. The resultant unemployment was aggravated by bad harvests, and hunger stalked the countryside. Much foreign grain was in storage, waiting for the domestic price to rise to that stipulated in the Corn Laws. Parliament hastily authorized the sale of this grain and thereby tacitly admitted that the Corn Laws worked hardship on the nation. Two years later a sliding scale of duties was introduced, decreasing as grain prices rose on the domestic market; and this principle remained operative until 1846. Parliament was willing to compromise in an emergency, but, once the crisis passed, the legislature put the welfare of the landed interest ahead of the general welfare.

For the moment the question of the Corn Laws was overshadowed by political developments. Early in 1827 a stroke incapacitated Lord Liverpool, the titular head of the government since 1812, and a bitter battle ensued for the succession. Canning won, at the cost of disrupting his party. Rank-and-file Tories distrusted his liberal views, especially on Catholic emancipation, and also distrusted him. He was too brilliant for more pedestrian men, and he could not blunt the shafts of his wit: every time he delivered a major speech, it was said, he made an enemy for life. When he was named prime minister, six of his colleagues resigned, including Peel and Lord Eldon; and Tories harassed him more than Whigs during his term of office. It was brief. In August 1827 he died, and without him his few followers could not carry on. After a short interlude the duke of Wellington formed a government, in January 1828, that appeared to be a return to the Toryism of an earlier day. But in fact that Toryism was dying, torn by factions and haunted by the ghost of Canning, and the duke was forced to surrender its principles one by one.

The first surrender seemed to be insignificant. The new cabinet unwillingly accepted a Whig bill, introduced by Lord John Russell in 1828, to restore dissenters to full citizenship by repealing the Test and Corporation Acts that barred them from local and national office. This legislation of the Cavalier Parliament had lost most of its teeth after 1727, thanks to annual suspending acts, but had remained on the books as a nostalgic Tory symbol of the day when Anglicans had monopolized political power.[7] The chief effect of repeal was psychological rather than legal: it gave new force to the movement for Catholic emancipation. If Protestants outside the established church deserved full recognition, why not Roman Catholics?

The man who posed this question dramatically was Daniel O'Connell. Ever since 1801 Irish Catholics had been agitating for repeal of the union and for emancipation, and O'Connell, a successful Dublin lawyer, had recently come to the fore as the leader and organizer of their discontent. He welcomed not only gentlemen but also tenant farmers—who paid dues of a penny a month—into his Catholic Association, an increasingly powerful pressure group that utilized the cause of "emancipation" to make its members more conscious of their Irish identity. O'Connell was a big man in every way—in body and intellect and humor—and he was as patient as he was astute. He had no faith in persuading the British by logic or coercing them by violence; his aim was to generate irresistible political pressure, and in this he succeeded. In 1828 he stood for Parliament from the Irish county of Clare, and experts were startled to discover that a Catholic might legally be nominated and even elected, though he might not sit. The Anglo-Irish gentry were solidly opposed to the candidate, and they were used to controlling county elections. But the peasants in their thousands marched to the polls, regimented by their priests, to vote for O'Connell. He was triumphantly returned.

The Clare election put Wellington's government in a serious dilemma. The duke and Peel, his leader in the House of Commons, were against Catholic emancipation on principle; so were the king and the great majority of the House of Lords. But to refuse to seat O'Connell might well have led to new rebellion in Ireland—over an issue that had the support of at least half the members of the House of Commons. The followers of Canning, true to his memory, championed the Irish cause, as did most Whigs. If

---

[7] See Chapter 2.

emancipation were to be carried at all, Wellington would have to carry it; only he could overcome the opposition of the upper house. The bill was introduced, to the scandal of the diehard Tories. For a moment it seemed as if Wellington would be stopped as Pitt had been: the king balked. George had taken on all his father's bigotry, which he mistook for principle, but, after haranguing his ministers for six hours while he helped himself to brandy, he gave way before their threat to resign. In April 1829 the bill became law.

The effect was profound. Emancipation created in the House of Commons a third party, composed of Irish Catholics, which was not committed to Whig or Tory principles but solely to the interests of Ireland; for more than a century that party was to play a role in British politics out of all proportion to its numbers. The way in which O'Connell had achieved his ends showed that efficient organization, backed by the threat of violence but operating within legal channels, could force the hand of a reluctant British government, and the lesson was not lost on the Irish. In domestic politics the emancipation crisis was a further step in the disruption of the Tory party that had begun at Liverpool's retirement. Wellington and Peel were discredited with their own rank and file, and the Canningites were driven into coalition with the Whigs. While the impetus to change was accelerated, the barriers to it were revealed as feeble when the king and the House of Lords, those champions of the status quo, gave way before the ministry. The path was open for changing the structure of Parliament itself, and the drive for reform began that culminated in 1832.

The Tory defenses crumbled rapidly. In June 1830 George IV performed what many of his subjects regarded as his one good deed: he died. Whatever his virtues as a patron of the arts, as a monarch he had proved opinionated, meddlesome, and inconsistent, and he had brought the popularity of the crown to its nadir in modern times. Despite his sympathy for Fox in his earlier years, he had become an adamant opponent of constitutional reform. His younger brother, who succeeded him as William IV, was a far less ponderous obstacle. He was a bluff and genial man, with some pretensions to liberalism but little political common sense, and as conscientious and well-meaning as he was irresolute.

His accession necessitated a new parliamentary election, which coincided with a revolution in France. It was a moderate revolution, like that in England in 1688, because it was carefully managed by the upper classes; out of it came not a Jacobin Reign of Terror but a staid bourgeois regime with a bourgeois king, Louis Philippe. Developments in Paris made a deep impression across the Channel. If even the volatile French could change their government without opening the floodgates of democracy and chaos, surely the British could.

In the new Parliament the Tories had a shaky majority, which melted away as soon as Wellington made clear that he would not consider any measure of reform. He stood for a Toryism that had starved to death for want of ideas, and his speech in the House of Lords in November 1830 was its funeral oration. Parliament as it then existed, he said, "possesses the full and entire confidence of the people. I will go further. If at the present moment I had imposed upon me the duty of forming a legislature ... for a country like this, in possession of great property of various descriptions, I do not mean to assert that I could form such a legislature as we possess now, for the nature of man is incapable of reaching such excellence at once, but my great endeavor would be to form some description of legislature which would produce the same results." At a time when the people were clamoring for change and were backed by holders of "great property of various descriptions," the duke could only extol the surpassing excellence of the status quo. Two weeks later he was forced to resign, and the battle for reform began.

THE REFORM PROGRAM

The Industrial Revolution, by creating a new wealth that demanded power, began the process that culminated in the Reform Bill. Preindustrial Britain had seen agitation for making the House of Commons more representative of the people, as witness the mobs that had rioted for John Wilkes; this left-wing radicalism, which continued under the surface and sometimes broke through it, as in the Battle of Peterloo, was essentially popular and carried a threat of social revolution that alarmed the propertied classes. Against that kind of reform the factory owner was united with the landowner; both, as employers, could foresee that extending the suffrage to the laborer would eventually mean, if only because of his overwhelming numbers, government that was more in his interests than in theirs. By the 1820s, however, the progress of industrialization was creating pressure for reform of quite another sort. A large propertied group, the magnates of foundry and mine and mill, now stood outside the narrow world of Parliament and demanded entrance into it. These new plutocrats dreaded radicalism as much as the bluest-blooded Tory did. What they wanted was a share of political power for themselves, not for the people; and they backed their demand with a logic that was hard to refute.

Until the accession of George III the composition of the House of Commons, despite all the anomalies of rotten boroughs, had borne some rough relationship to the distribution of wealth and population. The country had still been chiefly engaged in trade and agriculture, and a case could be made for a legislature in which the commercial and landed interests predominated.[8] But by the time George III died, a vast new interest had come into being, and it had no representation worth the name. The great industrial centers were in parts of the British Isles that had hitherto been sparsely populated, and in which parliamentary boroughs were few and far between. Most of the mushrooming cities sent no members to Parliament, and the barons of industry who dominated those cities had almost no voice in na-

---

[8]For the composition of the eighteenth-century House of Commons see Chapter 4.

tional politics. These men accepted wholeheartedly the oligarchical principle that no one deserved a voice unless his property gave him a stake in the social order; what they repudiated, just as wholeheartedly, was the Tory identification of property with land. Why, they asked, should industrial wealth be discriminated against in favor of landed wealth? The question was hard to answer, and they pressed it more and more insistently with every year that passed.

The Tories refused to budge. Although they had in their ranks a few scions of industrialists, such as Robert Peel, the party was in essence that of the landed interest. The heads of the great territorial houses still made up the bulk of the peerage, and their relatives and dependents the bulk of the House of Commons. That house could not be enlarged to take in the clamorous outsiders without becoming hopelessly unwieldy; the only way to accommodate them was to wipe out most of the rotten boroughs in order to make room for new industrial constituencies—in other words to destroy the system by which the oligarchs had governed for more than a century. A change of such magnitude would be revolutionary, and the prospect horrified conservatives.

On this issue many Whigs were by instinct as conservative as Tories, from whom they were indistinguishable in their social connections and landed roots. But the Whigs as a party were different from the Tories in one important respect. They were out of power. They had been out since the days of Fox, and clinging to their old ways gave them little chance of getting in again. A political party that feels itself condemned to perpetual wandering in the wilderness is a party that sooner or later will be ripe for new ideas, even unpalatable ones, if they offer some hope of tasting once more the fruits of office. So it was with the Whigs. In the course of the 1820s they not only clung to the tradition of civic and religious liberty identified with Charles James Fox; they also embraced the cause that some of their party had advocated forty years earlier, parliamentary reform, and by 1830 they were its champions.

They knew that the cause was popular, but this was not their reason for embracing it. They were willing to use the people for generating pressure, and even to exploit the theme that Whiggism had always stood for popular rights; but they had no intention whatever of obtaining a popular franchise. The unenfranchised whose support they really sought were the wealthy, not the masses. The Whigs held to Edmund Burke's view that the vote, far from being a right, was a privilege necessarily associated with property, and that universal suffrage would be the prelude to despoilment of the rich by the poor. They were as oligarchical as the Tories and differed from them only in advocating the enlargement of the oligarchy.

The Whigs' political program had two parts—the rationalization of the franchise and the reapportionment of borough representatives. Landed property, they argued, deserved no more influence in government than any other form, and voting qualifications should be adjusted so that all men of substance had an equal voice. The existing electoral system was chaotic: at one extreme were boroughs with only a handful of voters, and at the other a few democratic constituencies, such as Westminister, in which almost all adult males voted. Here too the whigs proposed to create greater uniformity by giving seats taken from the smaller boroughs to the newly populous areas, particularly the industrial cities of the north. Some anomalies might be left, but the system in general would be based on the realities of wealth and population.

The long-term effects would be sweeping, as both conservatives and radicals were well aware. Once admit the principle that the constitution needed amending, then no amendment could be regarded as permanent; the same logic that impelled the first change would lead inexorably to others, in a never-ending process of innovation. Removing the rotten boroughs would shake the gentry's control of local government; unseating the gentry there would be a prelude to attacking their economic power as maintained by the Corn Laws; destroying the Corn Laws in the interest of the people at large would lead on to enfranchising the masses, and then how would any kind of property be safe? This line of thinking was behind the Tory's dread of reform and the radical's enthusiasm for it. And both were right.

EPILOGUE

When the Whigs introduced their Reform Bill in March 1831, Britain had reached a watershed in its history. No previous ministry of the crown had ever proposed to Parliament such a deliberate and drastic constitutional revision. The Glorious Revolution and the Hanoverian accession had certainly brought drastic revision, but it had not been deliberate; the intent had been to safeguard the existing constitution. In the eighteenth century the gradual and subtle process of constitutional growth had gone largely unperceived by the oligarchs themselves. They had not created the cabinet or the rotten borough or government by "interests" but had merely used the means that came to hand for conducting the business of the state. "In what we improve," said Burke, "we are never wholly new; and in what we retain, we are never wholly obsolete." He was speaking for a ruling class that proved itself capable of moving with the times, slowly and hesitantly, but that had no thought of revolution even by statute.

Now, a generation after Burke's death, one segment of that class was converted to changing fundamentals of the constitution. During the previous half-century, Britain had undergone an economic revolution, and perceptive Britons could no longer blind themselves to the truth, however unwelcome, or to the need of acknowledging it in political terms. The greatest imperial and mercantile nation in the world had reached that position because it had new sources of strength. This giant was not Antaeus, who drew his power from the earth as the aristocracy did. Power now flowed as well from steam engines and factories, mines and blast furnaces. When the wielders of this industrial force, having grown rich by it, were moved to reach for political influence commensurate with their wealth, the concept of government as an aristocratic monopoly became obsolete.

Aristocracy, oligarchy, and the ruling class had hitherto been substantially synonyms for the landed interest. But oligarchy is a broader term than aristocracy and covers any form of rule by a minority. The Britain of 1830 had two wealthy minorities—the agrarian, and the commercial and industrial. The question at issue was whether the former, the traditional aristocracy, would share power with the latter, thereby compromising the aristocratic principle in order to maintain the oligarchical—abandoning the obsolete predominance of land, in other words, to preserve a system of government by the few. The aristocrats agreed to this compromise because at bottom they had no choice. The extinction of oligarchy was unthinkable and the only way to maintain it was to broaden its base.

This the Reform Bill did. The newcomers brought with them concepts of administration, of poor relief, of colonial and economic policy, that rapidly altered the character of government; and soon the accelerating pace of industrialization brought an even more basic change as the working classes came of age and demanded further adjustment of the franchise. When the settlement of 1832, which Whigs and Tories hoped would be permanent, disappeared in the second Reform Bill of 1867, the whole principle of oligarchy was eroded. The practice of a ruling class persisted until recent times and in some degree still persists. But the principle that power should be vested in a small minority, and secured to it by constitutional means, survived the first Reform Bill by only thirty-five years.

A survey of the age of aristocracy may reasonably end in 1830, for the tumult that followed Wellington's resignation that autumn belongs more to the new age that was dawning than to the twilight of the old. The Britain of 1830 was a far cry from that of Lord Chesterfield. The frock coat and top hat had replaced the finery of a gentleman's brocade and sword and wig; factories, clattering in the middle of workers' slums, had appeared in parts of the countryside that had hitherto known nothing busier than grazing cows; the workshop of the world was a bustle of activity, and portents were everywhere of the greater bustle to come. The first Atlantic crossing by a steamship, British-built, had occurred in 1827; and in 1830 the opening of a rail line between Liverpool and Manchester, designed to carry passengers, inaugurated the railroad age. Steam and machinery, as they came into their own, were making the social order of the eighteenth century more and more archaic. Since the 1790s the Tories had defended and preserved that order by setting their faces flintlike against change in the structure of Parliament, when change was prerequisite for adapting public policy to the needs of the new era. Now the Tory party, and the society out of which it had grown, were disintegrating together.

That eighteenth-century society need not evoke nostalgia, but it does demand respect. Aristocrats ruled it as never before or since; they loved their country, and by and large they served it well. The list of their accomplishments is long, and a few examples in conclusion may stand as a summary of their rule. They did not resolve the Irish problem, but they did consolidate the British Isles into a single kingdom and direct the armies and navies that brought it out of insularity to world empire. They maintained a financial structure that was both stable and flexible enough to survive disruptive economic change. They governed in a manner that was sometimes lax, sometimes repressive, and always inefficient but that permitted in the long run the growth of individual freedom. Their self-confidence matched their energy. They had a refinement and sureness of taste that made both the Jacobean and the Victorian era seem boorish by comparison, and they were experts in the fine art of living.

Most important of all, they knew by instinct when their power was ebbing and were able to surrender it with good grace. The grace did not come easily, yet in the end they achieved it; for, hard as they battled against the inevitable, they did not battle to the death. They had a saving gift for compromise, which may be one of the humdrum but is also one of the great political virtues; and by compromising they made peaceful change possible. Their best epitaph is the observation of a shrewd foreigner, Prince Louis Napoleon, the heir and eventual successor of his uncle as Napoleon III. "In England you make reforms," said the prince; "in France we make revolutions."

BIBLIOGRAPHY

BIBLIOGRAPHIES AND REFERENCE WORKS

Brown, Lucy, and Ian Christie, eds. *Bibliography of British History, 1789–1851.* 1977.

Chaloner, W. H., and R. C. Richardson, eds. *British Social and Economic History: A Bibliographical Guide.* 1976.

Davies, Godfrey, ed. *Bibliography of British History: The Stuart Period.* 2nd rev. ed. 1971.

Dictionary of National Biography. 1882–1900.

Elton, G. R., ed. *Annual Bibliography of British and Irish History.* Since 1975.

Falkus, Malcolm, and John Gillingham, eds. *The Historical Atlas of of Britain.* 1982.

Kanner, Barbara, ed. *The Women of England from Anglo-Saxon Times to the Present: Interpretive Bibliographical Essays.* 1979.

Mitchell, Brian, and Phyllis Deane, eds. *Abstract of British Historical Statistics.* 1962.

Morrill, J. S., ed. *Seventeenth Century Britain, 1603–1714.* Critical Bibliographies in Modern History. 1980.

Pargellis, Stanley McC., and D. J. Medley, eds. *Bibliography of British History: The Eighteenth Century, 1714–1789.* 1951.

GENERAL WORKS

Beckett, J. C. *The Making of Modern Ireland.* 1966.

Briggs, Asa. *The Age of Improvement, 1783–1867.* Vol. VIII. A History of England, edited by W. N. Medlicott. 1959.

Bryant, Arthur. *The Years of Endurance, 1793–1802.* 1942.

———. *The Years of Victory, 1802–1812.* 1945.

———. *The Age of Elegance, 1812–1822.* 1950.

Churchill, Winston S. *A History of the English-Speaking Peoples,* vol. 3. 4 vols. 1956–1958.

Clark, George N. *The Later Stuarts, 1660–1714.* Vol. X. The Oxford History of England. 2nd ed. 1956.

Ferguson, William. *Scotland: 1689 to the Present.* 1968.

Gash, Norman. *Aristocracy and People: Britain, 1815–1865.* New History of England. 1979.

Halévy, Elie. *A History of the English People in the Nineteenth Century,* vols. 1 and 2. 6 vols. 2nd ed. 1949–1952.

Holmes, Geoffrey, ed. *Britain After the Glorious Revolution.* 1969.

Jones, J. R. *Country and Court: England, 1658–1714*. New History of England. 1978.

Lecky, W. E. H. *A History of England in the Eighteenth Century*. 8 vols. 1878–1890.

———. *A History of Ireland in the Eighteenth Century*. Edited by L. P. Curtis. 1972.

Marshall, Dorothy. *Eighteenth-Century England, 1714–1783*. 2nd ed. 1975. A History of England, edited by W. N. Medlicott.

McCaffrey, Lawrence. *Ireland: From Colony to Nation State*. 1979.

MacDonagh, Oliver. *Ireland: The Union and Its Aftermath*. 1977.

McDowell, R. B. *Ireland in the Age of Imperialism and Revolution, 1760–1801*. 1980.

Ogg, David. *England in the Reigns of James II and William III*. 1955.

Owen, John B. *The Eighteenth Century, 1714–1815*. Norton Library History of England. 1974.

Plumb, John H. *England in the Eighteenth Century*. 1963.

Speck, W. A. *Stability and Strife: England, 1714–1760*. New History of England. 1977.

Trevelyan, George Macaulay. *England Under the Stuarts*. Vol. V. A History of England, edited by Charles W. C. Oman, 21st ed. 1949.

———. *England Under Queen Anne*. 3 vols. 1930–1934.

———. *British History in the Nineteenth Century and After, 1782–1919*. 2nd ed. 1938.

Trevelyan, George O. *The American Revolution*. 4 vols. 1905–1912.

———. *George the Third and Charles Fox: The Concluding Part of the American Revolution*. 2 vols. 1915.

Watson, J. Steven. *The Reign of George III, 1760–1815*. Vol. XII. The Oxford History of England. 1960.

Willcox, William B. *Star of Empire: A Study of Britain as a World Power, 1485–1945*. 1950.

Williams, Basil. *The Whig Supremacy, 1714–1760*. Vol. XI. The Oxford History of England. 2nd ed. 1962.

Woodward, E. Llewelyn. *The Age of Reform, 1815–1870*. Vol. XIII. The Oxford History of England. 1938.

LEGAL, CONSTITUTIONAL, AND GOVERNMENTAL HISTORY

Ashley, Maurice. *The Glorious Revolution of 1688*. 1966.

Beattie, John M. *The English Court in the Reign of George I*. 1967.

Brewer, John. *Party Ideology and Popular Politics at the Accession of George III*. 1976.

———, and John Styles, eds. *An Ungovernable People: The English and Their Law in the Seventeenth and Eighteenth Centuries*. 1980.

Brock, W. R. *Lord Liverpool and Liberal Toryism, 1820–1827*. 2nd ed. 1967.

Brown, Philip A. *The French Revolution in English History*. 1918.

Butterfield, Herbert. *George III and the Historians*. 1957.

Christie, Ian R. *Myth and Reality in Late Eighteenth-Century Politics and Other Papers*. 1970.

———. *Wilkes, Wyvill and Reform*. 1962.

Cone, Carl B. *Burke and the Nature of Politics*. 2 vols. 1957–1964.

———. *The English Jacobins*. 1968.

Cookson, J. E. *Lord Liverpool's Administration: The Crucial Years, 1815–1822*. 1975.

Davis, Richard. *Political Change and Continuity, 1760–1885: A Buckinghamshire Study*. 1972.

Dickinson, H. T. *Liberty and Property: Political Ideology in Eighteenth Century Britain*. 1978.

Feiling, Keith G. *A History of the Tory Party, 1640–1714*. 1924.

———. *The Second Tory Party, 1714–1832*. 1938.

Foord, Archibald S. *His Majesty's Opposition, 1714–1830*. 1964.

Goodwin, Albert. *The Friends of Liberty: The English Democratic Movement in the Age of the French Revolution*. 1979.

Harvie, Christopher. *Scotland and Nationalism: Scottish Society and Politics, 1709–1977*. 1977.

Hill, B. W. *The Growth of Parliamentary Parties, 1689–1742*. 1976.

Holdsworth, William S. *A History of English Law*, vols. 10–16. 16 vols. 3rd ed. 1922–1938.

Holmes, Geoffrey. *British Politics in the Age of Anne*. 1968.

———. *The Trial of Doctor Sacheverell*. 1973.

Horwitz, Henry. *Parliament, Policy, and Politics in the Reign of William III*. 1977.

Jones, J. R. *The Revolution of 1688 in England*. 1972.

Keir, David L. *The Constitutional History of Modern Britain, 1485–1950*. 1953.

Kenyon, J. P. *Revolution Principles: The Politics of Party, 1689–1720*. 1977.

Langford, Paul. *The Excise Crisis: Society and Politics in the Age of Walpole*. 1975.

Machin, G. I. T. *The Catholic Question in English Politics, 1820–1830*. 1964.

Mitchell, Austin. *The Whigs in Opposition, 1815–30*. 1967.

Namier, Lewis B. *England in the Age of the American Revolution*. 1933.

———. *The Structure of Politics at the Accession of George III*. 2 vols. 2nd ed. 1957.

———, and John Brooke. *The House of Commons, 1754–1790*. 3 vols. History of Parliament Series. 1964.

O'Gorman, Frank. *The Rise of Party in England: the Rockingham Whigs, 1760–82*. 1975.

———. *The Whig Party and the French Revolution*. 1967.

Pares, Richard. *King George III and the Politicians*. 1953.

Peters, Marie. *Pitt and Popularity: The Patriot Minister and London Opinion During the Seven Years' War*. 1981.

Petrie, Sir Charles. *The Jacobite Movement*. 2 vols. 1948–1950.

Plumb, J. H. *The Origins of Political Stability in England, 1675–1725*. 1967.

Porritt, E., and A. *The Unreformed House of Commons*. 2 vols. 1903.

Prall, Stuart E. *The Bloodless Revolution: England, 1688.* 1972.

Reitan, E. A., ed. *George III: Tyrant or Constitutional Monarch?* 1964.

Riley, P. W. J. *The Union of England and Scotland: A Study in Anglo-Scottish Politics of the Early Eighteenth Century.* 1979.

Robbins, Caroline. *The Eighteenth-Century Commonwealthman.* 1959.

Roberts, Michael. *The Whig Party, 1807–1812.* 1939.

Rudé, George. *Wilkes and Liberty.* 1962.

Sack, James J. *The Grenvillites, 1801–29: Party Politics and Factionalism in the Age of Pitt and Liverpool.* 1979.

Sedgwick, Romney. *The House of Commons, 1715–1754.* 2 vols. History of Parliament Series. 1970.

Straka, Gerald M., ed. *The Revolution of 1688 and the Birth of the English Political Nation.* 2nd ed. 1973.

Thomas, P. D. G. *The House of Commons in the Eighteenth Century.* 1971.

Thompson, Edward P. *Whigs and Hunters: The Origins of the Black Act.* 1978.

Walcott, Robert. *English Politics in the Early Eighteenth Century.* 1956.

Webb, Sidney, and Beatrice. *English Local Government from the Revolution to the Municipal Corporation Act.* 9 vols. 1906–1929.

Williams, E. Neville. *The Eighteenth Century Constitution, 1688–1815: Documents and Commentary.* 1960.

ECONOMIC AND SOCIAL HISTORY

Altick, Richard D. *The Shows of London.* 1978.

Ashton, Thomas S. *An Economic History of England: The Eighteenth Century.* 1955.

———. *The Industrial Revolution, 1760–1830.* Rev. ed. 1964.

Buck, Anne. *Dress in Eighteenth Century England.* 1979.

Carswell, John. *The South Sea Bubble.* 1960.

Chambers, J. D. *Population, Economy, and Society in Pre-Industrial England.* 1972.

———, and G. E. Mingay. *The Agricultural Revolution, 1750–1880.* 1966.

Clapham, John H. *An Economic History of Modern Britain,* vol. 1. 3 vols. 1930–1938.

Clarkson, Leslie. *Death, Disease, and Famine in Pre-Industrial England.* 1975.

Cockburn, J. S., ed. *Crime in England. 1550–1800.* 1977.

Cowherd, Raymond G. *Political Economists and the English Poor Law.* 1977.

Cullen, L. M. *An Economic History of Ireland Since 1660.* 1972.

Deane, Phyllis. *The First Industrial Revolution.* 2nd ed. 1979.

———, and W. A. Cole. *British Economic Growth, 1688–1959: Trends and Structure.* 2nd ed. 1967.

Dickson, P. G. M. *The Financial Revolution in England: A Study in the Development of Public Credit, 1688–1756.* 1967.

Dobson, C. R. *Masters and Journeymen: A Prehistory of Industrial Relations, 1717–1800.* 1980.

Ehrman, John. *The British Government and Commercial Negotiations with Europe, 1783–1793.* 1962.

Emsley, Clive. *British Society and the French Wars, 1793–1815.* 1979.

Flinn, M. W. *British Population Growth, 1700–1850.* 1970.

———. *Origins of the Industrial Revolution.* 1966.

George, M. Dorothy. *London Life in the Eighteenth Century.* 1925.

Girouard, Mark. *Life in the English Country House: A Social and Architectural History.* 1978.

Habbakuk, H. J. *Population Growth and Economic Development Since 1750.* 1971.

Glass, D. V., and D. E. C. Eversley, eds. *Population in History.* 1965.

Hammond, John L. Le B., and Barbara. *The Town Laborer, 1760–1832: The New Civilization.* 1917.

———. *The Skilled Laborer, 1760–1832.* 1920.

———. *The Village Laborer, 1760–1832: A Study in the Government of England Before the Reform Bill.* 4th ed. 1932.

Hargreaves, E. L. *The National Debt.* 1930.

Hartwell, R. M. *The Industrial Revolution and Economic Growth.* 1971.

Hay, Douglas, et al. *Albion's Fatal Tree: Crime and Society in Eighteenth-Century England.* 1975.

Hecht, J. Jean. *The Domestic Servant Class in Eighteenth-Century England.* 1956.

Hibbert, Christopher. *King Mob: The Story of Lord George Gordon and the Riots of 1780.* 1958.

Hilton, Boyd. *Corn, Cash, Commerce: The Economic Policies of the Tory Governments, 1815–1830.* 1978.

Hobsbawm, E. J. *Industry and Empire.* 1968.

Laslett, Peter. *The World We Have Lost: England Before the Industrial Age.* 1965.

Lipson, Ephraim. *The Economic History of England,* vols. 2 and 3. 3 vols. 1937–1953.

Malcomson, R. W. *Popular Recreation in English Society, 1700–1850.* 1973.

Mantoux, Paul J. *The Industrial Revolution in the Eighteenth Century in England.* Rev. ed. 1928.

Marshall, Dorothy. *Dr. Johnson's London.* 1968.

———. *English People in the Eighteenth Century.* 1956.

———. *The English Poor in the Eighteenth Century: A Study in Social and Administrative History.* 1926.

Marshall, J. D. *The Old Poor Law, 1795–1834.* 1968.

Mathias, Peter. *The First Industrial Nation.* 1969.

———. *The Transformation of England: Essays in the Economic and Social History of England in the Eighteenth Century.* 1979.

Mingay, G. E. *English Landed Society in the Eighteenth Century.* 1963.

———. *The Gentry: The Rise and Fall of a Ruling Class.* 1976.

Musson, A. E., and Eric Robinson. *Science and Technology in the Industrial Revolution,* 1969.

Nef, John U. *The Rise of the British Coal Industry,* vol. 2. 2 vols. 1932.

Olson, Donald J. *Town Planning in London: The Eighteenth and Nineteenth Centuries.* 1964.

Owen, David. *English Philanthropy, 1660–1960.* 1964.

Pawson, Eric. *The Early Industrial Revolution: Britain in the Eighteenth Century.* 1979.

Perkin, Harold. *The Origins of Modern English Society, 1780–1880.* 1969.

Pinchbeck, Ivy. *Women Workers and the Industrial Revolution.* 1930.

_____, and Margaret Hewitt. *Children in English Society.* 2 vols. 1969–1972.

Plumb, J. H. *The Commercialization of Leisure in Eighteenth-Century England.* 1973.

Poynter, J. R. *Society and Pauperism: English Ideas on Poor Relief, 1795–1834.* 1969.

Prothero, Rowland E. *English Farming Past and Present.* 1913.

Quinlan, Maurice J. *Victorian Prelude.* 1941.

Rostow, W. W. *The Stages of Economic Growth.* 1960.

Rudé, George W. *Hanoverian London, 1714–1808.* 1971.

_____. *Paris and London in the Eighteenth Century.* 1973.

Stone, Lawrence. *The Family, Sex, and Marriage in England, 1500–1800.* 1977.

Summerson, John. *Georgian London.* 3rd ed. 1978.

Taylor, A. J., ed. *The Standard of Living in Britain in the Industrial Revolution.* 1975.

Taylor, P. A. M., ed. *The Industrial Revolution in Britain: Triumph or Disaster?* 2nd ed. 1970.

Thomis, Malcolm I. *The Luddites.* 1970.

_____. *Responses to Industrialization: The British Experience, 1780–1850.* 1976.

_____. *The Town Laborer and the Industrial Revolution.* 1975.

_____, and Peter Holt. *Threats of Revolution in Britain, 1789–1848.* 1977.

Thompson, Edward P. *The Making of the English Working Class.* 1963.

_____. "The Moral Economy of the English Crowd in the Eighteenth Century," *Past & Present,* no. 50. February 1971.

_____. "Patrician Society, Plebeian Culture," *Journal of Social History,* Summer 1974.

Traill, Henry D., ed. *Social England: A Record of the Progress of the People . . . by Various Writers,* vols. 4–6. 6 vols. 1893–1897.

Trevelyan, George Macaulay. *English Social History.* 3rd ed. 1946.

Trumbach, Randolph. *The Rise of the Egalitarian Family: Aristocratic Kinship and Domestic Relations in Eighteenth-Century England.* 1978.

Turberville, A. S. *English Men and Manners in the Eighteenth Century.* 2nd ed. 1929.

Webb, Sidney, and Beatrice. *English Poor Law History,* vol. 1. 3 vols. 1927–1929.

West, E. G. "Literacy and the Industrial Revolution," *Economic History Review,* August 1978.

Williams, E. Neville. *Life in Georgian England.* 1962.

Wilson, Charles. *England's Apprenticeship, 1603–1763.* 1965.

Wrigley, E. A. *Population and History.* 1969.

INTELLECTUAL AND RELIGIOUS HISTORY

Altick, Richard D. *The English Common Reader.* 1957.

Becker, Carl. *The Heavenly City of the Eighteenth-Century Philosophers.* 1932.

Bossy, John. *The English Catholic Community, 1570–1850.* 1975.

Clive, John. *Scotch Reviewers.* 1957.

Davies, Horton, *Worship and Theology in England,* vol. 3 [1690–1850]. 1961.

Endelman, Todd M. *The Jews of Georgian England, 1714–1830: Tradition and Change in a Liberal Society.* 1979.

Gay, Peter, "Carl Becker's Heavenly City." *The Party of Humanity.* 1964.

_____. *The Enlightenment: An Interpretation.* 2 vols. 1967–1970.

Gilbert, Alan D. *Religion and Society in Industrial England: Church, Chapel, and Social Change, 1740–1914.* 1976.

Girouard, Mark. *The Return to Camelot: Chivalry and the English Gentleman.* 1981.

Gooch, George P. *English Democratic Ideas in the Seventeenth Century.* 2nd ed. 1927.

Halévy, Elie. *The Growth of Philosophic Radicalism.* 1928.

Harris, R. W. *Reason and Nature in the Eighteenth Century, 1714–1780.* 1968.

_____. *Romanticism and the Social Order, 1780–1830.* 1969.

Henriques, Ursula. *Religious Toleration in England, 1787–1833.* 1961.

Humphreys, A. R. *The Augustan World: Society, Thought, and Letters in Eighteenth-Century England.* 1954.

Jacob, Margaret. *The Newtonians and the English Revolution.* 1976.

Laqueur, Thomas Walter. *Religion and Respectability: Sunday Schools and Working Class Culture, 1780–1850.* 1976.

Laski, Harold. *English Political Thought from Locke to Bentham.* 1920.

LeMahieu, D. L. *The Mind of William Paley: A Philosopher and His Age.* 1976.

Maccoby, Simon. *English Radicalism,* vols. 1 and 2. 5 vols. 1935–1955.

Plumb, J. H., ed. *Man and Society in Eighteenth Century Britain.* 1968.

Priestley, J. B. *The Prince of Pleasure and His Regency, 1811–1820.* 1969.

Pruett, John. *The Parish Clergy Under the Later Stuarts: The Leicestershire Experience.* 1978.

Quennell, Peter. *Romantic England: Writing and Painting, 1717–1851.* 1970.

Rendall, Jane. *The Origins of the Scottish Enlightenment, 1707–1776.* 1978.

Semmel, Bernard. *The Methodist Revolution.* 1974.

Stephen, Leslie. *History of English Thought in the Eighteenth Century.* 2 vols. 3rd ed. 1902, 1963.

Stromberg, Roland. *Religious Liberalism in Eighteenth-Century England.* 1954.

Sykes, Norman. *Church and State in England in the XVIIIth Century.* 1934.

Vann, Richard T. *The Social Development of English Quakerism, 1665–1755.* 1969.

Wearmouth, Robert F. *Methodism and the Common People in the Eighteenth Century.* 1945.

_____. *Methodism and the Working Class Movements of England, 1800–1850.* 1937.

Webb, Robert K. *The British Working Class Reader, 1790–1848.* 1955.

Willey, Basil. *The Seventeenth Century Background: Studies in the Thought of Age in Relation to Poetry and Religion.* 1934.

_____. *The Eighteenth Century Background: Studies on the Idea of Nature in the Thought of the Period.* 1941.

IMPERIAL AND DIPLOMATIC HISTORY

Anstey, Roger. *The Atlantic Slave Trade and British Abolition, 1760–1810.* 1975.

Christie, Ian R. *Crisis of Empire: Great Britain and the American Colonies, 1754–1783.* 1966.

———, and Benjamin Labaree. *Empire or Independence, 1760–1775: A British-American Dialogue on the Coming of the American Revolution.* 1976.

Curtin, Philip D. *The Atlantic Slave Trade: A Census.* 1969.

Davis, Ralph. *The Industrial Revolution and British Overseas Trade.* 1979.

Drescher, Seymour. *Econocide: British Slavery in the Era of Abolition.* 1977.

Derry, John. *English Politics and the American Revolution.* 1976.

Gipson, Lawrence H. *The British Empire Before the American Revolution* [1748–1776]. 15 vols. 1958–1970.

Harlow, Vincent T. *The Founding of the Second British Empire, 1763–1793.* 2 vols. 1952–1964.

Horn, D. B. *Great Britain and Europe in the Eighteenth Century.* 1967.

Knorr, K. E. *British Colonial Theories, 1570–1850.* 1944.

Langford, Paul. *The Eighteenth Century, 1688–1815.* Modern British Foreign Policy Series. 1976.

Marshall, P. J. *East India Fortunes: The British in Bengal in the Eighteenth Century.* 1976.

———. *The Impeachment of Warren Hastings.* 1965.

———. *Problems of Empire: Britain and India, 1757–1813.* 1968.

Moon, E. P. *Warren Hastings and British India.* 1947.

Perkins, Bradford. *Prologue to War: England and the United States, 1805–1812.* 1961.

Ritcheson, Charles R. *Aftermath of Revolution: British Policy Toward the United States, 1783–1795.* 1969.

Rose, John Holland, et al., eds. *The Cambridge History of the British Empire,* vols. 1–2. 8 vols. 2nd ed. 1929–1936.

Semmel, Bernard. *The Rise of Free Trade Imperialism.* 1970.

Seton-Watson, R. W. *Britain in Europe, 1789–1914.* 1937.

Sosin, Jack M. *Whitehall and the Wilderness: The Middle West in British Colonial Policy, 1760–1775.* 1961.

Sutherland, Lucy S. *The East India Company in Eighteenth-Century Politics.* 1952.

Temperley, Harold. *The Foreign Policy of Canning, 1822–1827.* 1925.

Thomas, P. D. G. *British Politics and the Stamp Act Crisis: The First Phase of the American Revolution, 1763–1767.* 1975.

Ward, Adolphus W., and George P. Gooch, eds. *The Cambridge History of British Foreign Policy, 1783–1919,* vol. 1. 3 vols. 1922–1923.

Webster, Charles K. *The Congress of Vienna.* Rev. ed. 1934.

———. *The Foreign Policy of Castlereagh.* 2 vols. 1925–1931.

Williamson, James A. *A Short History of British Expansion.* 2 vols. Rev. ed. 1943–1945.

Woodruff, Philip. *The Men Who Ruled India: The Founders.* 1954.

MILITARY HISTORY

Atkinson, Christopher T. *Marlborough and the Rise of the British Army*. 1921.

Baugh, Daniel A. *British Naval Administration in the Age of Walpole*. 1965.

Bond, Gordon. *The Grand Expedition: The British Invasion of Holland in 1809*. 1979.

Corbett, Julian S. *England in the Seven Years' War: A Study in Combined Strategy*. 2 vols. 2nd ed. 1918.

Fortescue, John W. *History of the British Army*, vols. 1–10. 13 vols. in 20. 1899–1930.

Glover, Michael. *Wellington as Military Commander*. 1968.

Glover, Richard. *Britain at Bay: Defense Against Bonaparte, 1803–14*. 1973.

_____. *Peninsular Preparation: The Reform of the British Army, 1795–1809*. 1963.

Kopperman, Paul E. *Braddock at the Monongahela*. 1976.

Mackesy, Piers. *The War for America, 1775–1783*. 1964.

_____. *The War in the Mediterranean, 1803–1810*. 1957.

Mahan, Alfred T. *The Influence of Sea Power upon History, 1660–1783*. 32nd ed. 1928.

_____. *The Influence of Sea Power upon the French Revolution and Empire*. 2 vols. 10th ed. 1898.

Marcus, G. J. *The Age of Nelson: The Royal Navy, 1793–1815*. 1971.

_____. *Heart of Oak: A Survey of British Sea Power in the Georgian Era*. 1975.

Oman, Carola. *Britain Against Napoleon*. 1942.

Oman, Charles W. C. *A History of the Peninsular War*. 7 vols. 1902–1930.

Potter, Elmer B., and Chester W. Nimitz, eds. *Sea Power: A Naval History*. 1960.

Stevens, William O. and Allan Westcott. *A History of Sea Power*. 1944.

Wallace, Willard M. *Appeal to Arms: A Military History of the American Revolution*. 1951.

Ward, Christopher. *The War of the Revolution*. Edited by John R. Alden. 2 vols. 1952.

Western, J. R. *The English Militia in the Eighteenth Century: The Story of a Political Issue, 1660–1802*. 1965.

BIOGRAPHY

Ashley, Maurice. *James II*. 1978.

Ayling, Stanley. *The Elder Pitt, Earl of Chatham*. 1976.

_____. *George the Third*. 1972.

_____. *John Wesley*. 1979.

Barnett, Correlli. *Marlborough*. 1974.

Bartlett, J. C. *Castlereagh*. 1967.

Bate, W. Jackson. *Samuel Johnson*. 1977.

Baxter, Stephen B. *William III and the Defense of European Liberty, 1650–1702*. 1966.

Beaglehole, J. C. *The Life of Captain James Cook*. 1974.

Boswell, James. *The Life of Samuel Johnson, LL.D.* 1791.

Brooke, John. *King George III.* 1972.

Brown, Peter Douglas. *William Pitt, Earl of Chatham.* 1978.

Browning, Reed. *The Duke of Newcastle.* 1975.

Butler, Geoffrey G. *The Tory Tradition: Bolingbroke—Burke—Disraeli—Salisbury.* 1914.

Churchill, Winston S. *Marlborough, His Life and Times.* 6 vols. 1933–1939.

Coupland, Reginald. *Wilberforce: A Narrative.* 1923.

Derry, John W. *Castlereagh.* 1976.

———. *Charles James Fox.* 1972.

Dickinson, H. T. *Walpole and the Whig Supremacy.* 1973.

Ehrman, John. *The Younger Pitt: The Years of Acclaim.* 1969.

Fulford, Roger. *George the Fourth.* Rev. ed. 1949.

Furneaux, Robin. *William Wilberforce.* 1974.

Gash, Norman. *Mr. Secretary Peel.* 1961.

Green, David. *Queen Anne.* 1971.

———. *Sarah, Duchess of Marlborough.* 1967.

Gregg, Edward. *Queen Anne.* 1979.

Hatton, Ragnhild. *George I: Elector and King.* 1978.

Hedley, Olwen. *Queen Charlotte.* 1975.

Hibbert, Christopher. *George IV, Prince of Wales, 1762–1811.* 1972.

———. *George IV, Regent and King, 1811–1830.* 1974.

Holme, Thea. *Caroline: A Biography of Caroline of Brunswick.* 1980.

Kemp, Betty. *Sir Robert Walpole.* 1976.

Kenyon, John P. *The Stuarts: A Study in English Kingship.* 1959.

Kronenberger, Louis. *The Extraordinary Mr. Wilkes.* 1974.

Lang, Paul Henry. *George Frederick Handel,* 1970.

Longford, Elizabeth. *Wellington: The Years of the Sword.* 1969.

———. *Wellington: Pillar of State.* 1973.

Macalpine, Ida, and Richard Hunter. *George III and the Mad Business.* 1969.

Mahan, Alfred T. *The Life of Nelson,* 1897.

Marshall, Dorothy. *John Wesley.* 1965.

Miller, John. *James II: A Study in Kingship.* 1977.

Mingay, G. E., ed. *Arthur Young and His Times.* 1975.

Mossner, Ernest Campbell. *The Life of David Hume.* 2nd ed. 1980.

Ogg, David. *William III.* 1956.

Oman, Carola. *Nelson.* 1947.

Osborne, John W. *William Cobbett: His Life and Times.* 1966.

Plumb, John H. *The First Four Georges.* 1956.

———. *Sir Robert Walpole: The Making of a Statesman.* 1956.

———. *Sir Robert Walpole: The King's Minister.* 1960.

Postgate, Raymond. *That Devil Wilkes.* 1930.

Quennell, Peter. *Hogarth's Progress.* 1955.

Richardson, Joanna. *George IV: A Portrait.* 1970.

Robertson, Charles Grant. *Chatham and the British Empire.* 1948.

Rose, John Holland. *William Pitt* [the Younger]. 2 vols. 1911.

Thomas, P. D. G. *Lord North*. 1975.

Trevelyan, George O. *The Early History of Charles Fox*. 1904.

Turner, F. C. *James II*. 1949.

Valentine, Alan. *Lord North*. 2 vols. 1967.

Wain, John. *Samuel Johnson*. 1974.

Wallas, Graham. *The Life of Francis Place, 1771–1854*. 4th ed. 1925.

West, E. G. *Adam Smith: The Man and His Works*. 1976.

Wickwire, Franklin, and Mary. *Cornwallis: The American Adventure*. 1970.

———. *Cornwallis: The Imperial Years*. 1980.

Wilkes, John W. *A Whig in Power: The Political Career of Henry Pelham*. 1964.

Willcox, William B. *Portrait of a General: Sir Henry Clinton in the War of Independence*. 1964.

Williams, Basil. *The Life of William Pitt, Earl of Chatham*. 2 vols. 1913.

INDEX

France (continued)
166–67, 190, 198–99, 211–17
after Waterloo, 266–68, 270–72,
274–75, 292–93, 302
See also Army, French; Bourbon,
House of; French Revolution; Navy,
French
Francis, Philip, 202, 205
Frederick, prince of Wales (son of
George II), 69, 100–101, 105, 120,
134
Frederick II, king of Prussia, 109, 112,
115–18, 120, 124–26
Frederick William III, king of Prussia,
286
French Revolution
first (1789–1815), 187, 196, 207,
211–33, 236–67, 270, 277
second (1830), 297

Gage, General Thomas, 152–55
Gainsborough, Thomas, 137
Garrick, David, 138
Gay, John, 81
Gentleman's Magazine, 138
Gentry, landed, 4–5, 15, 44–50, 66,
68–69, 71–77, 171–73, 187–91,
279, 299–301
and Walpole, 94–95, 97
George I, king, 12, 38, 63–65, 69–70,
72, 87, 91–94, 96, 133
George II, 43, 65, 69–70, 72, 95–97,
99–100, 104, 105, 113–14, 118–21,
124, 133, 135, 137, 178
George III
before 1783, 70, 120–21, 125,
133–38, 140–43, 145, 149–51, 154,
163, 164, 166, 179
later years, 187, 194, 197, 200, 206,
213, 232, 236, 255, 285–87
George IV
as Prince of Wales and regent, 70,
200, 255, 266, 269, 272, 282,
285–87
as king, 285–88, 297
George, prince of Denmark, 25
Georgia, 104–5, 152, 158
Germain, Lord George (Sackville),
120–21, 154, 156
Ghent, Treaty of (1814), 259
Gibbon, Edward, 63, 78
Gibraltar, 29, 37, 106, 227
Gin Lane, 58, 80
Gin mania, 56–58, 119n., 169
Glasgow, 78–79, 175

Glencoe, Massacre of (1692), 32
Glorious Revolution (1688–1689), 3–22,
32, 212, 297, 300
Godolphin, Lord (Sydney Godolphin),
26, 28, 31
Goldsmith, Oliver, 138–40
Gordon, Lord George, 163–64
Gordon Riots (1780), 163–65
Grafton, duke of (Augustus Henry
Fitzroy), 142, 145, 150–51
Grand Alliance (1689), 14–16
Grand Tour, 76, 85, 188
Grasse, Admiral Comte de, 161–62
Grattan, Henry, 162, 233
Graves, Admiral Thomas, 161–62
Greeks, revolt against Turks, 274,
290–93
Greene, General Nathanael, 159, 161
Grenville, George, 141, 143, 149

Habeas Corpus, 143, 221, 282
Habsburg, House of, 23–24, 36–37,
100, 102–3, 108–9, 271. *See also*
Charles VI, Maria Theresa
Handel, George Frederick, 72, 86
Hanover
electorate of, 12, 35, 37–38, 63, 70,
96, 109, 113, 117–20, 137
House of, 9, 12, 37–39, 63–65,
68–70, 88, 96
Kingdom of, 269
See also George I, II, III, IV; Sophia;
William IV
Hardy, Thomas, 221
Hargreaves, James, 180
Harley, Robert (later Earl of Oxford), 36
Hastings, Warren, 202–3, 205–6
Herschel, William, 137
Hessians, in America, 155–56
Highlanders, Scottish, 31–32, 88, 113–14
Hogarth, William, 58–59, 68, 79–80, 86
Holland, Henry, 286
Holy Alliance (1815), 272–74, 276, 290,
292
Hood, Admiral Sir Samuel, 161–62
Houghton Hall, 95
Howard, John, 194
Howe, General Sir William, 152, 155–57
Howe, Lord (Richard Howe), 155,
157–58
Huguenots, 6, 17
Hull, 173
Hume, David, 79–80
Hunter, John, 78
Huskisson, William, 290, 294

Low countries
  in eighteenth century, 27, 29, 37,
    114–15
  in Revolutionary and Napoleonic wars,
    211, 218, 239, 257
  after Waterloo, 268, 270
  See also Belgium; Netherlands, Dutch
Luddite riots, 256, 282

Madison, James, 258
Madras, 102, 115, 201–3
Mahan, Alfred, 112n.
Malplaquet, Battle of (1709), 35
Malta, 227, 230–31, 237, 257, 270
Malthus, Thomas, 280
Manchester, 178, 183, 282–83, 301
Mansfield, Lord Chief Justice, 164, 195
Maria Theresa, archduchess of Austria
    and queen of Hungary, 103, 108–9,
    112–13, 115–18
Markham, William, 164
Marlborough, duchess of (Sarah
    Churchill), 25, 27, 31, 36
Marlborough, duke of (John Churchill),
    7, 25–29, 31, 35–36, 73, 95, 112,
    113, 118, 124, 218, 246, 253
Mary II, queen, 5–9, 11–12, 17, 26, 31,
    212
Mary of Modena, 5
Masham, Abigail, 36
Massachusetts, 115, 151–52
Masséna, André, Napoleonic marshal,
    255, 257, 260
Mauritius, 257, 270
Medical profession, 78, 169–70
Mediterranean
  in eighteenth century, 28, 29, 37, 106,
    122, 157
  in Revolutionary and Napoleonic wars,
    224, 227–32, 239, 241–42, 257
  after Waterloo, 270, 293
Messiah, The, 72
Methodism, 191–95, 215, 222
Metternich, Prince Klemens von, 262,
    271, 273, 277, 289, 292–93
Minden, Battle of (1759), 120–21, 154
Ministry of All the Talents (1806–1807),
    246–47
Minorca, 29, 37, 106, 117, 119, 121,
    166, 230
Mohammed Ali, 292
Monarchy, role of
  late seventeenth and early eighteenth
    century, 9–12, 34–35
  after 1714, 63–66, 92–93, 96–97,

    134–37, 140–42, 146, 150–51, 163,
    164, 196–97, 203
Monroe Doctrine, 275–76
Moore, General John, 254
Music, 55, 72, 136
Mutinies, British naval (1797), 225–26
Mutiny Acts (1689 and after), 11–12

Napoleon, Prince Louis, 302
Napoleon Bonaparte
  as general and first consul, 218,
    226–28, 230–32, 234, 237–40
  as emperor, 109, 118, 120, 126,
    240–42, 244–58, 260–63, 265–68,
    271–72, 302
Nash, John, 286, 289
National Assembly, French (1789–1791),
    211–12, 216–17
Nations, Battle of the (1813), 238, 261
Navarino, Battle of (1827), 292
Navy, British
  in late Stuart period, 4, 6, 16–17, 21,
    28–29, 34–35
  in Hanoverian period, 67, 71, 105–6,
    108, 111–12, 115, 121–24, 147,
    153–55, 157–62
  role in American history, 167, 240,
    257–60, 275–76
  in Revolutionary and Napoleonic wars,
    223–34, 238–46, 250–52, 257–59,
    266–67
  See also Blockade
Navy, French
  of Louis XIV, 17, 21, 37
  of Louis XV, 122, 124, 126
  of Louis XVI, 157–62
  in Revolutionary and Napoleonic wars,
    223–31, 233–34, 239–45
Navy, Spanish
  in eighteenth century, 37, 104–5, 124
  in Revolutionary and Napoleonic wars,
    224–25, 241–42, 245
Nelson, Admiral Horatio (later Lord Nel-
    son), 224–25, 227–28, 230, 232,
    242, 244–45
Netherlands, Austrian. *See* Belgium
Netherlands, Dutch
  in seventeenth and eighteenth centu-
    ries, 6, 14, 16, 22, 24, 26, 28, 37,
    52, 70, 102, 103, 114, 164
  in Revolutionary and Napoleonic wars,
    217–18, 224, 231, 237, 239, 241,
    263
  kingdom of (1815), 268, 270
Netherlands, Spanish. *See* Belgium

Newcastle, duke of (Thomas Pelham-
Holles), 106, 118–20, 124–25, 140
Newcomen, Thomas, 181
New Orleans, Battle of (1815), 259
Newton, Isaac, 44, 77–78
New York City, 155–59, 161
New Zealand, 195
Nicholas I, tsar of Russia, 292–93
Nile, Battle of the (1798), 228–30, 245
North, Lord (Frederick North), 142,
150–51, 154, 163–64, 166, 187,
197, 200, 201
North America, Anglo-French rivalry in,
101, 115–17, 122–23, 125–26
North Briton, 143
Norwich, 51

Occasional conformity, 13, 38
O'Connell, Daniel, 296–97
Ottoman Empire, 230, 290–93
Oudenarde, Battle of (1708), 35
Oxford, Lord. *See* Harley
Oxford University, 4, 6, 71, 76, 78, 191

Paine, Thomas, 216–17
Palmerston, Lord, 279
Pardo, Convention of (1739), 105–6
Paris, Peace of (1763), 125–26, 141,
143; (1783), 166–67
Parker, Admiral Hyde, 232
Parliament, English
in late Stuart period, 3, 5, 7–12, 15,
22, 26, 31–37
in Hanoverian period, 53, 65–70,
91–99, 101, 105–7, 134–35,
140–42, 145, 149–50, 187,
234–35, 281–82, 293–94
reform of, 145–46, 199–201, 220,
282, 296–302
See also Commons, Lords
Parliament, Irish, 16, 18, 162–63, 197,
233–35
Parliament, Scottish, 31–33
Patents, 175
Paul I, tsar of Russia, 230–32
Peel, Robert, 290, 294, 296–97, 299
Pelham, Henry, 118–19
Peninsular War (1808–1814), 252–57,
259, 261, 263, 267
Pennsylvania, 155–57
Peterloo (or Manchester) Massacre
(1819), 282–83, 298
Philhellenes, 290–91
Philip V, king of Spain, 24, 29, 37, 103,
135

Pitt, William, later Lord Chatham, 101,
105, 113, 118–25, 140–43, 147–49,
151, 159, 197, 219
Pitt, William, the Younger
peacetime ministry of, 196–201, 203,
206, 217, 273
as war leader, 217, 220, 222, 227,
232–38, 241, 246, 253, 256, 267,
283
Place, Francis, 184
Placemen, 67, 93, 135
Poland, 100, 260–61, 269
Polish Succession, War of (1733–1735),
100
Pompadour, Madame de, 143
Pontiac's Rebellion (1763–1764), 148
Poor relief, 57, 60, 75, 173, 176, 207,
220, 222, 248, 280
Pope, Alexander, 77, 80–82, 85, 143
Portugal, 26, 29, 102, 122, 251–55, 260,
270, 273
Pragmatic Sanction, 102, 109
Presbyterians, 13, 18, 31, 79, 233–34
Press, newspaper, 14, 55, 60, 97, 104,
143, 145–46, 221, 281, 283, 286
Pretenders. *See* Stuart, Charles Edward;
Henry; James
Price, Richard, 213
Priestley, Joseph, 212, 217
Prime minister, role of, 92–93, 107,
140–42, 187, 197, 206
Prince Regent. *See* George IV
Privy Council, 4, 65, 289n.
Promotion of Christian Knowledge, Soci-
ety for, 14
Propagation of the Gospel, Society for,
14
Protestant Association, 163
Prussia
in eighteenth century, 70, 109–12,
115–18, 120–21, 123–26
in Revolutionary and Napoleonic wars,
211, 217–18, 231, 247, 261–63,
265–67
after Waterloo, 268–70, 276, 286, 292
See also Frederick II

Quadruple Alliance (1814), 262, 272
Quakers, 13, 195
Quebec Act (1774), 152

Radicalism, 145–46, 211–13, 217, 221,
279, 281–83, 289, 298
Railroads, 182, 301
Ramillies, Battle of (1706), 35

Stanhope, Lord (James), 91
Steam engine, 175, 177, 181–82, 185,
  206, 301
Sterne, Lawrence, 188
St. Helena, 228, 266
St. John, Henry. *See* Bolingbroke
Stuart, Charles Edward, Young Pre-
  tender, 113–14
Stuart, Henry, Cardinal and Pretender,
  114
Stuart, House of, 6, 12, 24, 35–39, 62,
  87–88. *See also* Anne; James II;
  Mary II; Stuart, Charles Edward,
  Henry, and James; William III
Stuart, James, Old Pretender, 5, 7, 24,
  36, 38, 63, 87–88, 99, 113
St. Vincent, Lord. *See* Jervis
Sunderland, Lord (Charles Spencer), 92
Sweden, 14, 231, 245, 260
Swift, Jonathan, 81
Switzerland, 231, 237, 239

Tariffs. *See* Corn Laws; Customs duties
Taxation, 15, 35, 38, 57, 68, 97–99,
  127, 141, 146, 219–20, 248–49,
  277, 279. *See also* Customs duties;
  Excise; Poor relief
Temple, Lord (George Nugent-Temple-
  Grenville), 143
Test Act (1673), 13, 38, 63, 296
Theater, 81, 97, 138
Third Coalition, War of the (1805–1807),
  245–48
Tilsit, Treaty of (1807), 247–50, 252,
  255, 260
Toleration Act (1689), 13, 62
Tories
  in late Stuart period, 3, 7–9, 11–15,
    21, 26, 29, 31, 35–38, 62–63, 68,
    89, 100, 124
  after 1714, 62–64, 87
  after 1815, 215, 222, 276–77, 279–83,
    289–90, 293–301
Torres Vedras, Lines of, 255
Toulon, French naval base at, 29, 122,
  157, 227–28, 234, 242, 244
Townshend, Charles, 149–50
Townshend, Charles "Turnips," 77
Trade
  domestic, 54, 82, 173
  foreign, 50–51, 54, 88–89, 91, 173,
    180, 197–99, 220, 237, 239,
    248–52, 258, 294–95
  with Ireland, 197–98, 235

Trafalgar, Battle of (1805), 245–46,
  266
Transportation methods, 73, 173–75,
  182
Treasonable Practices Act (1795), 221
Treasury, 34–35, 44
Triennial Act (1694), 35
Troppau, Congress of (1821), 273
Turks. *See* Ottoman Empire
Turnpike roads, 60, 173, 182, 220, 280
Two Sicilies, Kingdom of the, 230, 273
Tyrconnel, Earl of, 16

Ulster, 16–17, 233–34
Union, Act of
  with Scotland (1707), 9, 31, 33–34,
    39, 87, 235
  with Ireland (1801), 142n., 234–36,
    296
Unitarians, 13
United States, 157, 166–67, 213, 217,
  240, 251, 257–60, 266, 275–76,
  290
Utrecht, Treaty of (1713), 37–38, 87,
  90, 99–101, 112, 115

Vanbrugh, Sir John, 73, 189
Vauxhall Garden, 54
Verona, Congress of (1822), 274
Vienna, Congress and Peace of
  (1814–1815), 261–63, 268–72
Villeneuve, Pierre de, Napoleonic admi-
  ral, 242, 244–45

Walpole, Sir Robert, 88, 91–108,
  113–15, 122, 133, 142, 145, 197,
  199
Ward, Ned, 55
Warfare, nature of
  before French Revolution, 109–12
  after 1792, 218–19
War of 1812 (1812–1815), 167, 257–60,
  263
Warwick, 280
Washington, General George, 117,
  155–57, 159, 161–62, 259n.
Watchmaking, 52
Waterloo, Battle of (1815), 238, 245,
  263–66
Watt, James, 175, 181, 212
Wellesley, Arthur. *See* Wellington
Wellesley, Lord (Richard Wellesley),
  253
Wellington, duke of (Arthur Wellesley)
  in Napoleonic wars, 110, 253–55,

2 3 4 5 6 7 8 9 0